A Concise Companion to
American Fiction 1900–1950

Blackwell Concise Companions to Literature and Culture
General Editor: David Bradshaw, University of Oxford

This series offers accessible, innovative approaches to major areas of literary study. Each volume provides an indispensable companion for anyone wishing to gain an authoritative understanding of a given period or movement's intellectual character and contexts.

Published

Chaucer	Edited by Corinne Saunders
English Renaissance Literature	Edited by Donna B. Hamilton
Shakespeare and the Text	Edited by Andrew Murphy
Shakespeare on Screen	Edited by Diana E. Henderson
Milton	Edited by Angelica Duran
The Restoration and Eighteenth Century	Edited by Cynthia Wall
The Victorian Novel	Edited by Francis O'Gorman
Modernism	Edited by David Bradshaw
Postwar American Literature and Culture	Edited by Josephine G. Hendin
Twentieth-Century American Poetry	Edited by Stephen Fredman
Contemporary British Fiction	Edited by James F. English
Contemporary British and Irish Drama	Edited by Nadine Holdsworth and Mary Luckhurst
Feminist Theory	Edited by Mary Eagleton
American Fiction 1900–1950	Edited by Peter Stoneley and Cindy Weinstein

Forthcoming

Middle English Literature	Edited by Marilyn Corrie
Postwar British and Irish Poetry	Edited by C. D. Blanton and Nigel Alderman

A Concise Companion to

American Fiction 1900–1950

Edited by Peter Stoneley
and Cindy Weinstein

Blackwell
Publishing

© 2008 by Blackwell Publishing Ltd
except for editorial material and organization © 2008 by Peter Stoneley
and Cindy Weinstein

BLACKWELL PUBLISHING
350 Main Street, Malden, MA 02148-5020, USA
9600 Garsington Road, Oxford OX4 2DQ, UK
550 Swanston Street, Carlton, Victoria 3053, Australia

The right of Peter Stoneley and Cindy Weinstein to be identified as the authors
of the editorial material in this work has been asserted in accordance with the
UK Copyright, Designs, and Patents Act 1988.

First published 2008 by Blackwell Publishing Ltd

1   2008

Library of Congress Cataloging-in-Publication Data

A concise companion to American fiction, 1900–1950 / edited by
Peter Stoneley and Cindy Weinstein.
      p. cm.—(Blackwell concise companions to literature and culture)
   Includes bibliographical references and index.
   ISBN 978-1-4051-3367-8 (hardback: alk. paper)
   1. American fiction—20th century—History and criticism.   I. Stoneley, Peter.
II. Weinstein, Cindy.

PS379.B567 2007
813'.5209—dc22

                                                              2007020966

A catalogue record for this title is available from the British Library.

Set in 10/12.5pt Meridien
by Graphicraft Limited, Hong Kong
Printed and bound in Singapore
by Fabulous Printers Pte Ltd

The publisher's policy is to use permanent paper from mills that operate a
sustainable forestry policy, and which has been manufactured from pulp processed
using acid-free and elementary chlorine-free practices. Furthermore, the publisher
ensures that the text paper and cover board used have met acceptable
environmental accreditation standards.

For further information on
Blackwell Publishing, visit our website at
www.blackwellpublishing.com

Contents

Contents

Notes on Contributors

Florence Dore is Associate Professor of American Literature at Kent State University and author of *The Novel and the Obscene: Sexual Subjects in American Modernism* (Stanford University Press, 2005). She is working on a second book, entitled "White Secrets: Privacy Law and Sexual Identity in Southern Modernism."

Michael A. Elliott is Associate Professor of English at Emory University. He is the author of *The Culture Concept: Writing and Difference in the Age of Realism* (Minnesota, 2002) and *Custerology: The Legacy of the Indian Wars and George Armstrong Custer* (Chicago, 2007); he is also, with Claudia Stokes, the co-editor of *American Literary Studies: A Methodological Reader* (New York University Press, 2003).

Mary Esteve is Associate Professor of English at Concordia University in Montreal, where she teaches nineteenth and twentieth century American literature and culture. She is the author of *The Aesthetics and Politics of the Crowd in American Literature* (Cambridge University Press, 2003), as well as of numerous articles appearing in such journals as *ELH*, *American Literary History*, *Genre*, and *Yale Journal of Criticism*.

Jennifer L. Fleissner is Associate Professor of English at Indiana University–Bloomington. She is the author of *Women, Compulsion, Modernity: The Moment of American Naturalism* (University of Chicago Press, 2004) as well as articles in such journals as *Critical Inquiry*, *American*

Literature, Differences, and *Tulsa Studies in Women's Literature.* She is currently at work on two new projects, "Novel Appetites: Eating and Meaning in Modernizing America," and "Maladies of the Will."

Keith Gandal is the author of *The Virtues of the Vicious: Jacob Riis, Stephen Crane, and the Spectacle of the Slum* (Oxford University Press, 1997) and *Class Representation in Modern Fiction and Film* (Palgrave Macmillan, 2007). He is also the author of a novel, *Cleveland Anonymous* (North Atlantic Books, 2002). He received his PhD from the University of California, Berkeley and is Professor of English at Northern Illinois University outside of Chicago. His essay is part of a book forthcoming from Oxford University Press, "The Gun and the Pen: Hemingway, Fitzgerald, Faulkner and the Fiction of Mobilization."

Loren Glass is Associate Professor of English at the University of Iowa and author of *Authors Inc.: Literary Celebrity in the Modern United States, 1880–1980* (New York University Press, 2004). He has published articles on American literature and cultural studies in *Critical Inquiry, American Literary History,* and *American Literature.* His current book project, "The End of Obscenity: Vulgar Modernism and Literary Value," is forthcoming with Duke University Press.

Donald E. Hardy is Professor of English at the University of Nevada, Reno; he teaches linguistics and is the author of *Narrating Knowledge in Flannery O'Connor's Fiction* (University of South Carolina Press, 2003) and "The Body in Flannery O'Connor's Fiction: Computational Technique and Linguistic Voice," the latter to be published in 2007, also by University of South Carolina Press.

Jennifer A. Hughes is a doctoral candidate in English at Emory University. Her dissertation research is on humor in the literature of the late-nineteenth- and early-twentieth-century United States.

Gene Andrew Jarrett is currently Associate Professor of English and African American Studies at Boston University. He is the author of *Deans and Truants: Race and Realism in African American Literature* (University of Pennsylvania Press, 2006). He is the editor of *African American Literature beyond Race: An Alternative Reader* (New York University Press, 2006), and *A Long Way from Home* by Claude McKay (Rutgers University Press, 2007). He is co-editor with Thomas Lewis Morgan of *The Complete Stories of Paul Laurence Dunbar* (Ohio University Press,

2006) and, with Henry Louis Gates Jr., of *The New Negro: Readings on Race, Representation, and African American Culture, 1892–1938* (Princeton University Press, 2007).

Kathryn R. Kent is Associate Professor of English and Chair of the Women's and Gender Studies Program at Williams College. She is the author of *Making Girls into Women: American Women's Writing and the Rise of Lesbian Identity* (Duke University Press, 2003). She has also published work on the creation of queer identifications and community in the Girl Scouts.

John Carlos Rowe is USC Associates' Professor of the Humanities in the Department of English and the Department of American Studies and Ethnicity at the University of Southern California. His recent books are *Literary Culture and U.S. Imperialism: From the Revolution to World War II* (2000), and *The New American Studies* (University of Minnesota Press, 2002). His current scholarly projects are: "Culture and U.S. Imperialism since World War II," "The Rediscovery of America: Multicultural Literature and the New Democracy," and "Blackwell's Companion to American Studies."

David Schmid is Associate Professor and Director of Graduate Studies in the University at Buffalo's English Department, where he teaches courses in British and American fiction, cultural studies, and popular culture. He has published on a variety of subjects, including celebrity, Dracula, crime fiction, and African American literature anthologies. He is the author of *Natural Born Celebrities: Serial Killers in American Culture* (University of Chicago Press, 2005), and he is currently working on two book-length projects: "Mean Streets and More: Space in Crime Fiction" and "The Scarlet Thread: A History of Homicide and American Popular Culture."

Paul Simpson is Professor of English Language in the School of English at Queen's University Belfast. His research is mainly in stylistics and critical linguistics, and his books in these areas include *Language, Ideology and Point of View* (Routledge, 1993) and *Language through Literature* (Routledge, 1997). He is also the co-editor of *Language, Discourse and Literature* (Unwin Hyman, 1989). His most recent books are *On the Discourse of Satire* (Benjamins, 2003) and *Stylistics* (Routledge, 2004). Simpson currently edits the journal *Language and Literature* which is published four times a year by Sage Publications.

Peter Stoneley is Professor of English at the University of Reading, England. His research interests are the literary cultures of the United States from the mid-nineteenth century onward, and queer aesthetics and traditions. His books include *Consumerism and American Girls' Literature, 1860–1940* (Cambridge University Press, 2003), and *A Queer History of the Ballet* (Routledge, 2006).

Michael Szalay is the author of *New Deal Modernism: American Literature and the Invention of the Welfare State* (Duke University Press, 2001) and is Associate Professor of English at the University of California, Irvine, where he also serves as director of the Humanities Center. He is currently finishing his second book, called "Democratic Party Culture: Hip Liberalism and the US Political Novel, 1946–2000."

Alan Wald is Professor in the English Department and Program in American Culture at the University of Michigan. He is the author of seven books on US literary radicalism, including *Exiles from a Future Time: The Forging of the Twentieth Century Literary Left* (University of North Carolina Press, 2002) and *Trinity of Passion: The Literary Left and the Anti-Fascist Crusade* (University of North Carolina Press, 2007).

Cindy Weinstein is Professor of English at the California Institute of Technology. She is the author of *Family, Kinship, and Sympathy in Nineteenth-Century American Literature* (Cambridge University Press, 2004), *The Literature of Labor and the Labors of Literature: Allegory in Nineteenth-Century American Fiction* (Cambridge University Press, 1995), and the editor of *The Cambridge Companion to Harriet Beecher Stowe* (Cambridge University Press, 2004).

Chronology

1890   William Dean Howells, *A Hazard of New Fortunes*. Emily Dickinson, *Poems*. Jacob Riis, *How the Other Half Lives*. The population of the United States is 63 million; this represents an increase of 25 percent over the preceding decade. More than half the nation's wealth is owned by one percent of the population. The Sherman Antitrust Act is passed to counter the growing power of monopolies. There are nearly 200 lynchings of African Americans each year in the following decade.

1892   Mary E. Wilkins Freeman, *A New England Nun and Other Stories*.

1893   The stock market crashes; in the course of the year, over 15,000 businesses fail, including 600 banks and 74 railroads. Chicago World Columbian Exhibition.

1894   Mark Twain, *Pudd'nhead Wilson*. The labor unrest of preceding and succeeding years is especially intense in this year, with the Pullman workers' strike.

1895   Booker T. Washington delivers "Atlanta Compromise" speech, urging African Americans to postpone their wish for equality with whites; Washington is sharply criticized by other African Americans, including W. E. B. Du Bois.

1896   Stephen Crane, *The Red Badge of Courage*; Sarah Orne Jewett, *The Country of the Pointed Firs*. Supreme Court rules in *Plessy v. Ferguson* that the segregationist policy of "separate but equal" is legal.

1897   Henry James, *What Maisie Knew*. Gold rush to the Klondike.

1898   The Spanish–American War over the issue of Cuban independence. The United States acquires an empire with Puerto Rico, the Philippines, and Haiti.

1899   Charles Chesnutt, *The Conjure Woman*; Kate Chopin, *The Awakening*; Charlotte Perkins Gilman, "The Yellow Wallpaper"; Frances E. W. Harper, *Iola Leroy: Or, Shadows Uplifted*; Henry James, *The Awkward Age*; Thorstein Veblen, *The Theory of the Leisure Class*.

1900   Theodore Dreiser, *Sister Carrie*; Robert Grant, *Unleavened Bread*; Pauline Hopkins, *Contending Forces*.

1901   Charles Chesnutt, *The Marrow of Tradition*; Frank Norris, *The Octopus*.

1902   Thomas Dixon, *The Leopard's Spots*, first in a Ku Klux Klan trilogy, to be followed by *The Clansman* (1905) and *The Traitor* (1907); Henry James, *The Wings of the Dove*; Owen Wister, *The Virginian*.

1903   Jack London, *The Call of the Wild*; Gertrude Stein, *Q. E. D.* Mother Jones leads children's march on Washington to protest child labor.

1904   Henry James, *The Golden Bowl*.

1905   W. E. B. Du Bois, *The Souls of Black Folk*; Mark Twain, "The War Prayer"; Edith Wharton, *The House of Mirth*.

1906   Jack London, *White Fang*; Upton Sinclair, *The Jungle*; Lincoln Steffens, *The Shame of the Cities*. San Francisco earthquake.

1907   Henry Adams, *The Education of Henry Adams*; Henry James, *The American Scene*. Immigration reaches a new peak, with over 1,285,000 arriving in this year.

1908 Henry Ford announces the Model T.

1909 Gertrude Stein, *Three Lives*.

1910 Jane Addams, *Twenty Years at Hull House*. The National Association for the Advancement of Colored People is founded. The census reveals that the population stands at nearly 92 million, with 50 million living in rural areas, 42 million in urban areas. Nearly nine percent of the population has arrived within the decade, with thirty-five percent of New York City being foreign-born. Standard Oil and American Tobacco forced by Supreme Court to divest and restructure under Sherman Antitrust Act.

1911 Ambrose Bierce, *The Devil's Dictionary*.

1912 Theodore Dreiser, *The Financier*; Zane Grey, *Riders of the Purple Sage*; James Weldon Johnson, *The Autobiography of an Ex-Colored Man*; Titanic sinks on maiden crossing of Atlantic.

1913 Willa Cather, *O Pioneers!*; Edith Wharton, *The Custom of the Country*. The controversial International Exhibition of Modern Art, known as the Armory Show, opens in New York, featuring work by Gauguin, Cézanne, van Gogh, Picasso; Cubist art is the most shocking, with Duchamp's "Nude Descending a Staircase" becoming the most talked of and derided painting.

1914 Theodore Dreiser, *The Titan*. Robert Frost, *North of Boston*. War begins in Europe; President Wilson declares United States' neutrality.

1915 Theodore Dreiser, *The "Genius"*; Charlotte Perkins Gilman, *Herland*. D. W. Griffiths' film, *The Birth of a Nation*, premieres; it is based on a best-selling Ku Klux Klan novel by Thomas Dixon, Jr.

1916 Easter Rising in Dublin. Federal Child Labor law is passed banning interstate commerce in products made by children under the age of 14. Repeated skirmishing brings the United States and Mexico to the brink of war.

1917 David Graham Phillips, *Susan Lenox: Her Fall and Rise*. German U-boat campaign against Atlantic shipping brings United States into the First World War. Margaret Sanger begins publication of *Birth Control Review*. Russian Revolution culminates in abdication of Tsar Nicolas II; he will be executed in the following year.

1918 The First World War ends.

1919 Sherwood Anderson, *Winesberg, Ohio*. T. S. Eliot, "The Love Song of J. Alfred Prufrock." The "Red Summer" of riots and lynching begins with trouble in Chicago. Creation of the League of Nations.

1920 Zona Gale, *Miss Lulu Bett*; Sinclair Lewis, *Main Street*. Eugene O'Neill, *The Emperor Jones*. Ezra Pound, *Hugh Selwyn Mauberley*. The population stands at 105,710,620, and less than half live in rural areas. The nineteenth Amendment, giving women the right to vote, is ratified. After the passing of the Prohibition Amendment in 1917, and its ratification in 1919, the United States goes "dry."

1921 John Dos Passos, *Three Soldiers*. Congress passes Emergency Quota Act, which sets a limit of 358,000 immigrants per year. The Italian anarchists, Sacco and Vanzetti, are found guilty of murder, in spite of a lack of evidence.

1922 James Joyce, *Ulysses*. T. S. Eliot, *The Waste Land*.

1923 Edith Summers Kelley, *Weeds*; Jean Toomer, *Cane*. Wallace Stevens, *Harmonium*.

1925 Willa Cather, *The Professor's House*; John Dos Passos, *Manhattan Transfer*; Theodore Dreiser, *An American Tragedy*; F. Scott Fitzgerald, *The Great Gatsby*; Janet Flanner, *The Cubical City*; *The New Negro*, edited by Alain Locke; Gertrude Stein, *The Making of Americans*; Anzia Yezierska, *Bread Givers*. The "monkey trial" in Tennessee, in which John Scopes is found guilty of teaching evolution.

1926 Ernest Hemingway, *The Sun Also Rises*. Langston Hughes, *The Weary Blues*. Book-of-the-Month Club established.

1927 Sinclair Lewis, *Elmer Gantry*; Gertrude Stein, *Tender Buttons*. Charles A. Lindbergh becomes the first to fly non-stop across the Atlantic. Sacco and Vanzetti are executed, to international disapproval.

1928 Djuna Barnes, *Ladies Almanack*; Jessie Fauset, *Plum Bun*; Rudolph Fisher, *The Walls of Jericho*; Radclyffe Hall, *The Well of Loneliness*; Nella Larsen, *Quicksand*.

1929 William Faulkner, *The Sound and the Fury*; Ernest Hemingway, *A Farewell to Arms*; Nella Larsen, *Passing*; Thomas Wolfe, *Look Homeward, Angel*. The various strands of crime fiction exemplified in this year with S. S. Van Dine's *The Bishop Murder Case*, Dashiell Hammett's *Red Harvest*, and W. R. Burnett's *Little Caesar*. Wall Street crashes; by 1932, there will be two million vagrants, and unemployment of over five million. Further symptoms of gambling and bootlegging empires with the St Valentine's Day Massacre.

1930 The first instalment in John Dos Passos's "U. S. A. trilogy," *The 42nd Parallel*, is published, to be followed by *1919* (1932) and *The Big Money* (1937). William Faulkner, *As I Lay Dying*; Dashiell Hammett, *The Maltese Falcon*. The Agrarian point of view is manifested in *I'll Take My Stand*. The "Scottsboro Boys" are convicted of rape. The Empire State Building is opened. Franklin Delano Roosevelt is elected, promising Americans a "new deal."

1932 Ernest Hemingway, *Death in the Afternoon*; James T. Farrell begins his Studs Lonigan trilogy with *Young Lonigan: A Boyhood in Chicago Streets*, to be followed by *The Young Manhood of Studs Lonigan* (1934), and *Judgment Day* (1935).

1933 Gertrude Stein, *The Autobiography of Alice B. Toklas*. The end of Prohibition. Judge Woolsey rules in *The United States v. One Book Called "Ulysses"* that *Ulysses* must be allowed into the US.

1934 James M. Cain, *The Postman Always Rings Twice*; Henry Miller, *Tropic of Cancer*; parts of Tillie Olsen's *Yonnondio* published in *Partisan Review*; Henry Roth, *Call It Sleep*; Zora Neale Hurston, *Jonah's Gourd Vine*.

1936 Djuna Barnes, *Nightwood*; William Faulkner, *Absalom, Absalom!* Marianne Moore, *The Pangolin and Other Verse*.

1937 Zora Neale Hurston, *Their Eyes Were Watching God*. Richard Wright, "Blueprint for Negro Writing."

1938 Richard Wright, *Uncle Tom's Children*.

1939 John Steinbeck, *The Grapes of Wrath*; Nathaniel West, *The Day of the Locust*. Clement Greenberg, "Avant-Garde and Kitsch." The Second World War begins in Europe, following Hitler's attacks on Czechoslovakia and Poland; the United States declares neutrality.

1940 Ernest Hemingway, *For Whom the Bell Tolls*; Richard Wright, *Native Son*.

1941 Eudora Welty, *A Curtain of Green*. The Japanese attack Pearl Harbor; the United States enters the war.

1942 The internment of Japanese Americans begins.

1944 Saul Bellow, *Dangling Man*. The GI Bill passes into law.

1945 Chester Himes, *If He Hollers Let Him Go*; Richard Wright, *Black Boy*. Atomic bombs are dropped on Hiroshima and Nagasaki. The Second World War ends.

1946 Carson McCullers, *The Member of the Wedding*; Eugene O'Neill, *The Iceman Cometh*. The United States grants independence to the Philippines. The United Nations meets.

1947 Norman Mailer, *The Naked and the Dead*. W. H. Auden, *The Age of Anxiety*. Tennessee Williams, *A Streetcar Named Desire*. Jackie Robinson becomes first African American to play major league baseball.

1948 Truman Capote, *Other Voices, Other Rooms*; William Faulkner, *Intruder in the Dust*. Ezra Pound, *The Pisan Cantos*. The United States recognizes the new state of Israel. Dr Alfred C. Kinsey publishes *Sexual Behavior in the Human Male*.

1949 Arthur Miller, *Death of a Salesman*. The North Atlantic Treaty is ratified.

1950 The United States enters the Korean War. Senator Joe McCarthy gains more publicity for his campaign against un-American activities, claiming that he has a list of 205 names of communists who are working in the State Department.

1951 J. D. Salinger, *Catcher in the Rye*. Julius and Ethel Rosenberg are convicted of espionage.

1952 Ralph Ellison, *Invisible Man*; Flannery O'Connor, *Wise Blood*.

1953 Arthur Miller, *The Crucible*. The Rosenbergs are executed.

1954 In the case of *Brown v. the Board of Education*, the Supreme Court declares the "separate but equal" policy unconstitutional.

1955 Rosa Parks is arrested when she refuses to give up her seat at the front of a bus; this leads to the boycott of Montgomery bus services. The United States sends military advisers to Vietnam.

Acknowledgments

It has been our pleasure to work with the contributors to this volume, and we thank them for their intellectual rigor, timeliness, and spirit of camaraderie. At Blackwell we wish to thank our commissioning editor, Emma Bennett; sharp-eyed copy-editor Felicity Marsh; and Louise Spencely, Rosemary Bird, and Jenny Phillips, who all pushed the project along at one point or another. We are also grateful to Professor Dave Grether and Susan Davis at CalTech, and to Jan Cox at Reading. Thanks, as always, to family and friends for encouragement, advice, and love.

Introduction

This Companion is designed to help readers make sense of the vast changes in US literature that took place during the period from 1900 to 1950. One need only look at some of the texts that fall under this temporal umbrella to realize that the literature at the turn of the century and the literature of the mid-century differ greatly, despite the obvious persistent examination of race, gender, and class relations. These essays offer a variety of explanations for a fifty-year period that includes texts as dissimilar as Theodore Dreiser's *Sister Carrie* (1900), Charles Chesnutt's *The Marrow of Tradition* (1901), Gertrude Stein's *Tender Buttons: Objects Food Rooms* (1914), Radclyffe Hall's *The Well of Loneliness* (1928), Ernest Hemingway's *Death in the Afternoon* (1932), and Richard Wright's *Native Son* (1940). To be sure, there are many ways to explore the diversity of literary production during these years: the impact of new mechanisms in the marketplace, such as agents and editors, for the writing and distributing of texts; the influence of communism on authors in the thirties; World War I, World War II; the advent of New Criticism, academic professionalization, and the valorization of irony, ambiguity, and modernity. There is no master narrative that contains and explains the creative forces of this, let alone any, period's literary production. That is not to say, however, that certain crucial issues, aesthetic practices, and cultural events are not recurrent and constitutive elements of this literature.

Several of the essays, in fact, make the case that something new was happening at the turn of the century, and that conventions of

1

nineteenth-century literature were inadequate to the task of identifying and expressing what had changed. Many twentieth-century authors knew it too, as they abandoned the comforts of realist representation for the ambiguities and ironies of modernism. The lures of the city, the heightened experience of consumption, the feeling of a lost agrarianism was expressed both in the content of the literature and in the form. Modernism was the term that described the experience of being in a kind of conceptual free-fall. Modernism was also the term that described the representation of that experience, as writers sought to articulate their shaken faith in the notions of stability, progress, equality, identity, to name just a few. The formal implications of this existential shake-up finds expression in William Faulkner's stream of consciousness narratives, or the hard-boiled style of Raymond Chandler, or the elliptical phraseology of Gertrude Stein. The question of modernism – when it began, what it means, what it meant – comes up repeatedly throughout this volume. In the introduction to Raymond Williams's *The Politics of Modernism*, Tony Pinkney observes, "as critics of many persuasions have pointed out, 'modernism' is the most frustratingly unspecific, the most recalcitrantly *un*periodizing, of all the major art-historical 'isms' or concepts" (3). Williams attacks Modernism on the grounds that "it stops history dead . . . the innovations of what is called Modernism have become the new but fixed forms of our present moment" (34–5).

Indeed, many of the authors discussed in this volume have the modernist seal of approval, and they worked very hard to get it. How they got it is the story told by several of the essays, whether it's a material culture analysis of book selling, an account of writers aiming to professionalize their craft and cordon it off from the onslaught of bourgeois sensibility, or a racialized story that pits Southern academics, armed with the apparatus of New Criticism, against the incursions of brilliant African American writers knocking down their institutional doors. Modernism, in other words, might well define and defend itself by calcifying time, aesthetic criterion, and canon-formation, but several of these essays, indeed this volume as a whole, attempt to respond to Williams's call, to "search out and counterpose an alternative tradition taken from the neglected works left in the wide margin" (35). Concision allows for some counterposition, but the margin is even wider than these essays can demonstrate.

As this last suggests, a concise account of fifty years of writing requires some difficult reckoning: which authors should be covered? which approaches should be represented? how does this concise account both revisit older imaginings of those fifty years and offer different paradigms? and why these fifty years? Expanding the canon is one of the goals of this collection, but expanding our understanding of the canon is another. We have not tried to replace one set of influential writers with another. Rather, by including essays that revisit canonical texts and authors from different perspectives and by expanding the texts that count as significant, our aim is to broaden an understanding of the literary field. Thus, the World War I mobilization of vast numbers of people, of US soldiers to Europe, is foregrounded as a key context for reading *The Great Gatsby* (1925). William Faulkner's *Absalom, Absalom!* (1936) becomes a vehicle for interrogating the relation between Southern agrarian fiction and African American literature. An essay on T. S. Eliot's "The Love Song of J. Alfred Prufrock" (1917) reads the poem in relation to Clement Greenberg's aesthetic theory as well as Hemingway's *Death in the Afternoon*. Other texts, such as Zora Neale Hurston's *Their Eyes Were Watching God* (1936), Charles Chensutt's *The Marrow of Tradition* (1901), and Richard Wright's *Native Son* (1940), appear throughout the volume as touchstones for considerations of race, gender, politics, and stylistic analysis.

Conventional ideas about this period, organized according to stale phrases such as "the Jazz Age" and "The Lost Generation," are abandoned in favor of more particular and inclusive conceptual categories. One of the consequences of revisiting this period with a different set of interpretive concerns and practices is that new narratives of the period arise that bring into focus authors and texts that have, for a variety of reasons, fallen off the critical radar. Thus, David Graham's *Susan Lenox: Her Fall and Rise* (1917), along with *Sister Carrie* (1900), becomes a vital text for demonstrating a foundational narrative of twentieth-century literature having to do with the endless task of female self-making. Or, Tillie Olsen's *Yonnondio* (1934) takes on new importance as part of a conversation, taking place in fiction, about its radicalizing potential. As diverse as the subject matter of the individual essays is, we have also sought to represent a variety of interpretive methodologies, ranging from a material culture analysis of the period's literary production to a technical stylistic discussion of vernacular. Similarly, readers will see how queer theory, cultural studies, and new historicism generate new insights into this literature.

However, these questions about methodology and literary periodization do not only fall within the purview of the editors of the volume, but to the contributors as well. Throughout these essays, authors ask readers to think about how a focus on this time period helps illuminate certain aspects of the literature, say of racial uplift or white masculinity or mass production and consumption, and yet constrains the full development of an account that would consider the antebellum world of slave narratives, separate spheres, and the beginnings of industrialization. Thus, it is impossible to begin a discussion of the politics of race in twentieth-century American literature without reference to the devastating *Plessy v. Ferguson* (1896) Supreme Court decision, which held that public space could be at once separate and equal. Similarly, no analysis of the place of the city in twentieth-century detective fiction makes a great deal of sense without reference to Poe's work in the 1830s. One could make this point by going in the opposite temporal direction. To talk about the origins of cosmopolitanism in this period without sustained attention to Don Delillo's *Cosmopolis* (2003) would be to abrogate that account in midstream. The story of best-sellers, editors, and censorship is not complete without reference to legal cases against edgy – to put it mildly – books, such as William Burroughs's *Naked Lunch* (1966), post World War II. The essays in this volume, in other words, are acutely aware that to put a text in a context, historical as that context is, is a necessary though arbitrary circumscription.

That said, the goal of this volume is to present readers with wide-ranging essays that give them a sense of the capaciousness of literary production during these years. Its riches are astonishing, and we have organized them in the following way. The opening three essays reflect upon and intervene in canon-formation, with Michael A. Elliott and Jennifer A. Hughes presenting canonical texts as producing, one would imagine unintentionally, a set of African American responses that combat assumptions about racial identity. The second and third essays offer a trajectory of the period that radically diverges from the customary, as Jennifer Fleissner delineates a pervasive narrative of female self-making and Kathryn R. Kent establishes the contours of a queer canon that vacillates between visibility and invisibility. The next three chapters represent quite different approaches to the literature of this period. Loren Glass's materialist account explains how a middle-brow reading audience was constructed through the marketing of bestsellers. Hemingway's avant-garde aspirations, according to Glass, actually paved the way for a "more low-brow accessibility to hard-boiled crime fiction," which is the subject of David Schmid's close reading of the detective genre. The tonal uniqueness of this set of texts is then explicated in Paul Simpson and Donald Hardy's essay, which demonstrates the usefulness of stylistic analysis for understanding modernist narrative experimentation. The three essays that follow explore how the literature of this period was profoundly engaged with political and aesthetic issues. Michael Szalay reads Eliot's poetry and Hemingway's prose as allegories of a modernist aesthetic that requires a recognition and communion with the dead. Keith Gandal meditates upon the impact that the three writers of "the Lost Generation" – Hemingway, Fitzgerald, and Faulkner – were "frustrated in their desires to serve in the US military's colossal war effort." Alan Wald's essay, like the others, chooses representative figures from the period, in his case James T. Farrell, Richard Wright, and Tillie Olsen, to discuss the proletarian impulse at the heart of much 1930s US literature. The final set of essays considers the place of race during this period. Florence Dore asks us to consider race in the context of modernism, specifically to what extent has Southern modernism defined itself as antithetical to African American literature. Like Wald, Gene Jarrett argues that Wright is a seminal figure in any delineation of an African American literary tradition. His essay explores the thematic of racial uplift, its limitations and possibilities for this fiction. The penultimate essay of the volume by Mary Esteve investigates race and identity politics in relation to questions of cosmopolitanism. Our contributors indicate various moments of exhaustion, competition, and adaptation within paradigms of Americanness. In moving beyond "American" or "fiction", or "1900–1950" to discuss a wide range of creative beliefs and practices, John Carlos Rowe's "Other Modernisms" signals an "anti-national" and "post-national" criticism, full of "historically conflicted, polyglot, transcultural intersections" within and beyond the Western Hemisphere. Once having thought about some of the configurations within "United States" and "fiction," we hope that readers will consider Rowe's argument that an understanding of the cultural productions of the period need not be limited by the boundaries of nation, genre, and medium.

It is with this over-arching organizational structure in mind that we now turn to specific summaries of individual chapters. In their far-reaching introductory chapter, "Turning the Century," Elliott and Hughes consider the idea that nineteenth-century fictional conventions could not represent modern experience. Such developments as increased technologization and racial and ethnic tensions seemed to take America beyond the reasoned, middle-class decencies of literary realism. Writers such as Dreiser, Sinclair, and Norris began to present a more heavily deterministic experience, in which potent biological and social pressures overwhelmed other aspects of subjectivity. These writers also saw their own function as overwhelmed by the emergence of mass culture: writers of literary fiction recognized that their work could not claim a decisive force in the lives that their work described. If modern living seemed a brutal biological and social struggle, writers also detected "over-civilization," whereby white men were in danger of losing out to other, more vigorous races. London's *The Call of the Wild* (1903) and *White Fang* (1906) sought to acknowledge and reawaken the primal powers that were necessary for the continued success of the race. Elliott and Hughes demonstrate, though, that struggle, awakenings, and ideas of the primal and the primitive take different forms when the writers are African American and/or female. Charles Chesnutt and Pauline Hopkins used their fiction to counter stereotypes of African Americans as stupid and animalistic (even as Thomas Dixon's Ku Klux Klan trilogy outsold their work many times over). Charlotte Gilman Perkins and Kate Chopin testify to the desire to move beyond the gentility that was required of middle-class women. Elliott and Hughes end by noting the death of Samuel Langhorne Clemens or "Mark Twain" in 1910. Twain serves as a paradigmatic figure in thinking about the turn of the century, in that he moved from an early career of humor and realist gestures towards "human goodness" to writing that was more concerned with determinism, arbitrariness, and alienation.

Fleissner's "Women and Modernity" indicates the major transformations in women's lives from the nineteenth century into the twentieth, and offers a gloss upon Adams's infamous claim that "the American woman had . . . nothing to rebel against, except her own maternity" (*The Education of Henry Adams*, 446). Greater numbers of women – especially from the white middle classes – entered higher education and the white collar workplace; they married later or not at all, and had fewer children than the women of earlier generations. Even girls and women from lower classes found new opportunities in large towns and cities – chances for self-determination and self-fulfilment that had not been available to them in the small town or in the country. Novels such as Theodore Dreiser's *Sister Carrie* (1900), Edith Wharton's *The Custom of the Country* (1913), and David Graham Phillips's *Susan Lenox: Her Fall and Rise* (1917) depict heroines whose experience of modernity becomes a "narrative of seemingly endless self-remaking." In an age in which industrialization led to over-production, consumerism was perceived less as a dangerous and disauthenticating self-indulgence, and more as a means to sustain a successful economy. But if writers depict women being trained for consumption, they also indicate that such women are being produced as items to be consumed: the "heroine" is not so much a distinctive entity as a "reproducible type." In the face of consumerized opportunities for self-remaking, other fiction focused on how women do or do not relate to a baseline natural reality in the modern age. Some writers saw women as more suited than men to the "artificial" aspect of a "machine age"; others suggest a woman's need to escape back into nature, while others again – including Edith Summers Kelley in *Weeds* (1923) – suggest that women are still, for the most part, limited by nature in the fact and consequences of child bearing. The problem of what the unencumbered, newly-educated woman might or should do features in Upton Sinclair's *Main Street* (1920), and also in "white-collar girl" novels such as Edna Ferber's Emma McChesney series. While the white woman's dilemma often turns on the opposition between love and work, in novels by writers from other racial and ethnic groups the exchange is sometimes more complicated. The Jewish American protagonist of Anzia Yezierska's *Bread Givers* (1925), and the African American protagonists of Jessie Fauset's *Plum Bun* (1928) and Nella Larsen's *Quicksand* (1928) find it hard to move beyond the affiliation to a community and its restrictions, partly because to do so would also be to disavow the oppressed group from which one had come. Further, to move beyond the group may also be to encounter the exoticized perceptions of one's self on the part of others. This uncertainty over how the female protagonist relates to her past and to the possibilities of modern life make her a compelling figure, not least because, as Fliessner points out, the heroine's "lack of a road map for her narrative of self-discovery makes her . . . emblematic of an era that has left traditional paths behind."

Whereas Fleissner "turns the century" by looking at it through the lens of women's continual self-fashioning, Kathryn R. Kent analyzes this period through a queer reading that considers the possibilities of representing lesbian experience. Her chapter, "Queer Modernity and Lesbian Representation" contends that it is not always easy to locate queerness in the fiction of a period in which it was almost impossible to write and publish an "out" narrative. Kent's response is not to "hunt for the lesbian in the text," but to look at texts that have some indication – formal or thematic – of queerness, and to look at how queer literary criticism can help us to re-read and understand the symptomatic crises and mysteries of certain narratives. Kent also wants, though, to critique some of the tendencies of queer studies. She points out that the modern conception of selfhood was formed around a newly clarified and hardened idea of sexual identity, whereby everyone was classified – or might be classified – according to a homo/hetero binary. Kent wonders, though, whether this split between the "normal" and the "deviant" was so strong, so consistent, and so clearly and relentlessly enforced in women's lives. Drawing her examples from the late nineteenth-century realism of Mary Wilkins Freeman, through Henry James and Gertrude Stein, to Djuna Barnes, Nella Larsen, and Zora Neale Hurston, Kent suggests that these writers use a range of different tactics to represent female–female erotics, and, in the process, they work against the notion of a modern lesbian identity even as they confirm its existence. Kent's earlier texts are interesting for the way in which they "resist the imposition of normative heterosexual closure," and suggest the "unrepresentability of protolesbian desire," which, Kent argues, "resists figuration even more than gay male desire does." Later works, on the other hand, such as Djuna Barnes's *Ladies Almanack* (1928), indicate that "lesbian identity itself is becoming the site of a standardization – something that can be routinized, mass produced, and marketed like a commodity." *Ladies Almanack* and *Nightwood* (1936) are anti-assimilationist, in that they resist the social and cultural contours of "the lesbian." There is a variant difficulty with assimilating desires and identities when race is also a factor. Kent looks at how, in Larsen's *Passing* (1929) and Hurston's *Their Eyes Were Watching God* (1936), same-sex erotics threatens to disrupt the narrative of racial uplift and the assertion of bourgeois black femininity. At every point, however, Kent is keen to show that the representation of female–female erotics is not a simple matter of telling, but is closely bound up with these writers' stylistic experiments.

If these opening chapters indicate the ways in which writers at the turn of the century and beyond represented the social changes that they saw around them, Loren Glass explores, in "Markets and 'Gatekeepers,'" the "sociology" of literature itself. He acknowledges that the novel is a commercial product that is "designed, promoted, and distributed by institutions organized for profit." In the early twentieth century, agents, editors, magazines and book-of-the-month clubs sought to shape the encounter between authors and readers. The market was most obviously divided into broad categories of "lowbrow" (cheap, often sensational mass entertainment) and "highbrow" (aesthetically ambitious writing by those who were supposedly indifferent to economic opportunity). But as, in the early to mid-twentieth century, publishers and promoters encouraged upwardly mobile readerships to identify literature as a means of fulfilment and self-improvement, there was a development of the "middlebrow" field. Readers looked to educate and elevate themselves through literature, and authors and publishers looked to provide for and profit from this readership. Glass observes the ironies of this situation: the attractive image of the reader was of a person of independent taste and judgment, but, in order to become such a reader, people joined the book clubs and followed the choices made for them by literary "gatekeepers." If the emergence of the middlebrow seemed to amount to a leveling off or homogenization of American literary taste, there were other developments. Many first- or second-generation immigrant Jews, who had been excluded from the established institutions of literature, made their publishing careers out of a willingness to promote fiction that was more experimental and that challenged the canons of literary, social, and sexual morality. They also pioneered the cheap reprinting and wide distribution of older "classics." Not only did these new publishers make available a wider repertoire of contemporary fiction but, in putting their reprints in department stores and on newsstands, they also made "great" literature a more accessible and everyday readerly option. The literary challenge to conventional morality was met with opposition from "purity" campaigners. Authors were often unwilling to eviscerate their work in deference to what they saw as an absurd and distasteful prudery. Glass looks at how perceived obscenity was mediated by agents and publishers, as they sought to placate writers, avoid costly trials, and, on occasion, use a novel's "frank honesty" as a selling point.

In "Manhood, Modernity, and Crime Fiction," David Schmid traces the "frank honesty" of the crime genre. He points out that crime fiction is not unified, but, rather, presents contrasting ideas of crime, morality, and gender. For Schmid, however, crime fiction nearly always offers readers – and implicitly, white male readers – a way of encountering and assimilating the threats of modernity. That threat might be defined in terms of urban life, in which one is surrounded by strangers; it might be seen in relation to new competition in professional life, in the form of women, African Americans, and immigrant groups. Equally, the sense of threat, of dislocation, or of incipient violence, might be seen in the context of other legal, economic, and social shifts, such as the crime wave that came, after 1919, with Prohibition, or the hardship and uncertainty that came with the depression of 1929. But, in response to a more generalized sense of the pace, brutality, and impersonality of modern experience, crime fiction offers two definitive models of thought and behavior: the superior figure of the "classical" detective, who remains aloof and who solves whatever puzzles come his way with intellectual detachment; or the hard-boiled figure who is somehow equal to, and partakes of the quality of, an exhausting and violent environment. Taking the hard-boiled school in particular, Schmid urges that we should not allow our sense of this fiction to simplify into a stereotype of tough masculinity. There are countervailing tendencies. Toughness is itself seen as a "forced reaction" rather than a "willed choice," and while the tough hero must cultivate an emotional distance in order to function, he is a hero precisely because, in a brutal and callous society, he retains a true, deep, and immediate ability to feel. Schmid's crime fiction hero is tough, but he is also, crucially, vulnerable and even sentimental. Similarly, the fictions themselves may be seen not simply as tough and contemporary but as part of a longer American tradition: Schmid cites George Grella to the effect that the crime fiction novel echoes and develops the Puritan "preoccupation with innate depravity."

Schmid's analysis of hard-boiled fiction is followed by a chapter on styles in modernism. Style is often invoked as a key concept for defining, organizing, and evaluating literature, but critics nowadays seldom give any sustained attention to the topic. Paul Simpson and Don Hardy, in their chapter on "American Sentences," explore a vocabulary drawn from the field of stylistics. They consider linguistic and literary devices as used by the writers of the period – dialect, labels, lexis, and syntax – before moving to a more developed analysis of the "hard-boiled" style. While parts of this chapter may seem "technical," Simpson and Hardy demonstrate that a stylistic focus can reveal aspects of a text that might seem "mere details" but which have far-reaching implications. In Zora Neale Hurston's use of African American dialect, for instance, a character's pronunciation of "I" and "my" are rendered as "Ah" and "mah," but the pronunciation of "sky" is rendered as "sky," not "skah." Similarly, what are we to make of "eye dialect," where a writer mis-spells a word to suggest a dialect pronunciation, when the correct spelling would have indicated the pronunciation just as well (as in the African American dialect rendering of "wuz" for "was")? Or, in hard-boiled fiction, what is the importance of "attenuated focalization," where an author opts for a noun phrase with indefinite reference ("a man's voice," "a man was hunkered on his heals")? We might feel that we assimilate and respond to such features without ever stopping to note them, or without checking that we have a vocabulary that enables us to describe them. If we make an explicit point of defining these features, the aim is not to isolate and explore style as an end in itself – to lose ourselves in "aesthetic appreciation." Rather, the point would be to think through the context and effects of such writerly choices, and also to think about what, if anything, can be completely isolated as "not style."

In the following chapter, Keith Gandal moves away from an "aesthetic appreciation" of Fitzgerald's style and instead contextualizes *The Great Gatsby* (1925) in a radically unstylistic way. He points out that, aside from the First World War itself, the experience of mobilization for war was a vast upheaval that had profound effects on American society and culture. Effectively, the fact of mobilization gave the military the power to grant or to withhold masculine status; even within the military machine, though, there were new hierarchies and new means of formulating hierarchies. Instead of granting authority to educated men from established backgrounds, the army introduced new intelligence and psychological testing. This meant that a man such as Gatsby, from a modest, non-WASP background, could gain a new social power on being made an officer, and it was this power that enabled him to meet and to court the Southern, upper-class girl, Daisy. Gandal gives fascinating details of the close match between Fitzgerald's narrative and the process of mobilization, and he suggests that Gatsby's subsequent experience is also reflective of the period in that it exemplifies a "post-war backlash against meritocracy." Gandal moves on to demonstrate the ways in which Daisy's narrative can be situated as mobilization fiction, inasmuch as the social and sexual risks that she takes in her romances correspond to widespread wartime phenomena and to government attempts to regulate the moral impact of the army camps. Moving away from the specifics of mobilization, Gandal sees the relationship between Gatsby and Daisy as a reversal of a longstanding novelistic theme, in that Gatsby comes to stand for the mythic innocent, the Jamesian naïve girl, while Daisy takes the role of the compromised, destructive, but compelling adventurer. Gandal concludes by pointing out recurrences of the mobilization effect in other works, including Hemingway's *The Sun Also Rises* (1926) and Faulkner's *The Sound and the Fury* (1929). Gandal observes the counterpoint to the meritocratic hero, in all these novels, in the figure of the "under-appreciated" Anglo whose masculine prowess is overshadowed by that of the ethnic outsider.

In a complex and powerful discussion of "Modernism's History of the Dead," Michael Szalay tests out different ways of defining the concept of "modernism" through the work of Hemingway and Eliot. He observes the idea that, in modernism, form and content become indistinguishable. As Clement Greenberg noted of the Abstract Expressionist painters, the work of art is "about" the paint and canvas. In such elitist, avant-garde work, the intention is not to express a self, but to explore the possibilities of the medium. This made for a highly specialized and difficult kind of art, an art that was willing to be at odds with traditional bourgeois expectations. Yet this art can be resituated within its capitalist moment, because it evinces the professional specialization that was widely apparent in a professional-managerial, corporate culture. Szalay traces these related aspects of form and "guild" specialization through representations of death and the dead. He shows that Eliot's professional practice or belief is that we bring the dead with us. While modernism is often seen as a breach with the styles and values of the past, for Eliot the writers who have gone before are precisely "that which we know." For Hemingway, however, the dead and death are more strongly related to his foundational experiences during the First World War. Having been witness to the massed horrors, for Hemingway death is the "irreducible element of experience." The point for him is that "all stories, if continued far enough, end in death," and so the professional guild to which he is drawn is bull-fighting, in which death is a close and recurrent possibility. Szalay compares Eliot's "art of death," with its professionalized reverence for those dead one can claim as precursors, to Hemingway's, which is "more baldly committed to the ugly fact of life's end." Hemingway's commitment to this "ugly fact" causes him to avoid abstraction and rhetoric. He pursues an immediacy in his writing which, returning to the issue of form and content, does not so much communicate or express a feeling or an experience, as recreate in the form of the writing the "material conditions" of the experience. Hemingway's form does not so much *tell*, as constitute in itself the sensation of the experience.

In "The Radical 1930s," Alan Wald considers the Great Depression of the 1930s as a feature in and influence upon the fiction of that decade. He delineates a generation of writers from the lower classes who, while not averse to literary experimentation, were committed to writing accessible narratives that might have a beneficial social effect. These writers often had some degree of Marxist belief or affiliation, and they were able to manifest their beliefs through the techniques of realism and naturalism, to which they added modernistic renderings of consciousness. Wald's rubric might embrace a wide range of otherwise un-like writers, from Steinbeck to Dos Passos. Wald focuses on James T. Farrell, Tillie Olsen, and Richard Wright. Farrell's Studs Lonigan trilogy explores lower- and lower-middle-class life through the Irish American Studs. Although Farrell's social and Marxist commitments are clear, he was somewhat at odds with a narrow Communist aesthetic, in that he did not idealize the working class. He can also be distinguished from the naturalists, in that, in true Marxist fashion, his characters are able, on occasion, to liberate themselves from the forces that otherwise determine their existence. Tillie Olsen's *Yonnondio* (sections of which were first published in the Communist *Partisan Review* in 1934), is set in the 1920s, but it is characteristic of radical 1930s fiction in its concern with the struggles of working-class families and, in this case, of women in working-class families. Again, though, there are elements that take Olsen beyond classic naturalism (and particularly the "gothic" aspect, as featured in the grotesque, and seemingly emblematic, characters). Wald's other key example, Richard Wright, again adopted Marxist ideas and preoccupations, but his faith in Marxist ideology was ultimately undermined by his sense that Marxism could not deal adequately with racial divisions.

The question of race is the subject of Gene Jarrett's discussion in "Racial Uplift and the Politics of African American Fiction." Jarrett focuses in particular on how writers negotiated the formidable cultural presence of Booker T. Washington, and the influential paradigm that Washington established in *Up from Slavery* (1901). Jarrett finds that, if turn-of-the-century writers found uplift a useful concept, later generations did not. Some either revised and critiqued uplift, as with the writers of the Harlem Renaissance, or they rejected it as a polite submission to white sensibilities, as was the case with writers from W. E. B. DuBois through to Richard Wright. Jarrett moves from Sutton Griggs's *Imperium in Imperio* (1899) and Frances E. W. Harper's *Iola Leroy: Or, Shadows Uplifted* (1899) through Charles Chesnutt's *The Marrow of Tradition* (1901), arguing that while uplift is sometimes used to assert equal status with whites, it is also used at times to assert a higher status in relation to other, supposedly inferior blacks. Writers of the Harlem Renaissance, such as Nella Larsen, were wary of Washington's influence, as he seemed to undermine black progress with his appeal to the supremacist sensibilities of white supporters. Larsen's novel *Quicksand* (1928) and Rudolph Fisher's *The Walls of Jericho* (1928) indicate the dangers of white patronage, which is seen to present African Americans as in need of constant elevation. Jarrett observes a new radicalism – and a further objection to the motif of uplift – in the 1930s, and especially with the magazine, *New Challenge*. The first issue of *New Challenge* published Richard Wright's "Blueprint for Negro Writing"; this and other essays declared the importance of writing about and for "the Negro masses." But this radical move would be replaced in turn, as later generations sought to perform a "kind of racial desegregation of American literature," which would allow black writers to move beyond the "Negro problem." Jarrett locates several writers, from Ann Petry and Zora Neale Hurston to Ralph Ellison, at different points on a scale that extended from Wrightean black solidarity to non-race-specific, "national" writing. And yet writers often refused to accept the polarizing of the field of black literature. They did not necessarily disavow blackness, but they did caution against trying to see African American writing as fitting into a "unique cultural pattern," or as affirming an identity of thought and feeling simply as a result of a "shared racial inheritance." Equally, as Ralph Ellison argued, African American experience might be seen as a central and powerful means for the definition and representation of American-ness as a whole.

In a chapter on "The Modernism of Southern Literature," Florence Dore investigates the idea of Southern literature and the place (or lack thereof) of African Americans in the writings of the Agrarians. This group of Southern writers declared that "the American progressive principle ha[d] developed into a pure industrialism without any check from a Southern minority." The Agrarians, though, defined Southern-ness in a way that precluded the idea of African American equality, and their resistance to modernity was in part a resistance to a racially confused present. In detailed and telling analyses of Faulkner's *Absalom, Absalom!* (1936), Flannery O'Connor's *Wise Blood* (1952) and "The Artificial Nigger" (1962), Dore finds that "Southern literature" is actually more closely aligned with a progressive modernist aesthetic than with the ideas of the Agrarians. Dore's chosen authors are interested in "crossed identities," whereby a would-be "pure" racial self is seen to dissolve into that which it defines as other to itself. A key scene for this argument is when Faulkner's Thomas Sutpen calls at the front door of a grand plantation house. A black butler whom Sutpen thinks of as a "monkey nigger" tells him to go to the back door. Sutpen then realizes that, in spite of his whiteness, his relative poverty makes him akin to the other back-door people – slaves – and this "crisis" inspires Sutpen's subsequent determination to rise. However, to confuse the butler with a monkey is to invoke a Darwinian idea of evolution, with the black man representing an earlier stage of existence. But this is also to suggest that Sutpen himself is evolved from – fathered by – the black man. Racist ideas, then, whether Sutpen's or the Agrarians', are threatened by narratives of progress, whether Darwinian or industrial, as such narratives imply change and dissolution. Faulkner's novel is concerned with showing Sutpen's futile attempts to ascend to wealth while moving away from any kinship with blackness. Dore traces similar evolutionary motifs, and resistance to them, in the work of Fitzgerald and, especially, O'Connor. She ends with Richard Wright, using his example – and especially his exclusion from the canon of Southern writing – to critique once more an idea of "Southern minority" that seeks to evade contact and confusion with blackness.

Whereas Dore analyzes the Agrarian ideal and the vexed status of modernism within it, Mary Esteve focuses on the effects of urbanization in big modern cities. In her chapter on "Cosmopolis," Mary Esteve quotes Louis Wirth's classic 1938 essay to the effect that the city had become "the initiating and controlling center of economic, political, and cultural life"; the city had "drawn the most remote communities of the world into its orbit and woven diverse areas, peoples, and activities into a cosmos." Esteve observes two important strands in thinking about the cosmopolis. On the one hand, there is a generalizing tendency, as the city gives broad shapes to life within and without its bounds. On the other hand, the cosmopolitan city is the scene of an increased and even threatening heterogeneity. Esteve marks out these twin aspects of generality and heterogeneity via a discussion of Don DeLillo's *Cosmopolis* (2003). Her interest then turns to the important differences to be found between DeLillo's "compressed, postmodern version" of the cosmospolis and the versions to be found in such novels as John Dos Passos's *Manhattan Transfer* (1925), Janet Flanner's *The Cubical City* (1926), Henry Roth's *Call It Sleep* (1934), and Anzia Yezierska's short story, "The Lost 'Beautifulness'." Esteve finds that the experience of the cosmopolis can lead to detachment, as the subject moves among and beyond various "parochial allegiances." At times, this detachment is undesirable as the protagonist in DeLillo's novel cannot escape from a narcissistic alienation. But the move beyond the parochial and into detachment might be positive in that it can give renewed life to the generality in the form of an abstract and universalizing ethics. The question might be, though, whether a cosmopolitanism that possesses "the sheen of universal inclusiveness" may not, in fact, absorb and homogenize all differences into a virtual whiteness. Esteve looks at fiction that gives various treatments of the "interlocking paradigms of assimilationism, pluralism, and cosmopolitanism." The different possibilities are explored in a series of vivid WASP-Jewish encounters. Crucially, the fiction demonstrates that cosmopolitanism enables a vision of identity which is chosen and acted out. Drawing on the work of Walter Benn Michaels, Esteve is keen to show that, in the cosmpolis, fictional protagonists arrive at an identity that is a creative reiteration of beliefs and practices. This is opposed to the defensive nativism that seeks to insist that one "derives one's beliefs and practices *from* one's cultural identity" (Michaels 1995: 16).

The volume concludes with an analysis of creative "beliefs and practices" not normally discussed in the same breath as Eliot, Faulkner, and other high modernists. Rowe demonstrates that our understanding of modernism, in particular, is limited by arbitrary boundaries. Hence, his essay expands the notion of what might count as modernist, such as Native American Ghost Dances and Mario Suarez's barrio fiction, and why they have not been counted. This last point is made by a recovery of the transnational aspects of texts, such as the anthropological writings of Zora Neale Hurston and the purposeful transgression of temporal borders. To this end, Rowe historicizes the modernism of post-World War II Chicano literature in relation to the 1848 Treaty of Guadalupe Hidalgo, and its creation of a Mexican American identity that "is historically the product of at least three different and competitive imperialisms: Spanish, Mexican, and US." His essay puts into dialogue texts and contexts that not only have not spoken to each other in the critical conversation about modernism, but have not spoken even for themselves; to wit, the Zoot Suit riots of the early 1940s and Ralph Ellison's *Invisible Man* (1952) occupy an overlapping discursive terrain or, in Rowe's own powerful formulation, "What Notes toward a Supreme Fiction (Wallace Stevens, 1947) did the Chinese immigrant write?"

As is evident, the essays in this volume speak to one another. They are intended to offer a variety of interpretations of authors, texts, and the cultural milieu in which they are produced. Many of the essays zero in on the same texts, while drawing out different aspects of them. Others produce new textual vistas that have heretofore been submerged, marginalized, or even erased. Our hope is that readers find these multiple interpretive approaches, and the texts that come into view or take on a different inflection as a result, illuminating, provocative, and useful for their own critical practices.

Chapter 1

Turning the Century

Michael A. Elliott and Jennifer A. Hughes

Satisfied that the sequence of men led to nothing and the sequence of their society could lead no further, while the mere sequence of thought was chaos, he turned at last to the sequence of force; and thus it happened that, after ten years' pursuit, he found himself lying in the Gallery of Machines at the Great Exposition of 1900, with his historical neck broken by the sudden irruption of force totally new.

The Education of Henry Adams (1907)

Henry Adams's meditation on "force" in the well-known "Virgin and the Dynamo" chapter of *The Education* climaxes in the language of physical violence. Throughout the chapter, Adams manages to describe the scientific discoveries on display at the Great Exposition in Paris with cool detachment but also to render the turbulence of his emotional state. "Force," as Adams represents it, is the source of revolutionary power, a turning from one world order (the spiritual order of the Old World epitomized by the Virgin) to another (the technological world of scientific discovery represented by the Dynamo). The "historian," Adams's self-nomination, can grasp the outlines of this shift, but only in the crudest of terms. The forms of historical knowledge that Adams has at his disposal no longer appear functional. He had sought a history that could produce more coherent meaning than mere sequence, that could create order out of the "chaos" of his time. The turn of the century, however, unleashed forces that rendered this project impossible and instead made Adams acutely aware of his own inadequacy to compass the turn of the century. The historian of the nineteenth century put himself at bodily risk in attempting to confront the twentieth.

The world of American fiction did not have a spokesperson who articulated the dilemma so baldly, but Adams's assessment of his inadequacy offers a useful starting point for considering where fiction found itself at the turn of the twentieth century. There was a growing sense that the nineteenth-century conventions that governed the production of fiction were not sufficient to the demands of an age in which so many forces were unleashed upon the United States: not only the scientific and technological forces to which Adams refers, but social and political ones that were altering the human landscape. The explosion of mass culture would drive the nascent film industry; massive immigration from eastern and southern Europe sparked fierce debates about the composition of American society; and African American leaders sharpened their response to the escalating racial violence suffered by their communities.

In the second half of the nineteenth century, the relationship of literature to society had been brokered in the United States by the ascendance of American realism, a mode of literary production and reception that prized the ability to document social realities with the premise that doing so would lead to a more just social order. Realist fiction prized the careful observation of social manners, questions of character over those of plot, and the articulation of local distinctions, including non-standard forms of English. On the one hand, it cultivated the drawing-room novels of Henry James; on the other, the regional fiction of Sarah Orne Jewett and Mary Wilkins Freeman. Hamlin Garland, a vocal advocate of realism, explained, "The sun of truth strikes each part of the earth at a little different angle; it is this angle which gives life and infinite variety to literature." Variety, indeed, was a cornerstone of realism, which placed an optimistic faith in the power of fiction to negotiate social distinctions, to render them on the page in such a way that they could be recognized, even celebrated, without becoming debilitating. William Dean Howells, whose work as an editor and novelist placed him at the center of American realism, sounded this optimistic note in an 1887 *Harper's Monthly* column: "Let fiction cease to lie about life . . . let it speak the dialect, the language, that most Americans know – the language of unaffected people everywhere – and there can be no doubt of an unlimited future, not only of delightfulness but of usefulness, for it."

By the end of the next decade, that optimism seemed less possible – and not only for Howells, but also for his contemporary Mark Twain, for the younger writers whom Howells promoted, like Stephen Crane, for naturalists such as Theodore Dreiser and Frank Norris, and for African American novelists such as Charles Chesnutt and Pauline Hopkins who chose to lodge their protests against the racism that too frequently seeped into American writing. Howells's own fiction offers a guide to the waning of this realist faith in the ameliorative power of mimetic fiction in his 1890 novel *A Hazard of New Fortunes*. There, Howells contrives to bring together an improbably divergent set of social types – a Midwest tycoon, a bohemian artist, an evangelist of the Social Gospel, an unreconstructed Southerner, a German-born socialist, and so on – to work on a literary magazine edited by Basil March, a recurring character in Howells's fiction whose experiences closely resemble his own. The periodical is clearly a microcosm of the nation, and the novel's first half includes comments by several characters about its possible social benefits. But the literary center cannot hold: The group first splinters after a turbulent dinner party and then fractures permanently when a violent streetcar strike precipitates the deaths of some characters and the departure of others. At the novel's conclusion, the magazine will continue, but with its staff reduced and its aspirations tempered. Even the size of the novel represents a departure from Howells's earlier writing; the book is among his longest, and reads as though the author was uncertain how to bring his characters to a state of satisfactory conclusion.

Realists like Howells had believed that fiction could produce a more equitable society, and the diminishing conviction in the power of fiction to have this effect becomes most visible in the turn-of-the-century literature that attends to the physical, economic, and psychological violence suffered by African Americans during this period. Considered by many scholars to be the nadir of American race relations, the 1890s and early years of the twentieth century saw a dramatic rise in the number of lynching deaths of African Americans. Over 100 of these gruesome murders were recorded each year from 1890 to 1900. In an 1896 decision that devastated hopes for social equality of the races, the Supreme Court ruled in *Plessy v. Ferguson* against integration in public facilities. In 1898, rioting whites stormed the black community of Wilmington, North Carolina, randomly murdering men in the street, driving black public figures from the town, burning a building that housed a local black press, and preemptively ousting a lame duck city government that had given municipal positions to African Americans. Decades after emancipation, African American authors found themselves still negotiating, in both the North and the South, a brutally racist national atmosphere. They did not have the luxury of describing, as Adams did, broken bodies in only metaphorical terms. The reality of the nation's racism kept expectations in check regarding what work literary realism or any other genre could do for the cause against racist violence; nevertheless, an awareness of the need for counter-narratives to racism compelled African American literary efforts. In other words, even though they may have been more guarded in their expectations, African American authors shared the reformist impulses of many of the writers associated with American realism. Indeed, the hope of producing racial equality may have been the most ambitious literary aim of the time.

Pauline Elizabeth Hopkins, in the preface to her 1900 novel *Contending Forces: A Romance Illustrative of Negro Life North and South*, asserts the role of fiction – both realist and romantic – to be "a preserver of manners and customs – religious, political and social" and the goal of her fiction, in particular, to do that which European American authors neglected to do: "faithfully portray the inmost thoughts and feelings of the Negro." However, Hopkins was not just working against a dearth of representation, but against an abundance of misrepresentation. Much literature, as well as the popular stage and the press, continued to propagate insidious antebellum stereotypes of African Americans as lazy, ignorant, conniving, degenerative, ridiculous, or childlike. In *Contending Forces* Hopkins disabuses her readership of the speciousness of these types, while interrogating narratives of moral and social progress in the years after emancipation. Although she is clearly committed to creating realistic portraits of African American lives, she departs from the conventions of the literary realist novel of manners by placing historical events in the foreground and delineating the role that history itself has played in shaping African American identities. Through plot-lines that unabashedly treat rape, incest, mob rule, and murder, Hopkins traces the legacy of slavery and the failure of Reconstruction: "While we ponder the philosophy of cause and effect, the world is horrified by a fresh outbreak [of violence], and the shocked mind wonders that in this – the brightest epoch of the Christian era – *such things are.*" Her italics mark the urgency of the effort to make real and known the suffering of African Americans through the art of fiction. Hopkins decidedly claims validity for her work through the values of realism – *"such things are"* – but the terrible necessity of testimony against outrage replaces realism's naïve enthusiasm for pure variety. In the sensational, melodramatic *Of One Blood* – serialized in 1903 – Hopkins pushed even harder against the conventions of mimetic fiction. Seances, the animation of the dead, and the search for a hidden Egyptian civilization are just a few of the fantastic plot elements of Hopkins' occult novel. The truth about race, she suggests, will not be found through the careful documentation of social niceties, but in the unseen forces that have driven Africans across continents and centuries.

The fantastic plot in *Of One Blood* was perhaps the most radical solution by an African American novelist to the problem of documenting racial violence in an age when so many turned a blind eye to it. Hopkins and other African American intellectuals, including Paul Laurence Dunbar and Charles W. Chesnutt, published their works alongside texts that cried "such things are *not*," texts that explicitly and implicitly denied African American experience. Dunbar, in an 1898 article entitled "Recession Never," points with indignation to the sinister language surrounding American racism: "Progress! Necessity! Expedience! But why is it necessary to excuse these acts of sophistry? Is not murder murder? Is not rapine rapine? Is not outrage outrage?" Fiction becomes a battleground for claims of history; Chesnutt joined Hopkins and Dunbar in that battle with his 1901 historical romance *The Marrow of Tradition*. He already enjoyed a respectable literary reputation among a mixed audience for his two 1899 collections of framed short stories, *The Conjure Woman* and *The Wife of His Youth*. While these stories manipulated dialect, sentimentality, superstition, and humor to address slippery and difficult issues of race relations in the post-Reconstruction South, they made no claim to address any specific historical event. *The Marrow of Tradition*, in contrast, directly responds to the 1898 Wilmington race riot and the media coverage that downplayed the violent actions of the white mob, glorified it as a "white revolution," and perversely represented nameless members of the black population as instigators of the riot.

At the center of *The Marrow of Tradition* are two families, the Millers and the Carterets, through whom Chesnutt details the ways in which the fates of both races depend, precariously, upon one another for survival. The central character, William Miller, a successful and respected African American doctor and a reluctant leader in the local black community, has a young son with his wife, Janet, the unacknowledged sister of Olivia Carteret who is wife to white supremacist newspaper editor Major Phillip Carteret. Olivia suppresses documentation of their father's marriage to his black servant, Janet's mother, and refuses to recognize her sibling. The novel opens with the birth of the Carterets' first and only child, the sickly son who is to be the sole heir to the

Carteret fortune and name. The Carterets, like many of the white characters in Wellington, North Carolina (Chesnutt changes the name of
the town, though the parallel to Wilmington remains clear), believe
that "Negro domination" and the burgeoning of a black community
will undermine the future of both their son and the nation at large.
However, the political and personal destinies of the two families meet
when Major Carteret uses his power as the editor of the local press
to foment the white riot that leaves the Miller's only son dead by a
stray bullet, and the Carterets' son dying of a breathing condition
with no doctors available to treat him. Chesnutt ends the story with
significant hesitation and lack of resolution: Dr Miller has been called
to the Carterets' home to operate on the dying child and he stands,
a father who has just lost his only son to an accident of racist hostility, at the base of the stairs. From the second floor comes the call,
"There's time enough, but none to spare." Chesnutt leaves off writing with these words, abandoning the reader with only the exigency
of the situation. Why should Miller help the family that destroyed his
own? One cannot help but read a parallel question into Chesnutt's
novel: Why should African Americans attempt to be helpful citizens
in a country that abuses them?

Howells wrote that he found *Marrow of Tradition* "bitter, bitter," a
comment that betrays how ill-prepared the conventions of literary
realism were for the harsh violence of the turn of the twentieth century. But the novels of Thomas Dixon suggest that Chesnutt's dire,
emotional climax to *Marrow* may not have been out-of-place at all.
Inflamed and inflammatory, Dixon was a prolific Southern writer who
infamously sentimentalized the history of radical racism and the rise
of the Ku Klux Klan in his first trilogy of novels: *The Leopard's Spots*
(1902), *The Clansman* (1905), and *The Traitor* (1907). The contemporary
popularity of these novels, which offer stories of valiant white heroes
of the Southern aristocracy defending pristine porcelain virgins from
the sexual voracity of degenerated "black brutes," evinces just how
invidious the debate around race was while Hopkins, Dunbar, and
Chesnutt were writing. Indeed, Hopkins, Dunbar, and Chesnutt each
enjoyed a humble readership compared to Dixon. Hopkins' writing was
published serially in *The Colored American*, which aimed specifically at
an African American audience, and reached a circulation of 15,000
subscriptions during the height of its popularity. Dunbar's popularity,
advanced tremendously among white readers by a positive review from
William Dean Howells, rested problematically upon his African American dialect poetry; his later novels did not enjoy many reprintings.

Chesnutt, similarly, would sell more books using the dialect framing of Uncle Julius than he would with a serious historical romance like *The Marrow of Tradition*. While Hopkins, Dunbar, and Chesnutt did reach many readers – albeit sometimes with ambivalence – they knew the enormity of the forces they were writing against. As a point of comparison, Dixon's *The Leopard's Spots* sold over one hundred thousand copies in the first few months of sales, and the other volumes of his trilogy met with similar success.

The Clansman, which Dixon adapted into the film *The Birth of a Nation* in 1915 with the help of D. W. Griffith, casts the Civil War, the assassination of Lincoln, and the implementation of Reconstruction as well as its collapse, as parts of an epic narrative of white America struggling to overcome the "Black Curse." Although reading Dixon brings insight into the high tension of white anxieties over black citizenship and enfranchisement during this era, modern readers will find Dixon's sensational storylines ridiculous in their blatant white supremacist agenda. For example, in *The Clansman*, the impetus for the formation of the Ku Klux Klan is the rape of a young white woman named Marion (whose only dream was to marry young and "to fill the world with flowers, laughter, and music") by a black man, Augustus "Gus" Caesar. After the rape, Marion and her mother decide to commit suicide together and thereby hide her shame. In one of the most outrageous moments of the text, Marion's effort to conceal her rape is thwarted by a doctor who looks into the eyes of the corpses with a microscope in order to discover "on the retina of these dead eyes the image of this devil as if etched there by fire." Whatever doubt lingers in characters' minds over this pseudo-scientific evidence is abolished when Gus, under hypnosis, reenacts the crime for a jury of clansmen. The white men lynch Gus, and begin to "reclaim" the South by terrorizing black communities. Dixon ends the novel with his young white hero asserting that because of the clan, "Civilisation has been saved, and the South redeemed from shame."

Dixon's white supremacist fantasies are read today by few people other than scholars seeking to contextualize racism in the early twentieth century. Though Dixon's ideologically and stylistically dated writing has descended into relative obscurity, it nevertheless serves as evidence for the prophetic assertion of W. E. B. Du Bois that "the problem of the Twentieth Century is the problem of the color-line." Du Bois's *Souls of Black Folk* (1905), which includes elements of autobiography, history, sociology, philosophy, fiction, and musical analysis, stands as one of the most lastingly relevant texts of the twentieth

century, as well as an influential experiment in terms of its varied
generic and aesthetic composition. The dynamic conceptualizations
and potent metaphors that he uses to probe the color-line influenced
the development of American Modernism and fueled the Harlem
Renaissance. In *Souls*, Du Bois locates the problem of race in the United
States as a problem of perspective, of viewing things from the outside
versus from the inside. A history of racism, argues Du Bois, created a
"veil" between the races, obscuring the vision of each, but giving African
Americans a particular insight into the forces that continued to divide
them from whites. Utilizing the language of psychology, a discipline
undergoing significant changes in the 1890s and early 1900s due to
the work of figures such as William James (Henry James's brother)
in America and Sigmund Freud in Europe, Du Bois proposes that black
folk in the United States have a "double-consciousness." He writes:

> It is a peculiar sensation, this double-consciousness, this sense of always
> looking at one's self through the eyes of others, of measuring one's
> soul by the tape of a world that looks on in amused contempt and pity.
> One ever feels his two-ness – an American, a Negro; two souls, two
> thoughts, two unreconciled strivings; two warring ideals in one dark body,
> whose dogged strength alone keeps it from being torn asunder.

Henry Adams describes forces that destroy intellectual coherence; Du
Bois describes forces that may ultimately engender creativity through
courageous endurance.

For Du Bois, the "two-ness" of African American experience enables
a new, authentically American art exemplified by the sorrow songs.
He opens each chapter of *Souls* with an excerpt of a piece of canonical
Western literature and a line of music from these songs, using this
juxtaposition to both validate and differentiate the artistry of the music.
Born from the horrors of slavery, songs such as "Nobody Knows the
Trouble I've Seen" and "Swing Low, Sweet Chariot" represent to Du
Bois the unflagging will of black folk to produce art and perform their
humanity. The acceptance of hybridity then, for Du Bois, provides the
ideological structure necessary to negotiating the "veil" that attempts
to partition black experiences from the dominant white culture and
to surviving the rending of "unreconciled" forces that would fragment
and diminish the black psyche. In this way, the sorrow songs are paradigmatic in *Souls*, and Du Bois concludes the book with an appreciative
and insightful analysis of this music. He emphasizes that the sorrow
songs are organic to African American experiences: exile, betrayal,
mourning, strife. Yet what Du Bois works to uncover for his readers

is the way that these songs represent a blending of displaced African and displaced European cultures on American soil. They carry centuries-old African melodies and rhythms even as they partially absorb the English language or the distortions of the minstrel stage. Du Bois avers that the sorrow songs refute the much-cited argument that the darker races are in a less-advanced stage in human progress. Rather, they signify the common struggles of humanity, and Du Bois proffers them to his readership as a hopeful gift, wondering: "Our song, our toil, our cheer, and warning have been given to this nation in blood-brotherhood. Are these not gifts worth the giving?"

Music and history collide in Du Bois' penultimate chapter, the fictional story "Of the Coming of John." When the title character John leaves his small town of Altamaha, Georgia, in order to be educated at Wells Institute, a fictional black college, he finds that his education leaves him with a disturbing paradox: knowledge of history and his place in that history occlude his happiness, and yet he would not be content without that knowledge. John's epiphany occurs when he wanders into an opera house and becomes infatuated with the music, only to be ejected because of his race. John's situation perfectly exhibits double-consciousness; he discovers through the music his own love of the beautiful, yet he is also made painfully aware that whites regard him merely as a black body without capacity for such appreciation or intelligence. John returns to Altamaha wise and somber, but resolute in doing what he can to serve his community by teaching. However, the white school superintendent closes his school because of John's "almighty airs and uppish ways," and John's complete downfall is ensured when he murders a young white man, also named John, for molesting his sister. The story ends with John standing at the scene of the murder, listening to the noise of an approaching lynch mob and conflating that sound with opera music. Du Bois' free indirect discourse elegantly captures John's confusion: "Hark! was it music, or the hurry and shouting of men? Yes, surely! Clear and high the faint sweet melody rose and fluttered like a living thing, so that the very earth trembled as with the tramp of horses and the murmurs of angry men." John's last thoughts are of Wagner's lyrics from the "Song of the Bride," and then of pity for white John's father. He turns in a gesture of surrender, with his eyes closed, toward the sea, and waits listening to the mingling of remembered music and the rumble of the mob. Such operatic gestures and references confer upon John's death an aura of aesthetic tragedy, as if to say such endings are inevitable when white cultural ideology directly confronts African American experience in one person. The music appears as much responsible for leading John into the "coiling twisted rope" as white John's inculcated sense of entitlement to black John's sister. As beautiful as the music is to John, it only reminds him of "the veil" that divides how he understands himself and how the white world apprehends him. Finally, the high cultural form of the opera helps Du Bois convey the terrible irony of John's intellectual and emotional sophistication being destroyed by the crude forces of white racism.

Appearing in a book that bridges autobiography and sociology, polemic and documentation, "Of the Coming of John" offers a particular function for the work of fiction at the turn of the century. It supplements social scientific descriptions of the violence of everyday life, but it also stands apart from non-fictional narrative in its effort to harness the energies being unleashed upon the world through a stronger sense of plot than the fiction of the previous generation had deployed. Moreover, with its collision of operatic drama and folk melodies, Du Bois positions his fiction as a mediating work among competing forms of mass culture. This role is significant, for it suggests something of a larger shift in American fiction during this period. As Nancy Bentley points out, Chesnutt's *Marrow of Tradition* follows an earlier tradition in its thorough skepticism of the cultural forms that circulate information and images through mass populations; both the newspaper and the stage feed the violence of the Wilmington riot in Chesnutt's account. Du Bois, on the other hand, remains more ambivalent, suggesting that forms of mass culture could make visible a history of African American suffering – a notion that would later capture the attention of the ragtime-playing protagonist of James Weldon Johnson's *Autobiography of an Ex-Colored Man* (1912).

This kind of engagement with forms of mass culture slowly developed in the literary fiction of the turn-of-the-century as literary authors grappled with a world in which their own art appeared to be diminishing in its social significance. No work of fiction more fully treats this question than Theodore Dreiser's *Sister Carrie* (1900), the novel of Carrie Meeber's immersion into the commercial society of the urban metropolis, her extramarital relationships with two men, and subsequent success as an actress. In Dreiser's Chicago and New York, the very geography of the city streets is configured so as to produce an orgy of display for the masses who walk them. Plate glass windows extend down to the sidewalks, soliciting consumers for the commodities housed inside, and the pedestrians themselves participate in the making of spectacle. "To stare seemed the proper and natural thing,"

Dreiser's novel tells us of the Broadway promenade. "Carrie found herself stared at and ogled." Looking and being looked at are the cornerstones of the social world that Dreiser depicts. The education of Carrie Meeber therefore shapes her into a font of longing for the material things that will enable her to succeed in this spectacular economy. "She did not grow in knowledge so much as she awakened in the matter of desire," Dreiser writes – and what Carrie learns to desire are those things that will make her more desirable to others. As Priscilla Wald has argued, Carrie is not seduced by the men she meets, but by the city itself.

Dreiser figures this economy of desire most evocatively in Carrie's achievements as an actress. In a crucial passage in which the novel describes Carrie's talents, Dreiser describes his heroine as being in possession of a "sympathetic, impressionable nature" as well as "an innate taste for imitation." Throughout the book, the question of which instincts and forces are "natural" and which are not recurs, and the genius of Carrie's thespian career seems to rest in her ability to walk a line: She is *naturally imitative*. This characterization depicts not just Carrie but the theatrical realm in which she succeeds as occupying a kind of borderland between the real and the false, between the slavish copy and the wholly original. Carrie is neither, and her inability to achieve a kind of self-consciousness about this position is a crucial component of this performance as well. In the final sections of *Sister Carrie*, Dreiser introduces Robert Ames, an inventor from the Midwest who seeks to instill in Carrie a proper sense of the value of things, as well as an aspiration for more serious drama than that in which she has appeared. However, if the novel intends Ames to provide a final (male) correction to Carrie's unfocused, constant (female) desire, then it is also deliberately ambiguous as to the possibility of success. At the conclusion of *Sister Carrie*, which exists in multiple versions because of editorial intervention, Carrie is reading Balzac and is newly aware of the social injustices of the kind European naturalism portrays. Yet there are no indications that high literature will remake Carrie's acting career or the stage on which she performs; the penultimate chapter informs us that "the old, mournful Carrie – the desireful Carrie, – unsatisfied" remains.

Literature, in other words, may be able to describe Carrie's desires, but Dreiser's novel is ambiguous about the extent to which literary narrative itself will have a decisive role in this new economy of desire. In an age of visual, mass culture, could literary art be enough of a force to sway, or even survive, Carrie's – or the masses' – superficiality and insatiability? Dreiser recognizes that *Sister Carrie* itself must compete for the attention of the public that it is trying to represent. Newspapers, though, are a different matter. Hurstwood, whose decline is juxtaposed in the novel with Carrie's success, becomes enraptured by the newspapers, which he uses to learn about the local events that affect his search for employment. Eventually, the newspapers paralyze Hurstwood; he sits reading rather than venturing into the city itself. In contrast, the Sunday newspaper offers one of the few depictions of unalloyed pleasure in the life of Jurgis Rudkis, the protagonist of Upton Sinclair's *The Jungle* (1906). A "most wonderful paper could be had for only five cents," he realizes. "There was battle and murder and sudden death – it was marvelous how they ever heard about so many entertaining and thrilling happenings; the stories must be all true, for surely no man could have made such things up, and besides, there were pictures of them all, as real as life."

The Jungle, of course, is full of its own "battle and murder and sudden death" in its grim account of the meat-packing industry in Chicago, and the purpose of the book was to show that the horrors it detailed "must all be true." While occasional rumors of media corruption are floated through the novel – and in one particular episode Sinclair blames the newspapers for exaggerating the violence of a labor dispute – in fact *The Jungle* suggests that the newspapers do on occasion provide a check against the capitalist excesses of industrial life. The novel mentions that they have exposed the mishandling of waste, the canning of horsemeat, and the medical experiments on indigent patients at a hospital – the kind of muckracking with which Sinclair himself was famously identified. Near the end of the novel, as Sinclair introduces his reader to the Socialist party, he even includes a paean to its national organ, *The Appeal to Reason*: "It had a manner all its own – it was full of ginger and spice, of Western slang and hustle: It collected news of the 'plutes,' and served it up for the benefit of the 'American working mule.'" *The Jungle*, in fact, does something different by collecting the stories of an immigrant family – "working mules," one might say – and using them to reflect on the working conditions created by the "plutes," or plutocrats. But what the novel shares with the propaganda newspaper as Sinclair describes it is a desire to circulate the truth among a mass public, and in doing so create an audience that understands itself *as* a mass public and is able to strike a blow for its own interests.

Sinclair's novel conceives of itself as a mass cultural event about the process of mass production, and it confronts the forces of mass production in two different arenas: The making of meat out of the bodies of animals, and the making of members of the American working class out of immigrants. While the exposé of the former received more attention in Sinclair's time – influencing legislation regulating the meat industry – the link between these two processes is in fact the burden of the novel. Early in the novel, Jurgis and his family tour one of the slaughterhouses and witness how the steers walk to their deaths under their own power. "[I]t was quite uncanny to watch them," Sinclair writes, "pressing on to their fate, all unsuspicious, a very river of death." At this point in the narrative, however, the recently-arrived immigrants fail to make the connections between the fate of the animals and their own voluntary migration to the meat-packing factories: Just as no part of the animal goes unused by the factory, all of the physical and mental energy of the laborers is extracted by their labor – and by their constant effort to secure for themselves the barest material existence. Just as the public prefers not to see how its sausage is made, it also turns a blind eye to the way that immigrant laborers are ground into the political process – led through the citizenship system and manipulated as voters by the bosses who run Packingtown.

Jurgis's epiphanic moment, which occurs upon his introduction to socialist politics near the conclusion of the novel, finally yields an identification with the beasts that he has slaughtered: "his new acquaintance showed him that a hog was just what he had been – one of the packers' hogs." *The Jungle* reinforces this relationship by repeatedly referring to Jurgis and other laborers using animal imagery; Sinclair has all of the subtlety of a propagandist. In fact, his characterization of the powerlessness of the Packingtown class is so effective that Jurgis's self-realization has less emotional force than the chapters that precede it. The optimism of Sinclair's conclusion, in other words, is less convincing than his *tour de force* of the brutality of the economic and social forces that have converged upon the lives of Jurgis, his family, and his peers.

This characterization of a human world driven by animal, bestial instincts was central to the naturalist fiction being published in the United States at the turn of the century. "Among the forces which sweep and play throughout the universe, untutored man is but a wisp in the wind," Dreiser writes in *Sister Carrie*. "Our civilisation is still in a middle stage, scarcely beast, in that it is no longer wholly guided by instinct; scarcely human, in that it is not yet wholly guided by reason." Chapter Four of this volume takes up the emergence of

American naturalism, and its relation to realism, in more detail. For now, we wish to note the way in which naturalists – among whom we might include Henry Adams – believed that these primitivist forces were being unleashed in the world. They contended that the forces of market capitalism existed as extensions of or arenas for this animality. Frank Norris titled the first part of his "Epic of the Wheat" trilogy *The Octopus* (1901) – a naming of the railroad as an insatiable beast whose hunger can neither be subdued nor whose will affected by human intervention. At the conclusion of the first chapter, a character imagines a passing locomotive as a "symbol of a vast power, huge, terrible, flinging the echo of its thunder over all the reaches of the valley, leaving blood and destruction in its path; the leviathan, with tentacles of steel clutching into the soil, the soulless Force, the iron-hearted Power, the monster, the Colossus, the Octopus." The locomotive is not simply these things itself, but a "symbol" of them, for the true force that Norris seeks to reckon with goes beyond any single object, but rather is elemental and universal; indeed, it extends to the land itself. The novel ends with an agent of the railroad, a speculator and land broker, buried in an avalanche of wheat: "a prolonged roar, persistent, steady, inevitable." The wheat is greater than any person who would attempt to control it, a symbol of the global, natural forces that will always prevail over the wills of even the most potent individuals.

The emphasis on animality in Norris has a definitively masculine cast. As Gail Bederman and others have described, the turn of the twentieth century was a moment in which white manhood was widely considered to be in jeopardy from both the emasculation of "over-civilization" and competition from non-white peoples. For this reason, just as fiction worked to expose the brutish nature of American men, Theodore Roosevelt was urging them to engage in the "strenuous life," and groups such as Ernest Thompson Seton's Woodcraft Indians (and later the Boy Scouts) were being founded to give a chance for white children to cultivate a relationship to American Indians. Jack London took this primitivist turn even further in his highly popular dog novels *Call of the Wild* (1903) and *White Fang* (1906). In the first, canine protagonist Buck is stolen from a Californian ranch and transported to Alaska, where he awakens to his primal memories of wild life and becomes transformed into the "Ghost Dog" of the wilderness. The latter novel reverses this movement by bringing a dog of the "savage, frozen-hearted Northland Wild" into the civilization and domesticity of the south. In both cases, London's novels attempt to dramatize the power of social environment over their male, animal protagonists. Progress is measured through the lens of a violent evolutionism, and can only occur when the forces of nature – figured as masculine – are properly recognized.

Male authors and male protagonists (animal or otherwise) were not the only ones, however, who felt the forces of everyday life outstripping the aesthetic conventions that realism and other cultural institutions had developed for the representation of their society. American realism had subsumed much of women's writing under the category of "regional" or the more diminutive label of "local color fiction," but the rich body of work by authors such as Sarah Orne Jewett and Mary Wilkins Freeman emphasized the role of women in negotiating the relationships among local, national, and even global forces. Terms like "regional" and "local color" may be problematic as names for the complexity of this fiction, but at least they suggest something of the uneasy relationship of such texts to an American realism that still placed male-authored novels at the center. On the other hand, both of these terms are wholly useless when accounting for the kind of female experience depicted by Charlotte Perkins Gilman in "The Yellow Wallpaper" (1899), her Gothic account of the "rest cure," a treatment used for women suffering from nervous ailments. With its first-person monologue, its narrative fragmentation, and its vision of both oppression and release, Gilman's story reads much more like the modernist fiction of the decades that followed it than the prose that had dominated the literary marketplace of the preceding one. She would later write a utopian novel, *Herland* (1915), but never an account of everyday domestic life as conceived by the realists.

Kate Chopin, on the other hand, did begin her literary career writing short fiction of the regionalist variety, two collections of Louisiana tales, *Bayou Folk* (1894) and *A Night in Acadie* (1897). *The Awakening* (1899) departs from this set of conventions, though, by focusing away from the material conditions of domestic life and its psychological pressures. Edna Pontellier, Chopin's protagonist, engages in both sexual and romantic affairs outside of her marriage, and decides to take up residence apart from her husband. Her "awakening" takes place only by degrees; she is unable to articulate what compels her to do what she does, it is not a process of clarity or even clarifying self-consciousness. In a passage that describes Edna as she is "beginning to realize her position in the universe as a human being," Chopin describes Edna's inner life as "tangled, chaotic, and exceedingly disturbing. How few of us ever emerge from such beginning!" What throws Edna into turmoil is her own kind of call from the wild: "The voice of the sea is seductive; never ceasing, whispering, clamoring, murmuring, inviting the soul to wander for a spell in abysses of solitude; to lose itself in mazes of inward contemplation."

Edna Pontellier, famously, listens to the voice of the sea, acting on the desires that it represents and then, when she comprehends the difficulty of achieving them, swims out into the ocean in what most readers interpret as a suicide. This kind of ending is more than the failure of consensus that fractures the unifying vision of, say, Howells's *Hazard of New Fortunes*. Rather, it registers a sense that modernity itself is incapable of assimilating the emotional and psychological currents that are driving Edna Pontellier into the sea. Chopin's narrative cannot fully explicate those currents. Suggesting them evocatively, rather than articulating them in detail, is part of the dilemma of the novel. The literary imagination of the turn of the twentieth century simply has no space in which a heroine like this can live. Nor is her demise an isolated example. Although written in a style much more fully conversant with the idiom of American realism, Edith Wharton's *House of Mirth* (1905) also ends with its protagonist's death, another possible suicide, this time the result of a complicated matrix of upper-class social mores and economics. Lily Bart simply cannot afford the life that she wants to live with what she conceives to be honor, and takes an overdose of sleeping medication as she repays her last debt. In doing so, she joins Henry Adams and Edna Pontellier on the honor roll of victims to the "sequence of force" that dominated their age.

By the time ten years had passed in the new century, the arena of American fiction was home to an emerging modernist aesthetic that would confront the forces of spiritual alienation, mass representation, and social violence in significantly different ways from the works of the late nineteenth century. By 1910, Gertrude Stein had woven the interior voices of women into the taut short fiction of *Three Lives* (1907); James Weldon Johnson was a short two years away from publishing his existential masterpiece of the experience of racialization in *Autobiography of an Ex-Colored Man* (1912); and in three years Willa Cather would publish *O, Pioneers!* (1913), the first of her novels that combined the regionalist devotion to place with the questions of feminine desire that sweep Edna Pontellier out to sea. The sense of transition into a new era of American literature was also highlighted by the passing of an icon, for 1910 was also the year of the death of Samuel L. Clemens, or Mark Twain, the preeminent figure in American letters during the preceding three decades.

Out of chance beginnings in journalism, Southwestern humor, and travel writing, Mark Twain rose to prominence at the end of the nineteenth century as a representative figure of American literature and culture. During the last decade of his life he enjoyed a fame that transcended conventional boundaries, puckishly (but perhaps accurately) describing himself as "the most conspicuous person on the planet." As important as his writing had been to the development of the national literary identity of the United States – readers championed his rough-and-tumble tales, his masterful use of dialect, and his balance of nostalgia and critique in narratives about the antebellum nation – was his literary *persona* as "Mark Twain" to marketing him as an American icon. Like Dreiser's Carrie, Mark Twain maintained an incredibly effective (and likeable) artificial naturalness that is at least partially responsible for his enduring reputation.

Still, in spite of his exceptional successes, Mark Twain was not immune to the wrenching forces of the turn of the century. The dynamic world of new technology captured his imagination, and his investments into printing innovations in the early 1890s devastated his finances. In order to repay his creditors and avoid bankruptcy, he started on a world lecture tour and made an agreement to publish anything that he managed to finish. The deaths of two of his three daughters, as well as his brother and his beloved wife, arguably affected just how much he would publish during the last fifteen years of his life, though abundant unfinished manuscripts evince that he persisted in writing through his mourning and personal struggles. Nevertheless, readers of Mark Twain's later writings – the travel narrative *Following the Equator* (1897) that accompanied his world tour, and short stories such as "The Man Who Corrupted Hadleyburg" (1899), "The War Prayer" (1905), and "What Is Man?" (1906) – will find darker evolutions from the writings that propelled him to fame.

Though the possibility for human goodness does not entirely disappear in the later works, never again is there a literary moment testifying to faith in humanity equal to Huckleberry Finn's "crisis of conscience," Huck's decision to "go to hell" rather than turn his friend Jim in to the authorities. Rather, in the late works we see sympathetic characters unable to free themselves from their cultural conditioning or transcend their natural frailty. When the honesty of a village is put to the test in "The Man Who Corrupted Hadleyburg," the righteous citizens self-destruct out of greed, as well as of pride in their own righteousness. When a prophet explains to a congregation in "The War Prayer" that any prayer for victory in war calls simultaneously for the suffering, death, and defeat of other human beings, the congregation reaches the consensus that "the man was a lunatic, because there was no sense in what he said." They ineluctably persist in the belief that their prayer is humane and just. The congregation's disturbingly blithe and narrow assessment of the prophet and his words may reference Mark Twain's own frustration with attempting to change the world through literature. In "What Is Man?," an Old Man instructs a Young Man in cynicism and determinism, teaching him that men are but machines which may have a degree of free choice, but certainly do not have free will. The Old Man avers that the choices that people make are choices offered by cultural training. Even virtues – heroism, self-sacrifice, love – all come down to the training of persons to desire them, nothing more.

In "The Turning Point of My Life" (1910), one of the last pieces Twain published before his death, he playfully applies his philosophy of determinism to the trajectory of his own life. He first refutes the title of his piece, declaring that there was no one point in his life that should be given "too much prominence, too much credit." Instead, he suggests that one point might be more "conspicuous" than others, though "in real importance it has no advantage over any one of its predecessors." Somewhat ironically, then, he compares young Sam Clemens' ridiculous decision to actively contract the measles (in order to end his tedious anticipation of contracting the illness) to Caesar's decision to cross the Rubicon. At once donning comic arrogance and applying determinism to its extreme ends, he asserts, "I was one of the unavoidable results of the crossing of the Rubicon." The bathetic humor of his approach distracts his readers from the story's espousal of entropy in the place of meaningful destinies and progressive narratives. Mark Twain maps out how his decision to have the measles led his frustrated mother to apprentice him to a printer to keep him out of trouble, and how his apprenticeship allowed him to wander, how his wandering led him to finding lost money, and how that money financed a journey down the Mississippi (with hopes of leaving for the Amazon), and how he ended up instead apprenticing himself to a river pilot, and so on. Whereas Henry Adams abandons historical narrative when it fails to offer him the force of sense and meaningfulness, Mark Twain revels in its chaos. The dogma of determinism may rob a life of glory, but it also cleanses a life of guilt: Circumstance, not any human being or nation, dictates history. Twain does not conclude with despair but with his characteristic risibility: "Leaving the Rubicon incident away back where it belongs, I can say with truth that the reason I am in the literary profession is because I had the measles when I was twelve years old." Twain's embrace of the absurdity of the modern condition made him the exception rather than the rule in the turn-of-the-century world in which he lived, but it would fit perfectly with the twentieth century that followed in his wake.

References and Further Reading

Adams, Henry 1984: *Novels; Mont Saint Michel; The Education*. New York: Library of America.

Bederman, Gail 1995: *Manliness and Civilization: A Cultural History of Gender and Race in the United States, 1880–1917*. Chicago: University of Chicago Press.

Bentley, Nancy 2005: Literary Forms and Mass Culture, 1870–1920. In Sacvan Bercovtich (ed.), *Cambridge History of American Literature, Volume Three: Prose Writing, 1860–1920*.

Bercovitch, Sacvan (ed.) 2005: *Cambridge History of American Literature, Volume Three: Prose Writing, 1860–1920*. New York: Cambridge University Press.

Bramen, Carrie Tirado 2000: *The Uses of Variety: Modern Americanism and the Quest for National Distinctiveness*. Cambridge: Harvard University Press.

Chesnutt, Charles W. 2002: *Stories, Novels, and Essays*. New York: Library of America.

Chopin, Kate [1899] 1996: *The Awakening*. New York: Simon and Schuster.

Dixon, Thomas 1905: *The Clansman: An Historical Romance of the Ku Klux Klan*. New York: Doubleday, Page, and Company.

Dreiser, Theodore [1900] 1997: *Sister Carrie*. New York: Doubleday.

Du Bois, W. E. B. [1905] 1996: *The Souls of Black Folk*. New York: Modern Library.

Dunbar, Paul Laurence [1898] 1975: Recession Never. Cited in full in Jay Martin (ed.), Foreword, *A Singer in the Dawn: Reinterpretations of Paul Laurence Dunbar*. New York: Dodd, Mead & Company, 25–9.

Elliott, Michael A. 2002: *The Culture Concept: Writing and Difference in the Age of Realism*. Minneapolis: University of Minnesota Press.

Evans, Brad 2005: *Before Cultures: The Ethnographic Imagination in American Literature, 1865–1920*. Chicago: University of Chicago Press.

Gillman, Susan Kay 2003: *Blood Talk: American Race Melodramas and the Culture of the Occult*. Chicago: University of Chicago Press.

Gilman, Charlotte Perkins [1899] 1993: *The Yellow Wallpaper*, eds. Thomas L. Erskine and Connie L. Richards. New Brunswick: Rutgers University Press.

Hartman, Saidiya V. 1997: *Scenes of Subjection: Terror, Slavery, and Self-Making in Nineteenth-Century America*. New York: Oxford University Press.

Higham, John 1988: *Strangers in the Land: Patterns of American Nativism, 1860–1925*. New Brunswick, NJ: Rutgers University Press.

Hopkins, Pauline [1900]1988a: *Contending Forces: A Romance Illustrative of Negro Life North and South*. New York: Oxford University Press.

Hopkins, Pauline 1988b: *The Magazine Novels of Pauline Hopkins*. New York: Oxford University Press.

Howard, June 2001: *Publishing the Family*. Durham: Duke University Press.

Howells, William Dean [1890] 2002: *A Hazard of New Fortunes*. New York: Modern Library.

Howells, William Dean 1993: *Selected Literary Criticism*. 3 vols, eds. Ulrich Halfmann, Donald Pizer, and Ronald Gottesman. Vols 13, 21, and 30 of *A Selected Edition of W. D. Howells*. Bloomington: University of Indiana Press.

Kaplan, Amy 1992: *The Social Construction of American Realism*. Chicago: University of Chicago Press.

Kern, Stephen 1983: *The Culture of Time and Space, 1880–1918*. Cambridge, MA: Harvard University Press.

London, Jack 1982: *Novels and Stories*. New York: Library of America.

Lott, Eric 1993: *Love and Theft: Blackface Minstrelsy and the American Working Class*. New York: Oxford University Press.

Michaels, Walter Benn 1987: *The Gold Standard and the Logic of Naturalism: American Literature at the Turn of the Century*. Berkeley and Los Angeles: University of California Press.

Norris, Frank 1986: *Novels and Essays*. New York: Library of America.

Pizer, Donald (ed.) 1988: *Documents of American Realism and Naturalism*. Carbondale: Southern Illinois University Press.

Rampersand, Arnold 1976: *The Art and Imagination of W. E. B. Du Bois*. Cambridge, MA: Harvard University Press.

Russett, Cynthia 1976: *Darwin in America: The Intellectual Response, 1865–1912*. San Francisco: W. H. Freeman.

Seltzer, Mark 1992: *Bodies and Machines*. New York: Routledge.

Shi, David E. 1995: *Facing Facts: Realism in American Thought and Culture, 1850–1920*. New York: Oxford University Press.

Sinclair, Upton [1906] 1988: *The Jungle*. Urbana: University of Illinois Press.

Sundquist, Eric J. 1993: *To Wake the Nations: Race in the Making of American Literature*. Cambridge, MA: Belknap Press of Harvard University Press.

Twain, Mark 1992: *Collected Tales, Sketches, Speeches, and Essays: 1891–1910*. New York: Library of America.

Wald, Priscilla 2004: Dreiser's Sociological Vision. In Leonard Cassuto (ed.), *The Cambridge Companion to Theodore Dreiser*. New York: Cambridge University Press, 177–95.

Warren, Kenneth W. 1993: *Black and White Strangers: Race and American Literary Realism*. Chicago: University of Chicago Press.

Chapter 2

Women and Modernity

Jennifer L. Fleissner

For advocates of the expansion of women's sphere in the United States and beyond, the arrival of the year 1900 marked an auspicious moment. A guidebook for girls trumpeted, "there has never been a period in the world's history when a girl was of more importance than she is just now . . . Some of our most able writers tell us that we are just on the threshold of 'the woman's century'" (Waterman 1910: 13–14).

In 1893, the African American novelist and activist Frances Harper spoke similarly of standing "on the threshold of woman's era"; a year later, a journal dedicated to black women's issues, Woman's Era, was born. Overall, magazines in the final years of the 1890s burst with articles bearing such titles as "The Modern Woman," "Woman: A Phase of Modernity," "Woman's Future Position in the World," and "The Evolution of the Sex" – not to mention "Are Womanly Women Doomed?"

Whether enthusiastic or skeptical, the writers of such essays stood united in their view that the figure often referred to as "the New Woman" was a cultural force to be reckoned with. She was commonly identified with certain unmistakable changes in the lives of white, middle-class women, in particular, in the decades following the Civil War: increasing rates of higher education (in 1870, 21 percent of American college students were female, by 1910, 40 percent); a new presence in the workplace, particularly in burgeoning white-collar fields such as clerical work (2.5 percent female in 1870; dominated by women by 1930); and, in the home, trends toward smaller families, later marriages or even lifelong singlehood, and an increasing acceptability of divorce.

These were, of course, broad social shifts that occurred over a number of decades and were often not noticed until their impact was already quite significant. By contrast, in the 1890s, the discourse of the New Woman's advent was much more proactive and self-conscious, a development in which not only magazine articles but novels led the way. By 1898, a writer for the popular journal *Munsey's* was able to joke that:

> By a judicious use of the woman problem, the modern novel writer can save himself the trouble of plot, situation, action, minor characters, and all the furniture that was once thought indispensable to a well fitted out book. So long as the central character is a woman who is developing with each chapter, nothing else needs to happen. She may progress from A to Z, or begin at Z and retrograde to primitive A, or she may show that the woman's era is dawning, or is over . . . she may prove anything or nothing. (1898: 149)

The "modern novel," for this writer at least, could be viewed as near-synonymous with the novel about the "developing" modern woman.

While many of the first such books appeared earlier in the 1890s in Britain, by the beginning of the twentieth century, they had become commonplace fare in the United States as well. The British novels tended to be psychological explorations by women authors writing explicitly from the stance of a "New Woman." By contrast, their American counterparts, just as likely to be the work of men, seized upon the modern woman's evolving story as a particularly apt lens through which to view the dizzying landscape of modernity itself. This was not so surprising, given that many of the most oft-noted features of that landscape – including urbanization, industrialization, and the rise of consumer culture – were arguably integral, as we will further see, to the shifts taking place in women's lives.

Two books published right on the new century's "threshold," in 1900, can give a preview of what was to come as American writers continued, at least through the 1920s and early 1930s, to explore women's changing stories as a signal emblem of changing times. One, Robert Grant's *Unleavened Bread*, was a bestseller in its day, yet has been all but forgotten now. The other, Theodore Dreiser's *Sister Carrie*, garnered little success at the time but has risen in stature since to become an acknowledged classic of American realism. Together, they begin to sketch out some of the most important elements in the development of the novel of women and modernity, itself an often overlooked category of early twentieth-century American fiction. Most broadly, we will see, both adopt a narrative mode characterized by constant self-reimagining on the part of a restless female protagonist.

At first glance, while both books are clearly interested in portraying a new kind of heroine appropriate to a shifting social landscape, they would appear to do so very differently. Grant's Selma White fits much more the *Munsey's* model of the modern woman obsessed with her own ongoing "development," a buzzword Selma herself uses throughout the book. Typically, it comes up when Selma is musing as to whether her present husband – she has three over the course of the novel – will allow her space for her personal "development." Selma's commitment to her era's ideal of female emancipation is quite explicit; as she asks one spouse-to-be, "Surely you are not one of the men who grudge women the chance to prove what is in them – who would treat us like china dolls and circumscribe us by conventions?" ([1900] 1906: 99). She speaks of becoming "one of the army of new American women" (237) who will, "side by side" with their mates, pursue "the important work of the world" (321).

Grant further links Selma to the New Women of the day through her energetic involvement in the local women's club, the Benham Women's Institute. Like many such clubs that sprang up across the United States in the 1890s and flourished in the early decades of the twentieth century, the Institute blends cultural uplift ("A paper on Shakespeare's heroines was read and discussed. Selections on the piano followed" [51]) with the advocacy of reforms such as women's suffrage, aid to the poor, and prohibition. America's actual women's clubs federated in 1892 and thereafter held national conferences, one of which Selma is shown to attend. She does so alone, over her husband's protests, and the result, on his end, is a one-night stand that ends up ruining their marriage.

Here, Grant's perspective on Selma's urgently pursued project of self "development" begins to become clear. For her, divorce appears synonymous with becoming "free – free – free" (84); it concludes a section of the book ironically titled "The Emancipation." Selma is further "emancipated" earlier in the same section by the death of her baby, which occurs at home while she is off looking into local architectural reforms with the man who will later become her second husband. Grant depicts her as initially viewing motherhood as an "unwelcome interruption of her occupations and plans" (51), and as relieved when her doctor "pronounce[s] the supply of her breast-milk inadequate," which she views as "an indication of feminine evolution from the status of the brute" (60); at the same time, two days prior to the baby's death, she reads a paper to the Institute on "Motherhood," which is "enthusiastically received" (65). The hypocrisy Grant conceives here is as significant, for him, as the turn against marriage's "natural" function (51). Despite Selma's strenuous feminist rhetoric, she is shown much preferring the perks of wedlock to ever more powerful men – finally, a US senator – to economic independence or even any significant work of her own. Her "modern woman"'s stance thus stands revealed as not only morally suspect; it is, in the end, nearly empty of content.

In this respect, she may be interestingly compared with Dreiser's Carrie Meeber. Carrie, coming to Chicago to look for work at eighteen in 1889, possesses none of Selma's self-conscious discourse of female emancipation. Naïve and knowing only that she enjoys creature comforts when she has them, she allows herself to be "kept" by two men in succession under the vague, misguided belief that they intend to marry her. By the end of the book, however, she has left both behind and achieved success in her own right on the Broadway stage. Hence, without explicitly having aimed at it, she in many ways arrives at the independence that Grant's Selma only claims to seek so passionately.

As such, Carrie may be said to embody, if not a New Woman, then another significant type of modern womanhood also receiving journalistic attention around the turn of the century. Often labeled the "woman adrift," this figure was, like Carrie, a young woman who deliberately cut family ties in order to seek a broader life for herself in the growing cities of the 1880s and 1890s. It is a striking historical fact that many more women availed themselves of this opportunity during this era than did men, attesting to a sense that the modern urban environment offered new kinds of opportunities to young women in particular at this time. Certainly, previously unknown categories of work, such as stenography, were opening up for them; Carrie, for one, expects to be employed as a "shop-girl" in one of the grand, newly unveiled department stores. Yet Dreiser's novel also reflects a real-life vagueness about the broader trajectory and meaning of these newly urbanized women's lives. "She would get in one of the great shops and do well enough," thinks Carrie's sister Minnie about her sibling, "until – well, until something happened. Neither of them knew exactly what. They did not figure on promotion. They did not exactly count on marriage" ([1900] 1970: 11). The famously inconclusive ending of *Sister Carrie* – Carrie continuing to move ever back and forth in her rocking-chair, still dreaming of what she has not yet achieved – thus speaks to this uncertainty about how to tell the full story of the modern woman "adrift."

At the same time, it shows what Dreiser's portrayal and Grant's do have in common. Selma White's story, too, is defined by a sense of constant dissatisfaction throughout. In both books, it is this desire for something more that leads the young, provincial woman to seek a more exciting life in the big city; and, again in both cases, the urban environment is depicted as stimulating rather than salving the sense that there is always another level of success to be attained. Instead of offering either a happy ending or a tragic fall, as Dreiser's narrator suggests at the outset we expect when a girl in a novel comes to the city, the new landscape produces a narrative of seemingly endless self-remaking. This process becomes quite literal in each book via the heroine's adoption of a series of different identities – stage names and aliases in Carrie's case; new surnames for Selma as she remarries again and again.

Importantly, this story of ongoing self-refashioning – in which the city street takes on the features of a theater or display window – is also linked, again in both novels, to the discourse of consumerism, with its lesson that one should never rest content with what one has. A sympathy note sent to Selma upon her child's passing leads her to ponder "whether she ought not to buy mourning note-paper" (Grant [1900] 1906: 71). Carrie, famously, imagines she hears seductive voices emanating from her "soft new shoes" and lace collar (75). The early years of the twentieth century marked a shift in the status of consumption in American culture; once viewed as a suspect means of indulging excessive desires, the purchase of unnecessary items and enjoyment of leisure activities began to appear, to a new generation of social scientists, key to a healthy economy, and thus to the public good. At the same time, seen as a particularly feminine pursuit, shopping drew women out of the home and thus blurred lines between public and private spaces demarcated by gender. As the title of one study of the period, *The Adman in the Parlor* (Garvey 1996), suggests, the same could be said of the new crop of advertisement-driven magazines. These, too, brought housewives into contact with a wider world and thus could play a role in stimulating the kind of dissatisfaction with traditional alternatives that brought real-life Sister Carries to the city in search of change.

Of course, the same developments could also be seen, as in *Unleavened Bread*, as a lamentable incursion of market values into the once-sacrosanct middle-class home. Selma thus drives her artistically

41

minded second husband, Wilbur Littleton, nearly to a breakdown (and perhaps his death) by encouraging him to speculate financially to back their social ascent. The critical perspective here finds an echo in two slightly later novels indebted to Grant's influence: Robert Herrick's *Together* (1908), conceived explicitly as a quasi-epic of modern American womanhood, and *The Custom of the Country* (1913), by a good friend and vocal admirer of Grant's, Edith Wharton. Wharton's ruthless social climber Undine Spragg similarly destroys a similarly sensitive spouse, Ralph Marvell; for her, marriage amounts to a "business partnership," and divorce a process to be "as carefully calculated as the happiest Wall Street 'stroke'" ([1913] 2001: 207, 224). For Herrick, more sweepingly still, the twentieth-century "emancipated woman"'s heated pursuit of "[her] own desires" cannot finally be separated from the growth of "the most material age and the most material men and the least lovely civilization on God's earth" ([1908] 1910: 517).

In both *Together* and *Custom*, indeed, the modern woman as Grant depicts her begins to harden into a highly standardized figure. These books, too, show her chafing against the limitations of her small-town world, eager for a "large, full life" packed with "pretty furniture" and "charity committees" (Herrick [1908] 1910: 46, 36), disgusted and debilitated by the unwelcome advent of motherhood, and ceaselessly dissatisfied, "ever trying to find something beyond the horizon" (195). (In the final lines of *Custom*, Undine, just married for the fourth time and living in "an exact copy of the Pitti Palace" on Fifth Avenue, discovers with chagrin one more token of success that has eluded her [Wharton [1913] 2001: 359].) In many ways, this sense of the heroine as a reproducible type forms part of the critique itself; she is not simply the ultimate consumer, but herself a consumer product – what the historian and social critic Henry Adams labeled in 1900 "the monthly-magazine-made American female" (in Adams [1918] 1931: 384).

More broadly, in an era when women reject their natural role as mothers, it is implied, the result is a modern generation made up not of nature's creatures but of human commodities. *Together*'s heroine Isabelle, raising her daughter according to all "the best modern theories," thus generates in the end a colorless "product," a "wooden doll" (Herrick [1908] 1910: 576). Wharton's Undine, daughter of a listlessly fashionable mother who herself resembles "a wax figure in a show window" ([1913] 2001: 4), has been named not for the water-sprite but after a hair-waver marketed by her father ("'It's from *un*doolay, you know, the French for crimping'" [50]). And in her later novel *Twilight Sleep* (1927), Wharton is even more scathing, depicting a relentlessly up-to-date matron who conceives of "babies [as] something to be turned out in series like Fords" ([1927] 1997: 18). The children here reflect the technologized state of their mothers, as in the case of the matron, who spends her days frenetically applying Frederick Winslow Taylor's principles for routinized factory management to her own battles with worry and age.

Her husband, by contrast, yearns for a simpler time when he might have accomplished "real things" instead of "spinning around faster and faster in the void" of "all this artificial activity" (71). It is a notable feature of all the books mentioned that the men who marry these determinedly modern women are themselves portrayed as throwbacks – helpless or appalled in the face of their wives' dizzying motion. Once impressed by them, the women soon grow beyond them; Dreiser's Carrie begins to see her sad, out-of-work lover Hurstwood as a millstone holding back her own career. In a remarkable reversal of nineteenth-century gender norms, the men thus become the conservative guardians of tradition, culture, and home, while the women represent a mechanized, ever-changing modernity. T. S. Eliot, accordingly, while raging against the modern world's ravages in "The Waste Land," embodies those who succeed in such a world in his passionless typist, who "smoothes her hair with automatic hand / And puts a record on the gramophone."

Eliot might have made his point even more bluntly had he called this female clerical worker a "type-writer," a term that in the early twentieth century referred both to the recently invented office machines and the women who used them. Both entered the previously male-dominated office around the same time, and the rationale for employing women had everything to do with their supposedly natural aptitude for routine, repetitive activity. Others noted that, in an industrialized era, barriers to women's work in many fields would surely break down, for physical strength no longer held the importance it once had for success within them. In various ways, then, women began to become subtly aligned not with nature, as we would expect, but with machinery. "Suppose . . ." Sherwood Anderson went so far as to muse in his 1931 *Perhaps Women*, "the whole modern age, the industrial age, the machine age, were women-made?" (55).

Anderson's point, in part, was that the very aspects of modernity that seemed to make men feel "crushed, humiliated," as if "the mystery of existence" has been taken from them – for "men need . . . direct connection with nature in work" – granted a new kind of power to women (48, 43–4). In Anderson's account, however, this was not necessarily because women had become more machinelike themselves. Rather, they appeared to be less affected by the advent of technology – perhaps, he argued, precisely because, while men saw themselves as competing with the machines and losing, the women retained a natural power, a distinctively "human," "personal" quality, that the machine could not take away (142).

The flip side, indeed, of the view of modern life as making woman more artificial can be seen in a number of counter-representations of her as more natural, because she has broken loose of Victorian conventions (literally, in the case of the discarded corset and other dress reforms) and has been given greater room for honest self-expression. The precursor text here is perhaps less *Unleavened Bread* or *Sister Carrie* – though Carrie, true as she is to the voice of her desires throughout Dreiser's novel, might be read along these lines – than a book published a year before both, Kate Chopin's 1899 *The Awakening*. In keeping with its more romantic than realist perspective, Chopin's book depicts female self-discovery as a matter not of social or economic success but of communion with the natural world, of lusty eating and unbridled sexual passion. Interestingly, occasional gestures toward this alternate viewpoint can be detected even in books like Herrick's *Together*, which softens its critique of modern femininity in presenting at least one character for whom a torrid affair is depicted as a legitimate, even ennobling means of expressing her own belief that "she had a soul, an inner life of her own, apart from her husband, her children" ([1908] 1910: 278). A much more fully developed version of it, however – and one in which the realist and romantic perspectives are shown more to merge – appears in David Graham Phillips's often overlooked two-volume epic (published in 1917, though written earlier), *Susan Lenox: Her Fall and Rise*.

The story of an illegitimate "fallen woman" from a small town who goes on to achieve great acclaim as an actress in New York, *Susan Lenox* resonates with some clear echoes of *Sister Carrie*. Even more than Dreiser, however, Phillips tells his story through a "naturalist" lens, giving a Darwinist thrust to Susan's worldly success. While Susan resembles an earlier breed of novelistic heroine in her beauty, intelligence, and resourcefulness, she stands apart in being characterized insistently throughout the book by her "health" and "strength." "'Grand heart action! . . . I've never seen anything more alive,'" cries the doctor who delivers her ([1917] 1930: I, 6, 8); later, she is distinguished from her "doll-like" cousin Ruth by her possession of "the greatest of all qualities," "naturalness" (I, 19). Yet Susan is perhaps less "natural" than, as she is characterized at one point, "supernatural" (I, 381) – an Amazonian figure who, in keeping with the book's title, finds over and over again that adversity (not to mention alcohol and opium) makes her stronger still. "I back you to win," she is told, admiringly, by two men in succession (I, 240); and what Susan learns is that to "win" in the urban jungle of New York means to comport herself "exactly like a man . . . free from the rules . . . A woman can't fight with her hands tied" (II, 268).

Phillips' portrayal of Susan's remarkable natural vitality, in other words, comes clearly yoked to a feminist message. Even more strikingly, many of the features that in the other books mentioned function as signs of the modern woman's egotism and artifice appear here recast as emblems of a salutary independence and natural liberation from social constraints. For Susan, New York is "the City of the Sun," "the isles of freedom"; she negotiates its crowds "like an expert swimmer adventuring the rapids" (I, 430; II, 82; II, 94). The modern feminine language of being "free" from familial ties – mocked in Grant's Selma White and Wharton's Undine Spragg – is here presented approvingly (I, 416), as is Susan's enjoyment of pretty things, which appears as a sign not of greed but of taste (II, 299). "*Ich bin ein Ich!*" she proclaims at the end of the book (II, 485); to become an "I," not a "we," appears as a triumphant female achievement. Indeed, *Susan Lenox* concords with the other books mentioned perhaps only in its pairing of the ambitious Susan, for most of the book, with a familiarly hapless male counterpart, a failed playwright who at one point confesses to his mate, " 'Yes, I *am* a whiner! Susie, I ought to have been the woman and you the man'" (II, 207).

One of Susan's appropriations of male prerogative in fact involves telling this same man she has no interest in marrying him, only in living together: "'I'm not in love with you . . . I simply like you . . . You're physically attractive to me'" (II, 269). While this frank admission of female sexual desire goes quite a few steps further than *Sister Carrie* – and helped get Phillips into hot water at the time of the book's publication – *Susan Lenox* does resemble its predecessor in notably sidestepping the issue of pregnancy. Had it been broached, that subject might (as in Chopin's *The Awakening*) have posed interesting complications for the book's sunny association of modern female independence simply with greater "naturalness."

In this respect, Phillips's novel might usefully be placed side by side with another text both published and also censored around the same time, Edith Summers Kelley's *Weeds* (1923). *Weeds*, too, offers a romanticist vision of feminine freedom in the figure of Judy Pippinger, who grows up poor in rural Kentucky yet consoles herself with the wild, beautiful, "vital" natural setting around her, with which she feels strongly in tune ([1923] 1972: 56). This portrayal of nature as a figure for "freedom from constraint" (88), however, changes drastically when Judy becomes pregnant and gives birth, processes Kelley describes in graphic physical detail. Suddenly, nature appears a constraining horror; the seemingly unstoppable arrival of one baby after another is likened to the proliferation of weeds, which she and her tobacco-farmer husband fight against daily. "The women who liked caring for babies could call her unnatural if they liked," Judy decides. "She wanted to be unnatural . . . Their nature was not her nature and she was glad of it" (240).

Like *Susan Lenox* and other naturalist texts about women, *Weeds* thus not only considers its characters within the framework of a larger natural order, but raises particularly modern questions about how to define "nature" itself. Particularly pertinent to *Weeds* was the growing influence of the movement for accessible birth control, a term coined by the activist Margaret Sanger in 1914. In her *Birth Control Review*, which began publication three years later, Sanger responded to such claims as Pope Pius XI's that birth control "frustrates nature" by stating, "'the Pope frustrates nature by getting shaved and having his hair cut'" (Kennedy 1970: 153). Similarly, the feminist sociologist Charlotte Perkins Gilman conceived her 1915 feminist utopia *Herland* as an exploration of what women's lives would look like under more "natural" conditions; in the case of her all-female Herland, these turned out to include an ability to become pregnant or not – without male intervention – simply by directing one's will toward the idea. In the real-life United States, however, the occasional eugenicist pronouncements of writers like Gilman and Sanger contributed to a birth-control movement often divided along class lines.

For authors of more realist fiction, birth control and, even more, abortion stood among the more strongly tabooed subjects in writing about changes taking place in American women's lives. One of the rare books to address both matters head on was Sinclair Lewis's late work *Ann Vickers* (1933). (Lewis, it is worth noting, had once been engaged to Edith Summers Kelley, and later helped her get *Weeds* into print.) With the aid of a feminist doctor friend, settlement worker Ann ends her first pregnancy after discovering her lover's unfaithfulness, and while she notes amusedly that "She did not at all feel 'ruined,'" she continues to mourn the child – a girl, she decides – that might have been (215). When she later marries a fellow social worker, however, she finds him more and more unpleasant (he calls her the "Little Woman" [434]) and determines to use birth control to ensure their union will not produce offspring. Instead, the end of the book finds her at forty defiantly having the baby of another lover, an unhappily married judge, and at last leaving her husband, as her lover leaves his wife, so that the three of them can begin a new life of freedom together.

Of the writers who emerged in the years following World War One, Lewis stands out as of particular interest for the way he, even more than Phillips, explicitly takes on and recasts many of the notions about the consumerist, antimaternal modern woman dating back to Grant's *Unleavened Bread*. While the staunch Ann Vickers is involved from her teens in much more clearly political causes, including feminism – she works for women's suffrage, then the settlement house, and, finally, women's penitentiary reform – Carol Kennicott of Lewis's earlier and more celebrated *Main Street* (1920) seems at first glance to share a great deal with the more vaguely dissatisfied, flighty heroines of Grant's book or Herrick's *Together*. Like them, she feels herself trapped by small-town life, and spends much of her time generating faintly absurd "village improvement" schemes such as the construction of a "Georgian town hall" or the creation of a drama club that ends up rejecting Shaw in favor of "The Girl from Kankakee." Bounding wildly from one activity to the next, puzzling her folksy husband with ongoing high talk of her "right to her own life" ([1920] 1961: 405), and "scared to death" that pregnancy will come along and interrupt all her plans (36), Carol could easily have been portrayed by her creator with the same mockery and scorn evident in Herrick and Grant. In the main, however, she is not. Instead, Lewis takes the dilemma of the newly college-educated woman with "a working brain and no work" quite seriously (86). While *Unleavened Bread*'s Selma wrecks her marriage by traveling with her women's club but without her husband, Carol saves hers by spending two years living alone with her child and working for a living (as a clerk) in Washington, DC.

The difference here may be chalked up in part to an interesting shift: in both *Unleavened Bread* and Wharton's *Custom of the Country*, the hyper-modern young woman is presented as herself representative of the vacuity of the American small town, the provincial ideals of which she then brings along to city life. The women's club becomes emblematic of the conjunction of a dubious feminine discourse of self-improvement with the cultural impoverishment and self-satisfaction that both Grant and Wharton saw as typical of the Midwest in particular. Yet whereas Lewis is if anything more scathing on the subject of Main Street, USA, he portrays his modern woman, Carol, not as its finest flower but as a rebel against the conventionalities it represents. Hence, her own experience with the local club, the Thanatopsis, is one in which enthusiasm quickly sours into chagrin as they reject her suggestions for discussions of Swinburne, science, and labor issues in favor of sessions on "furnishings and china" ([1920] 1961: 143).

By depicting the town of Gopher Prairie as a complacent middle, moreover, Lewis is able to portray Carol as at once freshly natural *and* more cosmopolitan than her neighbors. This is not to say that her many failed schemes are not gently mocked. The quest for something more that they represent, however, gets taken seriously. Lewis's novel sustains a judicious tone that can also be found in Zona Gale's *Miss Lulu Bett*, which was published in the same year and often compared to *Main Street*. The spinster Lulu shares few of Carol Kennicott's grand ambitions; she knows only that, daily, her small reserve of "individualism" finds itself at war with "that terrible tribal sense" as it is represented by her sister's family, who board her as a barely noticed domestic "slave" ([1920] 1994: 102). When Lulu at the end suddenly announces that she is leaving to marry the man the family had selected as a fiancé for their teenage daughter, the household reacts with shock that this meek woman could have any sort of life of romance and change at all. For a dramatic version that won the Pulitzer Prize a year later, Gale, herself a suffrage activist, at first chose an even more *Doll's House*-like ending in which Lulu spurns both her suitor and her family, instead lighting out for the city on her own. Although audience complaints forced a revision, critics were delighted: as one wrote, "Miss Gale has done authentically what perhaps only a *feminist*, and certainly only an *artist* can do. She has shown, in perfect American terms, the serious comedy of emancipation . . . that famous conflict between the tribe and the growing feminine individuality" (quoted in Williams 2001: 118).

Although the retiring Miss Lulu Bett hardly seemed the image of the "modern girl" as she increasingly appeared in the popular media of the 1920s, this way of putting the matter – as a struggle between "the tribe" and "the growing feminine individuality" – sounded a note right in tune with the times. Historians looking back at the 1920s have often distinguished the era's modern girl or flapper from her New Woman antecedents as being a "post-birth-control figure," "more interested in self-fulfillment than in social service . . . Like the heroine of a *McCall's* story in 1925, her philosophy was 'To live life in one's own way'" (Woloch 1984: 382). Of course, as we have seen, the feminists of the previous decades had already been caricatured since at least 1900's *Unleavened Bread* for using a high-flown rhetoric of social reform to disguise essentially narcissistic goals – a portrayal that re-emerges in Edith Wharton's portrait of the older generation of women in her Jazz Age satire *Twilight Sleep* (1927). In comparison, that generation's postwar children are depicted as being at once caught up in the new personal freedoms of the twenties – nightclubbing, fewer sexual inhibitions, more of a developed youth culture – and as less idealistic, more "disenchanted," at the same time ([1927] 1997: 12).

Overall, while the flapper – a figure who appeared in a similar form around the world, whether in the *girlkultur* of the Weimar Republic or as Japan's modern girl, the *moga* – could be easily identified with prevailing consumer trends in fashion, hairstyle, and popular music, her inner life, her hopes and goals, remained something of an enigma. Yet unmistakably, where such pre-1920s heroines as Lewis's Carol Kennicott or Ann Vickers emerge bewildered and a bit discomfited from their brief encounters with "bohemian" types in enclaves such as Greenwich Village, the young women of novels like *Twilight Sleep* embrace that culture without a second thought, as their birthright. It becomes, indeed, the sign of their "individualism" and separation from their elders – from the "tribe," even if the tribe is made up of the previous generation's more Puritanical feminist rebels.

In other novels of the era, however – notably, those by African American and immigrant women writers – this conflict between the "tribe" and the modern girl wishing to "live life in her own way" becomes a more vexed one. Published in 1928, both Jessie Fauset's *Plum Bun* and Nella Larsen's *Quicksand* represent takes on the "young woman comes to New York" story by writers themselves involved in that city's Harlem Renaissance. In each case, the mixed-race heroine flees a life in which she feels constrained by constant talk of duty to the black community; she hopes New York will bring a new world not only of pleasure but of "freedom and independence," in the words of Fauset's Angela Murray, who studies to become an artist ([1928] 1990: 88). At first, each heroine seems to find what she seeks. Angela, notably, meets for the first time fascinatingly bohemian young women making their own living by their art: Paulette, a smoke-ring-blowing siren who forthrightly pursues affairs with multiple men, and Martha Burden, a Village-dwelling intellectual and holder of salons. Like them,

Angela decides, "She would live her life as an individualist, to suit herself without regard for the conventions . . ." (207).

In fact, however, the goal of this "modern girl" grows decisively complicated, in each book, by the persistence and complexity of the issue of race. For Angela, the life of freedom she craves is synonymous with "passing" as white (under the name "Angele Mory"), a strategy that at first appears an exciting "game against public tradition . . . and family instinct" (146) but that soon leads her to the morally questionable ends of an affair with a racist man and, in order to placate him, a public rejection of her own darker sister. Larsen's Helga Crane, who finds herself too dogged by "the race problem" even in Harlem, escapes to the all-white world of her dead mother's native Denmark, similarly believing she will find there a way to "belon[g] to herself alone and not to a race," to "put the past behind her" ([1928] 1986: 64); instead, she finds she is treated by the Europeans as an exotic primitive, and begins to yearn for the community she left behind.

For these heroines, then, the modern elevation of the "individual" over the "tribe" is an aim that begins to appear not only harder to achieve than expected, but also less appealing. Fauset and Larsen choose to handle the dilemma, however, in markedly different ways. Fauset allows for the compromise-free fairy-tale ending, in which the young man Angela realizes she has loved all along turns out to have been passing himself. (She also gets to stand up to the art prize committee that disqualifies her on account of her race, and still take the money and go to Paris anyway.) Larsen, in stark contrast, shows Helga swinging violently back toward "tribal" loyalty in the form of marriage to a Southern reverend for whom she becomes a domestic drudge and childbearing machine; the book concludes as, weakened in body and soul and dreaming vaguely of "freedom and cities," she realizes she is pregnant once more with her fifth child ([1928] 1986: 135).

Some of the same problems recur in the Jewish immigrant writer Anzia Yezierska's autobiographical *Bread Givers* (1925); in addressing them, Yezierska plots something of a middle ground between the approaches of Fauset and Larsen. Sara Smolinsky's fight against the "tribe" takes the form of a more direct struggle against her Torah-scholar father, for whom "only through a man has a woman an existence." "Thank God," she throws back at him, "I'm not living in olden times . . . I'm going to make my own life" ([1925] 1975: 137–8). Much more in this novel, as Sara sees each of her sisters haplessly married off to unsuitable men, wage work and a "room all alone to myself" are presented as the means to a desired independence – a goal that Sara seems to achieve by the close, having earned her degree as a teacher. As such, however, she learns to recognize the continuity that actually connects her to her father's studies, despite his ongoing rejection of her choices. The book thus ends not with a sense of an achieved break between past and present, but with Sara musing over "the problem of Father – still unsolved," and not just him, "but the generations who made [him]," still "weigh[ing] upon me" (296–7).

The genuine difficulty, for the striving young woman, of negotiating a relation to a past she can neither simply embrace nor reject, achieves a vividness here not evident in the same degree in books from the same era about native-born white heroines. In them, one tends to find the dilemma of tradition versus modernity framed in the more familiar terms of love versus work. Indeed, as the "white-collar-girl" stenographer heroine becomes a familiar type in the texts of the 1920s and 1930s, workplace romance often serves as a narrative means to articulate the choices lying before her. Here, too, however, one finds some novels imagining (remarkably early on) a fairy-tale synthesis of old and new storylines, while others find it far harder to imagine such an idealized solution.

One of the most enjoyably fluffy of the fairy-tale scenarios can be found in Edna Ferber's three-volume homage to the indefatigable traveling saleswoman Emma McChesney, which began in 1913 with *Roast Beef Medium*, a collection of sketches about the same character previously published in magazines. Sidestepping the white-collar-girl plot by having entered the workplace following motherhood and a divorce that leaves her to raise her child on her own, Emma is shown occasionally yearning for domestic comforts, then always snapping back into business mode at the slightest whiff of a big sale. In the final installment, *Emma McChesney and Co.* (1915), it grows clear that her own long-belated marriage to the boss, T. A. Buck of Buck's Featherloom Petticoats, will merely enable an ideal balance of home life and work – and, into the bargain, Emma becomes not a mother, but a delighted grandmother to the daughter (named for Emma, of course) of her grown-up son.

Sinclair Lewis's pre-*Main Street* paean to the white-collar girl, *The Job* (1917), allows for a similarly rosy conclusion – heroine Una Golden climbs the corporate ladder *and* gets her man – although Lewis writes considerably more cuttingly about the obstacles faced along the way. While Una finds even clerical work to be fulfilling throughout the novel, she fears the future – "Always she saw the girls of twenty-two getting tired, the women of twenty-eight getting dry and stringy, the women of thirty-five in a solid maturity of large-bosomed and widowed spinsterhood" – and, endeavoring to escape such a fate, briefly leaves it all behind in favor of marriage to "the affably dull Mr. Julius Edward Schwirtz" ([1917] 1994: 234). A womanizer and drinker, jovially clueless about his wife's ambitions, Schwirtz is a composite of all the residual men of the era's novels, finally ending up a double of *Sister Carrie*'s Hurstwood as he loses his job and sinks into a state of home-bound abjection in which his once-harried wife can only pity him. In a reversal similar to that we see in Dreiser, the woman begins to find all her joy and companionship in the workplace, returning to which she rapidly rises to become a saleswoman, while the home becomes a male-identified space of stasis and drudgery. At the end, only marriage to a more enlightened fellow employee can ensure a desirable combination of the two.

Not all "white-collar-girl" novels end up as ready to imagine an idealized ending for their questing heroines, however. Booth Tarkington's 1921 *Alice Adams* keeps matters starkly ambiguous as his ambitiously social-climbing protagonist finally admits defeat and mounts the steps up to Frincke's Business College, to a fate she had always conceived of much as does Lewis's Una Golden: "pretty girls turning into withered creatures as they worked at typing-machines; old maids 'taking dictation' from men with double chins . . ." ([1921] 1997: 90). In the novel's final lines, however, Alice glimpses rays of sunshine at the top of the stairs – and we have no way of knowing whether this simply marks the return of her trademark optimism, so often shown to be charming but futile throughout the novel, or the genuine possibility that the stenographer's fate may not be as fatal as it seems.

By the end of the thirties, the plight of the clerical heroine receives its most explicit thematization in Christopher Morley's *Kitty Foyle* (1939), whose outspoken narrator waxes sociological about the unrecognized mass to which she belongs:

> I read about the guts of the pioneer woman and the woman of the dustbowl and the gingham goddess of the covered wagon. What about the woman of the covered typewriter? What has she got, poor kid, when she leaves the office? . . . I see them in subways and on buses, putting up a good fight in their pretty clothes and keeping their heebyjeebies to themselves. There's something so courageous about it, it hurts me inside. (261, 334)

As Kitty notes, newspaper columns on such topics as "the Working Girl's Budget" have little idea of what it takes even to dress properly for most office jobs (167). Her own work, as secretary to a Frenchwoman hawking perfume and beauty creams, seems merely part of the scam to which women like her are subjected. Morley, too, finds no fairy-tale ending for Kitty; like *Alice Adams*, his novel leaves his heroine still wondering what the future may or may not hold.

Although C. Wright Mills, in his sociological study *White Collar* (1956), took note of the advent of the white-collar-girl novel, the books discussed in this essay overall have virtually never been analyzed as a group. Indeed, they have rarely even been recognized as one, let alone seen as a significant strand in American realist fiction in the first half of the twentieth century. Interestingly, one of the only writers to have even begun to link them was Edith Wharton, who wrote to Zona Gale of her equal admiration for *Miss Lulu Bett* and *Main Street*, and who in her essay on "The Great American Novel" praised the latter, as among her own recent favorites, by comparing it to both *Unleavened Bread* and *Susan Lenox: Her Fall and Rise*. Within literary scholarship, Kenneth Lynn stands out singularly for asserting, in his *The Dream of Success: A Study of the Modern American Imagination* (1955), that "the American novel in this century has been, perhaps more than anything else, a continuing study of the emergent, still-changing, ever-new American woman. Undine Spragg, Alice Adams, Carol Kennicott, Kitty Foyle . . . these have been the characteristic figures of our modern fiction, and their various ambitions have supplied its dynamic power" (15).

One might ask, in what sense "characteristic figures"? How does it change our understanding of American fiction from 1900 through 1950 to conceive of these "emergent" women as somehow representative of their times? In calling them "still-changing" and "ever-new," Lynn supplies one possible way in – for, as we saw, the sense of this modern woman's story as a seemingly endless narrative of self-remaking is a thread that, from the first, connected works as disparate as our two pathsetters from 1900, *Unleavened Bread* and *Sister Carrie*. At first, such followers as *Together* and *Custom of the Country* seemed interested in this storyline only as a means to expose the emptiness of their heroines' ambitions, their similarity to the consumer's hopeless quest for ideal happiness.

In later novels such as *Susan Lenox*, *Main Street*, *Plum Bun*, and *Quicksand*, however, the pull of conflicting desires and goals, and uncertainty about how to achieve them, is portrayed with considerably more sympathy and concern. The modern heroine's lack of a road map for her narrative of self-discovery makes her indeed emblematic of an era that has left traditional paths behind, yet these novels make clear that it is possible to present her dilemma without nostalgia. She may appear, in her present form, disturbing, like the Louise Bentley whom Sherwood Anderson in *Winesburg, Ohio* (1919) characterizes as "a neurotic, one of the race of over-sensitive women that . . . industrialism was to bring in such great numbers into the world" ([1919] 1960: 87). Yet Anderson goes on to suggest that "Before such women as Louise can be understood and their lives made livable, much will have to be done. Thoughtful books will have to be written and thoughtful lives lived by people about them" (87). This more than simply literary imperative, we might then say, stands, finally, as the true legacy of the early twentieth-century American novel of women and modernity.

References and Further Reading

Adams, Henry [1918] 1931: *The Education of Henry Adams*. New York: The Modern Library.

Ammons, Elizabeth 1992: *Conflicting Stories: American Women Writers at the Turn into the Twentieth Century*. New York: Oxford University Press.

Anderson, Sherwood [1919] 1960: *Winesburg, Ohio*. New York: Viking.

Anderson, Sherwood 1931: *Perhaps Women*. New York: Horace Liveright.

Ardis, Ann 1990: *New Women, New Novels*. New Brunswick, NJ: Rutgers University Press.

Birken, Lawrence 1988: *Consuming Desire: Sexual Science and the Emergence of a Culture of Abundance*. Ithaca: Cornell University Press.

Botshon, Lisa and Meredith Goldsmith (eds.) 2003: *Middlebrow Moderns: Popular American Women Writers of the 1920s*. Boston: Northeastern University Press.

Carby, Hazel V. 1987: *Reconstructing Womanhood: The Emergence of the Afro-American Woman Novelist*. New York: Oxford.

Chopin, Kate [1899] 1994: *The Awakening*. New York: Norton.

Davies, Margery W. 1982: *Woman's Place Is at the Typewriter: Office Work and Office Workers, 1870–1930*. Philadelphia: Temple University Press.

Dreiser, Theodore [1900] 1970: *Sister Carrie*. Ed. Donald Pizer. New York: Norton.

DuCille, Ann 1993: *The Coupling Convention: Sex, Text, and Tradition in Black Women's Fiction*. New York: Oxford University Press.

Eliot, T. S. 1971: *The Waste Land*. Ed. Valerie Eliot. New York: Harcourt Brace Jovanovich.

Fauset, Jessie Redmon [1928] 1990: *Plum Bun: A Novel Without a Moral*. Boston: Beacon.

Felski, Rita 1995: *The Gender of Modernity*. Cambridge, MA: Harvard University Press.

Ferber, Edna [1913] 2001: *Roast Beef, Medium: The Business Adventures of Emma McChesney*. Urbana: University of Illinois Press.

Ferber, Edna [1915] 2002: *Emma McChesney and Co.* Urbana: University of Illinois Press.

Fleissner, Jennifer L. 2004: *Women, Compulsion, Modernity: The Moment of American Naturalism*. Chicago: University of Chicago Press.

Freedman, Estelle 1974: The New Woman: Changing Views of Women in the 1920s. *Journal of American History* 61.2, 372–93.

Gale, Zona [1920] 1994: *Miss Lulu Bett*. Oregon, WI: Wauseba Press.

Garvey, Ellen Gruber 1996: *The Adman in the Parlor: Magazines and the Gendering of Consumer Culture*. New York: Oxford University Press.

Gelfant, Blanche 1984: Sister to Faust: The City's "Hungry" Woman as Heroine. In Susan Merrill Squier (ed.) *Women Writers and the City*. Knoxville: University of Tennessee Press.

Gilman, Charlotte Perkins [1915] 1979: *Herland*. New York: Pantheon.

Grant, Robert [1900] 1906: *Unleavened Bread*. New York: Charles Scribner's Sons.

Hapke, Laura 1992: *Tales of the Working Girl: Wage-Earning Women in American Literature, 1890–1925*. New York: Twayne.

Herrick, Robert [1908] 1910: *Together*. New York: Macmillan.

Honey, Maureen 1992: *Breaking the Ties that Bind: Popular Stories of the New Woman, 1915–1930*. Norman: University of Oklahoma Press.

Kelley, Edith Summers [1923] 1972: *Weeds*. New York: Popular Library.

Kennedy, David M. 1970: *Birth Control in America: The Career of Margaret Sanger*. New Haven: Yale University Press.

Larsen, Nella [1928] 1986: *Quicksand and Passing*. New Brunswick: Rutgers University Press.

Lewis, Sinclair [1917] 1994: *The Job*. Lincoln: University of Nebraska Press.

Lewis, Sinclair [1920] 1961: *Main Street*. New York: Signet.

Lewis, Sinclair 1933: *Ann Vickers*. New York: Grosset and Dunlap.

Livingston, James 2001: *Pragmatism, Feminism, and Democracy: Rethinking the Politics of American History*. New York: Routledge.

Lynn, Kenneth 1955: *The Dream of Success: A Study of the Modern American Imagination*. Boston: Little, Brown.

Marks, Patricia 1990: *Bicycles, Bangs, and Bloomers: The New Woman in the Popular Press*. Lexington: University of Kentucky Press.

Meyerowitz, Joanne J. 1988: *Women Adrift: Independent Wage Earners in Chicago, 1880–1930*. Chicago: University of Chicago Press.

Mills, C. Wright 1956: *White Collar: The American Middle Classes*. New York: Oxford University Press.

Morley, Christopher 1939: *Kitty Foyle*. Philadelphia: J. B. Lippincott.

n.a. 1898: Evolutionary Novels. *Munsey's* xx. 1 (October), 149.

Phillips, David Graham [1917] 1930: *Susan Lenox: Her Fall and Rise*. New York: D. Appleton and Co.

Raub, Patricia 1994: *Yesterday's Stories: Popular Women's Novels of the Twenties and Thirties*. Westport, CT: Greenwood.

Tarkington, Booth [1921] 1997: *Alice Adams*. New York: Bantam.

Waterman, Nixon 1910: *Girl Wanted: A Book of Friendly Thoughts*. Chicago: Forbes.

Wharton, Edith [1913] 2001: *The Custom of the Country*. New York: Modern Library.

Wharton, Edith [1927] 1997: *Twilight Sleep*. New York: Scribner.

Wharton, Edith 1999: The Great American Novel. In Gordon Hutner (ed.) *American Literature, American Culture*. New York: Oxford University Press, 177–82.

Williams, Deborah Lindsay 2001: *Not in Sisterhood: Willa Cather, Zona Gale, and the Politics of Female Authorship*. New York: Palgrave.

Wilson, Christopher P. 1992: *White Collar Fictions: Class and Social Representation in American Literature, 1885–1925*. Athens: University of Georgia Press.

Woloch, Nancy 1984: *Women and the American Experience*. New York: Knopf.

Yezierska, Anzia [1925] 1975: *Bread Givers*. New York: Persea.

Chapter 3

Queer Modernity and Lesbian Representation

Kathryn R. Kent

Critics engaged in queer readings of literary texts face a unique dilemma. Claiming something as queer, or even more definitively, as lesbian, especially in the literary period that is the focus of this volume, is not always simple. Even using a biographical approach, in which the confirmed or rumored sexuality of the author becomes the standard of truth for queer readings of their works, cannot always produce an irrefutable "canon" of queer texts. There are historical as well as epistemological reasons for this: it would have been virtually impossible, given the literary and legal norms of the early-twentieth-century, to write an "out" literary text and have it published without risking legal action (as the obscenity trial subsequent to Radclyffe Hall's publication of *The Well of Loneliness* [1928] attests – although some writers, such as Djuna Barnes, succeeded nonetheless). Instead, critics of queer literature are often forced, through their readings, to justify the queer aspects of a text as part of their critical practice, rather than assume it.

In this chapter I analyze some of the American texts written during the period which might be said to constitute a queer female canon, while simultaneously demonstrating a multiplicity of critical, theoretical, and traditional literary methods that allow one to claim these texts as queer. This does not mean engaging in a hunt for the lesbian in the text, however. Instead I elucidate a variety of ways queer literary criticism contributes to a greater understanding of the formal, thematic, and epistemological aspects of a text. I interrogate the dominant critical assertion of queer modernity – that to be a modern self in this period entailed claiming a homo- or heterosexual identity. Finally, I engage critically with both the norms of realism and modernism, and especially the ways in which the literary innovations of modernism might have been particularly salient to or insufficient for representing queer sexualities.

Historians of sexuality argue that homo- and heterosexuality are recent inventions, particularly indicative of modernity and the formation of the modern self. In the late nineteenth century, a multiplicity of sexualities that had once been organized and regulated around acts became instead, through the workings of medical, psychological, and juridical discourse, organized around a compulsion to "have" a sexual identity defined by the gender of object choice, an identity thought to define the self. As Michel Foucault famously puts it, "the sodomite had been a temporary aberration; the homosexual was now a species" (Foucault 1978: 43). Eve Kosofsky Sedgwick extends Foucault's argument to claim that what defines the twentieth century is "the world mapping by which every given person, just as he or she was necessarily assignable to a male or a female gender, was now considered necessarily assignable as well to a homo-or a hetero-sexuality, a binarized identity that was full of implications, however confusing, for even the ostensibly least sexual aspects of personal existence" (Sedgwick 1990: 2). Elsewhere Sedgwick illustrates how such a binarized identity creates a crisis, "indicatively male," in which all men are required to identify on one side or another of the homo/hetero binary. The homosexual represents a set of culturally devalued traits, against which heterosexuality secures for itself a set of normative values (Sedgwick 1990: 1, 11). In this way, male homosocial relations and male–male sexual interactions that had once existed on a continuum now instead become defined in opposition to one another.

These theorists' works have been enormously influential in grounding the discipline of queer literary studies, yet their work focuses almost exclusively on white male identities and identifications. This focus raises several questions for the scholar interested in understanding the emergence of an American, specifically "female invert," "Sapphic," or "lesbian" identity. Was the imperative to identify as either homo- or heterosexual as relevant to women? Was there a definitive split between female homo- and heterosexual identifications parallel to those of men? Or do female–female erotics exist on a more fluid continuum with female–female homosociality? What connection if any does gender identification have with sexual desire? (Early sexologists asserted that "inverts" were improperly gendered, and that was what led them to desire the "same" sex – thus homosexuality was at heart a problem of gender identification, and desire for the opposite sex grounded even homosexual relationships.) Do texts by white and African American women in the United States of the early twentieth century employ the same strategies to represent female–female erotics and/or emerging lesbian identities as did their nineteenth-century counterparts? And how might these strategies parallel or challenge emerging modernist literary practices?

To answer these questions, this chapter examines a variety of literary styles, from the late-nineteenth-century realism of Mary Wilkins Freeman to the increasingly modernist, early-twentieth-century work of Henry James and the early Gertrude Stein, to the high modernist literary experimentation of later Stein, Djuna Barnes, Nella Larsen, and Zora Neale Hurston. It explores the range of representational tactics this diverse group of American literary texts employs to represent female–female erotics, identities, and identifications, especially in terms of articulating, resisting, or even critiquing a modern lesbian identity. It explores how the "open secret" (Sedgwick 1990) of queer desires might produce new representational possibilities for inscribing female–female desires and identifications. On the other hand, the chapter at times questions the imposition of queerness as necessarily secret, asking what happens if one reads lesbian and/or queer identifications and desires as visible – not assuming in advance the imperative of absence or secrecy.

Definitions of queer vary widely; for the purposes of this chapter, I employ the most inclusive: anything that falls outside the hetero- and gender normative (heterosexual identification and understandings of sex as primarily or centrally reproductive, or of sex acts defined most traditionally and narrowly as male–female genital intercourse, as well as normative notions of binarized gender identity and its relation to sexuality). While my aim is to be as expansive as possible in my deployment of the term, it is also important to assert, in the words of Sedgwick, that "given the historical and contemporary force of the prohibitions against every same-sex sexual expression, for anyone to disavow those meanings, or to displace them from the term's definitional center, would be to dematerialize any possibility of queerness itself" (Sedgwick 1993: 8).

Work that focuses specifically on the history of white women's sexualities in the United States argues that around the turn of the century a major shift occurred in how such women's relationships were viewed. Whereas in the nineteenth-century, "romantic friendships" between white women (and between some African American women) were often seen as natural and could even coexist alongside marriage (although even in the nineteenth century there is also evidence that some of these relationships were already stigmatized), by the late nineteenth century such relationships had begun to be viewed with some suspicion (Faderman 1981; Smith-Rosenberg 1985; Chauncey 1982–3; D'Emilio and Freedman 1997; Diggs 1995; Hansen 1996). Lisa Duggan argues persuasively that this was in part due to the visibility of the 1892 Alice Mitchell case, in which, enraged over the refusal of her female companion, Freda Ward, to see her anymore, Mitchell murdered her. What had previously been seen as harmless attachments were now increasingly viewed, in line with the emerging discourses of sexology, as deviant bonds (Duggan 2000).

Mary Wilkins Freeman's short story, "The Long Arm" (1895), fictionalizes the shift from the idealized romantic friendships of such nineteenth-century writers as Sarah Orne Jewett, as well as Freeman's own earlier work, to the creation of the gender deviant lesbian as perverse criminal (Faderman 1994: 372; Duggan 2000: 185–6). Sarah Fairbanks, a twenty-three year old girl eager to marry her suitor, Henry Ellis, narrates the story. Their union is thwarted, however, because of the threat of being disinherited by and alienated from her tyrannical, stereotypically patriarchal father. The story describes his brutal murder and the efforts made to solve the crime. After ruling out all the obvious suspects, guilt falls on Fairbanks; when there is no evidence to convict her, she sets out to clear her name with the help of her fiancé and an undercover detective.

Eventually suspicion falls on Sarah's neighbor, Phoebe Dole, a spinster woman who has lived for more than forty years with her companion and business partner, Maria Woods. In the process of the investigation, it turns out that Woods had previously had a romantic attachment to Fairbanks's father but was prevented from marrying him because she had earlier "promised Phoebe she would not marry" (395). The relationship between the two women, while already described as unequal in terms of Dole's dominant role in their business and personal dealings, is now revealed to be one of domination: Woods and Fairbanks's father, it is revealed, were finally planning to marry. When Dole confesses she exclaims in her defense, "There are other ties as strong as the marriage one, that are just as sacred" (396).

The story's title alludes to Dole's unusually long arm, which allows her to reach through a cat door to lock the house from the inside, thus creating the impression that no one could have left the house after the murder as all the doors were locked. It takes little imagination to see the long arm as a symbol for her phallic, masculine power, and this image is enhanced by the fact that Phoebe donned overalls to commit the murder. As if to pathologize her even more fully, Sarah refers to her actions as demonstrating "demoniacal possession" (397) (Diggs 1995: 334–5).

Such a story ostensibly illustrates the shift from viewing romantic friendships between white women as coexisting alongside heterosexual marriages to constituting a threat to them. It not only puts romantic friendships in tension or competition with marriage, but also portrays what will become a stereotype of female–female relationships: a masculine "inverted" woman, whose sexual difference is signified in biological or immutable terms, holds a feminine, weaker woman under her thumb. In turn, the feminine woman's subjectivity is always viewed as mutable: because of her "natural" femininity, she can be easily returned to heterosexuality. The model of an underlying essential heterosexuality as rooting even same-sex relationships as gender difference, rather than gender sameness, grounds Dole and Woods' relationship. (Krafft-Ebing [1886] 1998; Ellis [1901] 1975; Freud [1905] 1986).

Critics usually end their readings of the story here. However, if one examines the narrative in more detail, there is evidence, albeit rather incoherent, as reflected in Sarah's possibly unreliable narration, of ambiguity in Freeman's portrayal of the situation as merely a condemnation of Dole. Most obviously, by killing Fairbanks's father (whose prohibition of his daughter's engagement seems even more perverse in light of his own thwarted love), Dole's actions free up Fairbanks to marry her fiancé. Thus, we might read Dole's actions not only as an attempt to preserve her own proto-lesbian relationship, but also as attacking and usurping patriarchal authority in a way that allows for more feminist self-agency in heterosexuality, anticipating perhaps the vision of companionate marriage that will emerge in the early twentieth century. The story also alludes to Fairbanks's unconscious complicity in the crime as it details her efforts to wash out blood stains on her dress caused by Dole's attempts to clean her hands of the father's blood. That she and Dole, who takes the dress and dyes it in order to conceal the stains fully, never explicitly discuss Dole's actions, might also indicate an undercurrent of alliance that to some degree counteracts the emergence of a firm split between homo- and heterosexuality. At the very least this flags a subtext that describes, albeit perverse, alliances between women. In representing the complicity between heterosexual and homosexual desires, the expected heterosexual closure of the realist genre takes on a whole new valence, given that it requires the sacrifice of the masculine woman not only to save her own female–female relationship but to kill off a patriarchal authority that threatens both protolesbian desires and heterosexual female agency.

Henry James's "The Beast in the Jungle" (1903) also queers expectations of heterosexual closure. The story describes the enduring relationship between May Bartram and John Marcher, a relationship that centers around a secret Marcher waits to uncover about himself that he believes will change his life, and the ways in which he puts Bartram, and she puts herself, in the position of knowing what it is. Conventional readings of the story interpret the secret as the fact that Marcher misses the opportunity to love Bartram, and realizes this only after her death (heterosexuality as lost and mourned).

Echoing Oscar Wilde's famous pronouncement that homosexuality is "the love that dare not speak its name," Foucault and Sedgwick argue persuasively for the importance of silences as just as significant as speech or visibility, in and around what Sedgwick terms the performative space created by the closet (Foucault 1978: 27, 101; Sedgwick 1990: 3). In interpreting James's story, Sedgwick looks to gaps or ellipses in the text in order to consider the degree to which such aporias in fact are a representational strategy designed to resist the homo/hetero binary and the negative associations linked to homosexuality. While careful to preserve the possibility that the story might in fact be an experiment in how to sustain a narrative out of an empty signifier (the secret, while having no content whatsoever, still generates a plot), Sedgwick insists that reading for queer sexuality provides a (more satisfying) account of the secret and by extension, the work. Her seminal reading of the text argues that Marcher's situation illustrates the condition of modern male subjectivity, which is constructed around the imperative to identify as either hetero- or homosexual – thus his "willed ignorance" signals his refusal to accept this imperative (Sedgwick 1990: 3–10).

Her interpretation also revises traditional feminist readings of Bartram's situation *vis-à-vis* Marcher that portray her as simply a victim of male narcissism and representative of the feminine self-denial expected of women of her era. Instead, Sedgwick interprets Bartram's investment in Marcher's "secret" as being, in that choice phrase, a "fag hag (Sedgwick 1990: 209–10), especially in her recognition of the possibility of Marcher's homosexuality, something he steadfastly refuses to acknowledge.

Rather than see May as simple victim or as so specifically drawn to queer male self-ignorance and the possibility that Bartram will finally realize his own queer desires, what if we were to read her in light of the historical conditions under which lesbian identities and identifications emerge? Instead of viewing May and Marcher as gendered opposites, the story presents us with plenty of evidence to see them as in somewhat analogous situations. First of all, as my unconventional use of the former's first name and the latter's surname indicates, both contain within them not only the alliterative beginning consonant, but references to months of the year. That the beginning of Bartram also sounds similar to Marcher may lead readers to confuse the two characters when using their last names. Given James's intense attention to names, as evidenced by his notebooks, we might consider, then, that the story puts the two on somewhat parallel, rather than diametrically opposed, tracks. Indeed, the beginning of the story posits the two characters as sharing a similar status, as both are defined in opposition to the pairing off of various male–female couples, which James describes in quite scathing and explicitly eroticized terms:

> There were persons to be observed, singly or in couples, bending toward objects in out-of-the-way corners with their hands on their knees and their heads nodding quite as with the emphasis of an exited sense of smell. When they were two they either mingled their sounds of ecstasy or melted into silences of even deeper import, so that there were aspects of the occasion that gave it for Marcher much the air of the "look round," previous to a sale highly advertised, that excites or quenches as maybe, the dream of acquisition. (351)

As if to hammer home his criticism of heterosexual coupling, which includes a deep understanding of its literal and metaphorical overlaps with material accumulation, later James refers to the actions of the couples as "the movements of a dog sniffing a cupboard" (352). Both May and John remain on the margins of this activity; while John takes some satisfaction in her lower economic status, and thus her lower status in respect to himself, he also simultaneously enjoys the idea that "she remembered him very much as she was remembered – only a good deal better" (353). Nonetheless, while their asymmetry in regards to knowledge of Marcher's secret gives her the upper hand throughout the story, in other ways the work encourages us to see them also, at least in regards to what cannot be spoken within the text, as similar.

While John, given his sturdy willed ignorance, might refuse to recognize these similarities, May at moments explicitly alludes to them.

Consider one such moment: "She at least never spoke of the secret of his life except as 'the real truth about you,' and she had in fact a wonderful way of making it seem, as such, the secret of her own life too" (367). While it is possible to read this moment as one in which May indicates she has subsumed her whole existence into John's, it also is possible to read it as asserting that they both share a similar secret. When John asks her, "'What is it that saves you?'" May responds that, while their relationship may have made her "'talked about . . . if you've had your woman, I've had . . . my man'" (374). Elsewhere the text asserts that "beneath her forms as well detachment had learned to sit, and behaviour had become for her, in the social sense, a false account of herself. There was but one account of her that would have been true all the while, and that she could give, directly, to nobody, least of all to John Marcher" (368). May, then, may exist in her own closet. Because of John's investment in his own willed ignorance, and his narcissism, indicated by the phrase, "least of all," May would not consider confiding anything about herself in him. John's tragedy represents that of a compulsory heterosexual culture that requires the denial of desire between men, the solidifying of male self-ignorance, whereas May's secret remains unexplained by the narrator. Might it indicate the even more absolute unrepresentability of queer female desire, what Judith Butler has described as "a perpetual challenge to legibility," which both adds to the tragedy of the story but also pre-serves its complexities in refusing to be thematized at a time when the pathologizing of female–female relationships was on the rise (Butler 1993: 145)?

My interpretation of this text and Freeman's illustrates how they go against the grain of the imperatives of the form: they resist the imposition of normative heterosexual closure that would make Bartram simply a victim and Marcher simply a self-centered nar-cissist. These readings illuminate the complexities of the text in ways the former do not: they call into question the stability of the nar-rator in "The Long Arm," for example, and allow us to view "The Beast in the Jungle" as equally centered on the unrepresentability of pro-tolesbian desire, a secret that resists figuration even more than gay male desire does. In turn, this allows us to view "The Beast in the Jungle" as an example of an emerging modernism rather than a late realist work.

Gertrude Stein addresses similar formal conventions in her novella of the same year, *Q.E.D.* (1903), especially in the manner in which it demonstrates an awareness of the new prohibitions against lesbian identity. This work was not published during Stein's lifetime because, as she relates in the voice of Alice B. Toklas, her life partner, Stein put it away and "completely forgot about it for many years" (Stein 1933: 104), perhaps indicating Stein's own willed ignorance about the existence of the novella. Despite its posthumous publication, the work remains representative not only of Stein's early struggles to represent female–female erotics and an emerging queer identity, but also her earliest experiments with language.

Put most simply, the novel describes a love triangle between three women – Adele, Helen and Mabel. Adele, the main character, comes to understand her own desires and emerging sexual identity through falling in love with Helen, who cultivates their relationship only to return at the end of the novella to her lover and benefactress, Mabel, who appears to turn a blind eye to the affair. In the process Adele realizes that her personality and Helen's (and perhaps also their differing expressions of physical ardor) are incompatible.

To call this work a "coming out novel" may be to simplify the complexities of its exploration of Adele's trajectory. To some degree, her shift throughout the text is one of moving from her determined unknowing to a willingness to interpret that which is either not spoken or only obliquely hinted at; in other words, Adele's erotic development parallels her ability to interpret shifting signifiers of desire and its demise. But the novel presages much of Stein's later work in that it begins to substitute for the full development of a character's interiority expected of the genre an interest in experimenting with subtle changes in words' connotations, as well as in their associations with characters and affects.

One way to trace a path through the novella is to follow the ways in which silences are described. At the beginning of the text, we are presented with a description of Adele and Helen's first moment alone: "The two who were left settled down again quietly but somehow the silence now subtly suggested the significance of their being alone together. This consciousness was so little expected by either of them that each was uncertain of the other's recognition of it" (58). Adele responds to this silence by blathering on and on, until Helen interrupts her and presses her as to her feelings. As their relationship develops, the descriptions of silence shift: "Yet neither of them undertook to break the convention of silence which they had so completely adopted concerning the conditions of their relation" (77). The text uses silence to signify what it steadfastly refuses to represent, the emerging "conditions" of their erotic connection.

For example, one description of their time alone, "They were silent together a long time" (90), is echoed in the description that appears on the next page, "They had been together a long time" (91). Here silence and "be[ing] together" are connected explicitly. Subtle shifts in words' associations mirror and often, create, the plot. Thus, by the end of the novella, as their relationship painfully ends, Helen and Adele's interactions are described as "[an] intercourse . . . [that] now consisted in a succession of oppressive silences" (132).

This emphasis on the shifting meanings of silence within the text is linked to moments where the text refuses to specify action, but instead just notes the passage of time. For example, when Helen and Adele are alone together, their "intercourse" is described this way:

> They remained there together in an unyielding silence . . .
>
> The silence was not oppressive, but it lasted a long time. "I am very fond of you Adele" Helen said at last with a deep embrace.
>
> It was an hour later when Adele drew a deep breath of resolution, "What foolish people those poets are who say that parting is such sweet sorrow." (92)

At such moments, because the text refuses to specify what exactly is occurring between the two women, such gaps allow for the possibility of sex, while not providing a fully represented scenario. In so doing, they resist confining through specifying that imaginary relation (the reader is forced to fill in the action), while also avoiding the disciplinary scrutiny that might pathologize this relation. Thus these gaps also raise the possibility that a reader could assume a lesbian plot, rather than deny it.

As is true with the action in the piece, tracing other key words within the text as they "wander" and accrue or change significance, in a way analogous to Adele's own literal and metaphorical wandering, reveals as much about the development of Adele's character as anything else in the novella.

At the beginning of the work, Adele defends the American bourgeoisie, and accuses Helen of having "a foolish notion that to be middle-class is to be vulgar, that to cherish the ideals of respectability and decency is to be commonplace and that to be the mother of children is to be low" (56). Although she does not fully identify with this group, Adele associates middle-class identity with heterosexual reproductivity and gender normativity. Similarly, when returning to America, she employs the language of purity and whiteness to describe the country: "There was all America and it looked good; the clean sky and the white snow and the straight plain ungainly buildings all in a cold and brilliant air without spot or stain" (100). Deviance in the text, as represented by Mabel, is "yellow brown" and associated with "the decadent days of Italian greatness," which also indicates the repulsion Adele feels for female–female erotics, even as she finds herself drawn to Helen (55). Racial and national identity thus becomes associated with sexuality: America in the text is consistently linked to stable middle-class heterosexual and white identities, while Europe is connected to racial impurity. By the end of the novella, however, Adele has left behind America. The text describes her in Rome, striding towards Mabel and Helen, "a young woman, the cut of whose shirt-waist alone betrayed her American origin. Large, abundant, full-busted and joyous, she seemed a part of the rich Roman life . . . 'Why Adele,' exclaimed Helen . . . 'You look as brown and white and clean as if you had just sprung out of the sea'" (118). This passage blurs the binaries Adele originally upholds, as if to indicate her acceptance of a queer, nationally unstable, and perhaps racially marked subjectivity (Hovey 1996).

Associating brownness and wandering with sexual agency or erotic self-awareness takes on a more problematic cast when Stein rewrites *Q.E.D.* into a triangle between three African Americans, two women and one man, in "Melanctha," the most controversial of the three parts of her novel, *Three Lives* (1909). Here the associations the text makes between a more fluid sexuality and non-white identity reveal at the very least Stein's ambivalence about the connections between lesbians and other so-called deviant or primitive groups. Stereotypes about African Americans' supposedly more promiscuous and transgressive sexualities allow Stein to encode white female–female sexualities, as well as white female promiscuity ("wandering") (Hovey 1996). Instead of working against stigmatization through creating a Foucaultian reverse discourse of the idealized vision of the modern lesbian, Stein's novella, translating "perverse" white female desire into African American stereotype, nonetheless points towards a changing, unstable relation to gendered and sexual categories, albeit through promulgating a racist set of associations.

Common interpretations of Stein's later work assume that as she moved away from plot and characters into a more modernist abstract interest in language, she used this style as a way to closet lesbian erotics. However, if we assume the visibility and centrality of queer desires to her work, we are able to view it as an entirely different project.

As Stein's writing becomes even more centered on the play of words themselves, individual words still wander, in a way that connects sexuality with textuality. *Tender Buttons: Objects Food Rooms* (1914) contains numerous examples of the eroticization of language, the title itself alluding to, among other things, nipples and/or the clitoris, as well as the injunction to "tend her butt" (Kent 2003: 163). To read the prose poem with such erotics in mind allows one to view the whole work as "a perfectly unprecedented arrangement between old ladies" (24). This description, despite its use of the term "unprecedented," also demonstrates a continuity with, rather than a break from, and perhaps even an effort to refigure, the "romantic friendships" of the nineteenth century (Kent 2003). Such humorous and joyful explorations of female–female erotics continue in such prose poems as "Lifting Belly" (1915) and "Miss Furr and Miss Skeene" (1922).

That Adele needs to leave the United States in order to embrace her female–female desire also echoes an historical trend: many queer white women of the United States with the means to do so, including Stein and Toklas, left the country and settled in Paris and elsewhere in a self-imposed exile. These writers viewed Europe as offering more options for transgressing the stifling norms of gender and sexuality America was portrayed as upholding. In Paris, prominent queer white women writers and intellectuals such as Margaret Anderson, Jane Heap, Sylvia Beach, Janet Flanner, and Natalie Barney formed businesses, salons, and, at the very least, loose affiliations with one another (Benstock 1986).

One famous American exile, Djuna Barnes, known for her mastery of prose styles from Chaucer to the difficult, layered language, multiple, fragmented points of view, and emphasis on urban life that epitomizes high modernism, represents explicitly lesbian identity, inversion, and female–female desire, although not in a way that unequivocally celebrates any of them. In describing how "Dame Musset" recruits women into the pleasures of female–female sex in her witty send up of the coterie of Paris lesbians, *Ladies Almanack* (1928), Barnes compares the making of lesbians to other, less flattering forms of conquest and recruitment. She even goes so far as to use the language of war, wittily mixed with phallic humor: " 'Upon my Sword there is no Rust . . .' " Dame Musset exclaims ([1992] 55). In the racist language of imperial discourse, she describes the supposed differences between women of different regions and ethnicities:

I have learned on the Bodies of all Women, all Customs, and from their Minds have all Nations given up their Secrets. I know that the Orientals are cold to the Waist, and from there flame with a mighty and quick crackling Fire. I have learned that Anglo Saxons thaw slowly but that they thaw from Head to Heel, and so it is with their Minds. The Asiatic is warm and willing, and goes out like a Firecracker; the Northerner is cool and cautious, but burns and burns . . . (35)

In choosing the genre of the handbook, Barnes also implies that lesbian identity itself is becoming a site of standardization – something that can be routinized, mass produced, and marketed like a commodity. In so doing, she implies that lesbian identity itself has become a normative subject-position and implicated in modern capitalist culture (Kent 2003).

Perhaps this is one reason Barnes herself refused the label lesbian. As she famously insisted, "I'm not a lesbian, I just loved Thelma," alluding to her long relationship with Thelma Wood. *Nightwood* (1936) is often read as Barnes's account of their failed affair. Regardless of its biographical relevance, however, the novel, set mainly in Paris and written in a difficult, sometimes lyrical, sometimes impenetrable style often compared to Joyce, presents the queer cosmopolitan world of the night, an underworld that is the gathering place of all sorts of marginalized subjects, not only sexual deviants but also circus freaks, people of color, and Jews (Marcus 1991; Boone 1998). The novel takes to the extreme the notion of this world as an "inversion" of normative heterosexual (and, by extension, Christian) values. The invert, who is the reflection of this schema, is most centrally represented by the oracle-like figure of the flamboyant, transgendered Dr Matthew Dante O'Connor and by Robin Vote, whose slim hips and boyish appearance cast her as the classic masculine woman. The novel's center, the object of first heterosexual and then female–female desire, Vote first marries Felix Volkbein, a Jew desperate to create a history for himself as a Christian noble, then abandons him and their disabled child in favor of a kind of promiscuous wandering that leads her first to Nora Flood and then to Jenny Petherbridge. Significantly, we are never allowed much of a glimpse into Vote's consciousness; instead, she remains virtually an empty signifier who thwarts any attempt to comprehend her actions or contain her identity.

The novel makes no attempt to redeem any of its characters; it revels in, yet simultaneously despairs about all forms of unnatural subjectivities and acts. As Flood describes, " 'We give death to a child when we give it a doll – it's the effigy and the shroud; when a woman gives it to a woman, it is the life they cannot have, it is their child, sacred and profane . . .' " (142). Female–female desire may never, in this text, produce "life," but remains on the side of narcissism and death, just as it takes place in the night. Rather than seeing the text as simply queer-phobic or deeply ambivalent towards the world it describes, however, I would argue it anticipates the radical anti-assimilationism of some contemporary queer theorists such as Lee Edelman, who resists embracing normative values such as (gay) marriage and reproduction, arguing instead that to be queer is to reject "futurity" (instantiated in the figure of the child) in all its forms (Edelman 2004). Interpreting the novel in this fashion might explain this description of O'Connor's situation – "it was as if being condemned to the grave the doctor had decided to occupy it with the utmost abandon" (78) – as well as the sense that death hangs over the entire work. This rejection of futurity, reproductivity, and even life might also explain the novel's ending, in which Vote undergoes a kind of reverse evolution as she falls on all fours in what might be an attempt to engage erotically with a dog. Concomitantly, the novel resists any kind of thematic consistency or narrative structure, constituted as it is almost entirely of conversation (and often monologue) and structured more spatially than linearly, its only loose plot the rise and demise of Flood and Vote's affair.

Even more ambivalent about the contrast between bourgeois ideals of marriage and reproductivity and queer female possibilities is Nella Larsen's *Passing* (1929). The novel, through the unreliable point of view of Irene Redfield, tells the story of the reappearance of her childhood friend, Clare Bellew, a woman who has been passing as white and is married to a white man, and the crisis she causes in Irene's own racial and sexual identifications. This crisis is prefigured in the characters' first encounter after many years, in a café, where both are passing. Enduring Clare's intense stare, and strangely drawn to her presence, Irene converts or links what could be read as a scene of cruising into a racial panic, as she fears Clare might realize she is black (149–50) (McDowell 1986: xxvii–xxviii). As their relationship progresses, Irene fears that her husband, Brian, and Clare are having an affair, but the novel offers a much more complex understanding of the intertwining of racial and sexual anxieties Clare inspires in Irene. In Deborah McDowell's reading, the racial plot (Irene's continual disapproval of Clare's passing, even as she passes herself, and her need to eradicate the racial instability – and thus, domestic chaos – Clare introduces into her life) is a cover for a sexual plot in which Irene projects her own desires for Clare onto Brian, and in which the crisis Clare precipitates is one of sexual identity, as much or more so than race. This influential interpretation of the novel, has initiated a debate on how to theorize racial and sexual identifications (McDowell 1986: xxiii–xxxi). Extending even as she challenges McDowell's reading, Butler instead argues that it is Clare's instability in terms of race and desire that reveals the essential instability of both race and sexuality (Butler 1993: 167–85). Irene, throughout the novel, is portrayed as being desperate to preserve a stable, black, heterosexual identity, which is linked in the text to the imperatives of racial uplift, regardless of the toll it takes on her and her family. In this representation of Irene, Larsen reveals the enormous pressures black women have faced to silence and deny their sexual desires in order to counteract the stereotypes that have haunted them since at least the genesis of slavery, as well as the different political import marriage itself has taken on as a symbol of citizenship after the prohibitions against it during slavery (Carby 1987; Hammonds 1994).

We might also interpret Irene's relationship to Clare as challenging the Freudian dichotomy of identification and desire: Freud famously argues that homosexuality is a problem of confusing being and having. To be properly Oedipalized, and thus to achieve a "mature" gender and sexual identity, is to move, in a woman's case, from a desire to have her mother and an identification with her father, to a desire to be her mother and have her father. The female homosexual, then, suffers from a problem of failed gender identification: instead of renouncing her identification with her father, such a woman stubbornly clings to it (Freud 1905, 1920, 1921). Queer theorists have challenged this developmental narrative, arguing instead that polarizing identification and desire maintains heterosexuality and gender difference at the heart of all forms of subject formation. In the United States, at least since the nineteenth century, subject-forming efforts to make young girls into women have relied on the confusing of these two processes. In seeking to form girls' characters through encouraging them to emulate their teachers, older role models, etc., there is the risk that girls will end up desiring these models. (Fuss 1995; Kent 2003).

If we view having and being as not necessarily polarized, it may provide us with a new way to read Irene's relation to Clare. Consistently throughout the novel it is hard to distinguish Irene's desire to be Clare or at least acknowledge their similarities (and thus free herself from the constraints of the norms of the black bourgeoisie), as well as her violent disidentification from such desires, from her desire to have Clare (Butler 1993: 169, 177–9). Thus, when Clare dies at the end of the novel, perhaps because Irene pushes her out a window, the threat she poses to Irene's sense of self is contained, as presaged by the description of Irene's cigarette as she tosses it out the window and "watch[es] the tiny sparks drop slowly to the white ground below" (238) (McDowell 1986: xxix). Just as the spark of the cigarette is extinguished, so is the racial and sexual mobility Clare represents; thus, the novel presents a bleak picture of the possibilities of a black queer female sexuality, requiring as it does the extermination of passion. Furthermore, in interweaving racial and sexual identification, the work demonstrates the ways in which the hetero/homo dichotomy is complexly and inseparably tied to the dichotomy between black and white: just as the modern subject must "have" a sexuality, she must also "have" a race (Somerville 2000).

Zora Neale Hurston's *Their Eyes Were Watching God* (1936), as many critics have claimed, rejects fully the gendered norms of racial uplift. The novel represents the gradual coming to consciousness, including erotic awareness and fulfillment, of its main character Janie. Her famous first vision of sexual desire is a solitary one: lying under a pear tree,

> she saw a dust-bearing bee sink into the sanctum of a bloom; the thousand sister-calyxes arch to meet the love embrace and the ecstatic shiver of the tree from root to tiniest branch creaming in every blossom and frothing with delight. So this was a marriage! She had been summoned to behold a revelation. Then Janie felt a pain remorseless sweet that left her limp and languid. (24)

The passage ends with Janie's masturbatory release: her ability to pleasure herself, inspired by an erotic, idealized vision of what marriage might mean. Her trajectory through the novel carries her from one marriage to another, and at each stage she discovers more about her relation to gender constraints and sexual desires. She rejects the backbreaking labor associated with her first husband and the bourgeois security offered by her second husband, which requires that Janie become another object of display on the porch of her husband's store, to find (albeit complicated and fleeting) sexual fulfillment and gender equality in her life with Tea Cake in the Florida swamps. In so doing Janie rejects the norms of bourgeois black femininity under which Irene suffers and represents a form of "queer heterosexuality," as she lives among the lower class of the "Bottom" and finds pleasure without reproducing (as signaled by the fact that Janie never bears a child). However, the novel ends, not with heterosexual fulfillment, but with Janie, having been forced to kill her husband, striding back into town in her overalls, embodying an anti-gender normative singularity, which the novel implies epitomizes female erotic power (and perhaps is necessary for female agency). In other words, a queer erotics of self-fulfillment reminiscent of the masturbatory scene under the pear tree, rather than the expected female fulfillment of being a wife and mother, or even sexual pleasure with a male lover, grounds Janie's subjectivity.

Even more curiously, the frame of the novel sets up Janie's story as one she tells on her best female friend's porch. Janie tells Phoebe she may pass on her story to the rest of the townspeople: "Dat's just de same as me 'cause mah tongue' is in mah friend's mouf" (17). While on one hand, as a number of critics have argued, this indicates the power of communal storytelling within the African American oral tradition, one may also read this phrasing as sexual: Janie, still referring to the townspeople, remarks, " 'If they wants to see and know, why they don't come kiss and be kissed?' " (18). These references may indicate just the commonplace tradition of kissing as a form of social greeting, but the text seems more invested in the action's erotic implications. In making talk analogous to oral erotic exchange, and in calling Phoebe her " 'kissin-friend' " (19), Janie implies that female–female erotics are what finally allow her to give full voice to her heterosexual desires, as she narrates her story on Phoebe's porch (Kaplan 1996: 99–122, Rohy 2000: 91–116). To assert such a reading is to point out the ways in which the supposedly absolute split between homo- and heterosexuality might not always prove to be the structuring binary in African American women's queer narratives. Instead, the novel instantiates the possibilities of a more fluid set of gendered *and* sexual positions.

This chapter presents a selective overview both of the variety of queer representations of women in early-twentieth-century American texts and of the range of theoretical and formal strategies one might employ to interpret them. However, this group is by no means exhaustive. The writings of Willa Cather, for example, ambivalent and complex in their various relations to queer identifications and desires, remain central to any queer canon. I also have not discussed more realist, recently recovered texts of the period, including examples such as Gale Wilhelm's *We Too Are Drifting* (1935) and *Torchlight to Valhalla* (1938). Sui Sin Far's *Mrs. Spring Fragrance and Other Stories* (1912) interrogates the intertwining of ethnicity, gender, and the process and problems of Americanization in ways that also might reward a queer reading. Nonetheless, as is clear from the overview provided here, interpreting texts through the lens of gender and sexuality not only illustrates how they represent and metaphorize female–female erotics and/or the emergence of lesbian identity, but how these representations are intimately intertwined with the texts' experiments with literary style. It also demonstrates the degree to which the claim of that sexuality is *the* truth of the modern self, and that one must choose either a homo or a hetero identity, is both illustrated by but often also resisted or complicated by these works.

Note

1   For a reading of "The Long Arm" that in some way resembles and in some key ways differs from my own, see Rohy, 2001.

References and Further Reading

Barnes, D. [1928] 1992: *Ladies Almanack*. Elmwood Park, IL: Dalkey Archive Press.

Barnes, D. [1936] 1961: *Nightwood*. New York: New Directions.

Benstock, S. 1986: *Women of the Left Bank: Paris, 1900–1940*. Austin: University of Texas Press.

Boone, J. A. 1998: *Libidinal Currents: Sexuality and the Shaping of Modernism*. Chicago: University of Chicago Press.

Butler, J. 1993: *Bodies that Matter: On the Discursive Limits of "Sex."* New York: Routledge.

Carby, H. 1987: *Reconstructing Womanhood: The Emergence of the Afro-American Woman Novelist*. New York: Oxford University Press.

Chauncey, G. Jr. 1982–3: From Sexual Inversion to Homosexuality: Medicine and the Changing Conceptualization of Female Deviance. *Salmagundi* 58/59, 114–45.

D'Emilio, J. and E. Freedman 1997: *Intimate Matters: A History of Sexuality in America*, 2nd edn. Chicago: University of Chicago Press.

Diggs, M. 1995: Romantic Friends or a "Different Race of Creatures?" The Representation of Lesbian Pathology in Nineteenth-Century America. *Feminist Studies* 21, 317–40.

Duggan, L. 2000: *Sapphic Slashers: Sex, Violence, and American Modernity*. Durham: Duke University Press.

Edelman, L. 2004: *No Future: Queer Theory and the Death Drive*. Durham: Duke University Press.

Ellis, H. [1901] 1975: *Sexual Inversion*. New York: Arno Press.

Faderman, L. 1981: *Surpassing the Love of Men: Romantic Friendship and Love Between Women from the Renaissance to the Present*. New York: Morrow.

Faderman, L. (ed.) 1994: *Chloe Plus Olivia: An Anthology of Lesbian Literature from the Seventeenth Century to the Present*. New York: Penguin.

Far, S. S. [1912] 1995: *Mrs. Spring Fragrance and Other Writings*. Urbana: University of Illinois Press.

Foucault, M. 1978: *The History of Sexuality*. Hammondsworth: Penguin.

Freeman, M. W. [1895] 1994: The Long Arm. In L. Faderman, (ed.), *Chloe Plus Olivia: An Anthology of Lesbian Literature from the Seventeenth Century to the Present*. New York: Penguin.

Freud, S. [1905] 1986: Three Essays on the Theory of Sexuality. In J. Strachey and A. Richards (eds.), *On Sexuality: Three Essays on the Theory of Sexuality and Other Works*. Harmondsworth: Penguin, 31–169.

Freud, S. [1920] 1985: The Psychogenesis of a Case of Homosexuality in a Woman. In J. Strachey and A. Richards (eds.), *Case Histories II*. Harmondsworth: Penguin, 367–400.

Freud, S. [1921] 1989: *Group Identification and the Analysis of the Ego*. New York: Norton.

Fuss, D. 1995: *Identification Papers*. New York: Routledge.

Hall, R. [1928] 1990: *The Well of Loneliness*. New York: Anchor.

Hammonds, E. 1994: Black (W)holes and the Geometry of Black Female Sexuality. *Differences* 6, 126–45.

Hansen, K. 1996: "No Kisses Is Like Youres": An Erotic Friendship between Two African American Women during the Mid-nineteenth-Century. In M. Vicinus (ed.), *Lesbian Studies: A Feminist Studies Reader*. Bloomington: Indiana University Press, 178–207.

Hovey, J. 1996: Sapphic Primitivism in Gertrude Stein's *Q.E.D. Modern Fiction Studies* 42, 547–68.

Hurston, Z. N. [1937] 1978: *Their Eyes Were Watching God*. Urbana: University of Illinois Press.

James, H. [1903] 1962: The Beast in the Jungle. In L. Edel (ed.), *The Complete Short Stories of Henry James*. Philadelphia: Lippincott, 351–402.

Kaplan, C. 1996: *The Erotics of Talk: Women's Writing and Feminist Paradigms*. New York: Oxford University Press.

Kent, K. 2003: *Making Girls into Women: American Women's Writing and the Rise of Lesbian Identity*. Durham: Duke University Press.

Krafft-Ebing, R. V. [1886] 1998: *Psychopathia Sexualis*. New York: Little Brown.

Larsen, N. [1929] 1986: *Quicksand and Passing*. Ed. D. E. McDowell, New Brunswick, NJ: Rutgers University Press.

McDowell, D. 1986: "Introduction." In N. Larsen, *Quicksand and Passing*, ix–xxv.

Marcus, J. 1991: Laughing at Leviticus: *Nightwood* as Woman's Circus Epic. In M. L. Broe (ed.), *Silence and Power: A Reevaluation of Djuna Barnes* Carbondale: Southern Illinois University Press, 221–50.

Rohy, V. 2000: *Impossible Women: Lesbian Figures and American Literature.* Ithaca: Cornell University Press.

Rohy, V. 2001: "The Long Arm" and the Law, *South Central Review* 18.3–4, 102–18.

Sedgwick, E. K. 1990: *Epistemology of the Closet.* Berkeley: University of California Press.

Sedgwick, E. K. 1993: *Tendencies.* Durham: Duke University Press.

Smith-Rosenberg, C. 1985: *Disorderly Conduct: Visions of Gender in Victorian America.* New York: Oxford University Press.

Somerville, S. B. 2000: *Queering the Color Line: Race and the Invention of Homosexuality in American Culture.* Durham: Duke University Press.

Stein, G. [1903] 1971: *Fernhurst, Q.E.D., and Other Early Writings.* New York: Liveright.

Stein, G. [1909] 1990: *Three Lives.* New York: Penguin.

Stein, G. [1914] 1994: *Tender Buttons: Objects Food Rooms.* Los Angeles: Sun and Moon Press.

Stein, G. [1915] 1998: "Lifting Belly." In C. Simpson and H. Chessman (eds.), *Gertrude Stein: Writings 1903–1932: Q.E.D., Three Lives, Portraits and Other Short Works, The Autobiography of Alice B. Toklas.* New York: The Library of America, 410–58.

Stein, G. [1922] 1998: "Miss Furr and Miss Skeene." In C. Simpson and H. Chessman (eds.), *Gertrude Stein: Writings 1903–1932: Q.E.D., Three Lives, Portraits and Other Short Works, The Autobiography of Alice B. Toklas.* New York: The Library of America, *Gertrude Stein*, 307–12.

Stein, G. 1933: *The Autobiography of Alice B. Toklas.* New York: The Literary Guild.

Wilhelm, G. [1935] 1985: *We Too Are Drifting.* Tallahassee: Naiad Press.

Wilhelm, G. [1938] 1985: *Torchlight to Valhalla.* Tallahassee: Naiad Press.

Chapter 4

Markets and "Gatekeepers"

Loren Glass

It is easy to forget the many intermediary stages a novel must travel through between the hand of the author and the eye of the reader. We tend to romanticize novelists as solitary geniuses and to experience their books as personal communications directly from them to us; we tend to "suspend" our disbelief and "lose ourselves" in their fictional universes, forgetting the long process of fabrication and selection that enables this immersion; indeed, in order to enjoy fiction it seems we must deny that novels are, after all, commodities not entirely unlike shoes and cars and cereal, and therefore that they must be designed, discussed, promoted, and distributed by institutions organized for profit.

Of course, we generally tend not to worry about how and where what we consume was originally produced; Karl Marx famously called this commodity fetishism. But with literature this repression is reinforced by a common assumption that art, by its very nature, should not be concerned with matters of the marketplace. Furthermore, we tend to assume, and our legal system of copyright affirms, that ideas are separate from their material expression in texts, and that therefore the design and promotion of novels is somehow extrinsic to the stories told therein; as R. R. Bowker, discussing the Copyright Act of 1909, affirms, "the copyright is distinct from the property in the material object copyrighted" (Bowker 1912: 60). Our legal system of intellectual property, then, supports our assumptions about the immaterial nature of literature.

It was these persistent assumptions that led the cultural critic Van Wyck Brooks to argue in 1915 that culture in the United States was split between "highbrow" and "lowbrow," and these terms quickly entered the American vernacular as shorthand for the division between elite culture that is recognized as having aesthetic value and mass culture that is assumedly produced purely for economic profit. As Brooks phrased it, "in everything one finds this frank acceptance of twin values which are not expected to have anything in common: on the one hand, a quite unclouded, quite unhypocritical assumption of transcendent theory ('high ideals'), on the other a simultaneous acceptance of catchpenny realities" (Brooks 1934: 3).

Like all cultural critics, Brooks is overgeneralizing in order to make a point, but his categories do describe a crucial division in the modern literary marketplace which corresponds to a distinction between both authors and audiences. The highbrow indicates a relatively small community of educated individuals who privilege aesthetic over economic value, and who claim to write and read without consideration of profit or pay. Their novels are frequently experimental in form and sophisticated in tone. Their readers are assumed to be of equal sophistication, and to derive joy from what, to generations of high school students and college undergraduates, tends to feel like work. The lowbrow indicates that far larger mass of the general public to whom novels are marketed expressly for making money. This fiction is frequently formulaic, its authorship not uncommonly pseudonymous, and the pleasures derived from reading it tend to be compared to eating and drinking. Until recently, such fiction was never taught in college. This fundamental opposition, frequently framed as the incommensurability of culture and commerce, is crucial to any sociologically based understanding of modern American literature.

According to Brooks, "between academic pedantry and pavement slang, there is no community, no genial middle ground," and he wrote his essay partly as a call for a "middlebrow" literature that he did not name (Brooks 1934: 3). In fact, over the course of the first half of the twentieth century a broad field of overlap between high and low culture did develop, and arguably determined the process whereby most novels which we read in school were initially produced and consumed. After all, "highbrow" authors need to make a living, and many readers of "lowbrow" literature aspire to elevate their taste. In response to these twin pressures, a somewhat amorphous yet nevertheless distinct area of compromise between aesthetic sophistication and economic calculation emerged, in which authors with literary talent could make a living and literate Americans could purchase and read quality fiction.

This area became designated "middlebrow," and one of its defining features is the crucial role of gatekeepers, literary "experts" who regulate the relationship between author and audience by promoting certain kinds of novels and advising certain habits of writing and reading.

This was not always the case. In the colonial and revolutionary eras, writers frequently knew their readers personally, and there was little need for "marketing" literature. Furthermore, publishing was essentially a craft in which a single individual – who, though not necessarily a writer, tended to be on close social terms with those who were – personally chose, selected, printed, and distributed texts to a small community of essentially like-minded individuals. However, in the decades after the Civil War, an entire industry emerged to manufacture, distribute, and market literature, particularly fiction, which was becoming highly popular among the rapidly expanding reading public. As the historian Alan Trachtenberg details in his important study, *The Incorporation of America: Culture and Society in the Gilded Age* (1982), corporate forms of social and economic organization came to dominate this era, introducing hierarchies of control and divisions of labor into institutions that had previously been more informally and personally structured. Although publishing remained a "genteel" family business through much of the early twentieth century, it was not immune to these developments. The founding in 1872 of the industry journal *Publishers' Weekly*, an indispensable resource for any study of the modern literary marketplace, would be the first of a series of signs that publishing after the Civil War could no longer operate purely on informal and personal relationships.

Indeed, most of the occupations which are now indispensable to the literary marketplace, such as editors and agents, came into being in the late nineteenth and early twentieth centuries. The role of editor emerged when publishing houses became too large and complicated for the publisher to deal directly with authors. Increasingly, the publisher became responsible for the business end of the company, while editors, and soon a whole staff of editorial assistants, dealt with the literary end. The most influential editor of the early twentieth century was, without a doubt, Maxwell Perkins of Scribners, who worked with such significant novelists as Ernest Hemingway, F. Scott Fitzgerald, Thomas Wolfe, Marjorie Kinnan Rawlings, and Erskine Caldwell. Perkins was a man of both patience and taste, functioning not only as an editor but also as an informal banker and emotional advisor, providing these frequently troublesome figures with the time and money to complete their work. He paid endless advances to Fitzgerald while waiting for the dipsomaniacal and emotionally unbalanced author to finish *Tender is the Night*; he struggled stubbornly with Hemingway to tone down his language in order to avoid confrontations with censors; and he substantially revised the voluminous manuscripts of Thomas Wolfe after that author's untimely death. Perkins was called the "editor of genius" by his biographer, and he has long been a legend in the industry (Berg 1978). There can be little doubt that he not only enabled the economic livelihood of these now canonical authors, but influenced their aesthetic decisions as well.

The role of literary agent emerged as the increasing complexity of subsidiary rights and syndication made it incumbent upon authors to hire someone knowledgeable to represent them in these matters. Unlike editors, who were integral to publishing houses and therefore embraced by them as a necessary development, agents operated independently and their role was initially resisted. Agents had to fight to be accepted in the industry; publishers distrusted them, and felt that they threatened the culture of loyalty that publishing houses had established with authors. The profession began in the United Kingdom, but quickly spread to the United States. The first professional American literary agent was Paul Revere Reynolds, who worked with such authors as Stephen Crane, Frank Norris, F. Scott Fitzgerald, and Booth Tarkington. Reynolds' main job was to negotiate reprint rights between British and United States publishers. Thus agents such as Reynolds initially tended to deal with strictly economic and legal matters, such as translations, magazine serialization, and subsidiary rights in other media, and had less influence than editors on the actual composition of novels, but their influence on the relationship between editors and authors was significant insofar as they helped to dismantle the traditional loyalties between these figures. Indeed, over the course of the century, the agent would take on many of the tasks initially performed by the editor, and it would be the agent who would enable the competitive bidding that has led to the monumental advances that characterize the industry today, in which bestselling "blockbusters" provide the profits to subsidize the rest of a publisher's list.

Two significant developments in the late nineteenth century enabled the market for fiction to develop to the degree that agents and editors became necessary: the passage of an international copyright law and the rapid expansion of the magazine industry. Over the course of most of the nineteenth century, it was almost impossible for an American novelist to survive financially on writing alone, since most publishers pirated British fiction, which was enormously popular with the public in the United States. Authors on both sides of the Atlantic were unhappy with this situation (though most publishers tended to remain sanguine) and, after a century of agitation and negotiation, the United States Congress passed an international copyright bill in 1891 which, by criminalizing transatlantic piracy and leveling the international literary playing field, made it possible to make a living as a novelist in the United States. Like many other occupations that had previously been the bailiwick of gentleman amateurs, authorship became a profession open to anyone with talent and a work ethic; a Society of American Authors was formed in the same year, indicating that literature was adapting to the developing culture of professionalism that shaped the Progressive Era.

In the same decade, the market for fiction was rapidly expanding as a result of the so-called magazine revolution. As in book publishing, with which it was closely related, the magazine industry had been a relatively modest and genteel affair over the course of the nineteenth century, based mostly in Boston and having little national reach. Magazines such as *The Atlantic Monthly* and *The Century* were marketed to the educated upper middle classes and were only able to survive financially through subscription rates that were prohibitive for the less affluent. In the 1890s, a whole new genre of mass market magazine emerged which was addressed to a much larger public. Magazines such as *The Ladies' Home Journal* and *The Saturday Evening Post* had low subscription rates, since they made most of their money through advertising. Indeed, these magazines had partly been developed as a vehicle for the emergent advertising industry to market the vast proliferation of commodities being produced by the rapidly expanding industrial economy of the late nineteenth century. Instead of selling magazines to readers, they sold readers to advertisers. The very nature of reading would be transformed by this new economic relationship as, increasingly, advertisements and editorial matter were seamlessly integrated into the modern magazine format.

Fiction was a staple for these magazines, and many American authors during this era made more money on short stories and serialization than they did on published books. But this new venue didn't only provide a lucrative market; it also had a significant effect on the actual form and content of American fiction. On the one hand, a new generation of editors and authors became centrally concerned with the plight of the new urban poor and the depredations of industrial capitalism. Progressive-era editors such as the path-breaking Samuel

McClure employed muckraking journalists such as Lincoln Steffens and Ida Tarbell to expose the corruption of both government bureaucrats and corporate robber barons, while naturalist authors such as Jack London, Stephen Crane, and Frank Norris focused much of their fiction on the abject misery and hopelessness of the urban masses. Literary naturalism, in other words, was partly made possible by the magazine revolution.

However, insofar as they were beholden to their advertisers, more bottom-line oriented mass-market magazine editors such as Edward Bok at *The Ladies' Home Journal* and George Horace Lorimer at *The Saturday Evening Post* could be timid, especially when it came to moral and sexual issues; they wanted stories that would not offend any segment of their huge readership, and they tended to prefer moralistic narratives with happy endings. They edited and altered work which was submitted to them and frequently proposed and requested certain topics or ideas as work for hire. They were dismissive of literary experimentation and tended to prefer fiction written in simple accessible prose that focused on content over form.

Many successful authors were more than happy to adapt to these conditions, but others wanted to maintain sole control over their art, and were therefore disdainful of the entire middlebrow marketplace that emerged in these years. In the bohemian enclaves of America's major cities, a new genre of "little magazine" was born to address the needs of authors who refused to compromise. The editors of these magazines – such as Margaret Anderson and Jane Heap of *The Little Review* and James Oppenheim and Waldo Frank of *The Seven Arts* – were resolutely not interested in making money, and frequently their journals were subsidized by private wealth. Indeed, new forms of patronage emerged around these magazines, as the heirs of great industrial fortunes sought prestige through subsidizing avant-garde art. The little magazines had small circulations but large reputations (at least in certain circles), and much of the literature which would come to be called modernism originally appeared in their pages. They became the central testing ground for literary experimentation and a crucial venue for new talent. Ernest Hemingway, William Faulkner, Gertrude Stein, and many, many others broke into print in the little magazines.

To publish the novels that developed out of this experimental literature took both patience and courage, qualities that the more established publishing houses did not always possess. In the early twentieth century, a so-called new breed of publisher emerged whose central role would be to usher the more challenging modes of literature from the restricted field of little magazines into the more general field of middlebrow culture. Alfred and Blanche Knopf, Albert and Charles Boni, B. W. Huebsch, Bennett Cerf, and Horace Liveright all founded small entrepreneurial houses before and after the First World War that would have a profound effect on the history of American fiction. Virtually all of these figures were first- or second-generation immigrant Jews whose advancement in the established publishing industry was blocked by anti-Semitism. They were sympathetic to European aesthetic and political radicalism and gravitated to New York's Greenwich Village in search of a friendly environment to disseminate and share these beliefs and practices; they were far less invested than the more established publishers in the literary and cultural traditions of the Boston Brahmins. The new breed not only enabled the shift from Victorian to modern literature, but also hastened the gravitation of the publishing industry from genteel Boston to metropolitan Manhattan.

The new wave was not inattentive to classic literature, however. Indeed, they developed a mode of distribution for the (mostly European) "classics" that would transform the publishing industry. In 1915, the Boni brothers, along with their friend and colleague Harry Scherman, founded a series called the "Little Leather Library" that consisted of cheap reprints of classics and excerpts from classics sold by mail order and in department stores. Their success was an inspiration to their competitors; soon a number of publishing houses were targeting editions of the classics at the moderate-income market. The most successful of these would be the Modern Library which, when purchased by Bennett Cerf and Donald Klopfer of Random House in 1925, would become one of the most popular sources of cheap classic, and eventually modern, literature.

However, the most significant innovation to develop out of the mail-order concept was undoubtedly the Book-of-the-Month Club, incorporated in 1926 by Harry Scherman and his partners, Maxwell Sackheim and Robert Haas. Partly in order to distinguish his product from competitors, Scherman decided to convince publishers that contemporary literature could also be marketed and sold by mail. He developed a distribution method whereby texts would be selected each month by a panel of judges and sent to subscribers automatically unless they exercised a "negative option." Thus, not only did the Book-of-the-Month Club develop a whole new method of gatekeeping, it also promised to overcome the perennial problem of distribution that had vexed the industry from its beginnings. Many Americans in the early twentieth century did not have access to bookstores, which were mostly located in large urban centers, and simply getting books to readers outside of these centers presented an almost insurmountable challenge. Like the earlier subscription publishing method that enabled Mark Twain's enormous popularity, selling books by mail overcame this difficulty. The Book-of-the-Month Club grew slowly but steadily, spawning many competitors, and by the thirties the idea of the book club had transformed the publishing industry.

In their innovative incorporation of culture with commerce, book clubs would become, for both their supporters and detractors, the representative institution of American middlebrow culture in the literary field. On the one hand, the idea that a panel of experts would choose the best books appealed to the vast population of literate Americans who wanted to educate and elevate themselves but were without the time or the capacity to negotiate the bewildering range of options presented by the burgeoning publishing industry. On the other hand, by essentially ceding their agency to experts – a passivity apparently epitomized by the "negative option" method of distribution – club members also seemed to be sacrificing the very capacities of selection and distinction that made good readers in the first place. For some, then, book clubs democratized American culture, elevating the taste of the reading public; for others, they degraded American culture, homogenizing the taste of the reading public and reducing literature to a pre-packaged commodity.

The book club idea also offered one solution to a perennial problem in publishing: advertising. Walter Hines Page, in his influential memoir, *A Publisher's Confession* (1905), had baldly stated, "about the advertising of books, nobody knows anything" (Quoted in Gross 1961: 45). And Henry Holt, in an oft-quoted response to Page significantly entitled "The Commercialization of Literature," affirmed why: a book "is a thing in itself: there is nothing like it, as one shoe is like another, or one kind of whisky is like another" (Holt 1905: 596); books, in other words, are far more difficult, and far less cost effective, to advertise than mass produced commodities that are essentially identical. Since every novel is unique, it seemed to follow that every novel would also require an individual promotional campaign which, factoring in the unpredictability of public taste, seemed to make book advertising at best a risky investment.

Traditionally, reviewing had been the principle means of promoting books. Novels would be sent out to reviewers, and positive reviews would be culled for "blurbs" which could then be incorporated into advertisements and quoted on book jackets. But publishers were unable to control the personal favoritisms and animosities of the reviewers, and more independent modes of promotion accompanied the post-war expansion of the industry. By the last decade of the nineteenth century, in response to the so-called fiction boom, there was an exponential increase in advertising budgets and a slew of imaginative and even bizarre campaigns (the publisher of Charles Major's enormously popular *When Knighthood was in Flower* actually hired a man dressed in armor to ride through Manhattan on horseback), but it remained essentially impossible to measure any causal relation between advertising and sales. Then, as now, most novels lost money, regardless of advertising, and there were ongoing, and occasionally quite incendiary, debates in the industry about the utility of promotion.

The book club idea provided the possibility for publishers to advertise themselves, as opposed to their wares, and thereby stimulate consumption of a wide variety of novels under the logic of the brand name. Publishers such as Knopf and Liveright saw their lists as reflections of their own personalities, and they strove to inject these personalities into their advertising copy. Exploiting the new corporate concept of "brand loyalty," during this era many publishers developed "colophons," emblems whereby all their books could be recognized as a company product, such as Knopf's borzoi and Huebsch's candelabra, which were featured prominently both in advertisements and on book jackets.

Indeed, jacket design, which over the course of the nineteenth century had consisted mostly of functional identification of title, author, and publisher in simple fonts, became far more ornate and elaborate in the twentieth century, with entire staffs of designers and artists deploying new technologies of engraving and color reproduction in order to flout the traditional wisdom that you cannot judge a book by its cover. Many publishers were not beneath promoting simple possession of their books as a way to acquire the appearance of cultural distinction. This idea of the book as "cultural furniture" was symptomatic of the contradictions between culture and commerce that shaped middlebrow culture.

Publishers could also promote reading itself, and the middlebrow marketplace tended to emphasize the beneficial effects of novel reading and to play off public anxiety concerning the acquisition of knowledge and expertise. The modern era was characterized by a bewildering profusion of information and provocative challenges to traditional values, and many publishers attempted to convince readers that they needed to read modern novels in order to understand the profound social and political upheavals of the world following the First World War. Such tactics represented a fragile compromise between democratic ideals and commercial realities. On the one hand, the promotion of reading allowed publishers to position themselves as public servants, providing the American reader with tools for citizenship. On the other hand, many of these advertisements blatantly exploited social insecurities about cultural distinction in many ways indistinguishable from anxieties about halitosis and body odor that were used to market toothpaste and soap.

Another increasingly common response to the problem of advertising would be to promote the author, as opposed to the text, and literary celebrity during this era was widespread. Interest in the private lives of authors became particularly intense in the late nineteenth century, and prominent novelists were increasingly expected to give magazine interviews and go on book tours in order to promote their latest work. Photographs of authors and authorial signatures became standard components of both book jackets and advertising copy. In essence, the name "Mark Twain" or "Ernest Hemingway" became, in itself, a sort of trademark that guaranteed a certain reading experience. Writers, in turn, began to incorporate the experience of celebrity and renown into their fiction, partly because it was such a significant cultural phenomenon, but also as a sort of promotion of their own personalities. Thus, many classic novelists, from Twain and London up through Hemingway and Fitzgerald, wrote quasi-autobiographical *romans à clefs*, collapsing authorial personality into literary form, and making these novels, in essence, advertisements for themselves.

For authors who aspired to high cultural reputations, celebrity was particularly contradictory, as it was widely believed that true artists did not concern themselves with the marketplace. Commerce was seen as degrading, and many artistically ambitious and formally experimental authors, such as John Dos Passos and William Faulkner, shunned personal appearances and were disdainful of any marketing methods that used their "personalities" to promote their novels. This widespread attitude generated a noteworthy paradox whereby this very resistance to the market could be used as a mode of promotion. What the sociologist Pierre Bourdieu tellingly calls "an interest in disinterestedness" would come to characterize both authorial attitudes and advertising copy, such that publishers could make money precisely by claiming that their authors were not concerned with making money, and that their novels transcended economic value (Bourdieu 1993: 40). Bourdieu describes this process as the translation of symbolic capital – the social prestige of the author – into economic capital – the profits of the publisher and, ultimately, the income of the author.

In the twenties, celebrity authors such as Fitzgerald and Hemingway tended to be intellectual socialites whose lively activities frequently appeared in gossip columns; in the thirties, during the depression, political engagement became firmly part of the image, and novels correlatively shifted in focus. This shift was partly enabled by the New Deal entry of the federal government into the publishing industry. Under the auspices of the Federal Writers' Project (a part of the Works Progress Administration), many authors, such as Richard Wright and Meridel Le Sueur, collected folklore and wrote tour guides that would inflect both the content and form of their novels. Furthermore, the very fact that government support was available for creative writing altered the national understanding of the nature of authorship. New Deal subsidization of the arts affirmed the idea of art as a public service, and artists as a public resource. It also enabled artists to produce civic-minded work without worrying about marketability.

Academic criticism also became a significant gatekeeping force in the thirties. Traditionally, reviewers and critics had been a species of public intellectual affiliated with the magazines in which they published; university English departments tended to be conservative bastions of philological and historical scholarship focusing on European and British literature with little interest in modern American fiction. However, in the thirties American and modern literature increasingly became acceptable topics of study, and university-based critics such as Lionel Trilling and Alan Tate became influential figures in the mainstream literary field. Prestigious English Departments, such as Columbia and Vanderbilt, became homes to significant schools of literary criticism whose principles and practices began to have sway in the publishing industry. In particular, the New Criticism, which championed the formal complexity of texts over the purported "realism" of their referential content, helped ballast the reputations of experimental modernist authors such as Faulkner and Dos Passos. It would not be until the post-Second World War expansion of the university, however, that academia would become the central arbiter of literary taste, as whole generations of undergraduates would acquire their understanding of aesthetic quality through required literature and writing courses.

In the commercial industry, the depression caused marketability, and particularly pricing, to become an acute issue, despite the confidence many had that publishing was "depression proof." This crisis precipitated a return to a strategy that had had been a cyclical phenomenon in the industry since the early nineteenth century: cheap paperback reprints. In 1939, Robert Fair de Graff, along with Richard Simon, Max Schuster, and Leon Shimkin, launched a company called Pocket Books, which was explicitly designed to produce 25-cent books for the mass market. Starting out with reprints of such respectable classics as *Wuthering Heights* and *The Way of All Flesh*, alongside more contemporary, yet still respectable, fare such as *Lost Horizon* and *The Bridge of San Luis Rey*, the company was an immediate success. The so-called paperback revolution had begun.

Two aspects of the paperback revolution are worth noting. First of all, like the book clubs, cheap paperbacks responded to the desire for and anxiety about cultural distinction among the reading public. Whereas, on one level, paperback publishers seemed simply motivated by profitability, many of them had a genuine desire to make good literature more widely available. The slogan for the New American Library (NAL), a spinoff from the American branch of Penguin Books started by Victor Weybright and Kurt Enoch, was "Good Reading for the Millions." NAL published cheap reprints of the work of such major American novelists as William Faulkner, Erskine Caldwell, and James T. Farrell, as well as the African American novelists Richard Wright, James Baldwin, and Ann Petry. Thus the paperback revolution allowed many reputable authors to reach audiences that could not afford hardcover editions of their novels.

In order to access this mass public, the paperback houses did not use the standard distribution networks of the book industry. Rather, they piggy-backed on the magazine industry, selling their wares through department stores, drugstores, and newsstands. Indeed, the paperback reprint became a sort of hybrid between book and magazine; it was usually a single book by a single author (though "double" titles were produced), but it looked like, and was distributed alongside, magazines that were designed to sell rapidly and reliably on a weekly or monthly basis. Thus, in order to facilitate quick turnover and impulse buying, many of the new paperback houses developed sexy and salacious cover art that precipitated the attention of decency leagues and vice societies, local and state police departments and courts, and, eventually, the federal government.

Indeed, censorship was a persistent problem across the entire first half of the twentieth century, affecting both the content and marketing of the American novel. Modern censorship began in 1873, when dry goods clerk Anthony Comstock founded the New York Society for the Suppression of Vice and then lobbied the Federal Post Office Department to enact a law, which informally would become known as the Comstock Act, proclaiming that "no obscene, lewd, or lascivious book, pamphlet, picture, paper, print, or other publication of an indecent character . . . shall be carried in the mail." Comstock's unrelenting fervor inaugurated a battle between decency crusaders and modern novelists that would persist up until the "constitutionalization of obscenity" in the fifties and sixties, when the Supreme Court, in a series of landmark rulings, would essentially end the censorship of print in the United States.

The legal definition of obscenity in the late nineteenth century had been established by the British case of *Regina v. Hicklin* (1868), which stated that "the test for obscenity is whether the tendency of the matter charged as obscenity is to deprave and corrupt those whose minds are open to such immoral influences and into whose hands a publication of this sort may fall." Draconian as this seems in retrospect, it was initially embraced on both sides of the Atlantic and was not perceived as a threat to literary freedom. Indeed, Comstock initially had the cooperation of publishers since they, like him, tended to be conservative in moral matters, and had no desire to offend the sensibilities of their class. Most of the major publishers of the nineteenth century saw their careers in terms of ethical uplift and moral constraint, and they shared Comstock's concern about the availability of "indecent" matter. However, once influential literary figures such as William Dean Howells and Henry James started to champion European naturalist authors such as Emile Zola and Leo Tolstoy, spawning a generation of American naturalists such as Theodore Dreiser and Kate Chopin, the publishing industry increasingly found itself at odds with watchdog groups such as the New York Society and Boston's Watch and Ward Society. Once the "new breed" of publishers came on the scene, men who were deeply invested in modern European thought and had little patience with what they considered to be American provincial prudery, the stage was set for a major confrontation.

This confrontation would come in the twenties, when a series of highly public battles in Boston and New York would eventually result in resounding defeat for the anti-vice crusaders, and in the process put "modern" literature on the mainstream cultural map. In New York, a "Clean Books League" was founded in 1922 with the central objective of strengthening the anti-obscenity laws in the state which was, then as now, the center of the publishing industry. The industry as a whole was surprisingly meek in its response, but Horace Liveright lobbied vigorously against the bill, which eventually failed to pass after Senator Jimmy Walker made his famous claim, "No woman was ever ruined by a book." It would also be in the twenties that "Banned in Boston" would become a derisory catchphrase, as the Watch and Ward society became increasingly aggressive in its attempts to suppress such prominent bestsellers as Theodore Dreiser's *American Tragedy* and Sinclair Lewis's *Elmer Gantry.*

However, these highly public confrontations were only the tip of the iceberg in terms of the concrete effects of censorship on the content of modern American fiction. Almost every major American author of the early twentieth century struggled with their editors over the inclusion of sexual scenes and indecent language in their novels, and they almost invariably ended up conceding to the perceived prudery of the American public. Thus, most famously, Max Perkins convinced Ernest Hemingway to alter key scenes and dialogue in *A Farewell to Arms*, arguing that a censorship battle over the text would greatly diminish his audience at this key juncture in his career. Upon receiving the initial manuscript, Perkins wrote to his boss Charles Scribner, "Its story in outline is not objectionable but many words and some passages in it are: we can blank the words and the worst passages can be revised" (Bruccoli 1996: 88). He then insisted to Hemingway,

> There are things in the book that never were in another . . . There are points that enemies could make a good deal of . . . I don't think we can print those three words, Ernest. I can't find *anyone* who thinks so. That supreme insult alone might turn a judge right around against us, and to the post office, it and the others, I think, would warrant (technically) action. (Bruccoli 1996: 106)

(The words were "cocksucker," "fucking," and "balls.") Hemingway relented, but then wrote, "It's no fun for me on acct. of the blanks – Now I can never say shit in a book – Precedent – When you make your own precedent once you make the wrong precedent you're just as badly stuck by it – It takes away the interest in writing fiction" (Bruccoli 1996: 122).

It would be this "chilling effect," the pre-publication revision of novels, that would really constitute the power of the vice societies. Though their public struggles were almost always lost, the indirect consequences of these confrontations in the persistent struggles between authors and editors were wide-reaching and profound.

Of course, obscenity could also be exploited as a promotional device, and vice societies always had to struggle with the paradox that their crusades tended to bring attention to the texts they attacked. Although most publishers during this era wanted to avoid the cost and hassle of obscenity trials, and were afraid of being labeled as "pornographers," they were not averse to generating publicity through controversy, and advertising copy for modern novels frequently deployed euphemistic references to "frank honesty" or "vivid realism" to indicate sexual suggestiveness in modern fiction. Thus although Perkins convinced Hemingway to alter *A Farewell to Arms*, Scribners was also able to promote it as a novel that broke taboos in representing both the language of war and the realities of sex.

The cause of literary freedom achieved a signal breakthrough when the landmark case of *The United States v. One Book Called "Ulysses"* was decided in 1933. Judge John Woolsey's famous ruling allowing James Joyce's masterpiece into the country determined that the text must be considered as a whole, and that its purportedly corrupting effects must be measured in terms of the average, as opposed to the particularly susceptible, reader. The *Ulysses* case enabled a loosening of constrictions on American fiction, and representations of sex and sexuality became more explicit in the thirties and forties as the power of the vice societies waned. However, Catholic organizations such as the Legion of Decency were quick to fill the gap, and the paperback revolution spawned another wave of post-World War Two censorship that eventually brought the issue to the Supreme Court. It would not be until the exoneration of William Burroughs' wildly explicit experimental novel *Naked Lunch* in 1966 that censorship of print would essentially end in the United States.

A full appreciation of the significance of any novel depends on an understanding of the cultural field in which it is produced, promoted, distributed, and read. The stratification of this field into highbrow, lowbrow, and middlebrow is a good place to start, but it is important to remember that these terms are schematic abstractions from a far more complex concrete reality, and that many authors and texts may straddle categories, or shift over time. For example, Hemingway's famously sparse style was initially effective as highbrow experimentation, but it also centrally influenced the more lowbrow accessibility of hard-boiled crime fiction. Furthermore, though Hemingway's great success during his lifetime was due to his concessions to the middlebrow marketplace, he is now celebrated in American literature courses as a classic highbrow author on the level of Shakespeare. By contrast, Erskine Caldwell was initially celebrated as highbrow, but then became an author of mass-market bestsellers, and now he is almost entirely forgotten. Indeed, many of the more popular middlebrow authors of the first half of the twentieth century, such as Ellen Glasgow and Booth Tarkington, have been long out of print and are rarely, if ever, taught in American literature classes. Which is only to confirm that the classification of a novel depends at least as much on the decisions of gatekeepers – initially editors and critics, but ultimately English professors and high school teachers – as it does on the actual form and content of the text. The study of these decisions is usually called the sociology of literature, and it consists of placing the thematic and formal qualities of a given text in the context of its publication and reception. Authors write novels, but publishers, editors, agents, advertisers, reviewers, critics, professors, students, and readers all play a role in the form they take and the manner in which they are read.

References and Further Reading

Berg, A. Scott 1978: *Max Perkins: Editor of Genius*. New York: Pocket Books.

Bonn, Thomas 1989: *Heavy Traffic and High Culture: New American Library as Literary Gatekeeper in the Paperback Revolution*. Carbondale: Southern Illinois University Press.

Bourdieu, Pierre 1993: *The Field of Cultural Production*. Trans. Randal Johnson. New York: Columbia University Press.

Bowker, R. R. 1912: *Copyright: Its History and Its Law*. Boston: Houghton Mifflin.

Boyer, Paul S. 2002: *Purity in Print: Book Censorship in America from the Gilded Age to the Computer Age*. Madison: University of Wisconsin Press.

Brooks, Van Wyck 1934: *America's Coming-of-Age*. New York: Doubleday.

Bruccoli, Matthew (ed.) 1996: *The Only Thing That Counts: The Ernest Hemingway/ Maxwell Perkins Correspondence, 1925–1947*. New York: Scribners.

Cerf, Bennett 1977: *At Random: The Reminiscenes of Bennett Cerf*. New York: Random House.

Coser, Lewis A., Charles Kadushin, and Walter W. Powell 1982: *Books: The Culture and Commerce of Publishing*. New York: Basic Books.

Gross, Gerald (ed.) 1961: *Publishers on Publishing*. New York: Grosset and Dunlap.

Gross, Gerald (ed.) 1962: *Editors on Editing*. New York: Grosset and Dunlap.

Holt, Henry 1905: The Commercialization of Literature. *Atlantic Monthly* 96.5, 577–600.

Madison, Charles A. 1966: *Book Publishing in America*. New York: McGraw-Hill.

Radway, Janice A. 1997: *A Feeling For Books: The Book-of-the-Month Club, Literary Taste, and Middle-Class Desire*. Chapel Hill: University of North Carolina Press.

Reynolds, Paul R. 1972: *The Middle Man: The Adventures of a Literary Agent*. New York: William Morrow.

Rubin, Joan Shelley 1992: *The Making of Middlebrow Culture*. Chapel Hill: University of North Carolina Press.

Satterfield, Jay 2002: *"The World's Best Books": Taste, Culture, and the Modern Library*. Amherst: University of Massachusetts Press.

Schick, Frank L. 1958: *The Paperbound Book in America*. New York: Bowker.

Szalay, Michael 2000: *New Deal Modernism: American Literature and the Invention of the Welfare State*. Durham: Duke University Press.

Tebbel, John 1972–81: *A History of Book Publishing in the United States*. New York: Bowker.

Tebbel, John 1987: *Between Covers: The Rise and Transformation of American Book Publishing*. New York: Oxford University Press.

Trachenberg, Alan 1982: *The Incorporation of America: Culture and Society in the Gilded Age*. New York: Hill and Wang.

Turner, Catherine 2003: *Marketing Modernism Between the Two World Wars*. Amherst: University of Massachusetts Press.

West III, James L. W. 1988: *American Authors and the Literary Marketplace since 1900*. Philadelphia: University of Pennsylvania Press.

Wilson, Christopher P. 1985: *The Labor of Words: Literary Professionalism in the Progressive Era*. Athens: University of Georgia Press.

Chapter 5

Manhood, Modernity, and Crime Fiction

David Schmid

The critic writing about American crime fiction published during the first half of the twentieth century faces several daunting challenges. Quite apart from the huge number of short stories and novels in the genre published during this period, there is also significant diversity in terms of types of American crime fiction. That is, the genre itself is not a single entity, despite certain overlapping conventions and themes, but rather an amalgam of competing accounts of such subjects as crime, morality, gender roles, and violence. At one extreme, there are those writers who are influenced by British classical mystery fiction. The work of late nineteenth- and early twentieth-century British crime writers like Sir Arthur Conan Doyle (himself inspired by Edgar Allan Poe) and G. K. Chesterton, and more particularly that of "Golden Age" mystery writers of the 1920s and 1930s such as Dorothy L. Sayers, Agatha Christie, and Margery Allingham is often characterized by upper-class characters, rural (often country-house) settings, a limited number of suspects, unusual murder methods, an eccentric (usually amateur) detective, and a vast number of (frequently false or misleading) clues ultimately leading to the unmasking of the murderer by the detective in a climactic final scene. Violence in such narratives is usually limited to the murder or murders that form the focus of detection, and the representation of such violence is usually restrained. Perhaps most importantly, the crimes in classical British crime fiction are seen as extremely unusual, even shocking events that violently erupt into and upset the ordinariness of the social milieu in which they occur. The detective, in solving the crime, thus restores normality and order to his or her society in a fairly unambiguous fashion.

Although the American examples of the classical mystery school do not necessarily include every one of these details, the work of such writers as S. S. Van Dine, Ellery Queen, and Rex Stout can certainly best be described as classical mysteries influenced by the British tradition in the sense that they all include eccentric detectives, murders committed in an exceedingly complicated fashion requiring both erudition and creativity for their solution, and a final scene in which the murderer is revealed by the detective.

At the other extreme is the American hard-boiled mystery, most often associated with those writers who published in the pulp magazine *Black Mask*: Carroll John Daly, Erle Stanley Gardner, Raoul Whitfield, Dashiell Hammett, and Raymond Chandler, among many others. As these authors often explicitly reject the British classical mystery tradition, deliberately adopting styles, characters, and settings in every way alien to it – every aspect of their work is different. They tend to write about the working classes (and often how they are exploited by the rich); they use urban settings; they write about professional criminals; their detectives usually detect for a living, rather than being amateurs; the crimes about which they write could have been committed by almost anyone and so they do not present a limited number of suspects; they write about violence much more explicitly and include much more of it in their narratives; the crimes that drive their work are not interruptions of the social order, but instead practically constitute a normal part of everyday life because they are so frequent and ordinary; and, finally, the detective is rarely able to solve and resolve the mystery as neatly as Golden Age detectives because the corruption both exemplified and revealed by the initial crime has, by the end of the story, come to be seen as so pervasive as to be insoluble. As Ernest Mandel has remarked, "mystery always returns," and this is nowhere more true than in hard-boiled mysteries (Mandel 1984: 27).

Quite apart from the presence of both classical and hard-boiled mysteries during this period, the landscape of American crime fiction is further complicated by the simultaneous existence of a number of genres closely related to crime fiction – the Western, out of which many aspects of the hard-boiled mystery developed, with the cowboy becoming the private eye and moving from the range into the city; the gangster novel, which, in many ways, in works such as Paul Cain's *Fast*

One (1933), is the hard-boiled novel written from the point of view of the criminal rather than the detective; and the proletarian novel, which shares, in such works as Benjamin Appel's *Brain Guy* (1934), a complex of themes with the hard-boiled crime novel: violence, poverty, lawlessness, corruption, and especially class antagonism (see Haut 1995: 10). A representative example of American crime fiction's diversity can be provided merely by a perusal of the works published in 1929: this one year saw the appearance of classical crime novels, such as S. S. Van Dine's *The Bishop Murder Case*, hard-boiled novels, such as Dashiell Hammett's *Red Harvest*, and the gangster novel, exemplified by W. R. Burnett's *Little Caesar*.

What this list also indicates is a final complication in writing about American crime fiction between 1900 and 1950: rather than one school of crime fiction being neatly succeeded by another, they overlap with each other, making it incorrect to argue for a clear line of development in the genre. In some respects, hard-boiled crime fiction predates the most prominent examples of classical American crime fiction, with *Black Mask* beginning publication in 1920, while S. S. Van Dine does not publish *The Benson Murder Case* until 1926. Similarly, it is possible to argue that hard-boiled crime fiction outlasts the classical examples of the genre, the artificialities of which seemed increasingly irrelevant after World War Two. Certainly, examples of the hard-boiled genre have come to dominate both critical and popular understandings of what "counts" as American crime fiction, perhaps because of the way they encapsulate a language (colloquial, direct, and informal) and an approach to modernity (both cynical and idealistic) that have come to be coded as quintessentially "American." Moreover, the stubborn individualism and world-weary pragmatism of the private eye practically guaranteed the powerful influence of the hard-boiled form because the author was able to use the character to articulate the challenges facing the United States in an increasingly complex and conflictual twentieth-century world order.

Despite the hegemonic status of hard-boiled fiction in historical accounts of American crime fiction, however, we must also keep in mind the fact that classical mystery writers such as Ellery Queen and Rex Stout, who favored a style closer to the British model, go on publishing and enjoying great success until the 1960s and 1970s, so once again it is the simultaneity of these different forms of crime fiction that stands out as one of the most interesting features of the genre during this period. How can we explain this simultaneity? Both classical and hard-boiled American crime fiction, while different in so many ways, and appealing to different audiences, actually have a common purpose: offering imaginative resolutions to some of the most perplexing and threatening problems of modernity in general and of manhood in particular. Crime fiction, from its very beginnings, has always been engaged with the particulars of modern experience in order to provide reassurance and guidance (often through the model of the hero-detective) to its predominantly male readers (see Smith 2000 for a study of the readership of hard-boiled fiction) about how to negotiate the increasingly complex and threatening landscape of modernity.

Although some critics have questioned whether crime fiction is closely related to the modern, arguing that its obsession with revealing secrets hidden in the past gives the genre a strong Gothic (and therefore anti-modern) flavor (Scaggs 2005: 16–17, 66–8), in fact crime fiction was originally introduced and subsequently developed within the context of modernity, so that it "enables and constrains the creation and reception of mystery fiction" (Kelly 1998: 1). For the purposes of this chapter, I am using a definition of modernity taken from Marshall Berman's ground-breaking book, *All That Is Solid Melts Into Air*, because his definition correctly stresses its simultaneous creativity and destructiveness: "To be modern is to find ourselves in an environment that promises us adventure, power, joy, growth, transformation of ourselves and the world – and, at the same time, that threatens to destroy everything we have, everything we know, everything we are" (Berman 1982: 15).

Crime fiction captures both the negative and positive energies associated with modernity, not least because it both draws upon and critiques the socioeconomic processes that Berman sees as intrinsic to modernity: "demographic movements (for example, immigration and migration), industrialization, growth of cities, technological advances, and, above all, the extraordinary expansion of the capitalist market" (Berman 1982: 15). Of these processes, American crime fiction has concentrated in particular on the growth of cities, and in particular the fact that the new city dwellers were more likely than ever before to have daily encounters with strangers or with people they knew only slightly.

The consequences of this fact were not only a pervasive sense of insecurity and uncertainty, but also a pressing need to read the appearance and behavior of others correctly in order not to be taken advantage of or harmed by figures who came to personify both the seductive charm and the dangerous potentialities of the city, such as the confidence man. From the beginning of the genre, therefore, crime fiction paid particular attention to negotiating and interpreting the new urban environments. When Edgar Allan Poe published his genre-founding short stories, beginning with "The Murders in the Rue Morgue" in 1841, featuring his famous protagonist, Auguste Dupin, he used Dupin's ability to interpret and resolve the mysteries thrown up by the complex urban environment of Paris to provide his readers with reassurance that American cities, too, although potentially dangerous and destructive, could be mastered if one paid sufficient attention to detail.

The influence of Poe on later writers who wrote in the genre he founded was profound and various, but his focus on the detective's ability to read the city was one of Poe's most enduring influences, as we can see if we consider Sherlock Holmes' encyclopedic knowledge of London and its various mysteries in Sir Arthur Conan Doyle's short stories and novels. A less obvious influence, but one with equally profound ramifications, was Poe's choice of a male detective figure. In some ways, this choice was to be expected: men, after all, were on the streets of the new urban environments much more frequently and more extensively than women, and so they were exposed to the potentially dislocating and harmful, as well as the pleasurable, aspects of urbanization much more than women. In other ways, Poe's female victims and male investigators established a gender dynamic in crime fiction that the vast majority of subsequent writers would observe. Placing men in control was just one way in which Poe's crime stories provided reassurance and pleasure to his male readers.

With this said, the model of masculinity offered in crime fiction beginning with Poe was frequently different from ideal notions of American manhood at the time these stories were written. According to Michael Kimmel, the prosperous "Self-Made Man" was the dominant conception of American manhood in the middle of the nineteenth century, and yet Dupin does not fit this ideal at all, being a French aristocrat who had fallen on hard times (1994: 29). Moreover, Auguste Dupin was markedly different from the ideal of rough hewn, violent manhood provided in the frontier romances of James Fenimore Cooper writing at the same time as Poe. Although Dupin sometimes takes an active role in his investigations and occasionally even places himself in potential danger, it would not be accurate to describe him as either courageous or virile, and his many personal eccentricities (he only went out at night, displayed erudition about obscure subjects, and shunned society) make him an unlikely role model for American men. Bringing him closer to hegemonic definitions of American manhood, however, is Dupin's "demeanor of cool unflappability" when faced with a dangerous or difficult situation (Kelly 1998: 5). It is his confidence that brings him closest to being an urban version of Cooper's Deerslayer – a confidence that is expressed in his ability to read the urban jungle in the same way that Natty Bumppo, the "man who knows Indians," negotiates the frontier.

If Poe's Dupin was able to provide some beneficial guidance and confidence to his readers in the 1840s, however, it is doubtful that his ability to do so lasted very long. As the nineteenth century progressed, the forces transforming the meanings of American manhood – industrialization, the entry of large numbers of women into the public sphere, newly freed blacks, and immigrants of a more ethnically diverse background than had constituted the American until this point, along with the closing of the frontier – intensified steadily. As a consequence, many men of all types and backgrounds felt both threatened and dislocated from the elements that traditionally constituted their identities; these feelings were strengthened still further by the fact that their roles as breadwinner and dominant partners in marriage were undergoing constant redefinition (Kimmel 1994: 52).

Under these circumstances, it is unlikely that a reclusive French aristocrat could address the dislocating effects of modernity at all convincingly for an audience of American men. Just as Teddy Roosevelt becomes the symbolic apotheosis of American manhood at the turn of the twentieth century (Kimmel 1994: 120–4), so crime fiction adapts its icons of manhood to match a world transformed by the slaughter of World War One, the crime wave unleashed by the beginning of Prohibition in 1919, and the devastating economic consequences of the depression, beginning in 1929. Crime fiction launched this process of adaptation under the banner of greater realism, and its most famous rallying cry (albeit a largely retrospective one) was Raymond Chandler's 1944 essay, "The Simple Art of Murder":

> The realist in murder writes of a world in which gangsters can rule nations and almost rule cities, in which hotels and apartment houses and celebrated restaurants are owned by men who made their money out of brothels, in which a screen star can be a fingerman for the mob, and the nice man down the hall is a boss of the numbers racket . . . It is not a fragrant world, but it is the world you live in. (Chandler 1944: 17)

In differentiating the American hard-boiled mystery (for Chandler, exemplified by the work of Dashiell Hammett) from the classical British mystery and its American practitioners, Chandler argues that the former is more "realistic" in its view of the world in general and in its treatment of crime in particular. If iconic aspects of American modernity such as Prohibition, the rise of the gangster figure as epitomized by Al Capone, and the depression are referred to obliquely if at all in the classical American crime fiction of S. S. Van Dine and Ellery Queen, the hard-boiled school makes these subjects the heart and soul of what it does.

Part of the reason why hard-boiled crime fiction represents the world of the depression with such realism is that during the 1930s and 1940s many pulp fiction writers of all kinds (including writers of pulp crime fiction) were not only writing about the depression, they were living through it. Some, like Raymond Chandler, were driven into writing by the depression, and this illustrates the larger point that many hard-boiled crime fiction writers, especially those who never broke through into the "slick" magazines or into novels, are more accurately described as literary workers rather than artists; paid by the word, they ate only if they kept up a punishing rate of literary production. In such a situation, they were bound to be more attuned to the struggles of working people to make a living, and to the corruption and violence that surrounded both the acquisition and maintenance of wealth (Haut 1995).

Indeed, if we are looking for those qualities in hard-boiled American crime fiction that constitute its realism, the speed of this fiction's production is entirely relevant, because this speed was also a feature of hard-boiled narratives themselves. The immobility of Rex Stout's obese detective, Nero Wolfe, personifies the tendency of classical American mysteries toward stasis; their narratives are dominated by long conversations between characters about the various possible solutions to the crimes under investigation. In hard-boiled crime fiction, by contrast, there is constant movement. As Ernest Mandel has argued, the hard-boiled protagonist "will track . . . criminals down by obstinate questioning and constant moves from place to place, not through the painstaking analysis of clues and related analytical reasoning" (Mandel 1984: 36), and the pace of hard-boiled narratives is largely determined by such movement, whether it be the Continental Op's wanderings around Dashiell Hammett's Personville, Philip Marlowe driving from one part of Raymond Chandler's Los Angeles to another, or Carroll John Daly's Race Williams baldly summarizing his method: "When I wanted a man I stuck a gun in my pocket and went after him" (Daly [1927] 1984: 38). In such ways hard-boiled protagonists respond to a modern world in which every part of the capitalist process, from production, to distribution, to consumption is becoming increasingly rapid by attempting to match its pace.

Perhaps the most extreme example of relentless pace in a hard-boiled novel is Paul Cain's aptly titled 1933 novel, *Fast One*. The novel begins with the words "Kells walked north on Spring" (1) and from that point on Kells never stops, moving faster and faster, leaving a trail of bodies behind him, submitting himself to beating after beating, and only finally coming to a halt when, in the novel's memorable closing words, "life went away from him" (Cain 1933: 304). The pace of *Fast One* is so frantic that it almost becomes a character in its own right, dominating the novel to the extent that the details of plot and character development are often shoved to one side by the onward rush of events (Faust 1978: 311) and the speed that characterizes hard-boiled fiction is just one way in which the genre is attuned to the economic and technological conditions in which it is written.

The type and frequency of violence in hard-boiled crime fiction is another such example. Violence has a defining role in such fiction and this comes as no surprise when we consider the extent to which hard-boiled crime narratives were concerned with types of crime that were in the process of becoming part of the everyday fabric of American life rather than being rare and extraordinary. The rise of the gangster had changed the face of crime in the United States forever; not only did Prohibition dramatically increase the murder rate, it also impressed upon millions of Americans the fact that America was violent in a way it had never been before. But hard-boiled fiction was different not only because of the types of violence it dealt with; it also stood out because of the way it so often drained affect from the representation of violence. In the classical crime novels of S. S. Van Dine, the narrator frequently stresses the disgust and horror he feels when confronted with the body of a murder victim. In the world of the hard-boiled novel, however, peopled with characters who practice violence for a living, acts of brutality are accompanied by a singular lack of emotion: "He brushed himself off and went over and kicked Kells' head and face several times. His face was dark and composed and he was breathing hard. He kicked Kells very carefully, drawing his foot back and aiming, and then kicking very accurately and hard" (Cain 1933: 35).

If violence in classical American crime fiction was still seen overwhelmingly as a shocking eruption into the ordinariness of the everyday, in hard-boiled fiction such violence was precisely that ordinariness.

Faced with such an environment, the private eye had to be both courageous and enduring, and these qualities were seen not only in his ability to absorb punishment but also in his ability to "dish it out."

Indeed, one of the things that distinguishes run of the mill hard-boiled fiction from more interesting examples of the type is that whereas writers like Carroll John Daly exhibit a remarkable lack of interest in questioning the efficacy of violence ("Them that live by the gun should die by the gun, is good sound twentieth century gospel" [1927] 1984: 93), writers such as Dashiell Hammett examine the consequences for the psyche as well as the body of the detective of living and working with such brutality. Perhaps the most famous example of this aspect of the hard-boiled genre is what happens to the Continental Op in *Red Harvest*. Although he begins the novel enthusiastically killing and encouraging others to kill, by the middle of the novel the welter of blood implied by the book's title starts to get to the Op; he ponders the possibility that he is going "blood simple" in the sense that he is starting to enjoy the killing too much.

Speed and violence are undoubtedly useful ways of tracking both the differences between the classical and hard-boiled forms of American mysteries, and the ways in which hard-boiled writers attempted to respond to both the pace and brutality that defined economic competition and interpersonal relations in the contemporary United States. By far the most important aspect of the difference between the competing traditions of American crime fiction, however, and the aspect that speaks most eloquently of the problems and challenges of American modernity, is what examples of the genre have to say about American manhood. Once again, Raymond Chander's "The Simple Art of Murder" gives us a useful point of entry:

> But down these mean streets a man must go who is not himself mean, who is neither tarnished nor afraid. The detective in this kind of story must be such a man. He is the hero; he is everything. He must be a complete man and a common man and yet an unusual man. He must be, to use a rather weathered phrase, a man of honor – by instinct, by inevitability, without thought of it, and certainly without saying it. He must be the best man in his world and a good enough man for any world. (Chandler 1944: 18)

Chandler's famous evocation of the ultimate hard-boiled male hero emphasizes the extent to which the hard-boiled ideology not only Americanizes but also emphatically masculinizes the crime fiction genre, while the setting of the "mean streets" reminds Chandler's reader of the urban context of this type of fiction (Krutnik 1991: 42). Again, the most useful points of contrast are the heroes of classical American mysteries written during the same period, although comparing the two will also reveal the extent to which the differences between the two traditions can be overstated.

Philo Vance, the series character in S. S. Van Dine's mysteries, is a bohemian aesthete from an aristocratic family who was partly educated in England. As this thumbnail sketch suggests, Vance is presented to the reader as a decidedly unmanly and antimodern character. His speech is filled with foppish declarations (he particularly delights in calling other men "my dear") and he pays an inordinate amount of attention to his appearance. His attitude toward the modern world is best described as disdainful, as when he complains "our so-called civ'lization is nothing more than the persistent destruction of everything that's beautiful and enduring, and the designing of cheap makeshifts" (1926: 200). Vance's characteristics made him an easy target for early defenders of the hard-boiled school of crime fiction, but in some ways he is a more complex character than his detractors acknowledge. Although it is true that Vance's foppishness is emphasized *ad nauseam*, Van Dine occasionally has Vance take decisive, manly action, as when he overpowers the murderer at the climax of *The Benson Murder Case*. The fact that this display of physical prowess comes just after the murderer calls Vance a "sissy" only accentuates Vance's strength while also complicating the reader's attitude toward his effeteness.

The influence of Van Dine's work was widespread, and can be seen most clearly in the work of Ellery Queen, at once the pseudonym of cousins and collaborators Frederic Dannay and Manfred B. Lee. and the name of their detective. The early entries in the long-running series of novels featuring Queen, such as *The Roman Hat Mystery* (1929), show him to be both brilliant and arrogant, much like Vance. These early novels also feature challenges to the reader to solve the crime once all the evidence has been presented, another indication of the strong debt these novels owe to the classical British mystery tradition. By the late 1930s, however, perhaps in response to the great success of the hard-boiled mode, the Queen novels become, if not hard-boiled, at least noticeably more modern. Queen's *The Four of Hearts* (1938), for example, uses a Hollywood setting that would have seemed very out of place in the earlier novels.

If the "modernization" of the classical mystery à la Queen was one response to the rise of the hard-boiled mystery, another can be seen in the Nero Wolfe novels of Rex Stout, which combine elements of both schools. The deeply eccentric and brilliant Nero Wolfe seems like a figure straight out of the classical school, with his huge girth, passion for orchids, and refusal to leave his house under any circumstances in one way or another echoing not only Philo Vance, but also Sherlock Holmes as well as Auguste Dupin. Conversely, Wolfe's business partner, Archie Goodwin, seems much closer to the stereotype of the hard-boiled private eye: he handles all the physical aspects of an investigation and can be intimidating when necessary.

Stout not only presents us with personifications of the classical and hard-boiled schools of detection, but also suggests how the methods of those schools can conflict with each other. Toward the end of *Fer-De-Lance*, the first Nero Wolfe novel, Archie expresses his frustration with Wolfe's passivity: "Do you think all it takes to catch a murderer is to sit in your damn office and let your genius work? That may be most of it, but it also takes a pair of eyes and a pair of legs and sometimes a gun or two" (Stout 1934: 254). If the "pure" classical mystery tries to incorporate elements of a very different type of mystery, the results may not necessarily be harmonious. The conflict between Archie and Wolfe, in other words, is emblematic of the difficulties Stout had in combining the very different traditions of the classical and the hard-boiled mystery in a single volume.

The complexity that characterizes the representation of masculinity and the relation to modernity in classical American crime fiction suggests the danger of overstating the difference between such fiction and its hard-boiled counterpart. It also suggests that the popularity of writers like Van Dine, Queen, and Stout is not entirely predicated on a desire to escape from the dislocating effects of modernity but is also driven by a desire to master contemporary circumstances, by the power of brilliant men to demonstrate the continuing efficacy of rationality, even in the midst of a modern world that seemed to contradict such efficacy more and more. Hard-boiled narratives were also driven by a desire to master modernity through manhood, but through a very different kind of manhood and a very different kind of mastery.

These differences are immediately obvious in the work of Carroll John Daly, credited as the author of the first hard-boiled story, the first tough-guy private investigator, and the first hard-boiled novel, components he then brought together to truly originate the genre with his 1927 novel *The Snarl of the Beast*, which features the character of Race Williams, easily the most well known early example of the hard-boiled private eye. Williams' description of his philosophy and methods convey better than any summary exactly why Daly's contribution proved to be so powerful:

Right and wrong are not written on the statutes for me, nor do I find my code of morals in the essays of long-winded professors. My ethics are my own. I'm not saying they're good and I'm not admitting they're bad, and what's more I'm not interested in the opinions of others on that subject . . . I stand on my own legs and I'll shoot it out with any gun in the city – any time, any place. Thirty-fourth street and Broadway, in the five o'clock rush hour, isn't barred either. Race Williams – private Investigator – tells the whole story. Right! Let's go. (Daly [1927] 1984: 11–12)

The emphasis on violence, personal integrity, individualism, and ethical flexibility all inspired countless imitators, many of whom make Race look vacillating and pacifist by comparison. Even though *Black Mask's* most famous editor, Joseph "Cap" Shaw, did not have a particularly high opinion of Daly's work, he had to acknowledge that sales of an individual issue always jumped by about fifteen to twenty percent whenever a Daly story was included. What was the secret to Daly's success? A typical Race Williams story is a fable of manhood being tested and passing that test emphatically and triumphantly. Most importantly, the results of that test are ratified by other men. As Michael Kimmel has argued,

From the early nineteenth century until the present day, most of men's relentless efforts to prove their manhood contain this core element of homosociality. From fathers and boyhood friends to our teachers, coworkers, and bosses, it is the evaluative eyes of other men that are always upon us, watching, judging. It was in this regime of scrutiny that such men were tested. (Kimmel 1994: 19)

Williams' ability to pass the test of manhood made him a role model for many of his readers. Moreover, the idea that a single individual with physical strength, a personal code of ethics and brute force could take on and overcome the negative forces of modernity – gangsters, corrupt police officials, and politicians – was tremendously appealing.

Kimmel also reminds us, however, that American manhood has always been defined through opposition to women (1994: 40), so what role do women play in Daly's work and in hard-boiled fiction more generally? In many respects women were a prominent presence in American crime fiction between 1900 and 1950, both as writers and editors. One of the most popular mystery novelists writing during this period, for example, was Mary Roberts Rinehart, whose books, beginning with *The Circular Staircase* in 1908, generally featured intuitive and energetic middle-aged spinsters as their protagonists. Even that bastion of male hard-boiled writing, *Black Mask*, at one point subtitled "The He-Man's Magazine," "employed its first woman writer and heroine . . . as early as 1928 . . . Moreover, in 1936, F. Ellsworth, a woman, took over as editor of *Black Mask*" (Haut 1995: 112). By far the most interesting novel by a female writer during this period was Dorothy B. Hughes' *In a Lonely Place*, a brilliant study of the corrosive effects of war and modernity on the male psyche published in 1947. When Hughes writes of her homicidal and aptly-named war veteran protagonist, Dix Steele, that the "war years were the first happy years he'd ever known. You didn't have to kowtow to the stinking rich, you were all equal in pay; and before long you were the rich guy," (113) she concisely asserts a link between class resentment, misogynist blood lust, and the killing both enabled and justified by war.

Unfortunately, however, the work of such writers as Rinehart and Hughes tends to be the exception that proves the rule of how women are represented in American crime fiction during this period. In the classic examples of the genre, women are merely background figures – victims, wives, servants, mothers, daughters – who rarely play a central role in the narratives in which they appear. Such neglect can seem positively benign, however, compared to the ways women often appear in hard-boiled fiction. The hard-boiled male often claims, for example, that he is simply indifferent to women, so that Daly's Race Williams can declare: "Women mean nothing in my life. Some old mummy has said, 'He travels farthest who travels alone.' That's me. Venus de Milo or Cleopatra herself couldn't switch me from my purpose" (Daly [1927] 1984: 116). Williams' attitude implies that getting too close to a woman can be dangerous for a hard-boiled male, and this is borne out by Sam Spade's situation at the end of Dashiell Hammett's *The Maltese Falcon*. Part of the reason Spade produces such an elaborate list of reasons why he is going to turn Brigid O'Shaughnessy over to the authorities is because he has become emotionally involved with her, a fact that clearly contradicts both his personal and professional identities.

There are also a number of other, more explicitly violent ways to repudiate women in hard-boiled texts, ranging from Philip Marlowe's visceral disgust with the Sternwood sisters in Raymond Chandler's *The Big Sleep* to Mike Hammer's notorious execution of Charlotte Manning at the climax (and I use the word advisedly) of Mickey Spillane's *I, the Jury*. In as much as these acts are repudiations of whatever is conventionally unmasculine (as well as what is specifically feminine), it is viable to associate the attitude of hard-boiled men to women with their attitudes to "alternative" types of masculinities. Many examples of American hard-boiled crime fiction are notably hostile to effeminate male characters whose main purpose in the narrative often seems to be to make the hero's heteronormative masculinity stand out even more. It may even be that these effeminate men are a way in which the effeminate heroes of some examples of classical American crime fiction (for example, Philo Vance) make their way into hard-boiled fiction; perhaps this is an example of one form of crime fiction intertextually interrogating the other. Regardless, Philip Marlowe's disgust with homosexual characters in *The Big Sleep* rivals and perhaps even exceeds his disgust for women:

> I still held his automatic more or less pointed at him, but he swung on me just the same. It caught me flush on the chin. I backstepped fast enough to keep from falling, but I took plenty of the punch. It was meant to be a hard one, but a pansy has no iron in his bones, whatever he looks like. (Chandler 1939: 100)

A particularly complex and justly famous example of this tendency to present queer characters as abject occurs in Hammett's *The Maltese Falcon* in the person of Joel Cairo, who is presented as a strange aberration not only because of his "queer" sexuality, but his equally queer ethnicity: he is described as "Levantine" (Hammett 1929: 42). This point reminds us that the models of manhood in both the classical and hard-boiled types of American crime fiction are not only overwhelmingly heterosexual, but also overwhelmingly white. When non-white characters appear at all in crime fiction during this period, it is usually in the most appallingly stereotypical terms (see Chandler 1940: 10, Macdonald 1949: 117–18). About the only honorable exceptions to this rule are Raoul Whitfield's Jo Gar stories, featuring a private detective in the Philippines (where Whitfield, an Anglo-American, had been partially raised), and African American author Rudolph Fisher's extraordinary novel, *The Conjure-Man Dies: A Mystery Tale of Dark Harlem* (1932), filled with page after page of descriptions of black people behaving and talking as they do in no other piece of crime fiction in this period. Some of the characters have learned conversations on difficult subjects, and others participate in a vibrant and lively street culture that is portrayed with none of the sense of strangeness that would dominate such depictions in other examples of crime fiction from the period.

But if one can easily find multiple examples of the ways in which hard-boiled manhood is seen as mutually exclusive of both womanhood and associated "others" this is by no means the whole story. The same

Race Williams who claims to be indifferent to women ends *The Snarl of the Beast* by falling in love: "each conversation ended with the slip of a girl's head down on my chest . . . It was real and wonderful and hardly believable to me – but mush to the outsider. It all depends upon whose chest the head is on, I guess" (Daly [1927] 1984: 317).

If Race Williams, possibly the most representative and influential early example of hard-boiled manhood, can fall in love, this suggests that the meanings of hard-boiled masculinity are considerably more varied than many critics believe them to be, encompassing empathy and emotion as well as callousness and brutality.

In what remains of this chapter, I will argue that the relation between men and modernity in American crime fiction extends way beyond the model of mastering modernity, whether that mastery takes the form of rationality (in classical examples of the genre) or force (in hard-boiled fiction). Indeed, the major reason for both the phenomenal success of the genre and its striking stylistic, thematic, and generic diversity during the first half of the twentieth century is crime fiction's ability to provide a wide range of satisfactions to a wide range of readers by suggesting a multiplicity of ways to negotiate the challenges of modernity. Contrary to popular belief, hard-boiled masculinity in particular proves to be more accurately described as multiple, vulnerable, and sentimental rather than singular, violent, and realistic.

The first step is constructing this contrarian vision of hard-boiled masculinity is to emphasize that rather than the hard-boiled detective mastering his environment, frequently that environment masters, or at the very least, influences him, even if it is only by disallowing certain forms of manhood: "I looked down at the chessboard. The move with the knight was wrong. I put it back to where I had moved it from. Knights had no meaning in this game. It wasn't a game for knights" (Chandler 1939: 156). Such sentiments imply that the conventional code of tough, hard-boiled manhood may be a forced reaction to environmental factors as much as it is a willed choice.

With this point in mind, we should also emphasize that the conventional version of hard-boiled masculinity entails other features that may be experienced as impositions rather than freely made decisions by hard-boiled protagonists, such as the tendency for independence to shade into solipsistic isolation. As Chandler puts it in a 1959 letter, he always sees Marlowe "in a lonely street, in a lonely room, puzzled but never quite defeated" (quoted in MacShane 1987: 483). At its most extreme, the "aloneness" of the detective can ossify into an inability to form close friendships or emotional bonds of any kind with anyone, leading to a situation where the "positive" masculine trait of independence is in danger of becoming emotional paralysis.

And yet, the emotional distance cultivated out of necessity by hard-boiled protagonists never becomes the total absence of emotion because, according to Grebstein, "The tough hero's capacity for emotion constitutes the essence of his humanity. It is this quality which renders him most humanly attractive and credible to the reader and which provides the most important means of distinguishing him from his antagonists, the gangsters and thugs" (Grebstein 1968: 25). In other words, there remains, and must remain, a core of emotionality at the basis of hard-boiled masculinity in order for it to have meaning. Indeed, there is a type of hard-boiled fiction in which this emotionality is close to being the defining feature of hard-boiled masculinity, the so-called (in a term taken from Steve Fisher) the tough/tender school.

In the work of writers like Steve Fisher, David Goodis, and Cornell Woolrich, an alternative form of masculinity is developed in which emotions are always much closer to the surface and much more readily expressed than in the hard-boiled fiction of writers like Daly and Hammett. The "tough/tender" writers constitute a counter-type of hard-boiled masculinity, one which specializes in protagonists who are frequently wounded both physically and emotionally. Indeed, at its most extreme, this type of masculinity becomes openly masochistic, even abject, rather than tough. Goodis's protagonists in particular regularly submit themselves to savage beatings with no clear aim in mind other than to confirm the utter hopelessness of their situation. Although these protagonists are never identified explicitly as masochists, the label cannot be avoided as we watch them persistently put themselves into situations in which a beating is the inevitable result. They do so not so much because they desire pain, but rather because the pain gives them an objective correlative for their view of the world and their unquenchable desire for human connection. Goodis feels that a vulnerable, open and tender man cannot possibly expect anything else but pain in the brutal and isolating world of noir crime fiction.

If the tough/tender type seems a million miles away from the confident macho swagger of a Race Williams, however, once could also argue that this type merely develops a potentiality inherent in even the most unregenerately masculine of private eyes. Chandler's Marlowe is also beaten regularly for no apparent purpose, and the "toughness" of the hard-boiled hero often depends more on his ability to survive such violence than on his ability to inflict such violence on others. The strong masochistic dimension in the detective's voluntary submission to the physically challenging, dangerous circumstances in which the violence of hard-boiled crime fiction is played out demonstrates that the major role of this violence is not necessarily to glorify male mastery. The character of Ned Beaumont, the protagonist of Hammett's *The Glass Key* (1931), is perhaps the most extreme example of this tendency, referred to almost lovingly as a "massacrist" by another character who is amazed by Beaumont's extraordinary willingness to absorb yet another beating. These examples indicate that instead of one singular type of masculinity in hard-boiled fiction, there is a range of masculinities, so we cannot make the mistake of generalizing the tough private eye as a representative figure for the genre as a whole (Horsley 2005: 68).

The significance of this range of masculinities, however, extends beyond forcing us to rethink what defines masculinity in hard-boiled crime fiction, for it also forces us to rethink the much-vaunted "realism" of this fiction. Contrary to what Chandler argues in "The Simple Art of Murder," there are many aspects of hard-boiled crime fiction, including its representation of masculinity, that are decidedly sentimental rather than realistic. Although hard-boiled writers may have set out to write tough, contemporary fiction, what they in fact wrote were romanti-cized studies of the slide into universal sinfulness, "a modern expres-sion of the American Puritan preoccupation with innate depravity" (Grella 1980: 118). Even "The Simple Art of Murder," it has been argued, evinces a sentimental, even naïve, rather than a realistic attitude towards crime in the 1920s and 1930s, with its touching belief that "an indi-vidual confrontation with organized crime" in the person of the pri-vate eye can make a difference (Mandel 1984: 36). One might note in this respect that gangster novels such as *Little Caesar* and *Fast One*, with their much bleaker assessment of the possibilities of resistance against the rise of organized crime, have a much greater claim to be called "realistic" than most examples of hard-boiled crime fiction.

Recognizing the existence of a sentimental strain in hard-boiled crime fiction, and in the person of the "tough" protagonist of such fiction in particular, enables us to come full circle, and to realize the essential continuity between the varying types of masculinity in crime fiction during this period:

> Although the change in surroundings and atmosphere is real enough, there remains an unmistakable continuity with the private detectives of the traditional sort, with Sherlock Holmes, Lord Peter Wimsey, Albert Campion, Philo Vance, Ellery Queen and Nero Wolfe: the romantic

pursuit of truth and justice for their own sake. Sam Spade, Philip Marlowe . . . and Lew Archer may seem hard-boiled characters cynically devoid of any illusions in the existing social order. But at bottom they are still sentimentalists, suckers for damsels in distress, for the weak confronting the strong (Mandel 1984: 35).

I argued at the beginning of this essay that, despite their great variety, the different types of American crime fiction published between 1900 and 1950 shared a common purpose: offering imaginative resolutions to some of the most perplexing and threatening problems of modernity in general and of manhood in particular. This common purpose, however, is realized in startlingly complex and multi-layered ways. If it is the mode of mastery that has come to emblematize American crime fiction's engagement with manhood and modernity, I hope I have shown that this fiction did far more than master modernity. By means of vulnerable, wounded and masochistic male heroes, as well as their tough counterparts, American crime fiction attempted to show both the pleasures and the dangers of modernity, its seductiveness and destructiveness.

References and Further Reading

Appel, B. 1934: *Brain Guy*. New York: Knopf.
Berman, Marshall 1982: *All That Is Solid Melts Into Air: The Experience of Modernity*. New York: Penguin Books.
Burnett, W. R. 1929: *Little Caesar*. New York: Dial.
Cain, P. 1933: *Fast One*. Carbondale & Edwardsville: Southern Illinois University Press.
Chandler, R. 1939: *The Big Sleep*. New York: Vintage.
Chandler, R. 1940: *Farewell, My Lovely*. London: Penguin Books.
Chandler, R. 1944: The Simple Art of Murder. New York: Pocket Books.
Daly, C. J. [1927] 1984: *The Snarl of the Beast*. Boston: Gregg Press.
Faust, I. 1978: Afterword. In Paul Cain. *Fast One*. Carbondale & Edwardsville: Southern Illinois University Press, 305–13.
Fisher, R. 1932: *The Conjure-Man Dies: A Mystery Tale of Dark Harlem*. New York: Covici, Friede.
Grebstein, N. S. 1968: The Tough Hemingway and His Hard-Boiled Children. In David Madden (ed.), *Tough Guy Writers of the Thirties*. Carbondale & Edwardsville: Southern Illinois University Press, 18–41.
Grella, G. 1968: The Gangster Novel: The Urban Pastoral. In David Madden (ed.), *Tough Guy Writers of the Thirties*. Carbondale & Edwardsville: Southern Illinois University Press, 186–98.

Grella, George 1980: "The Formal Detective Novel." In Robin Winks (ed.), *Detective Fiction: A Collection of Critical Essays*. Englewood Cliffs, NJ: Prentice-Hall, 84–102.

Hammett, D. 1929: *Red Harvest*. New York: Knopf.

Hammett, D. 1930: *The Maltese Falcon*. New York: Knopf.

Hammett, Dashiell 1931: *The Glass Key*. New York: Knopf.

Haut, W. 1995: *Pulp Culture: Hardboiled Fiction and the Cold War*. London & New York: Serpent's Tail.

Horsley, L. 2005: *Twentieth-Century Crime Fiction*. Oxford: Oxford University Press.

Hughes, D. B. 1947: *In a Lonely Place*. New York: Duell, Sloan & Pearce.

Kelly, R. G. 1998: *Mystery Fiction and Modern Life*. Jackson, MS: University of Mississippi Press.

Kimmel, M. 1994: *Manhood in America: A Cultural History*. New York: Oxford University Press.

Krutnik, F. 1991: *In a Lonely Street: Film Noir, Genre, Masculinity*. London: Routledge.

Macdonald, R. 1949: *The Moving Target*. New York: Bantam Books.

MacShane, F. (ed.) 1987: *Selected Letters of Raymond Chandler*. New York: Delta.

Mandel, E. 1984: *Delightful Murder: A Social History of the Crime Story*. London: Pluto.

Queen, E. 1929: *The Roman Hat Mystery*. New York: Stokes.

Queen, E. 1938: *The Four of Hearts*. New York: Mercury.

Rinehart, M. R. 1908: *The Circular Staircase*. New York: Carroll & Graf.

Scaggs, J. 2005: *Crime Fiction*. London & New York: Routledge.

Smith Erin 2000: *Hard-Boiled: Working Class Readers and Pulp Magazines*. Philadelphia: Temple University Press.

Stout, R. 1934: *Fer-De-Lance*. New York: Pocket Books.

Van Dine, S. S. 1926: *The Benson Murder Case*. New York: Pocket Books.

Van Dine, S. S. 1929: *The Bishop Murder Case*. New York: Scribner.

Chapter 6

American Sentences: Terms, Topics, and Techniques in Stylistic Analysis

Paul Simpson and
Donald E. Hardy

It is impossible to imagine contemporary literature without the stylistic influences of Gertrude Stein, Ernest Hemingway, Zora Neale Hurston, William Faulkner, Willa Cather, and Raymond Chandler, among dozens of others. But if stylistic innovation is widely acknowledged to be a defining aspect of modern critical writing, the nature of these innovations is often assumed in the critical literature, or, at best, rendered in rather general and impressionistic terms. Stylistic analysis, however, offers both clearly-defined concepts and an explicit vocabulary that enable us to be more precise about how stylistic innovations are produced within a text. Some of the terms of stylistic analysis, such as, *dialect, vocabulary,* and *narrative,* will be familiar, although we intend to provide here both rigorous definitions and detailed explications of these concepts; other terms, such as *ethnophaulism, transitivity,* and *focalization* might seem abstruse and forbidding at first, but again, we will ground these concepts in clear linguistic criteria and explore their use and effects in the fiction of the period. We believe also that an understanding of these terms will not only enable a more incisive and explicit handling of general stylistic technique and method but, equally, demonstrate how individual authors from the period exaggerate, distort, ironize or otherwise experiment with their linguistic raw material. Reflecting contemporary stylistic practice, we develop our aims through two complementary approaches. The first is style-orientated: to help readers place into context the specific styles of individual authors of this period, we examine the broader techniques used with an emphasis on stylistic innovation and creativity. The second approach, developed in the later stages of the chapter, is genre-orientated, where a particular generic style from the period – in this instance, the "hard-boiled" movement – is illuminated using an array of stylistic concepts. In terms of the stylistic topics covered, we begin the chapter with dialect representation, paying particular attention to the use of African American English (AAE). Then we consider lexical issues such as ethnophaulisms and simplicity. The focus next shifts to syntactic issues framed in part by William Labov's discussion of oral narrative, an analysis that is remarkably illuminating of basic patterns in written narrative as well. Our final set of topics encompasses conversation, speech representation, transitivity, focalization, and point of view.

A *dialect* is a form of language which is identified through particular patterns of vocabulary and grammar and which is closely tied to the social, regional, and cultural identity of the speaker. A *register*, on the other hand, is a variety of language which is defined according to the particular use to which language is being put, so that the forms of language used for, say, a shopping list, an informal conversation, or a scholarly academic presentation are all shaped by their varying discourse contexts. It is important to make this distinction in order to highlight the interconnection between a dialect and the social characteristics of the user of language. All speech and writing is framed in a dialect of some sort, whether that dialect be standard or non-standard, high-prestige, or low-status. This is an important point because a common problem in many studies of "dialect" in literature is that critics sometimes talk too narrowly about the regional, non-standard dialects, often of a rural and conservative type, which are used by particular fictional characters in a story. Dialect embraces much more than this, and its numerous (and often competing) varieties serve as an important mechanism for differentiating narrator and character voices in a story, as well as establishing the general sociolinguistic backdrop to a work of fiction.

Although there are multiple complexities of dialect representation in American prose from 1900 to 1950, one of the most important and controversial uses is to represent AAE. As Lisa Minnick (2004) points out in a detailed analysis of literature that overlaps with this period, dialect representation of AAE is especially difficult for both blacks and whites after the plantation tradition of the nineteenth century, during which AAE was used to support racist calls for a return to heavily romanticized antebellum Southern social arrangements in which African Americans were supposedly "content" in slavery. Zora Neale Hurston's dialect-rich fiction has been criticized for representing black Americans speaking AAE. Minnick points out, for example, that although Hurston's 1937 masterpiece *Their Eyes Were Watching God* is dialect rich, there is little differentiation among the characters in the number of features of AAE that they use, presumably as an indicator that AAE is a marker of community in Hurston's fiction (2004: 127–31). This hypothesis is certainly borne out by Hurston's 1921 short story "John Redding Goes to Sea," which tells the story of John Redding, an African American man, from the time of his boyhood to early adulthood. The narrator tells us that people thought he "was a queer child": "Perhaps ten-year-old John *was* puzzling to the simple folk there in the Florida woods for he was an imaginative child and fond of day-dreams" (1). Specifically, he dreams of traveling and seeing the world. As a child, John produces many features of AAE, as in the following passage in which he expresses his frustration when his imaginary ships, his dry twigs, get stuck in the weeds of the local river:

> "Let go mah ships! You ole mean weeds you!" John screamed and stamped impotently. "They wants tuh go 'way. You let 'em go on!" . . .
>
> "Pa, when ah gets as big as you Ah'm goin' farther than them ships. Ah'm goin' to where the sky touches the ground."
>
> "Well, son when Ah wuz a boy Ah said Ah wuz goin' too, but heah Ah am. Ah hopes you have bettah luck than me." (2)

The speech styles of John and his father are rich in features of AAE, at the levels of both pronunciation and grammar. While we cannot offer a complete inventory of all of these features (although see the detailed treatments of literary dialect in Kretzschmar [2001], Minnick [2004] and Smitherman [1977]), one of the key features of pronunciation represented in the passage above is the monophthongization of diphthongs. This is the process of converting a glided double vowel sound into a single, long vowel: so, instead of *I* and *my*, both John and his father are represented as saying *Ah* and *mah*. Those dialect spellings represent the use of a simple vowel [a], close to the vowel of the first syllable of the word *father*, rather than a diphthongized vowel [ay], as in "standard" non-Southern American pronunciations of the word *sky*. At least two patterns are important to point out in this monophthongization. Firstly, like many but not all features of AAE, it is typical of many Southern accents, both white and black. Secondly, it is almost never consistently represented in any literary character's speech, whether that speaker would "in real life" be consistent or not (Leech and Short 1981: 169). So, for example, the word *sky* is not represented as *skah* in John's speech even though it would be pronounced with the same vowel as in *Ah* and *mah*. Other features of AAE include consonant clusters simplification (for example, *old* to *ole*), post-vocalic r-lessness (for instance, *here* to *heah*; *better* to *bettah*), and initial unstressed vowel deletion (for example, *away* to *'way*). Along with the change from glided double vowel to single, long vowel further substitutions of sounds form part of a common phenomenon in AAE, as in the following statement from Missie May to her husband Joe in Hurston's "The Gilded Six-Bits" when Joe has just told Missie that he believes Otis D. Slemmons' boastful claims because Otis himself made them; Missie responds, "Dat don't make it so. His mouf is cut cross-ways, ain't it? Well, he kin lie jes' lak anybody else" (90). An initial voiced *th* sound as in *that* is typically replaced with *d*, as in *dat*, and a final voiceless *th* sound as in *mouth* is typically replaced with *f*, as in *mouf*.

One of the most important and initially misleading patterns illustrated in the passage above is what is referred to as "eye dialect" (Minnick 2004; Lencho 1988). As Geoffrey Leech and Michael Short say of eye dialect "the impression of rendering non-standard speech by non-standard spelling is pure illusion" (1981: 168). In fact what the author does is use misspelling to represent a pronunciation that would have been indicated just as well by the conventionally correct spelling. As Leech and Short argue, "If we meet such a non-standard spelling in fiction, it is its non-standardness that strikes us, not the supposed phonetic reality behind it" (1981: 168). Clear examples of eye dialect in the passage from "John Redding Goes to Sea" above include *tuh* for unstressed *to* and *wuz* for *was*.

Further examples of eye dialect, as well as some complex grammatical features of AAE, are evident in the following passage from Faulkner's "That Evening Sun," in which Nancy tries to talk the Compson children into staying with her for the night because she is afraid of her husband Jesus: "Dilsey will tell um yawl with me. I been working for yawl long time. They won't mind if yawl at my house" (305). There are two uses of eye dialect in this passage: *yawl*, which is a misspelling of *y'all*, and *um*, which is a misspelling of *'em* (*them*). The syntactic forms of AAE that are represented here include the use of *been* in the perfect tense, as in the clause "I been working for yawl long time." This contrasts with the Standard English variant "I have been working . . ." in which the auxiliary "have" is retained. The deletion of the determiner *a* before "long time" is a result of the common deletion of unstressed vowels. Present here is another well-known syntactic feature of AAE known as copula deletion, in which the linking verb *to be* is removed in certain grammatical environments like "She [is] good" or "They [are] my friends." Copula deletion occurs in the dependent clause of "They won't mind if yawl at my house," which might otherwise be "if yawl are at my house."

Word choice is closely related to dialect and register, since systematic lexical variation occurs as one element of dialect and register representation. The use of offensive racial labels, as we discuss them below, can be argued to be more usually a reflection of register than dialect. There are several issues of importance in word choice among the American writers of 1900–1950, only a few of which we can treat here: labels of primary potency, semantic classes, and overall simplicity. Gordon Allport says that "labels of primary potency," such as *liberal* or *conservative*, are words that we use to label people and that sometimes prevent us from considering the real complexity of individuals and their identities, instead encouraging us to view them simplistically (1954: 174–7). Thus, to label someone as a "half breed" as the narrator does of Dick Boulton in Hemingway's "The Doctor and the Doctor's Wife" is in some ways to invite readers to perceive Dick Boulton one-dimensionally, perhaps as a poor and unskilled American Indian whose culture has been "half" destroyed by white predators (71). However, Boulton is not only fluent in Ojibway but also quite skilled in English as he demonstrates when he gets his way with Doctor Adams, whose title is also, by the way, a label of primary potency.

The word *nigger* is not just a label of primary potency; it is also, of course, a racial epithet the use of which reveals much about the sociocultural background of the user, whether that is the narrator or a character. A. A. Roback calls particularly offensive labels like this "ethnophaulisms," his coinage, *ethnophaulism*, having a Greek etymology (meaning, "a national group" and "to disparage," as Roback details) (1944: 251). Sometimes it is quite surprising to see whose prose these ethnophaulisms turn up; for instance, the following is from a very influential story by Gertrude Stein:

There was one, big, serious, melancholy, light brown porter who often told Melanctha stories, for he liked the way she had of listening with

> intelligence and sympathetic feeling, when he told how the white men in the far South tried to kill him because he made one of them who was drunk and called him a damned nigger, and who refused to pay money for his chair to a nigger, get off the train between stations. (135)

This passage from "Melanctha" illustrates the frequent subtlety of the use of ethnophaulisms in modern literature. The phrase "damned nigger" certainly originates from one of the drunken white men even though it is also certain that the porter uses the word in reporting the incident and the narrator uses the word in reporting the porter's report. The same is true for the use of the ethnophaulism *nigger* in the phrase "refused to pay money for his chair to a nigger." One stylistic way to tell that the label of primary potency *negro* is probably meant to be understood as more polite than *nigger* is that sympathetic narration from Melanctha's point of view uses the word *negro*, as in, "Melanctha liked this serious, melancholy light brown negro very well . . ." (135). Melanctha herself is referred to in the story as an African American; the text also reports that "she had been half made with real white blood" (125).

Although lexical analysis is long out of favor with contemporary literary critics, it is difficult to understand the texture of American fiction of the early twentieth-century without at least some brief attention to the matter, especially since one of the persistent and defining tendencies of American fiction of the period is specificity in lexical items. Part of this pattern comes, as Donald Sears and Margaret Bourland (1970) point out, from the fact that many of the writers of that period started first as journalists (for example, Hemingway, Barnes, Dreiser, Anderson), but the style of specificity and simplicity was generally in the air as well. Hemingway, of course, is famous for his studied intention to write using simple words with specificity. As Richard Bridgman points out in a chapter on Hemingway's style, "Objective reportage . . . remained one of Hemingway's favorite tools for rendering otherwise intolerable scenes" (1966: 209). The simplicity of diction and syntax is clear in the matter-of-fact way that Henry reports the fatal injuries of one of his fellow ambulance drivers after a shell attack in *A Farewell to Arms*: "His legs were toward me and I saw in the dark and the light that they were both smashed above the knee. One leg was gone and the other was held by tendons and part of the trouser and the stump twitched and jerked as though it were not connected" (55).

One well-known exception to the move to simplicity in diction in this period was Faulkner, whose sometimes outrageously multisyllabic complexity can be represented by this short description of Miss Rosa's childhood from *Absalom, Absalom!*: "In a grim mausoleum air of Puritan righteousness and outraged female vindictiveness Miss Rosa's childhood was passed, that aged and ancient and timeless absence of youth which consisted of a Cassandralike listening beyond closed doors, of lurking in dim halls filled with that presbyterian effluvium of lugubrious and vindictive anticipation . . ." (60).

Faulkner is even more famous for his convoluted syntax. As Walter Allen comments, "No novelist ever had less mercy on his readers . . . Sentences four pages long, containing parentheses within parentheses, are not rare" (1965: 113). However complex Faulkner's style might be, he shares some central stylistic tendencies with the likes of Stein, Anderson, and Hemingway, in particular parenthesis and repetition (Bridgman 1966: 13). One of the many problems in talking about the stylistics of narrative syntax in authors of this period is the enormous variability in their individual styles. This is compounded by the even larger complexity of the theory of syntax itself as well as by the variety of syntactic models that are available for description.

Of these models there is one that has proved especially effective in answering questions about variation in narrative syntax. This is the framework of *natural narrative* developed by the sociolinguist William Labov. Labov's model has enduring appeal largely because its origins are situated in the everyday discourse practices of real people in real social contexts. Working from hundreds of stories told by speakers from many different backgrounds Labov isolates the core, recurrent categories that underpin a fully formed natural narrative. Each of his categories serves to address a hypothetical question about narrative structure ("What is this story about?" "Where did it take place?" and so on) so each category fulfils a different function in a story. Although, as Michael Toolan points out, others' applications of William Labov's account of oral narrative structure to explain issues such as foregrounding and backgrounding can be challenged in interesting ways (1990: 103, 208), the Labovian model remains both a testable hypothesis and a useful heuristic for examining a number of different literary styles (see also Toolan [1988: 143–77], Hardy [2003], and Simpson [2004: 114–19]).

In Labovian narrative analysis, the core of a narrative is a series of clauses in the order in which they are imagined to have occurred in the real or imagined world. Such clauses are normally presented in the simple past (or preterite) although the simple present sometimes serves the same purpose. Thus, "The dog barked, and then he bit the burglar" is one narrative while "The dog bit the burglar, and then he barked" is another. These *core narrative clauses,* which address the hypothetical question "What happened?", tend not, however, to be of most use for literary analysis. Labov's "departures from narrative syntax" are syntactic and morphological deviations from the basic simple past clause, all of which serve to make the narrative more interesting, aesthetically or emotionally, than it would otherwise be. Hemingway's prose is, as everyone knows, relatively simple when compared to that of Faulkner. One of the reasons for that perception is the common occurrence of series of core narrative clauses like the following from Hemingway's *A Farewell to Arms,* in which Frederic Henry reports a simple sequence of events that occur upon his realization that he is in love with Catherine Barkley: "Everything turned over inside of me. [Catherine] looked toward the door, saw there was no one, then she sat on the side of the bed and leaned over and kissed me" (91). This passage contains six preterite verbs with no deviations from core narrative syntax, except the one simple embedded clause "there was no one."

Labov's four departures from basic narrative syntax are labeled "intensifiers," "correlatives," "explicatives," and "comparators." Each of these departures has several signals (for example, similes, metaphors, and negatives for comparators), and many of them are important for understanding the sentence styles of the authors under consideration in this book. One of the most sophisticated of applications of Labovian narrative analysis to the literature of the period is J. E. Bunselmeyer's (1981) distinction between Faulkner's "comic" style and "contemplative" style. He argues that the comic style is dominated by independent clauses with little subordination, as in the following sequence of events in "Shingles for the Lord," in which the narrator and his father accidentally burn down the church from which they are ineptly stripping the shingles: The lantern "hit the floor and bounced once. Then it hit the floor again, and this time the whole church jest blowed up into a pit of yellow jumping fire, with me and pap hanging over the edge of it on two ropes" (39). According to Bunselmeyer, the "contemplative" style is dominated not by relatively simple independent clauses but instead by much syntactic embedding, for example, of appositives and relative clauses, many of which interrupt the subject and verb of the main clause, as in the following passage from "That Evening Sun," in which Nancy is described as she tells a story in an attempt to divert herself and the Compson children from, at least, her fear of her husband: Nancy's "voice was inside [the cabin] and the shape of her, the Nancy that could stoop under a barbed wire fence with a bundle of clothes balanced on her head as though without weight, like a balloon, was there" (302); on Faulkner's syntactic style, see also Southard (1981).

The "intensifiers" include, for example, repetition, a device of importance in several writers of the period covered in this book (for instance, Stein, Hemingway, Anderson, and Faulkner). As Frederik Smith says is true especially of *As I Lay Dying*, Faulkner's "typical stylistic density is in large measure the result of his frequent weaving of the same words and phrases into new permutations and combinations of meaning" (1985: 66). Consider the word *stoop* in Faulkner's "Barn Burning." The Snopes girls, the sisters of Sarty, stoop: "The two sisters stooped, broad lethargic; stooping, they presented an incredible expanse of pale cloth and a flutter of tawdry ribbons" (13). The second clause begins with the repetition of the root *stoop* from *stooping* in the main clause in the present participle *stooping*, heavy use of participles being another syntactic characteristic of Faulkner (Toolan 1990: 94–124). One effect of this repetition is to stress the burdened fate of the Snopes family, sharecroppers, who are weighed down not only by their poverty but also by the violence of their father, Abner. When Major de Spain comes to say that his wife's rug has been ruined by Abner's attempt to clean it, the narrator reports with a series of participles: *looking, stooping, buckling, stooping*: "his father merely looking up once before stooping again to the hame he was buckling, so that the man on the mare spoke to his stooping back" (15–16; our italics here and *passim*). Here Abner's "stooping" takes on the paradoxical characteristics of oppression and resistance, since he turns his stooping back on de Spain.

The correlative occurs when events or descriptions are signaled to be concurrent in time, many happening at the same time. One of the most common realizations of the "correlative" is through participles, both present and past. As Bridgman points out, the present participle in particular is a recognizable element in Gertrude Stein's style (1966: 175–6), as in the following from "Miss Furr and Miss Skeene," a story which is very rich in participles: "Helen Furr and Georgine Skeene were regularly living where very many were living and cultivating in themselves something. Helen Furr and Georgine Skeene were living very regularly then, being very regular then in being gay then" (309–10; see also Perloff 1990: 674–75 on the style of this story and Hemingway's "Mr. and Mrs. Elliot"). In a book-length analysis of *Go Down, Moses*, Toolan argues that the progressive (our "present participle") is used in Faulkner for many purposes, only one of which we have time for here, the "overlapping of adjacent events" (1990: 105), as in the following passage from "Death Drag," in which a scene of some stunt-men performing in an airplane is described. The use of multiple present participles is particularly good for reflecting confused and undifferentiated events:

> We saw that battered rented car *moving* down the field, *going* faster, *jouncing* in the broken January mud . . . we saw the dangling ladder and the shark-faced man *swinging* on it beneath the death-colored airplane . . . And the end of the field was *coming* nearer, and the airplane was *travelling* faster than the car, *passing* it. (200)

As in Toolan's analysis, we do not consider the prenominal, adjectival -*ing* forms as participles. In this excerpted passage, there are seven participles. The first three form a picture of all events described (*moving*, *going*, and *jouncing*) occurring as undifferentiated, at least in time overlapping with the main verb *saw*. In the second clause, *swinging* occurs as a correlative to the main verb *saw*. And in the final sentence, *coming*, *traveling*, and *passing* all occur as correlatives, indicating that the perception, or cognition, of all three events occurs in no particular real order.

Explicatives are dependent clauses of various sorts (for example, reason adverbials and relative clauses) that explicate or provide extra information about main clause material. In that sense they are evaluative. One of the many interesting patterns that Toolan has noticed in Faulkner is the use of reason adverbial clauses to provide "delayed disclosure" (1990: 244–5), these reason adverbial clauses being clauses that start with adverbial markers such as *because* and *since*. This pattern is common in Faulkner's fiction; Toolan analyzes it in *Go Down, Moses*, but the following, from "Barn Burning," provides a further illustration:

> The boy, crouched on his nail keg at the back of the crowded room, knew he smelled cheese, and more: from where he sat he could see the ranked shelves close-packed with the solid, squat, dynamic shapes of tin cans . . . this, the cheese which he knew he smelled and the hermetic meat which his intestines believed he smelled coming in intermittent gusts momentary and brief between the other constant one, the smell and sense just a little of fear because mostly of despair and grief, the old fierce pull of blood. (3)

The "other" thing that Sarty smells here at the beginning of the story is not identified until the last appositive – "the smell and sense just a little of fear" – and then, the reason for that smell of fear is given only in the last "because" construction that tells of his despair and grief that we will learn is connected to his father and the "old fierce pull of blood," the very emotions that drive the entire story. In a discussion of focalization, Toolan argues that this sentence "emphatically expresses the boy's orientation . . ." (1988: 61).

The comparators are, sometimes, literally comparatives, as in "just like" or "just as." Sometimes they are similes and metaphors. And sometimes they are negatives. All comparators have in common that they compare what happened or what is with another state of affairs, usually an imaginary state of affairs. Cather's general style is recognized as "pastoral" (Giltrow and Stouck 1992: 91; Allen 1965: 74), a style that typically, in part, longs for a pristine condition that once was but is no longer, as in the following passage from *My Ántonia*: "All the years that have passed have not dimmed my memory of that first glorious autumn. The new country lay open before me: there were no fences in those days, and I could choose my own way over the grass uplands, trusting the pony to get me home again" (28).

Cather's Jim Burden could have forgotten his first autumn in Nebraska as a child, but he did not, and there could have been "fences in those days" but there were not, these negatives indicating that he has not forgotten his pastoral home and in part why he has not.

Our final set of topics on narrative style shifts to a focus on both "ordinary language" and on speech and dialogue; these issues provide a link to a genre of American writing that we have thus far not touched upon. This is the wave of popular crime fiction that materialized in the post-Wall Street crash era of the 1930s and which is epitomized by the work of James M. Cain, Dashiell Hammett, and Raymond Chandler. Emerging during the Great Depression and in the subsequent context of the Roosevelt administration's "New Deal" for economic recovery, the "tough guy" or "hard-boiled" *roman noir* played against the prevailing socioeconomic emphasis on private enterprise to generate a new kind of private detective: a self-employed, self-reliant anti-hero whose callous and even brutish persona was foregrounded by a markedly laconic style of narrative delivery.

A cursory inspection of the stylistic composition of this body of work is enough to justify its status as a bona fide "genre" of American fiction, although literary critical opinion has not always been accurate – or indeed fair – about the creative accomplishment of the hard-boiled authors. Predictably, the tough guy writers' stylistic debt to Hemingway is acknowledged *passim* in the critical literature (Grebstein 1968, Horsley

2001, Marling 1995), and to be sure the re-mergence of many of the earlier writer's structural and syntactic patterns in Cain, Hammett, and Chandler is plain to see. However, it is the totality of language use, rather than any single strand of narrative organization, which is a true index of a writer's style, and while the hard-boiled writers do press into service many of the devices we have described thus far, there are additional features, chiefly to do with *transitivity* and *point of view*, which make for a very particular kind of fictional design. Some of these features are explored below with reference to the work of Cain and Hammett.

Running the "hard-boiled" metaphor, David Madden has described James M. Cain as "the twenty minute egg" of the tough guy genre (Madden 1968: xxix). Indeed, in *The Postman Always Rings Twice* (1934), the novel's first person narrator, the drifter Frank Chambers, seems very much the embodiment of the stylistic reticence that typifies the genre. In the construction of Chambers the character, Cain sets his stall out early through the use of an idiolect which draws heavily on both slang and on general aspects of non-standard American vernacular English. Both speech styles signal informality in *register* of discourse, and in an affective sense feel manifestly "unwriterly." For instance, Chambers narrates how he "blows into" a roadside sandwich "joint," a joint whose unpolluted air must be "swell" at night (1–2). There, one of Chambers' first chores is to assist "a guy that came along" who was "all burned up" (4). These features of colloquial vocabulary are supplemented with non-standard English: a preterite form works as a past participle when Chambers notes that "He had *drew* a new sign for himself" (8) while multiple negation is employed twice in the sequence "I don't know nothing about the tests. All I know is I didn't have no drink" (52). Rich in the signals of generalized vernacular American speech, Chambers' idiolect acts as the vehicle of narrative transmission in the novel.

This "unwriterly" idiolect is only one dimension in style, however, and there are other, arguably more sophisticated, devices at work in *The Postman*. In order to fulfill a number of particular plot-advancing functions, Cain makes extensive use of direct speech presentation techniques, those techniques representing the words of the characters as if they uttered them without modification by the narrator. One telling use of direct speech is in the extended sequence where the lawyer Katz explains retrospectively how he managed to get Cora and Chambers out of jail and, in the process, to dupe his rival Sackett. This episode serves to present narrative events through flashback, through *analepsis* to adopt Genette's term. Elsewhere, speech presentation plays its part in the art of seduction (or at least in tough-guy-style seduction) as in Chambers' breathtakingly minimal interchange with Madge Allen before their ill-fated elopement to Mexico. Within but a few lines of Madge's first introduction in the text (as "*. . . a girl . . .* trying to start her car" [91]), the duologue between the two fairly sizzles towards its resolution:

"I'll take you home."
"You're awfully friendly."
"I'm the friendliest guy in the world."
"You don't even know where I live."
"I don't care."
"It's pretty far. It's in the country."
"The further the better. Wherever it is, it's right on my way."
"You make it hard for a nice girl to say no."
"Well then, if it's so hard, don't say it." (91)

Rendered entirely in free direct speech ("free" of reporting clauses), this quick-fire sequence of utterances – undoubtedly stylistic meat and drink to a screenplay writer like Cain – manages in spite of the absence of reporting clauses to anchor each speaker in the exchange. Notice how character differentiation is sustained through self-referential noun phrases like "a nice girl" and "the friendliest guy in the world" which leave no doubt as to the identity of who is talking.

This type of speech presentation, in which the removal of reporting clauses tends to diminish the presence of the narrator, can be better understood in the context of the broader concept of *point of view*. We define point of view as the perspective from which or through which a story is focalized, whether that perspective be the first person framework of a participating character-narrator or, alternatively, of a third person narrator whose "omniscience" facilitates privileged access to the thoughts and feelings of individual characters. As far as the hard-boiled genre goes, the axiom "tell but don't explain" seems to be a key focalizing principle where narrative action takes precedence over the psychological interpretation of thought and motive. This technique, in which the orientation is towards an objective-realist account of events as they unfold, is what Paul Simpson has referred to elsewhere as a "neutrally shaded" point of view category (1993). Although it is admittedly unusual to find an *entire* story so written, here is a good illustration of the technique at work in *The Postman*:

> I got him up, and laid him over the edge of the tub, and then got out myself, and dragged him in the bedroom and laid him on the bed. She came up, then, and we found matches, and got a candle lit. Then we went to work on him. I packed his head in wet towels, while she rubbed his wrists and feet. (19)

Notice here how the passage is comprised entirely of Labovian-style core narrative clauses, all temporally ordered, and without any of the "departures" from narrative syntax that we observed earlier in the chapter. Among other things, the effect of this pattern is to drive the plot along quickly and purposefully, and in a way that is free from the intercession of a narrator's or character's opinions of the events as they unfold.

As with all of the authors surveyed thus far, it is better to talk of stylistic tendencies than to make wholesale generalizations about a particular writer's craft. So, while the "external" point of view we have just observed is the dominant mode of focalization in Cain's novel, this is not to deny that other supplementary devices are at work at other levels of stylistic organization. A common misconception of hard-boiled writing is that it is long on action and short on metaphor. True, *The Postman* is not exactly a study in figurative thought, but it still embraces certain metaphorical themes. For example, the conceptual "mind style" of both Chambers and Cora is developed through one of the most core metaphors in human cognition. This is the broad orientational metaphor that gives the concepts of happiness and joy an upwards orientation, and sadness and misery a downwards orientation. Common linguistic manifestations of this metaphor include the following three source concepts which are ascribed to the sentiment being described: HAPPY IS UP, HAPPY IS OFF THE GROUND, and HAPPY IS BEING IN HEAVEN (Kövecses 2002: 85). So, when Chambers feels relief at Cora's departure to visit her sick mother, he employs the "off the ground" source domain: "I felt funny, like I was made of gas and would float off somewhere" (90). Elsewhere, two source domains ("up" and "heaven") are locked into the same expression, as in "I looked up at the sky. It was all you could see. I thought about God" (26) or in "It looked like the sweet chariot had swung low and was going to pick me up" (65). Cora inhabits the same metaphorical worldview ("We were up on a mountain. We were up so high Frank . . ." [84]) and at a key moment in the story delivers one of the most commented upon sequences in the novel: "It's a big airplane engine, that takes you through the sky, right up to the top of the mountain. But when you put it in a Ford, it just shakes it to pieces . . ." (85). William Marling has quite correctly highlighted the cultural significance of the technological imagery Cora employs, but the metaphor itself is not, as Marling suggests, "curious" (1995: 41). The metaphor itself is basic to human conceptual thought; it is rather the vehicle, so to speak, of the metaphor's construction which is novel.

Whereas *The Postman* is narrated through the necessarily restricted perspective of its participating central character, Dashiell Hammett's *The Maltese Falcon* (1930) offers a third person narrative framework which throws up some subtle variations on the hard-boiled generic style. The narratorial voice of *The Maltese Falcon* is "heterodiegetic" in the sense that it is "different" from the exegesis that comprises the story. What is especially striking about this framework, however, is that its narrator relinquishes the sort of third person omniscience that normally permits privileged access to the thoughts and feelings of individual characters. Instead, a kind of restricted focalization is developed where the narrator wrestles with features of external appearance in order to make interpretations of what characters *might* think and feel. In this respect, while the point of view category remains external to the psychology of the characters, it is overlain with a pattern of focalization in which a heterodiegetic narrator *tries* to make sense of what physical and visual details belie.

There are a number of stylistic reflexes of this special type of focalization in *The Maltese Falcon*, most notably in its exploitation of a set of expressions which Roger Fowler calls "modal words of estrangement" (Fowler 1986: 142). These expressions include *inter alia* modal auxiliaries like *must* and *might*, modal lexical verbs such as *looked* and *seemed* and modal adverbs like *evidently* and *apparently*; they also include the quasi-similes *as if* and *as though*, which we touched upon earlier. These features of style function both to draw attention to a speaker or writer's warrant for what they say and to offer explicit judgment or perceptual justification for the particular proposition expressed. Thus, in the novel's opening paragraph, the simile which develops a satanic parallel with Spade is activated through a modal verb of perception: "He *looked* rather pleasantly like a blond satan" (our italics). Similarly, in the following short fragment, in which Brigid O'Shaughnessy is apparently less than comfortable with Sam Spade's reference to the police, notice how narratorial interpretation is predicated upon reference to visual detail: "She squirmed on her end of the settee and her eyes wavered between heavy lashes, *as if* trying and failing to free their gaze from his. She *seemed* smaller, and very young and oppressed" (32).

Markers of this modality of estrangement are abundant in *The Maltese Falcon* and they are supplemented by a point-of-view sub-strategy which also involves the willful relinquishing of narratorial omniscience. *Attenuated focalization* is the term for a spatial viewing perspective which places a character, who might otherwise have been familiar to the reader, in a blurred, distant or impeded focus (see Simpson 2004: 29). A feature that commonly signals such a restricted viewing position is a noun phrase with indefinite reference such as "*a* man" or "*a* woman." Thus, at the opening of Chapter Two of the novel, when "a man's voice" answers a ringing telephone in the darkness, resolution of the man's identity (Sam Spade) is temporarily delayed. A few paragraphs later, the same tactic occurs in the narrative fragment "a man was hunkered on his heels before a bill board" (10), this time disguising the identity of Spade's dead partner, Miles Archer. Transposing this fragment to one containing a full reference would of course instantly nullify the stylistic effect: "*Miles Archer* was hunkered on his heels before a bill board." With the feeling of claustrophobia, suspense, and imprecision it can sometimes engender, attenuated focalization does indeed make for a very "*noir*-ish" point of view technique.

An aspect of narrative organization which goes hand in hand with the system of point of view we have just elaborated is *transitivity*. In stylistics, this grammatical concept is used in an expanded sense to refer to the way meanings are encoded in the clause and to the way different types of process are represented in language. When language is used to represent the "happenings" of the physical or abstract world in this way, to represent patterns of experience in spoken and written texts, it is encoded in texts through different patterns of transitivity. And what is of interest to stylisticians is why one type of structure should be preferred to another, or why, from possibly several ways of representing the same "happening," one particular type of depiction should be privileged over another.

What is striking about the transitivity profile of *The Maltese Falcon*, and indeed of many *romans noirs*, is its foregrounding of material processes of action at the expense of mental processes of cognition. There is marked absence of *verba sentiendi* (Uspensky 1973), that is, of words denoting thoughts, feelings and perceptions of the sort encoded in mental processes such as "I felt", "they realized," or "she understood." Even when the text cries out for an articulation of felt experience, it is withheld. Thus, when Joel Cairo becomes excited, the quality of excitement is employed by Hammett as a material process acting as an external physical agent on Cairo: "Excitement opened Cairo's eyes and mouth, turned his face red, made his voice shrill . . ." (48). By the same token, when Spade becomes angry, the predicted mental process is replaced by a physical action: "[Spade] made angry gestures with mouth, eyebrows, hands and shoulders" (37).

Transitivity patterns are especially marked in fight sequences where unreflective physicality takes precedence over any kind of emotional engagement with the victim. Just as Chambers beats up the blackmailer Kennedy, so Sam Spade deals out a beating to Joel Cairo with only the most "external" of physical action processes represented. Particularly striking in the latter episode is the employment of a stylistic strategy known as *meronymy* (Nash 1990: 139), which expresses a part-to-whole relationship:

> Spade's right heel on the patent-leathered toes anchored the smaller man in the elbow's path. The elbow struck him beneath the cheekbone, staggering him so that he must have fallen had he not been held by Spade's foot on his foot. Spade's elbow went on past the astonished dark face and straightened when Spade's hand struck down at the pistol . . . (43–4)

The actions of both Spade and his victim are presented through meronymy insofar as individuated body parts fulfill the role of agent in material processes of action. The crucial point, of course, is that this pattern of transitivity is not normally associated with anatomical meronyms simply because the carrying out of such processes requires conscious volition from a complete and sensate being.

Choices in style, even if unconsciously made by writers, are significant because they have a profound impact on the way texts can be both structured and interpreted. For example, in spite of its ostensibly "omniscient" narrative framework, Hammett's novel relinquishes the opportunity to delve into characters' thoughts and feelings. This is a diametrically opposed technique to that of a writer like Henry James who creates a "centre of consciousness," such as Strether in *The Ambassadors*, through sustained focalization from that character's perspective. Furthermore, Hammett supplements this "external" point of view – the stylistic mainstay of hard-boiled focalization – with a particular kind of modality of estrangement, to the extent that parts of his novel have more in common with Edgar Allan Poe's description of the House of Usher than with anything written by Hemingway. Similarly, the fastidious scrutiny of often atomized features of physical description, as a means of retrieving some understanding of character predisposition, has broad echoes of the prose of Kafka and Beckett, and more narrow parallels with the portrayal of grotesques in the work of Peake or Dickens.

Innovations in the language of American literature of the period 1900–1950 are almost as varied as the authors discussed in this book. Language in many ways became the subject of modernism in particular (Wales 2001: 257–8). Brent Harold paraphrases George Lukács as arguing that "the three modes [of modernism] may be roughly characterized as positivism (detached observation, a transparent medium); art for art's sake (literary solipsism, an opaque medium); and primitivism (deference to states of existence unrealizable in art and unavailable to its audience)" (1975: 214).

No single American author used any one of these modes to the exclusion of others, and many were not restricted to the choice among the three, the latter point being made by Harold about Faulkner. The strategies that we have explored in this chapter should facilitate discussions of the complexity in style of any of the authors considered in this book.

Further Reading

Allen, W. 1965: *The Modern Novel in Britain and the United States*. New York: Dutton.

Allport, G. W. 1954: *The Nature of Prejudice*. Reading, MA: Addison Wesley.

Bridgman, R. 1966: *The Colloquial Style in America*. New York: Oxford University Press.

Bunselmeyer, J. E. 1981: Faulkner's Narrative Styles. *American Literature* 53.3, 424–42.

Fowler, R. 1986: *Linguistic Criticism*. Oxford: Oxford University Press.

Giltrow, J. and D. Stouck 1992: Willa Cather and a Grammar for Things "Not Named." *Style* 26.1, 91–114.

Grebstein, S. N. 1968: The Tough Hemingway and his Hard-Boiled Children. In D. Madden (ed.), *Tough Guy Writers of the Thirties*. Carbondale and Edwardsville: Southern Illinois University Press, 18–41.

Hardy, D. 2003: *Narrating Knowledge in Flannery O'Connor's Fiction*. Columbia: University of South Carolina Press.

Harold, B. 1975: The Value and Limitations of Faulkner's Fictional Method. *American Literature* 47.2, 212–29.

Horsley, L. 2001: *The Noir Thriller*. Basingstoke: Palgrave.

Kövecses, Z. 2002: *Metaphor: A Practical Introduction*. Oxford: Oxford University Press.

Kretzschmar, W. (ed.) 2001: Special Issue: Literary Dialect Analysis with Computer Assistance. *Language and Literature* 10, 2.

Labov, W. 1972: The Transformation of Experience in Narrative Syntax. In *Language in the Inner City: Studies in the Black English Vernacular*. Philadelphia: University of Pennsylvania Press, 354–96.

Leech, G. N. and M. H. Short 1981: *Style in Fiction: A Linguistic Introduction to English Fictional Prose*. London: Longman.

Lencho, M. W. 1988: Dialect Variation in *The Sound and the Fury*: A Study of Faulkner's Use of Black English. *Mississippi Quarterly* 41.3, 403–19.

Madden, D. (ed.) 1968: *Tough Guy Writers of the Thirties*. Carbondale and Edwardsville: Southern Illinois University Press.

Marling, W. 1995: *The American Roman Noir: Hammett, Cain and Chandler*. Athens, GA, and London: University of Georgia Press.

Minnick, L. C. 2004: *Dialect and Dichotomy: Literary Representations of African American Speech*. Tuscaloosa: The University of Alabama Press.

Nash, W. 1990: *Language in Popular Fiction*. London: Routledge.

Perloff, M. 1990: "Ninety Percent Rotarian": Gertrude Stein's Hemingway. *American Literature* 62.4, 668–83.

Roback, A. A. 1944: *A Dictionary of International Slurs (Ethnophaulisms): With a Supplementary Essay on Aspects of Ethnic Prejudice*. Cambridge, MA: Sci-Art Publishers.

Sears, D. and M. Bourland 1970: Journalism Makes the Style. *The Journalism Quarterly* 47, 504–9.

Simpson, P. 1993: *Language, Ideology and Point of View*. London: Routledge.

Simpson, P. 2004: *Stylistics*. London: Routledge.

Smith, F. N. 1985: Telepathic Diction: Verbal Repetition in *As I Lay Dying*. *Style* 19, 66–77.

Smitherman, G. 1977: *Talkin and Testifyin: The Language of Black America*. Detroit: Wayne State University Press.

Southard, B. 1981: Syntax and Time in Faulkner's *Go Down, Moses*. *Language and Style* 14.2, 107–15.

Toolan, M. 1988: *Narrative: A Critical Linguistic Introduction*, 2nd edn. New York: Routledge.

Toolan, M. 1990: *The Stylistics of Fiction: A Literary-Linguistic Approach*. New York: Routledge.

Uspensky, B. 1973: *A Poetics of Composition*, trans. V. Savarin and S. Wittig. Berkeley: University of California Press.

Wales, K. 2001: *A Dictionary of Stylistics*, 2nd edn. London: Longman.

Chapter 7

The Great Gatsby as Mobilization Fiction: Rethinking Modernist Prose

Keith Gandal

Critics have almost exclusively assessed American modernist fiction in terms of stylistic innovation. Meanwhile, disillusionment with, and a consequent break from, tradition following the catastrophe of World War One have often been seen to precipitate this stylistic invention. The notion of a postwar break with tradition has indeed become a received idea; to take just a couple of examples, Wendy Martin writes of the "the gap of meaning that opened after World War I," while John W. Aldridge argues, "World War I had the effect of seeming to annihilate past history and the old styles of history. Hence, the generation that had fought in the war felt urgently the need to establish new premises, to redefine the terms of existence."[1]

Though cutting-edge New Historicists have been critical of the mid-twentieth-century New Criticism that granted modernism its literary importance and suspicious of such a notion of an epistemological break, they have nonetheless continued to focus on the issue of modernist style in the postwar context.[2]

In approaching well-known American novels of the 1920s and 1930s, though – and, in particular, the supposedly quintessentially modernist texts of Fitzgerald, Hemingway, and Faulkner, namely *The Great Gatsby* (1925), *The Sun Also Rises* (1926), and *The Sound and the Fury* (1929) – there are good reasons to recover the singular history of US mobilization in the Great War, and also to turn the attention to narratives and characters. This mobilization took place as Fitzgerald, Hemingway, and Faulkner were coming of age, and all three of these "major" writers were frustrated in their desires to serve in the US military's colossal war effort. Hemingway and Faulkner were disqualified or rejected by the military on physical grounds; Fitzgerald was denied promotions he expected. Only Hemingway made it to Europe – as an ambulance driver. At the same time these men observed, among other startling developments (including a wartime female promiscuity), Americans from ethnic minorities being granted essentially egalitarian treatment for the first time in the history of the United States in the army's selection of officers – a piece of the historical record that is only now re-emerging. Of course, much has been written about this 1920s literature as following from the traumatic experience of the war, but very little attention has been paid to the dramatic social experience of the mobilization and the trauma experienced by these Anglo writers who were in one way or another kept from the war or its main action, rejected or "passed over" by a military that, at the time, had what was essentially the power to confer or deny masculinity. This essay thus addresses, not Fitzgerald's style in the postwar context, but the content of his novel in the context of the war.

In 1917, when the United States entered the Great War, Jewish gangster Samuel "Nails" Morton enlisted in the army and went overseas. As the historian Robert Rockaway puts it:

> Nails rose through the ranks to become a first lieutenant. He received the *Croix de Guerre*, France's highest decoration for bravery, for capturing a machine gun nest despite being wounded. He returned to Maxwell street [a Jewish neighborhood in Chicago] a hero, became a bootlegger, and put his training in weapons and warfare to practical use. Morton was [after the war] a stylish dresser and high liver who loved horseback riding . . . After his death, Nails was characterized as a man who led a number of lives. To one set of acquaintances he was a gallant soldier . . . And to the police, a notorious gangster.[3]

If this thumbnail biographical sketch sounds eerily like the fictional career and double-sidedness of Jay Gatsby (romantic soldier–officer and "rough-neck" [53][4] bootlegger)[5] it is probably not because Fitzgerald modeled Gatsby on "Nails" Morton, but rather because the author of *The Great Gatsby* was describing, in Gatsby's experience, not a fantastical and romantic aberration, but a believable, if historically unprecedented, trajectory for ethnic Americans during and after the war. This possible social career of an ethnic American, from obscurity to wealth, founded on a wartime rise "through the ranks" in military training camps and on the front, interested Fitzgerald intensely. It is also something that, at our historical remove from the era of the Great War and in a world used to meritocratic placement and promotion, critics and readers now routinely miss in the novel.

Of course, Gatsby's own account of his success in the war and afterwards is a mix of fact and fiction, and Nick pieces together the truth over the course of the novel – sometimes in quite minute detail. For example, Nick eventually corrects Gatsby's romantic family-saga history of his military service in which he began the war by "accept[ing] a commission as first lieutenant" and was promoted to major after proving himself in combat in the Argonne Forest (70): Nick informs us that "he was a captain before he went to the front" (158). This correction of a seemingly minor omission on Gatsby's part seems indeed nitpicking and pointless. What difference does it make whether Gatsby was promoted to captain in camp before he saw action or was bumped up from lieutenant to major at the front, all as a result of his combat performance?

It obviously makes some difference to Fitzgerald, and what is at issue here is *how* Gatsby succeeds. It is generally, but mistakenly, understood that instrumental to German American and lower-class born Gatsby's later social success was a combination of self-mythification and a Ragged-Dick instance of good luck: he invented a new name and family pedigree for himself, and he ran into the rich Dan Cody and his yacht on Lake Superior at an opportune moment (104). The irony, or Fitzgerald's Jazz Age revision of Horatio Alger, is supposed to be that Cody did not teach Gatsby how to be moral but how to be rich or upper class and so pull off his self-fabrication as an Anglo from a good family; thus does Fitzgerald seem to anticipate historian Warren Susman's insight that what makes for success in the modern, corporate age is personality or likeability, not moral character.[6] Clearly, Gatsby's name change is significant and historically relevant; this is, after all, the era in which ethnic Americans routinely adjusted their names for the purposes of succeeding. Gatsby's fakery and his "singularly appropriate education" with Cody (107) is only part of the story of his success, however; there is another, separate ingredient in his story that is absolutely fundamental to his rise and has everything to do with his making captain before he went to the front.

Daisy's husband Tom Buchanan will be " 'damned' " if he sees how Gatsby " 'got within a mile of [Daisy] unless [he] brought groceries to the back door' " (138). Of course, what allowed Gatsby through the front door of her house during the Great War was not his polished manner or his false name but his officer's uniform, and that was something he could not grant himself, nor could Cody have given it to him.

The war gave Gatsby a new social status when it made him an officer; he in fact crossed the "indiscernible barbed wire" separating different classes and different "races" when he put on the "invisible cloak of his uniform" (155–6): "he went to her house, at first with other officers from Camp Taylor" (155). Gatsby's own account of how he came to be part of this officer cadre – that his upper-class background had secured his commission – is another piece of his story that Nick has reason to doubt. To get a commission in his circumstances, Gatsby would have had to take and pass a qualifying exam, just as Fitzgerald did.[7] It would seem Gatsby made it into officers' training, not on the basis of any personal wealth or connections to the rich and powerful. In short, the particular American mobilization for the Great War, with its new and very particular methods for selecting officers – which Fitzgerald knew all about, as an officer in training at Camp Taylor – meant that a nobody like Gatsby could be chosen for officer training, and specifically promoted to captain, while still at camp, on the basis of his own measurable abilities, in the context of a new meritocratic moment. The novel reflects this moment.

Indeed, the American army of World War One was like no other American army to that date: for the first time in United States history, an army was to a large extent mobilized on the basis of intelligence and other testing and personnel methods imported from industry and developed by psychologists and businessmen. Such unprecedented agencies as the Committee on the Psychological Examination of Recruits and the Committee on Classification of Personnel in the Army in the Adjutant General's Office were developed and coordinated to help distribute recruits to appropriate ranks and jobs in the military.[8] In a letter written in June 1918, the Psychology Committee of the National Research Council reported:

> In April 1916, President Wilson . . . expressed the desire that this mobilization should include the scientific resources of the entire country . . . The psychologists of the country . . . have made notable contributions to the national defense. Their program has included: the psychological examining of recruits in order that the mentally unfit may be eliminated, and the remainder classified according to intelligence . . .[9]

The "psychological tests" were also meant "to assist in selecting men of superior mental ability, who should be considered for promotion,"[10] or, more specifically, in "the selection of, as material for officers training course, those men who are best qualified intellectually for command."[11] Near the war's end (in November 1918), the Committee on Psychology was able to report that "approximately one million, seven hundred thousand individuals have been examined to date."[12]

By early 1918, such intelligence tests[13] "were commonly used . . . at the various cantonments for the examination of men for promotion and special work," and of particular relevance to *The Great Gatsby*, there were "tests used in the qualification of Army Captains."[14] The Committee on Classification of Personnel in the Army also developed a companion method for selecting officers,[15] *specifically captains*, an "Individual Rating Sheet for Selecting Candidates In Each Training Unit" and later a "Rating Sheet for Selecting Captains."[16] Evaluators were asked to rate a candidate in comparison with the ratings given to five existing captains in the group, on the basis of "the personal history record and the efficiency record, as well as upon your own observation." Candidates for "Officers' Training Camps" in 1917 were to be judged on:

1. Physical Qualities. Consider how the candidate will impress his men by his physique, bearing, neatness, voice, energy, and endurance . . .
2. Intelligence. Consider ease of learning and ability to grasp easily and to solve new problems . . .
3. Military Leadership. Consider self-reliance, initiative, decisiveness; and the ability to command the obedience, loyalty, and co-operation of men . . .
4. Character. Consider stability, freedom from general bad habits, regard for authority and spirit of service and general helpfulness in the . . . unit . . .
5. General Value to the Service. What is your general impression of the candidate's probable value for a company officer?[17]

It is easy to make the case that Gatsby has many of the characteristics that the army was identifying in this rating sheet: as concerns "Character," the novel tells us "he formed the habit of letting liquor alone" after seeing what drink did to Cody (107); as for "Physical Qualities," the book stresses Gatsby's bearing, neatness, and energy in various ways; his behavior in the war also seems to bear out some of these desirable traits for officers listed under the third rubric, "Military Leadership," such as initiative and decisiveness – for instance, Gatsby "took two machine-gun detachments so far forward that there was a half mile gap on either side of us where the infantry couldn't advance" (70).

In fact, Camp Taylor, Gatsby's camp, was definitely one of the first cantonments that used intelligence tests, in part to distinguish potential officers. The "tests [were] tried out . . . in the four cantonments at Camps Devons, Taylor, Dix, and Meade."[18] A document from the Committee on Psychology, entitled "Interpretation of Scores in Intelligence," contains the hand-written note, "Results at Camp Taylor." A score of 100–249 indicated a "Private (type)" and accounted for 57 percent of those tested; a score of 250–99 indicated an "Officer (type)" and accounted for 12 percent; a score of 300–49 indicated a "Superior Officer" and accounted for 5 percent, and a top range of 350–414, reached by only 1 percent, indicated "Skilled thinker in abstract relations" (at the bottom were another 25 percent encompassing "Unskilled laborers," "dull laborer," and "Feebleminded or bordering on fm.").[19] For a soldier like Gatsby to be considered for promotion to captain at Camp Taylor, he would have had to score in the top 6 percent on the intelligence test.[20]

Fitzgerald would certainly have known that captains were being generated in some of the training camps in 1917, and at Camp Taylor in particular, according to the new personnel methods, because he was in officer training at Camp Taylor, in Louisville. Interestingly, Fitzgerald put Gatsby at Camp Taylor though it was at Camp Sheridan near Montgomery, Alabama that Fitzgerald met his future wife Zelda – for many critics, the obvious inspiration for Daisy.[21] Most likely, Fitzgerald chose Camp Taylor for German American Gatsby and put Daisy in Louisville because Camp Taylor had the new personnel methods for officer testing, rating, and selection in 1917 during his tenure there while they were only in place at Camp Sheridan later (by early 1918 all the camps had the tests).[22] Moreover, with a population of 1,492 the largest ethnic group at Camp Taylor at the end of the war was comprised of Germans.[23] One other thing is for certain: Fitzgerald spent time in army camps (including Taylor and Gordon) that had substantial immigrant and first-generation ethnic, as well as specifically German American, populations, and these camps generated numerous ethnic officers: he no doubt encountered plenty of potential models for Gatsby.

The point of all this is that Gatsby had his real start, as a captain in the military – and thus came near Daisy – as a result of the unprecedented opportunities that the Great War offered to lower-class and ethnic American men of intelligence, education, and other leadership traits. For all his self-fabrication, Gatsby apparently did not fake his way into the officers' corp. In fact, one of benefits of the intelligence tests used at Camp Taylor and elsewhere was to eliminate, as the wartime Committee on Psychology put it, "the danger of charletans [*sic*]."[24] Gatsby was the beneficiary of new meritocratic techniques developed to rapidly mobilize a huge and effective American army to fight in World War One.

Given the seriousness of the crisis that confronted the United States, the "luxury" of ethnic prejudice was to a significant degree put aside in the interest of winning the war – though the traditions of racial prejudice against blacks were, by contrast, mostly retained and reaffirmed (there were very few black officers commissioned and black troops were segregated from whites).[25] While blacks made up about 15 percent of the draft,[26] a significantly larger percentage still of men drafted for the war were immigrants or the children of immigrants: about 33 percent of the total draft was made up of ethnic Americans or what were called "hyphenated-Americans."[27] The War Department expressly stated that it would not solve the country's "so-called race problem" between blacks and whites.[28] But the military simply could not afford, on top of this white–black conflict, a nativism that would provoke widespread ethnic disaffection with the military.[29] They also needed officers who could speak the various languages of foreign-born troops.[30]

President Wilson called for a mobilization strategy that was "undramatic, practical, and of scientific definiteness and precision."[31] The army's "scientific" system of the selection of officers, though biased culturally and toward the educated, was otherwise class and ethnicity blind though not at all color blind, and it was thus a far cry from the elitist traditions the American military had employed in the past.

In the early years of the Great War, American authorities had watched, and learned a lesson, as "England offered an especially compelling example" of how *not* to mobilize for war: "In the first two years of the war [the British] had seen their besteducated and most talented young men rush willy-nilly to the colors and as quickly and haphazardly die in the mud in Flanders. That non-policy wrought a terrible loss of leadership cadres that seriously crippled the British military effort."[32]

Wilson and his aides were determined to do things very differently, and one of the results, particularly relevant in terms of Fitzgerald's novel, was that ethnic Americans could indeed end up as officers, due to a new process of "scientific" selection.

The received wisdom on the military's intelligence testing is that it was biased against ethnic Americans, and that the results *only* served to confirm the stereotypes of Anglo racists and immigration restrictionists, who exploited these results after the war to argue for and effect their cause in the dramatic immigration restriction legislation of 1921 and 1924.[33] Though these tests certainly functioned in this invidious way after World War One, they – along with the other personnel methods for selecting officers – also undeniably gave unprecedented opportunities for status and advancement in the army to talented and educated ethnic Americans during the Great War.

For all its glaring faults in the treatment of blacks and women, the First World War army stood out as an institution in the nation when it came to the treatment of ethnic Americans.[34] Records show that in the case, for example, of Jewish Americans – against which group there was by all accounts a robust Anglo prejudice in the era of the teens and twenties – the army was very even-handed, in terms of officer commissions, except perhaps at the very highest ranks (above colonel).[35]

One can find striking anecdotes – besides the one concerning the Jewish gangster Morton – that reflect the special opportunities afforded by the Great War meritocracy to ethnic Americans such as Gatsby, along with the wartime practice of setting aside prejudice. For example: "in 1916 a Jewish intern [at King's County Hospital in Brooklyn] was overpowered in his room, bound, gagged, and taken by force to a train station and told not to return. That same intern became an Army medical officer in the first World War."[36]

And what happened after the war to men like Gatsby, whom the army appreciated and promoted? "In 1927, at the same hospital, an estimated twenty Gentile interns kidnapped, physically intimidated, and warned three Jewish interns to leave the 'Christian institution.'" The perpetrators were all let off.[37] Indeed, after the war, there ensued a backlash by the traditionally, ethnically privileged against a rising, ethnically-blind meritocracy. On the level of the law, an intensified nativist concern about alien immigrant masses was, of course, registered in the restriction of immigration in a nation that had become markedly immigrant. But more to the point here, given that the publicly-debated immigrant restriction acts of Congress were a *fait accompli* before the publication of *The Great Gatsby*, was the subtle, covert, non-judicial, non-legislative backlash against meritocratic forces that was taking place with the invention or intensification of ethnic and specifically Jewish quotas at universities and medical schools.

Tom Buchanan represents, or speaks for, the forces of Anglo backlash in the novel, including that of ethnic quotas. Thus, he is not only a reader of pseudo-scientific, racist literature that claims that the Nordic race is being overrun by the "lower races"; Tom, who went to Yale (135), expresses disbelief and dismay that a man of Gatsby's ethnic and lower-class origins could go to Oxford (136). Gatsby's attendance at Oxford "'was an opportunity they gave some of the officers after the Armistice'" (136): another example of Great War meritocracy. It is a new experience for Tom – whose matriculation at Yale was no doubt predicated on a family legacy or family money or both – to find his impeccable university credentials potentially equaled by an ethnic American such as Gatsby, who made it to Oxford not because of family tradition or wealth but on the basis of merit – in his case, meritorious military service.

Just as Tom resorts to assertions of traditional privilege in response to ethnic "upstart" Gatsby's attendance at Oxford, alarmed university and medical school administrators of the Anglo old guard were resorting throughout the 1920s to ethnic quotas.[38] As historian Charlotte Borst has put it, "Higher education was emerging as a substantial institutional force in American cultural and political life by the early twentieth century," and, in the same period, "middle-class, native-born white men" were attempting to "maintain their political and cultural hegemony" in the face of a rising challenge from ethnic Americans.[39]

Viewing this confrontation between Daisy's lovers in terms of its effect on Gatsby, one might say that Anglo-elite Tom's confrontation with Gatsby over educational pedigree – and his ultimate loss of Daisy to Tom, his defeat by him – makes Gatsby's experience after the war, as well as during it, emblematic of the ethnic experience of the entire wartime and postwar era. Gatsby's wartime rise in the armed forces and postwar fall at the hands of a representative of Anglo prerogative reflects the rapidly shifting status of meritocracy in the period – although, of course, Gatsby's ups and downs are still a tabloid or melodramatic version of very real trends. The novel can be thought of as a sort of historical fable about the meritocratic mobilization and the ensuing postwar backlash against meritocracy. Gatsby's training-camp promotion to captain and postwar dressing down and defeat by a self-proclaimed guardian of Anglo or Nordic privilege makes Gatsby a historically recognizable figure, and one with a remarkable specificity. And, as an examination of Daisy's relationship to Gatsby will make clear, this historical correlation is more specific still.

Another common misreading of *The Great Gatsby*, again predicated on a lack of attention to and familiarity with the era of mobilization for the Great War, is to perceive Daisy as a traditional woman and a foil to Jordan Baker's New Woman. Critics and readers tend to read the novel with an eye to the historical phenomenon of the New Woman of the 1920s, and, as a result, to contrast unmarried, sexually promiscuous Jordan to Daisy, mother and wife to a domineering philanderer. Concentrating on the postwar moment and dating a new female sexual activeness to the 1920s and a supposed "gap of meaning that opened after World War I,"[40] they see Jordan as a newfangled flapper and Daisy as a conventional – and traditionally submissive – woman.[41] What is missed or forgotten in this opposition is not that Daisy is sexually active insofar as she cheats on her husband (with Gatsby), but that, before her marriage and the end of World War One, she was involved with a number of men and her behavior would have been considered promiscuous at the time, even if Gatsby was the only man with whom she actually had premarital sex.

In fact, as a flirtatious and sexually-active teenager during the war, Daisy was initially Jordan's sexual role model. In an extraordinary narrative interlude in which Nick momentarily cedes the narration to Jordan, she recalls the day during the war when Daisy calls her over to her roadster, and, at 16, on her way "to the Red Cross to make bandages," she is "flattered that [Daisy] wanted to speak to me because of all the older girls I admired her most." Jordan is impressed by Daisy's example as she flirts with Gatsby: "The officer looked at Daisy while she was speaking, in a way that every young girl wants to be looked at sometime, and because it seemed romantic to me I have remembered the incident ever since . . . That was nineteen-seventeen." And Jordan quickly followed in Daisy's footsteps. Indeed, "By the next year [1918] I had a few beaux myself" (79–80). Which is to say, Jordan, like Daisy, became sexually active during the war: if Jordan has all the traits of a flapper, it is a role she adopted during the war before the vogue word had become a cultural phenomenon.

In terms of her wartime experience, Daisy, like Gatsby, has her own quite specific historical correlative: rather than the flapper, she resembles the "charity girl" or "silly girl" that the moralistic US wartime Commission on Training Camp Activities (CTCA) fretted were compromising servicemen, morally and hygienically, because of a sudden or surprising promiscuity apparently occasioned, not by an epistemological gap produced by the trauma of the war, but by the excitement of the mobilization for war and specifically its collections of thousands of uniformed men in American camps all over the country. As one CTCA pamphlet put it, "The 'lure of the uniform' is more than a phrase; it is an actuality. Girls often lose their heads in a whirl of emotion brought about by these unusual conditions."[42] These girls were often called "charity girls" because – unlike prostitutes, who also swarmed the camps and presented a similar kind of problem for moral and health reformers[43] – these girls had sex with the soldiers for free. As a CTCA report on "charity girls" near Camp Dix, New Jersey, explained:

> In all towns, both large and small, in the vicinity of the camp or access-ible to the soldiers by jitney, trolley or train, there still is considerable volume of "charity" intercourse. There seems to be a psychological feature to this particular evil in that young girls between the ages of 14 and 20 are inordinately susceptible to any man in uniform whether he be an officer or one of lesser rank.[44]

Daisy at 18 might not have been typical of the "hundreds of young girls" who became "hysterical at the sight of buttons and uniforms"[45] – admittedly, most of them were not economically privileged like Daisy – but she nonetheless "playe[d] around with" a number of soldiers (80), and "many men had already loved Daisy" (156) by the time she slept with lieutenant Gatsby from Camp Taylor. (Whether Daisy actu-ally had sex with the men who "loved" her and she "playe[d] around with" is an ambiguous point, but this ambiguity may be due prin-cipally to Fitzgerald and Scribner's desire to avoid outraged reviews or even censorship.) The behavior Daisy engaged in, which supposedly undermined the morals of the soldiers and, in the case of Gatsby at least, potentially spread venereal disease, was one of the major issues addressed by the Commission on Training Camp Activities, and this wartime organization pursued an unprecedented crackdown on sexual vice – precisely because, on account of the national emergency of the war and the necessity of having healthy troops, it was given an unprecedented power to do so.[46] Under the Selective Service Act and what was called the American Plan, "the military could arrest any woman within five miles of a military cantonment." And under "the new health laws, when women were arrested, their civil rights were suspended."[47]

Probably because of her social status, and perhaps also because she knew to stay – or to appear to stay – on the right side of such regula-tions, Daisy was spared the direct intervention of the social-work-based Committee on Protective Work for Girls, created in September 1917, which tried to befriend sexually-active girls who were not prostitutes, warn them of their danger, subsequently visit them and perhaps refer them to other protective agencies.[48] She was also spared the intervention of the repressive Section on Women and Girls, which, as the wartime mobilization dragged on and "soldiers and civilians continued to resist the new behavioral strictures passed by the federal legislature and implemented by the CTCA,"[49] came essentially to replace the Committee on Protective Work for Girls and addressed itself to the policing and internment of prostitutes and promiscuous girls alike.[50] Perhaps Daisy's wealth shielded her from the sort of "complaint" by neighbors that could be directed against any girl between "the ages of 10 and 21," who was perceived as sexually active, "the so-called charity girl and professional prostitute, whether diseased or not, also [including] women having venereal disease."[51] But perhaps her family's crackdown on her sexual dalliances with soldiers also kept her from being one of the approximately 30,000 women and girls held in detention houses, reformatories, or local jails by the CTCA's progressively misogynistic law enforcement program and the Interdepartmental Social Hygiene Board. After all, only a third of the females detained during the war were charged with prostitution; most were merely found to have violated a sexual code that could extend to speech, clothing, and styles of dancing.[52]

Though Daisy does not experience any of this governmental sexual policing, the novel and specifically Jordan (who narrates this section of the book) subtly registers its looming threat. Jordan recalls of the day in 1917 when she first saw Daisy with Gatsby: "I had a new plaid skirt that blew a little in the wind and whenever this happened the red, white and blue banners in front of all the houses stretched out stiff and said *tut-tut-tut-tut* in a disapproving way" (79). The American flags are disapproving because Jordan is violating the "dress code" with her skirt.

Interestingly, Daisy's family puts a stop to her sexual fraternization with military recruits, but not her promiscuity *per se*. When Daisy's "mother had found her packing her bag . . . to go to New York and say goodbye to a soldier who was going overseas," she "was effectually prevented, but she wasn't on speaking terms with her family for several weeks. After that she didn't play around with the soldiers any more but only with a few flat-footed, short-sighted young men in town who couldn't get into the army at all" (80).

Which is to say, Daisy's family's response, or the compromise she and her family come to, is not moralistic, but practical. Though Fitzgerald does not explain, two issues seem to be in play. Firstly, perhaps Daisy's family understands that she is indeed just the sort of "silly girl" the government is worried about, the girl who loses all (moral and social) sense when she sees a uniform. That is, they are concerned about Daisy's falling in love and wanting to marry a soldier who is not of her class (after all, she wants to travel to New York for just such a soldier, namely Gatsby) – while at the same time her family understands she is not in danger of falling in love with a socially inappropriate young man who is rejected by the army. Secondly, perhaps Daisy's family is indeed concerned that, even if she gives up Gatsby and the idea of marrying a soldier who is socially "beneath her," but not her social or sexual intercourse with officers, she may wreck her reputation and her future by attracting the ire of neighbors and government watchdogs.

While the War Department seems to have little effect on the sexual practices and attitudes of Daisy and Jordan, it seems to have everything to do with those of Gatsby. Critics have long noticed that Gatsby's sexual outlook is unconventional for a male of the 1920s, especially a former soldier – compare that of Nick, or of Jake Barnes, Hemingway's narrator in *The Sun Also Rises* – but its historical significance has not received wide attention. Gatsby's "romantic readiness" (6), a theme singled out by Nick and numerous critics, is manifested in his extraordinary commitment to Daisy, his undying belief in true love, and his misguidedly chivalrous attempt to protect her from her husband, Tom, who is only really rough with his lower-class mistress – and with whom Daisy is ultimately suited. The connection that critics have failed to make is with the "new man" that the wartime camp authorities sought to generate; Gatsby's "feminine" romanticism is entirely consonant with this figure, who could, for one thing, resist the temptations of sex with a potentially infected woman.

It is, of course, Gatsby who feels inextricably bound to Daisy when they have premarital sex, not the other way around (as in a seduction or romance novel); "He felt married to her, that was all" (157); she meanwhile continues her promiscuity with non-recruits, goes on to become engaged to a man from New Orleans, and then marries Tom (80). As a believer in the myth of true love, it makes sense for Gatsby to ask Daisy to tell Tom "'that you never loved him'" (139); in the romantic mythology of Gatsby's schema, a woman loves only one man, just as the man, Gatsby, loves only one woman, Daisy. Set against the tradition of sentimental literature, it is perhaps merely the reversal of emotional roles that is strange; for romantic Gatsby it is shocking that Daisy can claim to have loved two men at the same time: "I did love [Tom] once – but I loved you too" (140).

The transposition of "the mythic roles and values of male and female," Fitzgerald's recreation of "Clarissa in Lovelace's image, Lovelace in Clarissa's" in *The Great Gatsby* have been noticed by critics since Leslie Fiedler: "In a real sense, not Daisy but Jay Gatz, the Great Gatsby, is the true descendant of [Henry James's] Daisy Miller: the naïf out of the West destined to shock the upholders of decorum and to die of a love for which there is no object."

Quite rightly Fiedler points out that "thematically, archetypally even such [a] chief male protagonist . . . as Gatsby" is "female" inasmuch, at least, as he occupies in his story "the position of Henry James's Nice American Girls"; it is he who embodies "innocence and the American dream, taking up the role the flapper had contemptuously abandoned for what was called in the '20's 'freedom.'"[53] But what Fiedler and other critics do not explain is where, historically speaking, this "feminized" man comes from (or what, historically speaking, prompts a male with Gatsby's background to take up this unlikely role), or, more specifically, why Fitzgerald identifies this "feminized" man with Gatsby, the ethnic American promoted to lieutenant then captain then major and decorated as a war hero, and not, say, with Nick, an Anglo who also serves in the war, but whose rank and wartime achievements are never mentioned.

Focused, like most critics of *The Great Gatsby* on the 1920s and not the wartime experience, Fiedler misconstrues the order of events involved in this transposition of roles, a transposition that was taking place not simply in creative literature but also in public discourse and propaganda. If "public attitudes toward the 'fallen woman' . . . changed" in the first two decades of the twentieth century, and "woman as victim of environment or economics was replaced by woman as threat and pariah," as Dorothy M. Brown puts it in her study of the 1920s, it was not because of the flapper, but because, again, "During World War I, the federal Commission on Training Camp Activities had rounded up prostitutes" and – we can add – promiscuous women "to safeguard soldiers from the 'greatest destroyer of manpower.'"[54] Meanwhile, faced with the threat posed to soldiers by venereal disease and the moral contamination of prostitutes and "charity girls," the American army looked not only to the detention of women but to the re-education of soldiers. That is, in the face of women apparently abandoning sentimentality for promiscuity, the army tried to prompt regular recruits to step into the role of defender of chastity, a role traditionally belonging to women or to highly cultured males.

Army encampments were traditionally places where "alcohol abuse, prostitution, and venereal disease were rampant"; this had been true in the Revolutionary War, the Civil War, and very recently for the American public, in the conflict along the Mexican border in 1916.[55] But President Wilson and his progressive-reformer officers in the war department, notably Secretary of War Newton Baker and Raymond Fosdick, head of the CTCA, attempted to sanitize military camp culture. The military cost of venereal disease was a very real problem among Europe's armies during World War One. For example, the "French had recorded over a million cases of gonorrhea and syphilis . . . and British forces had continually suffered an average loss of 23,000 men for seven-week hospital stints due to sexually transmitted diseases."[56]

American masculinity came to be tied (by the army) to sexual purity, not only to combat the spread of venereal disease but also because of the ideology concerning the involvement of the United States in the war. Wilson himself publicly articulated the notion of the morally pure new man embodied in the programs of the CTCA. Partly because Wilson saw his country's involvement in the war as a moral crusade, "a war to end all wars," he instructed the troops, in a published communication, "Let it be your pride, therefore, to show all men everywhere not only what good soldiers you are, but also what good men you are, keeping yourselves fit and straight in everything and pure and clean through and through."[57] A CTCA propaganda pamphlet made explicit the connection between the American military's moral crusade and the chastity of its troops: "You are going to fight for the spirit of young girlhood raped and ravished in Belgium by a brutal soldiery . . . But in order to fight for so sacred a cause you must be worthy champions. You must keep your bodies clean and your hearts pure."[58]

Wartime government propaganda posters reflected the various rationales for male chastity: future health, morality, immediate fitness for service. One showed "The Folks at Home" and reminded soldiers, "Go back to them morally clean and physically fit / Don't allow a whore to smirch your record." Another, titled "Taking Chances," pictured a sailor walking with a girl outside the movie house, below this scene was another showing three soldiers loading an artillery gun; the finer print read, "A real sailor is not afraid to take chances BUT – If he takes a foolish chance – he may lose his chance to get into the **BIG GAME**."[59] The language of these posters could become extreme: a third read, "A German Bullet Is Cleaner Than A Whore."[60]

The military backed up its educational and propaganda campaign with teeth, especially when it came to soldiers overseas. Less than a week after the first American troops arrived in France, where they were greeted "hospitably" and offered "the run of local amenities, which included, of course, the use of local bars, cafes, and houses of pro-stitution," General Pershing issued General Order (GO) No. 6, which "called for semi-monthly inspections . . . and in addition required that soldiers report to special stations for administration of chemical pro-phylaxis within three hours of any sexual contact. Finally, the most radical provision of the order made the contraction of venereal dis-ease an offense punishable by court-martial." A few months later, the army followed up with GO No. 77, which not only made command-ing officers responsible for infections among its men, but officially barred American troops from houses of prostitution, including regulated ones, and thereby "committed the AEF [American Expeditionary Force] to an official continence."[61]

In addition to sexual abstinence, the new man of the training camps was to pursue physical fitness and athletic prowess: as a publicist for the CTCA put it, "Never before in the history of this country have so large a number of men engaged in athletics . . . Men are learning to get bumped and not to mind it."[62] Finally, this new man would exert a "chivalry towards women" that would extend to personal relationships and to marriage. "America is the land where women are partners, not chattels," asserted a CTCA spokesperson.[63]

Gatsby, of course, embodies all of these virtues expected of the new man by the training camps and the AEF. His remarkable chastity – after his slip-up with Daisy – is comparable to that of the heroine of a seduction plot, the traditional fictional character focused on the issue of chastity: having fallen, he remains sexually faithful (over years) to the woman with whom he had sex, practicing abstinence and pur-suing single-mindedly the dream of a marriage based on love that will redeem his misstep. Though he throws wild parties at which most others flirt and many act badly, Gatsby stays aloof from the women and remains proper. In fact, "he grew more correct as the fraternal hilarity increased . . . girls were putting their heads on men's shoulders in a puppyish, convivial way, girls were swooning backward playfully into men's arms . . . but no one swooned backward on Gatsby and no French bob touched Gatsby's shoulder" (54–5).

Because of his devotion to Daisy, Gatsby apparently does not have sex as a soldier overseas, and, despite the tremendous efforts of the military to promote chastity for its recruits, this continence certainly put him in the small minority. Only about 30 percent of American soldiers who went to Europe in the Great War refrained from sex.[64] His temperance (with alcohol) and his chivalry would equally have singled him out from the mainstream.[65]

The literary figure of the chaste and chivalrous American officer from the Midwest who resists sexual temptation while American soldiers all around him overseas carry on with foreign women would have been familiar to the reading public by the time *The Great Gatsby* appeared – and most likely to Fitzgerald as he was writing it. A few years earlier, in 1922, Willa Cather had published the very popular Pulitzer-Prize winning novel, *One of Ours*, in which Lieutenant Claude Wheeler from Nebraska practiced a standout celibacy in France. A British officer in the air service, who proposes Wheeler go "nutting" (picking up girls) with him, explains the realities of the soldier's life and gives him advice on how to break the American military rules and find women in France.

> He began to explain to a novice what life at the front was really like. Nobody who had seen service talked about the war, or thought about it . . . Men talked about . . . [their] next leave, how to get champagne without paying for it, dodging the guard, getting into scrapes with French women and out again.

He advises Wheeler, "I hear your M.P.'s are very strict. You must be able to toss the word the minute you see a skirt, and make your date before the guard gets onto you." Wheeler also learns that "French girls haven't any scruples." But while "every doughboy [American soldier] has a girl already," Wheeler stays chaste.[66] As for Wheeler's chivalry, "He believed he was going abroad with an expeditionary force that would make war without rage, with uncompromising generosity and chivalry."[67]

Gatsby is not only chaste, additionally – again like Cather's Wheeler – he stays true to the role of protector of women advocated by the army for soldiers: he, from time to time, imagines himself rescuing Daisy from a loveless and unequal marriage in which she has been demeaned, dominated, and misused. He sees Tom as nothing more than the man who treats his wife without proper respect, as a chattel. When Daisy started rehearsing Tom's infidelities to his face, "Gatsby walked over and stood beside her. 'Daisy, that's all over now,' he said earnestly. 'It doesn't matter anymore. Just tell him the truth – and it's all wiped out forever'" (139). And later on that evening, when things had come to a crisis, Gatsby stood in the yard, ready to watch over Daisy " 'all night if necessary.'" "'I'm just going to wait here and see if he tries to bother her about that unpleasantness this afternoon . . . if he tries any brutality she's going to turn the light out and on again' " (151–2).

And though Gatsby's physical fitness and athletic prowess is understated, it is nodded to, and its "Americanness" is clearly registered, in a striking paragraph: "He was balancing himself on the dashboard of his car with that resourcefulness of movement that is particularly American – that comes, I suppose . . . with the formless grace of our nervous, sporadic games. This quality was continually breaking through his punctilious manner . . ." (68).

But why should Gatsby reflect the "new man" the training camp authorities aimed at creating? Why Gatsby and not, for example, Nick, who obviously is not an example of this "new man" – who by contrast has, in the course of the novel, affairs with two women he does not love, Jordan and "a girl from New Jersey who worked in the accounting department" (61)? After all, Nick was a soldier in the war as well. Why might the army-camp propaganda fail with him? Or, conversely, since the CTCA's propaganda aimed at creating the "new man" failed for most soldiers (with the consequence of the increasingly repressive nature of its programs for women as the war went on), why might it succeed with Gatsby? Why, that is, is Gatsby the army camps' ideal product – both a war hero and a chivalrous, chaste new man?

Perhaps precisely because Gatsby is the beneficiary of the army camp's new meritocracy he is disposed to pay attention to its moral and social training program as well – especially if he comes from a poor, ethnic background and is thus predisposed to idealize rich, Anglo women. In fact, Gatsby's famous double-sidedness, over which critics have long puzzled – chivalrous lover and cold-blooded killer (from time to time in the novel Nick remarks, "He looked . . . as if he had 'killed a man'" [142]) – may not be as mysterious, eccentric, or peculiar as has been imagined. Of course, Gatsby has learned to kill men in the war, and if he has killed in civilian life as well, he has been prepared for criminal violence by his wartime experience (as was the case with the real-life gangster Nails Morton). That is, Gatsby's doubleness may not be a bizarre invention of Fitzgerald's. Rather, it may sit within the broader reaches of the historical mainstream: his doubleness may be a straightforward, if an ideal or even extreme product of the peculiar American military camp training of World War One. If anything, Gatsby is one with whom the military has succeeded all too well: he is both too much the killer and too much the chivalrous and chaste "new man." Trained to kill he becomes homicidal, and, in his chivalry he eventually becomes suicidal. It is in fact possible and plausible to read *The Great Gatsby* as Fitzgerald's extended, agonized missive addressed to the US military on the subject of *The Great War* (the novel's title is of course an echo of the contemporary term for World War One): "yes, you have helped win the conflict by creating soldiers and new men like Gatsby, but look too at what you have thereby created in our postwar world."

In any case, it makes sense that someone promoted to captain in the camps, like Gatsby, would be more disposed to the army's propaganda than an officer, say, who is stymied in his promotions at camp and underused or undecorated in the field. Nick may have been such an officer; we hear nothing about his rank, his promotions, or his combat exploits, except that he was in the "Third Division," "Ninth Machine-Gun Battalion" (51). The omission is suggestive because Fitzgerald was unquestionably such an officer; though he was eventually promoted from second to first lieutenant in the camps, he did not make captain there like Gatsby; he was deprived of the platoon he was promised at Camp Taylor because "his superior officers felt he couldn't be entrusted with a command," and, at Camp Sheridan, "his brother officers refused to take him seriously and made him the victim of pranks."[68] The war ended before Fitzgerald was due to be shipped overseas; likewise, Nick in some sense failed to have his fill of war: "he enjoyed [it] so thoroughly" that he "came back restless" (7). Gatsby, by contrast, "after the Armistice . . . tried frantically to get home." Of course, he wanted to get back to Daisy, but it is also made clear that he had significant combat adventure and responsibility: he had his Argonne Forest thrills and heroics and after that "command of the divisional machine guns" (158).

The point of this comparison is not only that Gatsby is a prime candidate to be a true believer in the military's "new man" ideology, but, also that an Anglo officer with, like Nick and Fitzgerald respectively, a fairly nondescript or simply frustrated military experience might naturally look at a figure with Gatsby's army career with some resentment – a resentment that would easily translate into a light ridicule of his embrace of the military's propaganda concerning chivalry and chastity. This would be especially so, again, if this Gatsby was a poor ethnic American who would, because of such a background, already have a "naïve" tendency to romanticize a rich, Anglo girl like Daisy whose very voice rings of money.

An officer such as Nick or Fitzgerald would not, of course, belittle combat prowess or Gatsby's account of his very real combat exploits, except to make clear that his Argonne Forest bravery and initiative achieved his promotion to major only from captain, and not from lieutenant, that he was already a captain before he went to the front.

The soldierly aspect of his masculinity would be unassailable, unless of course he failed to put away his talent for killing once he returned to civilian life – as Gatsby the gangster apparently does.

In contrast to Gatsby, Nick, suffering from no outsider illusions about Anglo women and smarting a little from his relative rejection or underemployment by a military that would make a Gatsby its darling, might be mildly critical of the military's production of killer soldiers who do not stop killing when the war is over. It would certainly be natural to him to reject the same military's prissy propaganda about protecting females and pursuing personal chastity, and to be at least gently critical of a Gatsby's romantic illusions. Thus Nick is poised to play the role of clear-eyed realist when Gatsby, somewhat pathetically, goes on about repeating the past or tries to rationalize the fact that Daisy was unable to deny that she loved Tom too (" 'Of course she might have loved him, just for a minute, when they were first married – and loved me more even then, do you see?' " [159]).

For, after all, what refuge is there for a sophisticated Anglo who has bumped up uncomfortably against the new meritocratic realities of the mobilization by which he is not exactly favored? One does not want to come off as a hateful, vulgar racist like Tom Buchanan: that reveals too much insecurity. (In fact, Tom is a foil to Nick whose presence in the novel demonstrates Nick's relative lack of racism and sexism.) So one naturally turns one's relative social failure into spiritual success: the successful are blinded by illusions; they tend to believe too uncritically in the system that has promoted them, along with the system's illusions. This is their vulnerability. Gatsby believes in his chivalry and fidelity. Meanwhile, the relatively failed have the freedom to reject such self-delusion and to know truth: so Nick says, "I am one of the few honest people that I have ever known" (64), and "I'm . . . too old to lie to myself and call it honor" (186). Such honesty is imagined as a protection against the vulnerability of the successful and deluded, who justify their own criminality and await a fall.

Add to this strategy of face-saving Nick's familial relationship to Daisy (his cousin), and his detached, anti-romantic superiority is complete. "Unlike Gatsby and Tom Buchanan I had no girl whose disembodied face floated along the dark cornices and blinding signs," Nick reports, and "so I drew up the girl beside me" and kissed Jordan (85), whom he will later peremptorily dump. But for all his talk of finding Gatsby "worth the whole damn bunch of them put together" (162), he will never clear Gatsby's name and betray Daisy to the police for her responsibility in Tom's mistress's death.

And there we have the distinctive profile of the narrator of a particular *post-mobilization* brand of modernist novel: Anglo; under-appreciated by the army or overshadowed by a pet of the military who is ethnic or an outsider; and in a special, nonsexual relationship with the promiscuous Anglo princess whose sexual career has been shaped by men in uniform. For Hemingway's Jake from *The Sun Also Rises* (1926) and Faulkner's Quentin and Benjy from *The Sound and the Fury* (1929) also fit this bill. Jake was relegated by the military to a "joke front" and is in competition with Jewish Robert Cohn, who, though not a soldier, graduated from "military school"; Quentin is humiliated by an outsider to the town who happens to be a returning soldier, Dalton Ames; feebleminded Benjy is precisely the sort of person the army testing program was initially developed to weed out; and their sexually-inaccessible partners Brett and Caddy have sexual pasts with soldiers (Lord Ashley and Ames).

The American modernist prose writers Fitzgerald, Hemingway, and Faulkner have successfully put one over on us. I am not referring primarily or simply to the singular, but usually ignored, fact that none of the lasting American literature about the Great War was written by soldiers in that conflict: neither Hemingway, nor Faulkner, nor Fitzgerald (nor Dos Passos, nor Cummings, for that matter) was a soldier in World War One. Rather, the larger ruse is that decades and decades later, these modernists' supposed *invention* of a brand new, modern literary style in the postwar 1920s, free in some significant way from the past – but actually involving a careful camouflage of their embarrassing wartime mobilization *histories* that underlie their most famous novels – still holds sway. Their unwitting allies, the New Critics, ratified their myth of themselves and of a "modernist" literature in which literary style is the supreme issue, the primary issue. But even the rejection of the New Criticism and the rise of the New Historicism have not deprived the prose modernists of the protection they continue to receive from their identification with literary style, with the materiality of the signifier: their personal and social histories in the "pre-modernist" 1910s, while in evidence in their biographies, have remained critically cordoned off from their 1920s novels. Though often deeply critical of the modernists' politics, New Historical and Cultural Studies critics, dubious of biographical study like the New Critics, have mostly taken the modernists' bait and followed their cues: praised or criticized, the modernists continue to be assessed in terms of the meaning of their stylistic innovation, in the postwar context.

Given the American prose modernists masterful self-invention and the literary critical movements that have dominated the last half century – along, of course, with the interesting-enough achievements in style of the modernists – it becomes easy to begin to see how issues of the First World War mobilization have been missed even in these most read and most taught American novels. But the fact that these issues have been missed in Fitzgerald's novel, where there is relatively little displacement or transposition, indicates that there has been much accident involved in the successful obfuscation, over the long term, desired by the likes of Hemingway and Faulkner. These modernists could not have counted on the fact that the US Army's extension of meritocracy to ethnic (but not black) Americans would long be forgotten – and is only *slowly* being re-learned now, in the early years of the twenty-first century. Nor could these modernists have counted on the rise of another received idea that would play into their hands: namely, the fact that the army's World War One intelligence-testing program, which, backed by other personnel methods, played a role in this *wartime* meritocracy, would be remembered today exclusively for its *postwar* interpretation in the discriminatory service of immigration restriction. The modernists were geniuses of self promotion, and they also got unusually lucky in their project of self definition. We are now poised to reassess them.

Notes

1   Wendy Martin, "Brett Ashley as New Woman in *The Sun Also Rises*," ed. Linda Wagner-Martin, *New Essays on* The Sun Also Rises (New York: Cambridge University Press, 1987), 115. John W. Aldridge, "Afterthoughts on the Twenties and *The Sun Also Rises*," *New Essays on* The Sun Also Rises, 67.

2   Perhaps the most influential recent example is Walter Benn Michaels, *Our America: Nativism, Modernism, and Pluralism* (Durham: Duke University Press, 1995). The important 1920s development for Michaels is not postwar malaise, but rather postwar nativism.

3   Robert A. Rockaway, "Hoodlum Hero: The Jewish Gangster: Defender of His People, 1919–1949," *American Jewish History*, 82.1–4 (1994–5), 217.

4   Page numbers in parentheses refer to F. Scott Fitzgerald, *The Great Gatsby* (New York: Scribners, 1992).

5   For an example of the theme of Gatsby's double-sidedness, see Roger Lewis, "Money, Love, and Aspiration in The Great Gatsby," ed. Matthew J. Bruccoli, *New Essays on* The Great Gatsby (Cambridge: Cambridge University Press, 1985), 43.

6 Warren Susman, *Culture as History: The Transformation of American Society in the Twentieth Century* (New York: Pantheon, 1984), xxii.

7 Matthew J. Bruccoli, *Some Sort of Epic Grandeur: The Life of F. Scott Fitzgerald* (New York: Harcourt Brace Jovanovich, 1981), 75.

8 Records of the Committee on Psychology and Committee on Classification of Personnel in the Army, National Archives. Robert M. Yerkes, "Psychological Examining in the U.S. Army," *Memoirs of the National Academy of Sciences*, Vol. XV, 1921, 424.

9 8 June 1918 letter from Robert M. Yerkes, Medicine and Related Sciences of the National Research Council, Committee on Psychology, National Archives.

10 Yerkes, "Psychological Examining in the U.S. Army," 424.

11 "Memorandum for Dr. George E. Hale Relative to Psychological Work, Medical Department," 1917, Committee on Psychology, National Archives.

12 "Committee on Psychology" report, dated "1918," 8, Medicine and Related Sciences of the National Research Council, Committee on Psychology, National Archives. See also Raymond E. Fancher, *The Intelligence Men: Makers of the IQ Controversy* (New York: W.W. Norton & Co., 1985), 119.

13 There were actually two versions of the US Army intelligence test: what came to be called "*Army Alpha* for literate subjects and the *Beta* for illiterates." Fancher, *The Intelligence Men*, 119. More precisely, the Army Beta test was supposed to be "for those recruits who did not speak English, could not read, or got low scores on Form Alpha." Robert M. Thorndike and David F. Lohman, *A Century of Ability Testing* (Chicago: Riverside, 1990), 45.

14 Letter from E. I. Du Pont De Nemours and Company, Military Sales Department, 23 February 1918, Medicine and Related Sciences of the National Research Council, Committee on Psychology, National Archives.

15 These two different methods of identifying potential officers – the intelligence tests and the rating systems – were both used during the war. Thorndike and Lohman, *A Century of Ability Testing*, 43.

16 "Rating Sheet for Selecting Captains," 1917–18, Committee on Classification of Personnel in the Army, National Archives.

17 "Officers' Training Camps, 1917. Individual Rating Sheet for Selecting Candidates In Each Training Unit," Committee on Classification of Personnel in the Army, National Archives.

18 Letter titled "The Training School at Vineland New Jersey," from E. R. Johnstone of the Committee on Provision for the Feeble-Minded to Mr R. Bayard Cutting of the same committee, Committee on Provision for the Feeble-Minded (1918), National Archives.

19 "Interpretation of Scores in Intelligence," 1918, Medicine and Related Sciences of the National Research Council, Committee on Psychology, National Archives.

20 Such a score on the intelligence test was deemed indicative of superior officer potential, but other qualities, such as those considered in the "Rating Sheet for Selecting Captains," were also taken into consideration. As Robert Yerkes put it, a grade of A on the intelligence test indicated "a high officer type when backed by other necessary qualities." Yerkes, "Psychological Examining in the United States Army," 424.

21 For example, John F. Callahan, "F. Scott Fitzgerald, 1896–1940," ed. Paul Lauter, *The Heath Anthology of American Literature*, Vol. 2, 3rd edn. (Boston: Houghton Mifflin, 1998), 1433.

22 David M. Kennedy, *Over Here: The First World War and American Society* (New York: Oxford University Press, 1980), 187.

23 Nancy Gentile Ford, *Americans All!: Foreign-born Soldiers in World War I* (College Station, TX: Texas A&M University Press, 2001), 80, 82.

24 "A Suggested List Of Topics That May Be Treated Under The Six General Problems Of The Course Of Study In Human Action For The S.A.T.C.," Psychological Course for Student Army Training Corps (SATC), 1918, Committee on Psychology, National Archives.

25 See Arthur E. Barbeau and Florette Henri, *The Unknown Soldiers: Black American Troops in World War I* (Philadelphia: Temple University Press, 1974), 20, 38, 37, 114–15. See also Kennedy, *Over Here*, 160–2.

26 See Ronald Schaffer, *America in the Great War: The Rise of the War Welfare State* (New York: Oxford University Press, 1991), 82. See also "Report of Second Conference on Control of Morale," 15 May 1918, Medicine and Related Sciences of the National Research Council, Committee on Psychology, National Archives.

27 Byron Farwell, *Over There: The United States in the Great War 1917–1918* (New York: Norton, 1999), 60.

28 Richard Slotkin, *Lost Battalions: The Great War and the Crisis of American Nationality* (New York: Henry Holt, 2005), 7.

29 Ford, *Americans All!*, 14–15.

30 Ibid., 76–8, 81.

31 President Wilson, quoted in Kennedy, *Over Here*, 149.

32 Kennedy, *Over Here*, 147.

33 See, for example, Kennedy, *Over Here*, 188–9, or Slotkin *Lost Battalions*, 226–31, in a section called "Racism Ratified: The Army IQ Tests."

34 See Slotkin, *Lost Battalions*, 93, 110.

35 Rabbi Lee J. Levinger, M. A., *A Jewish Chaplain in France* (New York: Macmillan, 1921), 121, 123.

36 Edward C. Halperin, "The Jewish Problem in U.S. Medical Education, 1920–1955," *Journal of the History of Medicine and Allied Sciences* 56.2 (2001), 153.

37 Halperin, "The Jewish Problem in U.S. Medical Education, 1920–1955," 153.

38 The use of quotas affected not only Jews but also Catholics and blacks. Halperin, "The Jewish Problem in U.S. Medical Education, 1920–1955," 143.

39 Charlotte G. Borst, "Choosing the Student Body: Masculinity, Culture, and the Crisis of Medical School Admissions, 1920–1950," *History of Education Quarterly* 42.2 (2002), 186, 185.

40 Martin, "Brett Ashley as New Woman in *The Sun Also Rises*," *New Essays on* The Sun Also Rises, 67.

41 See, for example, Laura Mulvey, "The Original 'It' Girl," ed. Marie Rose Napierkowski, *Novels for Students*, Vol. 4 (Detroit: Gale, 1998), 77.

42 CTCA pamphlet quoted in Nancy K. Bristow, *Making Men Moral: Social Engineering During the Great War* (New York: New York University Press, 1996), 113–14.

43 Mary E. Odem, *Delinquent Daughters: Protecting Adolescent Female Sexuality in the United States, 1885–1920* (Chapel Hill: University of North Carolina Press, 1995), 122. Bristow, *Making Men Moral*, p. 126.

44 Report quoted in Bristow, *Making Men Moral*, 117.

45 Raymond Fosdick, chairman of the CTCA, quoted in Bristow, *Making Men Moral*, 113.

46 Bristow, *Making Men Moral*, 135–6.

47 Ruth Rosen, *The Lost Sisterhood: Prostitution in America, 1900–1918* (Baltimore: Johns Hopkins University Press, 1982), 35. Allan M. Brandt, *No Magic Bullet: A Social History of Venereal Disease in the United States Since 1880* (New York: Oxford University Press, 1985), 85–6.

48 Bristow, *Making Men Moral*, 114–15.

49 Ibid., 116.

50 Ibid., 126.

51 Bulletin describing the Section on Women and Girls, quoted in Bristow, *Making Men Moral*, 126.

52 Bristow, *Making Men Moral*, 127, 129–30.

53 Leslie Fiedler, *Love and Death in the American Novel* (New York: Stein and Day, 1966), 313–14.

54 Dorothy M. Brown, *Setting a Course: American Women in the 1920s* (Boston: Twayne, 1987), 54–5.

55 Bristow, *Making Men Moral*, 5.

56 Brandt, *No Magic Bullet*, 101.

57 Wilson, quoted in Bristow, *Making Men Moral*, 18.

58 CTCA pamphlet quoted in Bristow, *Making Men Moral*, 20.

59 Posters displayed in Bristow, *Making Men Moral*, following 112.

60 Quoted in Brandt, *No Magic Bullet*, 101.

61 Brandt, *No Magic Bullet*, 98, 101–4.

62 CTCA publicist quoted in Bristow, *Making Men Moral*, 21.

63 Edward F. Allen in a book-length study of the CTCA, assisted by its chairman, quoted in Bristow, *Making Men Moral*, 21.

64 Brandt, *No Magic Bullet*, 112–13.

65 See, for example, Mark Thomas Connelly, *The Response to Prostitution in the Progressive Era* (Chapel Hill: University of North Caroline Press, 1980), 147.

66 Willa Cather, *One of Ours* (London: Virago, 1986), 331, 289, 435.

67 Cather's *One of Ours*, quoted in Hermione Lee, "Introduction," Cather, *One of Ours*, xxii.

68 Bruccoli, *Some Sort of Epic Grandeur*, 86.

Chapter 8

Modernism's History of the Dead

Michael Szalay

Some of the most useful definitions of what we now refer to as "modernism" are those penned by American critic Clement Greenberg, especially the ones found in "Avant-Garde and Kitsch" (1939), "Toward a Newer Laocoon" (1940) and "Modernist Painting" (1961). This essay will examine American literary modernism principally in light of T. S. Eliot and Ernest Hemingway, but it is useful to begin with Greenberg because he so accurately describes the many concerns that united these and other literary figures. Greenberg's earlier essays are written from an essentially Marxist understanding of Europe and the United States, and they use broadly political and economic categories to explain how "one and the same civilization produces simultaneously two such different things as a poem by T. S. Eliot and a Tin Pan Alley song."[1] This kind of distinction is crucial to Greenberg; an unapologetic elitist, he admires the first and scorns the second. His specific reasons for doing so, however, provide us with our first real clue to his account of modernism. The popular song is to Greenberg "kitsch"; a mechanical contrivance that operates by formula, it is mass produced for a popular audience and given to "vicarious experience and faked sensations" (*PJ* 12). On the other hand, Greenberg admires Eliot's avant-garde poetry because of its desire to dissolve "content . . . completely into form." An Eliot poem "cannot be reduced in whole or in part to anything not itself" (8). This is a difficult claim to parse, and it helps in this respect to compare Eliot's poetry to the abstract expressionist painting that Greenberg so admired. When you look at this painting, he reasoned, you could not help but understand the raw material of the paint and canvas as itself the subject of the painting. Thus an abstract expressionist painting, like all modernist art, achieves what "Avant-Garde and Kitsch" calls "the imitation of imitating" (9). The painting is about itself, and about the kind of painting that it is. He implicitly suggests that the same is true for Eliot, whose poetry is modernist because it "imitates the disciplines and processes of art and literature themselves" (8). Much of what follows is devoted to explaining what this means for works like Eliot's "The Love Song of J. Alfred Prufrock" (1919) and Hemingway's *Death in the Afternoon* (1932).

When was modernist art made? According to Greenberg, such art first emerged at the end of the nineteenth century, from within the low-rent, politicized enclaves of cosmopolitan European cities. Denizens of these enclaves – he calls them the "first settlers of bohemia" – opposed themselves to "bourgeois" values. But the overtly revolutionary ambitions that initially helped define the avant-garde eventually fell away; indeed, in a strange twist of fate, it became the aim of the avant-garde to eliminate from art anything resembling political ideology. In place of ideology, the avant-garde lionized "greater immediacy with sensations, the irreducible elements of experience" (30). According to Greenberg, romantic art had aspired to communicate the ideas and feelings of the artist; particular aesthetic media were in this respect only vehicles for a quick and effective transfer between artist and audience. But Greenberg's avant-garde was "both child and negation of romanticism" (28), and therefore "in flight from the undisciplined, bottomless sentimentality of the Romantics" (30). Its members aimed not to express the artist but his or her medium – to use the work to exemplify the particular kinds of sensations available to that medium. This is why, where Romanticism's populist spirit aimed at large numbers, the avant-garde's experiments in form had a much narrower appeal. Rejecting the middle class amounted to rejecting a large potential market. What remained were the ruling and working classes. The former was comprised of precisely "the rich and the cultivated" that the avant-garde despised, but to whom they remained "attached by an umbilical cord of gold" (11). The latter was ill-equipped to appreciate avant-garde art. Appreciating such work required a great deal of learning, of the kind unavailable to those toiling long hours in miserable conditions. On the other hand, it required no effort at all to enjoy someone like Norman Rockwell. Thus "the great mass of the exploited and poor" (17) turned to kitsch, a mass-produced commercial culture that Greenberg deems a kind of romanticism.

When Greenberg published "Modernist Painting" at the start of the 1960s, the world had changed enough to warrant revisiting the two essays cited above. The hopeful and progressive 1930s had given way to the resigned and conservative 1950s. But perhaps more important, Greenberg was now a specialist rather than a critic of large cultural and political trends. His vision of modernism reflected this change. Where his earlier essays discuss what they call "the avant-garde's specialization of itself" (10) in terms of politics and patronage, "Modernist Painting" understands this specialization in terms of the formal properties of the work of art itself. Missing is any account of bohemia or the struggle for power between classes; also missing is any account of what "Avant-Garde and Kitsch" calls the "professional" (18) dimensions of modernism. Greenberg now defines modernism as "the use of the characteristic methods of a discipline to criticize the discipline itself – not in order to subvert it, but to entrench it more firmly in its area of competence." His own area of competence was abstract expressionism; in 1961 he was perhaps most famous for his seminal essays on Jackson Pollock, written when critics were still struggling to understand the young painter's unique style. All the same, Greenberg believed that the process of self-criticism obtained in most modernist media. Reducing a discipline down to its most characteristic methods required understanding what made each unique; as he put it, "the unique and proper area of competence of each art coincided with all that was unique to the nature of its medium."[2]

This process led him to the conclusion that modern painting's most essential properties were "flatness and the delimitation of flatness."[3] Only terms as broad as these, he suggests, could account for the evolution of modernist painting. Even so, and despite what seems the anti-figural and even anti-representational nature of such painting, Greenberg means in this later essay to insist on one additional fact about this evolution: it is gradual. Only the untutored, or "journalists" writing for popular audiences, mistake modernism for a wholesale rejection of what came before. "Modernist art," he insists, "continues the past without gap or break, and wherever it may end up it will never cease being intelligible in terms of the past." Far from representing a decisive departure from either remote or recent artists and styles (such as romanticism), modernism pursues the self-criticism of artistic media by taking "its place in the intelligible continuity of taste and tradition" (110). Greenberg's equivocation – his initial claim that avant-garde art breaks with the past, and his later claim that such breaks are rather signs of a steady and consistent evolution – go to the heart of modernism, and matter a great deal to what follows. For in addition to describing what makes their work characteristically modernist, this essay examines Eliot and Hemingway in light of their shared tendency to allegorize "the intelligible continuity of taste and tradition" within their respective disciplines, as relations with the dead.

The artist, Eliot declares in his essay "Tradition and the Individual Talent" (1917), should apprentice himself to a tradition shaped by those already gone; "Some one said: 'The dead writers are remote from us because we *know* so much more than they did.' Precisely, and they are that which we know." Thus Eliot could imagine that "We are born with the dead: / See, they return, and bring us with them."[4] Hemingway, on the other hand, invoked the dead to very different ends. He was one of many to respond, numb and stricken, almost beyond language, to the unprecedented carnage of the First World War.[5] Much of the literature written after the First World War is "pregnant with disaster," explains Eric Auerbach, gripped by "universal doom." We find in this literature "a turning away from the practical will to live, or delight in portraying it in its most brutal forms."[6] This holds true of both Hemingway and Eliot. But unlike Eliot's, Hemingway's dead are not the hallowed voices of a steadily evolving tradition. They are instead mangled corpses, the points at which the literary hunt for a "greater immediacy with sensations" runs up against Hemingway's conviction that death itself is the most "irreducible element of experience."

"American literature is tricky for the critic," writes Hugh Kenner, the twentieth century's most accomplished interpreter of literary modernism. Kenner's modernism is in many ways similar to Greenberg's: he maintains that American literature is most recognizably modernist when "its writers invent the criteria by which we must understand them."[7] Even so, American modernism proves difficult for Kenner to define in any conclusive manner. This is the case in part because many of the movement's most important writers left the United States to work abroad: as with Eliot, Hemingway, Henry James, John Dos Passos, Robert Frost, Marianne Moore, Ezra Pound, H. D., Gertrude Stein, and F. Scott Fitzgerald. Was Eliot, who became a British citizen in 1927, an American? A Missouri-born poet who moved to London before the conclusion of the First World War, Eliot wrote much of the period's most influential criticism (his thought was extremely important to Greenberg). Faulting *Hamlet* for dramatizing a character gripped by emotions that Shakespeare does not adequately express, he called for an "objective correlative," something palpable within a poem or the environment of a play, to capture otherwise elusive subjective states. Advocating a "unified" as opposed to a "dissociated sensibility," he described the seamless fusion of thought and feeling that he found in John Donne and other "metaphysical" poets possessed of "the essential quality of transmuting ideas into sensations"; he wanted poets who looked "into a good deal more than the heart. One must look into the cerebral cortex, the nervous system, and the digestive tracts" (*SE* 249, 250). Rejecting the romantic cult of expressive personality (and the dissociated sensibility that it caused), he insisted on the "impersonality" of poetry and championed a "classicism" that might support it. Eliot pronounced, perhaps most famously, on what seemed to be the poet's single-handed ability to alter the tradition in which he works: as he put it, "what happens when a new work of art is created is something that happens simultaneously to all the works of art which preceded it. The existing monuments form an ideal order among themselves, which is modified by the introduction of the new (the really new) work of art among them" (5).

But he more consistently held that it was better for "minor poets" to produce slight adjustments to what had come before than for "the really new" to produce sudden or dramatic changes. Thus he maintained that John Milton, undeniably brilliant though he was, ruined the English language for hundreds of years; Milton offered an inimitable mold, and placed his own genius above the tradition that he inherited.

These are just some of the claims that characterize Eliot's modernism. But his poetry was only partly representative of what was most strikingly new at the time. Though his lines are often written in free verse, they display a formality and scholastic sensibility alien to someone like William Carlos Williams, whose more unadorned phrasings typically describe objects in their stark and sensuous clarity, and who produces in these descriptions what Kenner calls "analogies for the experience of the eye as it passes along the contours or across the surfaces of the seen world" (*HW* 93). For Williams, this world is made up of red wheelbarrows and chickens rather than, say, the ancient texts cited in the footnotes to *The Waste Land*. Likewise, Eliot's somber pretension and vatic gravity contrasts sharply, to take another example, with the ease and agility of Wallace Stevens, whose poems turn on fanciful phrasings and intricately-traced relations between what he called reality and the imagination. Stevens was no less preoccupied by death; he called it "the mother of beauty." Yet he often found consolation not in long-established collective practice, as did Eliot, but in the drenching beauty of the natural world:

Deer walk upon our mountains, and the quail
Whistle about us their spontaneous cries;
Sweet berries ripen in the wilderness;
And, in the isolation of the sky,
At evening, casual flocks of pigeons make
Ambiguous undulations as they sink,
Downward to darkness, on extended wings.[8]

More than the Atlantic itself kept Eliot from writing like this. For these are observations made from beyond the densely-layered customs and rituals of a social world – layerings that Eliot wanted and found in England. As the critic Lionel Trilling puts it, American writers "all in one way or another said that American society was 'thinly composed,' lacking the thick, coarse actuality" that the artist so often needs. The relative newness of the American scene rendered it unable to provide "the palpable material, the stuff" essential to what Trilling calls "the highly formulated departments of culture."[9] In more than a few instances, Americans left for Europe to find these highly formulated departments, even if, like Hemingway, they remained committed to the naturalism that these emigrations seemed designed to transcend, or if, like Pound, they embraced both a backward looking tradition and a "futuristic" vision of technology and industry.

Of course many important American modernists stayed home or traveled minimally, even as they closely followed and defined themselves with one eye on what transpired in the literary centers of Europe; this was the case for Williams, Stevens, Hart Crane, William Faulkner, Henry Roth and Willa Cather. Faulkner claimed, tongue in cheek, that he had never read James Joyce; nobody believed him, so transparently did his style echo that of the wildly influential Irish novelist. All the same, it is hard to place all of these figures within one movement. How, for example, to describe the modernism shared by the verbose Faulkner and the minimalist Hemingway? Faulkner said that it was his ambition "to put everything into one sentence – not only the present but the whole past on which it depends and which keeps overtaking the present, second by second" (cited in *HW* 198). Hemingway mocks this ambition in *Death in the Afternoon*: "My operatives tell me that through the fine work of Mr. William Faulkner publishers now will publish anything rather than to try to get you to delete the better portions of your works."[10] Hemingway wanted to boil it all down; Faulkner wanted, as Kenner puts it, "to expand, expand" (*HW* 205). As striking as it is, this difference between two of our most self-evidently modernist novelists does not begin to account for the variety we find in numerous of their contemporaries:

pillars of the Harlem Renaissance such as Jean Toomer, Nella Larsen, Zora Neale Hurston, and Langston Hughes, radical writers such as Mike Gold, Tillie Olsen, and Tess Slesinger, liberal sentimentalists such as John Steinbeck and Betty Smith, masters of noir detective fiction such as Dashiell Hammett, James M. Cain, and Raymond Chandler.

We might agree, though, that, on the whole, modernism names a particularly self-conscious and equivocal relation to an accelerating literary tradition, a relation understood to require strikingly innovative and intentionally difficult conceptions of form. These new conceptions of form often involved debate over whether art was made of objects or performances, and over whether it existed within history or beyond it. They also involved experiment with different kinds of spatial, fragmented, non-linear or mythic narrative structures, and with highly articulated uses of self-reference and irony.[11] Whether taken separately or together, these characteristics often appeared boldly new: no American novel before Faulkner's *As I Lay Dying* (1930) had made a whole chapter out of one obscure sentence – "My mother is a fish" – just as no writing before Stein's *Tender Buttons* (1927) had fused poetry and prose to such elliptically sexual effect – "**Peeled Pencil, Choke** / Rub her Coke."[12] Still, the fact that these works might have been intended to shock their readers should not be taken as an example of the avant-garde's supposed rejection of tradition; modernist authors might have used difficulty to reject the sensibilities of their reading public, but they did so precisely to register the cultural philistinism of that public – its amateurish inability to understand the essential effects and inner laws of particular media. It was a characteristically modernist assumption that approbation of a large audience, or popular success in any form, signaled a compromised aesthetic integrity. Thus Eliot and Pound scorned the unschooled masses and genteel middle classes steeped in Victorian cultural values; they wrote instead for each other and for members of their circle likewise interested in refining the rules and regulations of their shared discipline. They styled themselves, we will see in one moment, professionals.

Most critics agree that culturally-ambitious writing at the start of the twentieth century aimed to distinguish itself from new forms of mass media then flooding the United States. The introduction of linotype machines in 1885 and the subsequent production of faster presses contributed to the rise of national newspapers, newly adorned with front-page photographs, comic strips, and Sunday supplements. Many of these same printing technologies allowed for the introduction of book factories and book clubs, for the cheap production of dime novels and popular paperbacks, as well as for reprints of literary classics and a welter of new niche magazines. And then there was Hollywood, expanding at a fantastic clip, reinventing the tastes and styles of a new mass audience. All of these changes were results of the rise of corporate capitalism within the United States, and produced consumption communities that were alternately homogenized and highly differentiated – national and also subdivided along proliferating distinctions of class, region, and taste. The modern professions arose from the superfluity of increasingly specialized and saleable knowledge attendant on these changes; each in its own way generated authority (or "symbolic capital") around codes of expertise and competence aimed at the dissemination and appropriate processing of information. Professions insisted on their autonomy, and on their capacity for self-regulation, but they insisted, also, on their own importance to a changing form of capitalism. They justified their existence, one historian remarks, as "a way to *insure* that each audience would find its proper guide."[13] They would alter the basic nature of the class that Greenberg described, too simply it turns out, as "bourgeois." The middle classes were changing rapidly; historians have described these changes by giving name to a "Professional-Managerial Class" (or PMC) of "salaried workers" that "emerged with dramatic suddenness [*sic*] in the years between 1890 and 1920."[14] Increasingly, the middle class would include fewer small business and land owners and greater numbers working as managers, administrators or technicians, in the service sectors, or in professions organized by new national associations.

The cultural changes accompanying the emergence of the PMC were profound. To take an important example, the university as we know it, another historian points out, "came into existence to serve and promote professional authority in society."[15] And with the university came a new conception of the cultural life available to those possessed of such authority. Indeed it is possible from this vantage to say that, despite individual artists' hostility to "the bourgeoisie," modernism names the cultural effervescence of an ascendant PMC – a form of expertise that required the explication of the specialist, and that eventually found an especially suitable home in the newfound research university, whose own authority it helped consolidate. As one critic notes, "It would not be too much to say that the university has established in our century the legitimacy and continuity of a cultural realm that we can readily identify as meaningful, valuable, and worthy of careful analysis, and has done so in large measure by canonizing modernists and their aesthetic principles."[16]

This is misleading from one standpoint. Certainly modernism became a recognizable field of study after the Second World War, when English departments of the so-called "new university" used its texts to establish their own social value and mission. But with the notable exception of Eliot and Frost, few of those mentioned above wrote for or thought much of the Academy (and even Eliot believed that the artist "is hindered rather than helped by the ordinary processes of society which constitute education for the ordinary man" [*SE* 276]). Greenberg's avant-garde was especially hostile to what he sees as the "academicism and commercialism" (11) of bourgeois culture. Many of the avant-garde artists that mattered to Greenberg made their start either by refusing or being refused by the official "academies" that organized the training and dissemination of art in nineteenth-century France. Members of the avant-garde painted and wrote for each other and, in an important sense, were each other's best critics and educators. Moreover, the term "avant-garde" implied a pace of change far beyond the capacity of mainstream institutions to track. In this respect, "Avant-Garde and Kitsch" deems academic art too slavishly invested in styles of the past. This meant that "all kitsch is academic; and conversely, all that's academic is kitsch. For what is called academic as such no longer has an independent interest, but has become the stuffed shirt 'front' for kitsch" (12–13).

The avant-garde did not need the university, Greenberg might have added, because it was from the start already engaged in an implicitly professional mode of pedagogy – modernism was by its very nature a self-conscious, even scholarly inquiry into the properties and effects particular to different media – which, appropriately, Greenberg calls "disciplines." Seen from this vantage, modernism and the university pursued different paths toward the specialization of literary criticism: each developed what art critic Harold Rosenberg called an "incomprehensible . . . lingo" in order to identify "the profession as such and [elevate] it out of the reach of mere amateurs and craftsmen."[17] But Greenberg and many of the modernists were committed to the notion that individual works of art were their own sites of instruction: not subject matter for a classroom, but themselves a kind of classroom. Each instance of modernist art was, from this vantage, itself a site of instruction in the history of form, its own version of what the Irish poet William Butler Yeats had called "the long schoolroom."[18] What made this schoolroom uniquely modernist, at least according to Greenberg, was its emphasis on a given work's sensuous, "material" properties – as opposed to its explicit meaning or content. Eliot often viewed poetry in just this manner; he believed Dante to be "the one universal school of style for the writing of poetry in any language" (*SE* 228), not because he presumed that all readers of Dante understood Italian, but because he believed that "genuine poetry can communicate before it is understood" (*SE* 200) – because, in essence, he believed that the sound of the poem could teach readers before they understood the language in which it was written.

But though individual artists and writers eschewed the official institutions of higher learning, modernism did in fact find its apotheosis in the university, where professionally credentialed critics codified its basic attributes. And the speed with which the energies of bohemia relocated to the college campus after the Second World War, in the wake of widespread urban development and the GI Bill, suggests at the very least a certain compatibility of interest from the start between modernism and the project of "universal" middle-class education. As Greenberg had it, the avant-garde set out to find "new and adequate cultural forms for the expression of [bourgeois] society" (28). As it turned out, this was research and development for more mainstream organizations.[19] Greenberg began himself to discover these forms during the thirties, while taking New Deal art classes in Manhattan. Was this more like working in bohemia or the university? One thing is sure: the Federal Government fundamentally altered the nature of American bohemia by supporting tens of thousands of artists over the course of its brief existence from the mid-thirties to the early forties. In a very obvious sense, it would support the GI Bill for the same reasons it had supported the Federal Arts Projects: better to keep potential revolutionaries in the fold (and on the payroll), than to leave them hungry and angry in bohemia where they might fall in with any number of radical organizations. The John Reed Clubs, for example, adeptly nurtured writers during the thirties; they were reading clubs supported by the Communist Party that in turn supported some of the era's most important writers (like James T. Farrell, Ralph Ellison, and Richard Wright). It is probably fair to say that hundreds of writers moved from these clubs to the Federal Writers Project when it was founded in 1935 (just as its probably fair to say that even greater numbers than this moved after the Second World War from government payrolls to the new university).

Familiar to just about everyone in London's bohemia, and a qualified supporter of England's British Arts Council, Eliot might at first appear a part of this larger environment (especially given Greenberg's endorsement of him). He praised Dante, after all, for his ability to offer a "universal school." But however inclusive this sounded, and however much he may have played down his own facility in medieval Italian, few modernists were as committed to exclusivity (or had as many years of graduate study under their belt) as Eliot. Modernism was not for everybody, even if its particular species of difficulty refused an existing audience at the moment it began to make a new one. As Louis Menand puts it in his study of Eliot's modernism, this tension between exclusivity and equal access is a function of professionalism itself, which

> belongs to the movement toward a democratic social system and a free market economy: it promises to open careers to talents; it extends the characteristic capitalist division of labor to all areas of work; it provides the specialists necessary to serve the legal, financial, and technological needs of a competitive and highly interdependent economy. But some of its attributes seem neither democratic nor *laissez-faire*: it threatens to replace class elitism with elitism of another kind; it seeks to monopolize not only the production of certain highly rewarded social services but even, by dictating the requirements for the vocational training of the professional class, the production of services' producers; its ideology emphasizes self-consciously pre-capitalist "quality of life" values over the competition for profits.[20]

Literary modernists became professionals by disavowing the blandly bourgeois connotations of an amateur middle class interested in money more than the rigors of guild-specific expertise. Celebrating traditional literary values, even in the process of radically changing them, provided a perfect means of making these fine distinctions. For as Menand puts it, "the modern artist belongs to the moment when capitalism, entering its corporate phase, provided its professional class with a set of values that present themselves as pre-industrial in origin." On the face of it, these pre-industrial values seem antagonistic to the world around them, in the same way that Greenberg's avant-garde is in "opposition to bourgeois society." But these values are, rather, the bedrock condition for the professions at that moment: "the cultivation of tastes and principles that seem antagonistic to the capitalist world view, that appear to have derived from the culture of some other, more venerable social formation, is, of course, an activity highly valued in late capitalist society."[21] This is another way, then, of framing Greenberg's later assertion that modernism is in some sense an inherently conservative endeavor, committed to establishing links with the old even when it seems most radically new.

An avowed enemy of most things democratic, Eliot promised his readers precisely the "pre-capitalist 'quality of life'" that Menand associates with professionals (and this despite the poet's day job as a bank clerk at Lloyds of London). He advocated poetry of the early seventeenth century because the feudal society of that moment possessed an "organic" wholeness inimical to commerce and liberalism. In such a world, literary values reinforced political and religious values: there was a king, who kept poets at court and acted as true head of the national church. But such a harmony of commitments – had it ever existed at all – was harder to maintain in the twentieth century, even though Eliot described himself as "classicist in literature, royalist in politics, and Anglo-catholic in religion."[22] Eliot decried "the increasing isolation of élites from each other"; he thought "that the political, the philosophical, the artistic, the scientific, are separated" from each other "to the great loss of each of them."[23] All the same, good conversation across disciplines proved no substitute for properly expert knowledge – and Eliot was an expert in every respect. He insisted that "the artist must concentrate upon his canvas, the poet upon his typewriter, the civil servant upon the just settlement of particular problems as they present themselves upon his desk, each according to the situation in which he finds himself."[24] He also derided what he called "dislike of the specialist." He insisted that "the opposite of the professional is not the dilettante, the elegant amateur, the dabbler who in fact only attests the existence of the specialist. The opposite of the professional, the enemy, is the man of mixed motives." He continued, "surely professionalism in art is hard work on style with singleness of purpose."[25]

For Eliot as for Greenberg, only a professional could "eliminate from the specific effects of each art any and every effect that might conceivably be borrowed from or by the medium of every other art." The professional's "singleness of purpose" therefore describes not only the production of the poem, but also the energies of the community of specialists able to understand it. Indeed, for modernists such as Eliot and Hemingway, the work of art allegorizes the kind of professional community it most wants for readers. For example, a poem such as "The Love Song of J. Alfred Prufrock" doesn't simply narrate the story of a timid man afraid to leave his flat and enter a garish and hostile world – it also describes a poet unsure of how boldly he should with his own lines venture forth into the poetic tradition, of how decisively he should modernize the conventions already established within the discipline of poetry. "And how should I presume?" asks this character.

The "decisions and revisions" that postpone this presumption describe not simply the enfeebling actions of a timid man, but the self-effacement of a poet who signed his early work "T. Stearns Eliot" and who wrote that same year that "the progress of an artist is a continual self-sacrifice, a continual extinction of personality" (*SE* 7). A study in the stalled relation between an individual talent and the community of dead authors and readers whose company it wants to enter and reanimate, "Prufrock" frets about catering to a degraded world of mass culture on the one hand and an overly-refined and mannered enclave of women on the other. Eliot's style-conscious narrator worries over the manner of his dress, how to part his hair and roll his trousers, as he steps forth from his cloistered retreat into the tawdry world of "cheap hotels / And sawdust restaurants with oyster shells." The only alternative to this gaudy limbo between life and death is the one presided over by women, who cause the narrator marked sexual anxiety: "Do I dare to eat a peach?" he wonders. Even as they intimidate him in bed, Eliot's women serve as cultural arbiters committed to the out-of-date, to an excessively mannered preoccupation with "toast and tea" and "coffee spoons" and, of course, "Michelangelo." Eliot's poem repeats the famous stanza "In the room the women come and go / Talking of Michelangelo"; presumably our self-limiting protagonist hears this lulling chatter – captured in iambic tetrameter and an easy rhyme – and refrains from making his mark: he does not "dare / disturb the universe" (*CP* 4). If there's a problem in this poem, it is that Eliot imagines his audience as alternately tacky and genteel, crassly popular, or overly effeminate and refined.

The year before "Prufrock" was published, Eliot described the ideal artist as possessing two attributes noticeably absent from Prufrock himself: "The artist is more primitive, as well as more civilized than his contemporaries," he declared.[26] These sentiments were Hemingway's exactly. But where Eliot turned to the seventeenth century for "pre-capitalist 'quality of life values,'" Hemingway typically found these in exotic locales: Spain, Cuba, and Africa. As he said of Spain, for example, it was "the real old stuff."[27] Such a place therefore offered what *Death in the Afternoon* calls the "Lower Things" (190). Encapsulating his experience watching bullfights in Spain during the late twenties and early thirties, *Death in the Afternoon* anatomizes a traditional art form steeped in what was to him the very lowest of the low: the experience of "one of the simplest things of all and the most fundamental . . . violent death" (2). It is Hemingway's definitive account of how to conjoin the primitive and the civilized. It is also his definitive account of how to conjoin the artful and the professional; bullfighting is a fast-disappearing "minor art" (73) but also, at the same time, a highly codified trade. Thus he exhaustively catalogs the canon of expertise necessary to "a sound scientific education in bullfighting" (166), and the standards used to evaluate "ranking in the profession" (206) that he takes bullfighting to be. He grants that such "a technical explanation" often makes for "hard reading" (179). But such reading aims to educate and leave the reader able to evaluate "the ranking in the profession" not only of bullfighters but of artists generally. *Death in the Afternoon* means to produce "the aficionado": that member of "the most intelligent part of the public" who "understands bullfights in general and in detail and still cares for them" (380). It does the same for readers of modernism, who presumably leave this work able to understand that a "purity of line" and an "ordered, formal [and] passionate . . . disregard for death" (207) constitute the "dangerous classicism" (212) of both "the new style" (199) of bullfighting and the new style of Hemingway's own prose.

Like Eliot, Hemingway at moments understands the practice of classicism to depend less on exceptional talent than a dutiful regard for precedent; as much as modern professions required outsized explorers to blaze a path for others, they required, even more, standardized codes available to greater numbers. Thus Hemingway will urge his reader to appreciate the bullfighter of middling talent: "You should, as a spectator, show your appreciation of the good and valuable work that is essential but not brilliant. You should appreciate the proper working and correct killing of a bull that it is impossible to be brilliant with" (163). Whether or not the bullfighter is brilliant, he is likely to be a specialist, and his devotion to perfecting one aspect of his art is purchased by his remaining expert in that one aspect alone. Indeed, bullfighting generally is divided into specialties, and almost nobody can master them all. Only "rarely, extremely rarely, do you get a matador who is both a great killer and a great artist with either cape or muleta. As rarely as you would get a great boxer who is also a first rate painter" (178).

But at the same time, Hemingway has mixed feelings about the specialist; by the thirties, he observes, matadors had "become as much specialists as doctors":

In the old days you went to a doctor and he fixed you up, or tried to fix up, whatever was wrong with you. So in the old days you went to a bullfight and the matadors were matadors; they had served a real apprenticeship, knew bullfighting, performed as skillfully as their ability and courage permitted with cape, muleta, banderillas, and they killed the bulls. It is of no use to describe the state of specialization doctors have reached, nor speak of the aspects of this which are most repellant and ridiculous because every one has some contact with them sooner or later. (85)

As he has it, "the modern formal bullfight" (26) is in crisis because of its reliance on specialization and because it has entered a phase of "decadence" after the passing of the real masters of the twenties. "The decay of a complete art," he tells us, comes about "through a magnification of certain of its aspects" (70). One master of the complete art was Juan Belmonte, who radically altered the tradition that he inherited. No minor talent, he "did not accept any rules made without testing whether they might be broken, and he was a genius and a great artist. The way Belmonte worked was not a heritage, nor a development; it was a revolution" (69). Here we see Hemingway's difference from Eliot and Greenberg, his proclivity for heroic and mold-defying change. In 1932, he wanted something more than what Greenberg called "the intelligible continuity of taste and tradition." The revolutionary change he desired would reverse a process of modernization. "What is needed in bullfighting to-day," he reasons, "is a complete bullfighter who is at the same time an artist to save it from the specialists . . . What it needs is a god to drive the half-gods out." This is a messianic vision at the heart of many a modernist (Eliot, Stevens, and Pound, for instance, each of whom expressed different degrees of sympathy for Italian Fascist Benito Mussolini). But as the thirties could not help but demonstrate, charismatic leaders gave way to highly routinized bureaucracies; and as the widely-read German sociologist Max Weber would have it, specialization was the very core of modern bureaucracy. Hemingway knows he needs expert doctors, as does "every one [who] has some contact with them sooner or later." Perhaps specialists were here stay. The truest note of this melancholic, nostalgic text is therefore the one struck on the last page: "it's all been changed . . . Let it all change. We'll all be gone before it's changed too much . . . We've seen it all go and we'll watch it go again" (278).

This bittersweet register, and the ambivalence surrounding specialization that it captures, gives shape to the short story lodged at the very center of *Death in the Afternoon* – "A Natural History of the Dead." The story is introduced as "written in popular style and . . . designed to be the Whittier's *Snow Bound* of our time" (133). We know this to be, at the very least, snide. Whittier was a fervent abolitionist and widely-read poet whose gentility and sentimentality – whose romanticism – made him the antithesis of the proudly macho Hemingway, that hard-boiled master of unadorned and simple pleasures. The story is thus announced and then commenced with considerable irony, at great distance from the hardnosed and clinically evaluative voice that elsewhere describes the art of bullfighting:

> It has always seemed to me that the war has been omitted as a field for the observations of the naturalist. We have charming and sound accounts of the flora and fauna of Patagonia by the late W. H. Hudson, the Reverend Gilbert White has written most interestingly of the Hoopoe on its occasional and not at all common visits to Selborne, and Bishop Stanley has given us a valuable, although popular, *Familiar History of the Birds*. (335)

This is not the voice of an aficionado of blood sport, but of a bookish pedant, a scholar in the field of Natural History.[28] Included here are some of the natural historians associated with the field at the middle of the nineteenth century; all save one were published before Charles Darwin's *Origin of Species* (1859) transformed a field that had for some time previous encompassed the popular on the one hand and the incipiently professional and academic on the other. From its start in the Royal Academy of Science in the seventeenth century, Natural History had offered an essentially holistic approach to human and natural life; it was a field for learned amateurs, a mode of study inimical to the creation of specialized disciplines. Thus far, this comports well with Hemingway's professed mission in *Death in the Afternoon*, which describes the science of bullfighting from the outside perspective of one relatively new to the field. But such naturalists also sign on to the divine, and to what the narrator of this larger work disparagingly calls "fineness of feeling" and "higher things" (1, 190). The natural historian commits not only to the "charming," the "sound," and the "rational," but also, and perhaps most damningly, to the kind of "extraordinary beauty" one might find in a flower (335). This is to Hemingway the very essence of gentility. "Can any branch of Natural History be studied," asks our narrator, "without increasing that faith, love and hope which we also, every one of us, need in our journey through the wilderness of life?" (335). The question, at least here, is rhetorical, and so the narrator takes his reader in hand: "Let us therefore see what inspiration we may derive from the dead" (335).

With this Hemingway makes reference not simply to the field of Natural History, but also, and to different effect, to those specialists who share his particular sense of the rules and requirements of modernist writing. Eliot began his "Prufrock" with a similar desire to see what inspiration might be derived from the dead – its epigram from Dante's *Inferno* reads, "If I thought that my reply would be to one who would ever return to the world, this flame would stay without further movement; but since none has ever returned alive from this depth, if what I hear is true, I answer you without fear of infamy" (27.61–6). The speaker of these lines is imprisoned in Hell, and speaks to Dante only because he believes that what he says cannot be brought back to the world of the living.

But of course the poem relishes this as paradox: reading this poem, we do hear from the dead, especially as they comprise the tradition into which the narrator wants to enter. As Eliot's poem "Little Gidding" (1942) will later put it, "And what the dead had no speech for, when living / They can tell you, being dead: the communication / Of the dead is tongued with fire beyond the language of the / living" (201). The specialized knowledge intrinsic to the poetic vocation, Eliot believed, came from knowing how to speak to the dead. Hemingway's injunction ("Let us therefore see") thus also picks up on the first line of "Prufrock" ("Let us go then, you and I"): both narrators invite their readers on a journey into the world of the dead.

What follows moves the narrator from "higher things" to "Lower Things," from "a disposition to wonder and adore" and take consolation from the natural world, to a more "indecorous" (139) apprehension of the plain and ugly brutality of death. With a sexism similar to Eliot's, Hemingway represents this movement as an affront to the refined sensibilities of women, representative as they are presumed to be of a more delicate and genteel cultural moment. His narrator recounts his natural history to a blushing "Old lady," who only thinks she want to know what war and carnage really are. (The character is reportedly modeled on Gertrude Stein, from whom Hemingway learned much of his craft, and who wrote on bullfighting before her famous pupil did.)[29] This interlocutor therefore disapproves when the narrator recalls the mass slaughter of pack animals during the First World War and, later, a battlefield "on which the quality of unreality and the fact that there were no wounded rob the disaster of a horror which might have been far greater" (337). As Hemingway has it elsewhere in the book, "Death is the unescapable [*sic*] reality, the one thing that man may be sure of; the only security; that it transcends all modern comforts" (266). Here in the story, its unreal reality contradicts the transcendental affirmations of the early nineteenth-century naturalist. Death does not seem, as it were, natural. And dead bodies destroyed by war do not, it turns out, conform to the elegant etchings of anatomy found in a textbook. "It's amazing," recounts the narrator, "that the human body should be blown into pieces which exploded along no anatomical lines, but rather divided as capriciously as the fragmentation in the burst of a high explosive shell" (337). Indeed, these gruesome bodies seem to have exploded in conjunction with books. "The surprising thing," the narrator tells us, "is the amount of paper that is scattered about the dead" (337). In one sense, the narrator means this to describe the manner in which the dead bodies he witnessed during the war were strewn with sheets of paper, ripped from uniform pockets; but in another sense, we are meant to understand this as a gesture to the story before us. Hemingway's natural history is itself made up of sheets of paper scattered about the bodies of the dead – it is a form of writing preoccupied with the dead, a form of writing that in this instance circles like vultures around decaying corpses.

As Kenner puts it, Hemingway "is never really writing about what he seems to be" (*HW* 152). Almost invariably, we might add, he is writing about his writing in surprisingly literal registers. As Hemingway once put it, "You know that fiction, prose rather, is possibly the roughest trade of all in writing. You do not have the reference, the old important reference. You have the sheet of blank paper, the pencil and the obligation to invent truer things than can be true."[30] There is no landscape or bowl of fruit or model sitting on a chair. The ultimate reference for his stories, this would seem to suggest, are rather the artistic tools used in their creation: blank page and pencil. Such a claim helps to explain, for example, his masterful short story "The Snows of Kilimanjaro" (1935), which represents the dying moments of a writer who regrets bitterly his failure to have written more. With considerable irony, we are invited into the consciousness of a character musing on what he might have written: following his thoughts we read the stories he wishes he had written but did not, as he lies dying on his cot in a remote part of Africa. But what begins as dramatic irony had at the expense of the character becomes irony had at the expense of the reader, who misses the precise moment at which the character dies. We read of him being rescued by a friend with a small plane, and then share his point of view as, soaring high in the air, he sees "great, high, and unbelievably white in the sun . . . the square top of Kilimanjaro."[31] As we discover only moments later, he sees no such thing – he has died sleeping in his cot. What we thought was the point of view of the character was, rather, a product of the conventional form most essential to prose writing: in this instance, the rectilinear and white blank page, a plane hovering above it just as a pencil might; the dying writer sees the top of the mountain as Hemingway sees the page on which he writes.[32]

One of the many narrative voices in *The Waste Land* would seem to see what Hemingway's character sees: "I was neither / living nor dead, and I knew nothing / Looking into the heart of light, the silence" (*CP* 54; ll. 40–2). As in "Kilimanjaro," we see something like the whiteness of the page itself, capturing a mind neither dead nor alive. *Death in the Afternoon* describes this heart of light in similar terms, as when it recounts "the clean, clean, unbearably clean whiteness of the thighbone" (20) exposed by a bull's horn in the leg of a matador, one of the many unfortunates in this text who are "neither / living nor dead." Hemingway tells us that he aims above all in his writing to look without flinching into this unbearable whiteness – this meta-phorical empty page – and thereby grasp "with the roughest trade of all" the indistinct line between the living and the dead. He wants to not "physically or mentally shut his eyes, as one might do if he saw a child that he could not possibly aid, about to be struck by a train" (2). Put another way, Hemingway inculcates in himself what he takes to be the most basic quality of the bullfighter. Both find creativity in their unwavering apprehension of death: "The matador, living every day with death, becomes very detached, [and] the measure of his detach-ment is of course the measure of his imagination" (56). As Heming-way has it, this imagination can lead only one place: back to death. "All stories, if continued far enough," he tells the Old lady, "end in death, and he is no true-story teller who would keep that from you" (122).

But in another sense, stories never end in death; they narrate death, but do not themselves die. Once asked by an interviewer, "What do you think is the function of your art?" Hemingway responded "You make something through your invention that is not a representation but a whole new thing truer than anything true and alive, and you make it alive, and if you make it well enough, you give it immortality. That is why you write and for no other reason that you know of."[33]

Unlike the characters that it describes, true writing never dies. By contrast, and as he tells us more than once, bullfighting is only a "minor art" because, he explains, it is "impermanent" (73). "Suppose," he asks us, "a painter's canvases disappeared with him and a writer's books were automatically destroyed at his death and only existed in the memory of those that had read them. That is what happens in bullfighting" (99). As he was acutely aware, a writer's books are not destroyed at his death. A great deal depends, then, upon those little pieces of paper circling about the dead bodies in "A Natural History of the Dead." They are literal instances of Hemingway's medium that survive the dead, upon whom they seem so parasitic. These papers have purchased a kind of immortality, but only by capturing and testifying to the transience of human life. These papers are immortal because they are, to Hemingway, "true" in their representation of death – not because they build upon bits and pieces of language borrowed from dead poets. Speaking of those who wish to ennoble death, or at least dress it up respectably, the narrator writes, "I hope to see the finish of a few, and speculate how worms will try that long preserved sterility; with their quaint pamphlets gone to bust and into foot-notes all their lust" (139). Our narrator borrows these lines from Andrew Marvell; "I learned how to do that by reading T. S. Eliot" (139) he tells her. All the same, Hemingway's was a different art of death, less reverential toward the repossessed words of those who came before, and more baldly committed to the ugly fact of life's end. There are indeed pieces of paper circling about the dead – but Hemingway will not use them to produce rhyme.

What he does, however, is reproduce the motion of descent – the catabasis – that Eliot so often borrowed from Dante. As the story progresses, we lose our initially lofty orbit, and come plummeting downward. We move from higher to lower things, from comforting transcendental homilies to the particularizing representation of immediate experience – and to a cave dug into the side of a mountain. In the process, the story becomes more and more what we expect from Hemingway: truncated and unadorned, with a deceptively calm surface barely covering a shell-shocked and traumatized interior. We now find "a man whose head was broken as a flower pot may be broken" (141) – a man whose broken head echoes the mountain cave to which he is brought. Like Eliot's narrator, he is neither alive nor dead. The doctor of the field hospital lodged within the mountain cave has placed this man with the dead, though he still lives. He cannot be saved, and lives for the moment only because his head is kept together artificially, "by membranes and a skillfully applied bandage now soaked and hardened" (141). Here also are papers that encircle the dead, but in still more self-conscious form: these paper membranes, barriers between consciousness and what is beyond it, are all that keep the soldier from his inevitable death. These membranes are figures for Hemingway's writing, for what it can and cannot do: for the artifice with which it holds the mind together, and for its inevitable failure in the face of that mind's vanishing.

In a still different sense, these papers accomplish, tenuously, the doctor's instructions to his orderlies, who have restrained a lieutenant angered at the arrogation of the wounded man to the dead: "Hold him tight," says the doctor. "He is in much pain. Hold him very tight" (144). The pain here is profound, and belongs to more than just this soldier. It is Hemingway's, as it is that of anyone who appreciates the tragedy of bullfighting and the inevitability of death. These are general registers and, to this extent, anathema to petty specialists eager to subdivide a large and complete reality. But at the same time, the existentially capacious admonition to "hold him tight" points back very specifically to the central action of the bullfight, which consists in the matador holding the bull tight, trying "to pass the points of the horn as mathematically close to his body as possible" (68). It points, also, to the highly specialized literary community of which Hemingway was a part – to its commitment to what Eliot called "the nervous system," and to its concomitant avoidance of abstract thought. Writing after the carnage of the First World War, and profoundly disillusioned by its grandiose rhetoric, Hemingway understood his medium to require an immediacy of feeling between medium and reader. In *A Farewell to Arms* (1929), the narrator famously states, "Abstract words such as glory, honor, courage, or hallow were obscene beside the concrete names of rivers, the numbers of regiments and the dates."[34] This was precisely what Greenberg called the avant-garde's "escape from ideas." As Irving Howe would later add, Hemingway "wrote for the nerves."[35] This novelist, "for whom life consists in keeping an equilibrium with one's nerves," therefore mastered what Howe calls a "moral style," a bodily dispensation which pretends "as if there were – the drama consisting in the fact that there is not – a secure morality behind it" (*AW* 65). Thus the "gestures" and "manners" of characters in a Hemingway novel everywhere bespeak "the hope that in direct physical sensation . . . there will be found an experience that can resist corruption" (*AW* 68), precisely that corruption into which ideologies, moral outlooks, and other fixed systems of thought invariably fall.

Ambitions such as these had been common to modernism at least since the first "imagist" manifesto was issued in 1913 by those gathered about Pound (whom Hemingway admired). As Menand tells it, imagism amounted to the belief that "since our sensations are more immediate than the ideas we derive from those sensations, words that describe what can be grasped by the senses are to be trusted more than words that describe what can only be thought about" (*DM* 36). *Death in the Afternoon* embraces this line of thought by endeavoring to produce an immediacy of sensation; the narrator wants to avoid recording "what you were supposed to feel, and had been taught to feel," and to instead "put down what really happened in action; what the actual things were which produced the emotion that you experienced" (2). This "sensory education" (11) matters because, with the passing of time, "you remember things that happened, but the sensation cannot be recalled" (138). Good writing, however, holds the reader tight: it produces in her, for the first time, the situation that caused the sensations in the writer. It holds her tight, also, because it renders irrelevant the author's actual experience. Thus it makes sense that "Natural History of the Dead" opens with a first-person narrator (given to "obscene" abstractions) but then moves to a third-person narrator capable of a more impersonal affective immediacy: Hemingway's goal is not to communicate *his* experience to the reader (as Greenberg accused the romantics of doing), but rather to reproduce in the writing the material conditions out of which such an experience might again be had. Indeed, he understands the writing as itself communicating the basis of these material conditions.

Whether holding the reader this tight meant renouncing everything but sensations – as the evolution of Greenberg's formalism seemed to suggest – remains an open question. As Kenner tells us, modernists were fascinated by what appear only as traces within the work of art. For example, he describes symbolism – a late nineteenth-century French aesthetic movement that greatly influenced Pound, Eliot, and Stevens – as an effort to capture the vestiges of what has "dropped out" from poems and from language itself.[36] We see in the symbolist poem only fragments of a lost history, evidence of meanings once whole and now only partial. Hemingway worked within close orbit of these concerns, especially in *Death in the Afternoon*, where he famously declares,

> If a writer of prose knows enough about what he is writing about he may omit things that he knows and the reader, if the writer is writing truly enough, will have a feeling of those things as strongly as though the writer had stated them. The dignity of movement of an ice-berg is due to only one-eighth of it being above water. (192)

For symbolists, elliptical textual clues trigger sensations a writer does not need actually to describe; similarly Hemingway's writing carries as freight all that it refrains from addressing. In this way, what the writer "knows" somehow becomes for the reader a kind of "feeling." This is "the long schoolhouse," but radically shortened: the reader learns, remarkably, via sensation. Such were the fruits of Eliot's "unified sensibility," a species of feeling that was at the same time a condensed and crystallized form of thought. Citing Marvell, Prufrock wonders, "would it have been worth it" "To have squeezed the universe into a ball"? Hemingway answers: "If I could have made this enough of a book it would have had everything in it" (270), such that "any part" would "represent the whole" (278).

These were all characteristically modernist fantasies of how a work might be seen to possess a content it did not explicitly avow. Thus a work might in some sense contain the world precisely by refusing it. As Fredric Jameson has it, modernist writing was less "a way of avoiding social content . . . as rather of managing and containing it, secluding it out of sight in the very form itself."[37] But as it turns out, Hemingway wanted his readers to see the submerged seven-eighths of *Death in the Afternoon*, and complained bitterly that they did not.[38] Doing so ourselves returns us, very briefly, to the revolutionary ideas with which we began – ideas with which Hemingway was closely preoccupied as he watched the birth of the Second Spanish Republic in 1931, only the second democratic government in that nation's history. In passing, Hemingway describes the emergence of the republic as nothing less than a "revolution" (168), and this epochal event is otherwise missing but everywhere implied in *Death in the Afternoon*.[39] The word "revolution" appears only once in this context; elsewhere, it describes the nature of Belmonte's visionary style of bullfighting. From the vantage of Greenberg's avant-garde, this makes perfect sense: political and aesthetic energies are, in the early days of the movement, one and the same.

The evolution of the modern bullfight is poignant to Hemingway because it captures the bittersweet process whereby an oppositional, anarchic force enters and is destroyed within an increasingly rationalized public arena. In this respect, the bullfight allegorizes not only the course of modernist writing, but the course of Spain's political revolution as well. Bullfighting evolves, Hemingway tells us, from "the amateur bullfight," as "unorganized as a riot" and "all chance and the temper of the populace," into "a commercial spectacle built on . . . planned and ordered death" (371). The advent of specialization was to Hemingway intimately bound up with the domestication of death and the bureaucratizing of the modern state. The specialist depends upon but tragically disenchants "the real old stuff"; his too-technocratic relation to death dissipates the wild energies of a revolutionary population. Hence Hemingway's tellingly equivocal description of the revolution: the last page of *Death in the Afternoon* notes that, along with the aesthetic declensions attendant on the specialization of the bullfight, "Republicans are all respectable" (278). Respectability: the kiss of death for any avant-garde revolution, political or aesthetic. Eliot craved respectability; he might have been pleased to know that he would be memorialized in Westminster Abbey and take his place among the many English dead with whom his poetry had aimed to speak. But respectability was the kiss of death for any writer as committed as Hemingway to populist revolution – and as unrelentingly hostile to the more prosaic fact of government.[40] Buried in *Death and the Afternoon*, then, we find a singular question: what happens to the opposition after it attains some measure of success? "Been following politics closely," he wrote Dos Passos from Spain in 1931. "Madrid loves the Republic – which, as soon as anyone takes power . . . they shift from left to right faster even than in France."[41] In typically allegorical fashion, *Death in the Afternoon* notes something like the same: "Bullfighters will say that a bull is killed more with the left hand which controls the muleta and guides the animal than with the right which shoves in the sword" (237). Which side guided the animal? In 1931, Hemingway did not know. But with all certainty, he knew just how the story would end.

Notes

1   The earlier essays, "Avant-Garde and Kitsch" and "Toward a Newer Laocoon" appear in Clement Greenberg, "Avant-Garde and Kitsch," in *Perceptions and Judgments, 1939–1944*, ed. John O'Brien (Chicago: University of Chicago Press, 1986), 6, 5–6. "Modernist Painting" is included in Volume 4 of the same series. Following Greenberg, the present essay uses the term "avant-garde" in very general terms to describe the various movements that produced what we now define as "modernism." For three more nuanced accounts of the relation between these two terms, see Ronato Poggioli, *The Theory of the Avant-Garde*, trans. Gerald Fitzgerald (Cambridge: Harvard University Press, 1968); Peter Burger, *Theory of the Avant-Garde*, trans. Michael Shaw, Foreword by Jochen Schulte-Sasse (Minneapolis: University of Minnesota Press, 1984); and Andreas Huyssen, *After the Great Divide* (Bloomington: Indiana, 1986).

2   Greenberg, "Modernist Painting," in *The Collected Essays and Criticism Volume 4: Modernism with a Vengeance*, ed. John O'Brien (University of Chicago Press, 1995), 85, 86.

3   Greenberg, "After Abstract Expressionism," in *New York Painting and Sculpture: 1940–1970*, ed. Henry Geldzahler (New York: 1969), 369. For a powerful reading of both this essay and "Modernist Painting," see Michael Fried, "How Modernism Works: A Response to T. J. Clark" in *Critical Inquiry* 9 (September, 1982), 217–34.

4   T. S. Eliot, *Selected Essays: 1917–1932* (New York: Harcourt, 1932), 6; and T. S. Eliot, *Collected Poems: 1909–1962* (New York: Harcourt, 1991), 208.

5   Sandra Gilbert notes that, for Wallace Stevens and others, "the war that was supposed to end all wars . . . [became] as crucial a turning point in the history of both death and elegy as it is in the history of warfare." See her "'Rat's Ally': The Great War, Modernism and the (Anti)Pastoral Elegy" *New Literary History* 30.1 (1999), 181. For an account of the relation between death and modern poetry, see Jahan Ramazani, *The Poetry of Mourning: The Modern Elegy from Hardy to Heaney* (Chicago: University of Chicago Press), 1994.

6   Eric Auerbach, *Mimesis: The Representation of Reality in Western Literature*, intro by Edward Said, trans. Willard Trask (Princeton: Princeton University Press, [1953] 2003), 551.

7   Hugh Kenner, *A Homemade World* (Baltimore: Johns Hopkins University Press, 1975), 13.

8   Wallace Stevens, *The Collected Poems* (New York: Vintage Books, 1982), 70.

9   Lionel Trilling, *Sincerity and Authenticity* (Cambridge: Harvard University Press, 1972), 113, and "Manners, Morals, and the Novel," (1947) in *The Moral Obligation to be Intelligent*, edited with intro. by Leon Wieseltier (New York: Farrar, Straus, Giroux, 2000), 106.

10 Ernest Hemingway, *Death in the Afternoon* (New York: Scribner), 173.

11 For an account of the modernist interest in the relation between art as object and art as performance, and how this bore on literary professionalism, see Michael Szalay, *New Deal Modernism* (Durham: Duke University Press, 2000), Ch. 1. For an account of what was most formally innovative in American modernist fiction, see Mark McGurl, *The Novel Art: Elevations of American Fiction, After Henry James* (Princeton: Princeton University Press, 2001). For an invaluable synthesis of the many claims made on behalf of modernism, see Astradur Eysteinsson, *The Concept of Modernism* (Ithaca: Cornell University Press, 1990).

12 William Faulkner, *As I Lay Dying, Novels, 1930–1935* (New York: Library of America, 1985), 54. Gertrude Stein, *Three Lives and Tender Buttons* (New York: Penguin, 2003), 262.

13 Thomas Haskell, cited in Thomas Strychacz, *Modernism, Mass Culture, and Professionalism* (Cambridge: Cambridge University Press, 1993), 22. Strychacz's book offers a number of different ways of thinking about

the relation between modernism and professionalism, some of them harmonious with the account offered here.

14   Barbara and John Ehrenreich, "The Professional-Managerial Class," in *Between Labor and Capital*, ed. Pat Walker (Boston: South End, 1979), 5–45.

15   Barton Bledstein, cited in Strychacz, 23.

16   Ibid., 32. See also John Guillory, *Cultural Capital: The Problem of Literary Canon Formation* (Chicago: University of Chicago Press, 1993), Ch. 3.

17   Harold Rosenberg, "Everyman a Professional," in *The Tradition of the New* (New York: Horizon, 1959), 64.

18   William Butler Yeats, "Among School Children" (1928), in *The Collected Works of W. B. Yeats* (New York: Macmillan, 1989), 215.

19   See for example Andreas Huyssen, *After the Great Divide*.

20   Louis Menand, *Discovering Modernism: T. S. Eliot and his Context* (Oxford: Oxford University Press, 1987), 113.

21   Ibid., 132.

22   T. S. Eliot, *For Lancelot Andrewes: Essays on Style and Order* (London: Haskell House, 1928), ix.

23   Eliot, "Notes Toward the Definition of Culture" (1942) in *Christianity and Culture* (New York: Harcourt, 1976), 110.

24   Ibid., 92.

25   Cited in Menand, 123, 125.

26   Eliot, *Egoist* V (1918), 105.

27   Ernest Hemingway, *Selected Letters, 1917–1961* (New York: Charles Scribner, 1981), 131.

28   Most critics incorrectly assume that Hemingway counts himself a naturalist in this story, as opposed to a humanist; he actually lumps the two together in their tendency to exalt and render transcendental the experience of life and death. For an exception to this misreading, and a good account of Hemingway's relation to both naturalists and humanists, see Susan F. Beegle, " 'That Always Absent Something Else': 'A Natural History of the Dead' and Its Discarded Coda," in *New Critical Approaches to the Short Stories of Ernest Hemingway*, ed. Jackson J. Benson (Durham: Duke University Press, 1990), 73–96.

29   See Linda Wagner-Martin, " 'I Like You Less and Less': The Stein Subtext in *Death in the Afternoon*," in A Companion to *Death in the Afternoon*, ed. Miriam B. Mandel (New York: Camden House, 2004).

30   Hemingway, *Selected Letters*, 837.

31   Hemingway, *The Complete Short Stories of Ernest Hemingway* (*The Finca Vigia Edition*), forward by John, Patrick and Gregory Hemingway, preface by Charles Scribner Jr. (New York: Scribner, 1987), 56.

32   For a longer version of this reading, see Michael Szalay *New Deal Modernism: American Literature and the Invention of the Welfare State* (Durham: Duke University Press, 2000), Ch. 2. A similar structure obtains in *Death in the Afternoon*, where Hemingway tells us that "the sun is the best bullfighter,

and without the sun the best bullfighter is not there. He is like a man without a shadow" (15). In one sense, this reinforces Hemingway's claim that the brutal heat of the midday bullfight takes its toll on the matadors, many of whom, locked up in elaborate and over-warm formal dress during the fight, later succumb to tuberculosis. But exactly who is without a shadow? The sun likened to a bullfighter or the bullfighter to which the sun is likened? The point is not that men in the ring cast no shadow when fighting under the midday sun, though, interestingly, the man is "there" only because the sun is above him. The point is to understand the sun as itself something like such a man, which only makes sense if we imagine a perspective beyond the sun's – in which case we might say that the fictional sun is not there without the author looking down on it. Recall: it is not that we do not know the bullfighter to be there without the sun, it is that he is not there. In the same way, we are asked to understand that even the sun here is not simply fictional but somehow called forth by the sightline of an author who looks down onto the page on which he writes.

33 Ernest Hemingway, "An Interview with George Plimpton," in *Hemingway*, ed. Harold Bloom (New York: Chelsea, 1987), 136.

34 Hemingway, *A Farewell to Arms* (New York: Macmillan, 1986), 185. For an account of the relation between "A Natural History of the Dead" and *A Farewell to Arms*, see Margot Norris, "The Novel as War: Lies and Truth in *A Farewell to Arms*," *Modern Fiction Studies* 40 (4) (Winter, 1994), 689–710.

35 Irving Howe, *A World More Attractive: A View of Modern Literature and Politics* (New York: Horizon Press, 1963), 32.

36 Kenner, *The Pound Era* (Berkeley: University of California Press, 1971), 123.

37 Fredric Jameson, "Reflections in Conclusion," Afterword by Fredric Jameson, *Aesthetics and Politics* (London: New Left Books, 1977), 202.

38 Hemingway, *Selected Letters*, 378.

39 As Penas puts it, Hemingway's bullfight is about "the shifting power relations as the nation moved from feudalism to national unification, and the subsequent construction of a uniform national identity that was exported during the imperial conquest that engaged Spain between the fifteenth and eighteenth centuries." The tip of the iceberg, about bullfighting, "is supported by Spain, which just manages to appear briefly above the water-line in Chapter Twenty. Spain's history and institutions, which are embedded in the meanings of the bullfight, are kept just below water-level in *Death in the Afternoon*. And totally submerged below Spain and the historical, social, and philosophical contexts of the bullfight, we can find American and the American literary scene, unvoiced and invisible but bearing most of the iceberg's weight." Beatriz Penas Ibanez, " 'Very Sad but Very Fine,' *Death in the Afternoon's* Imagist Interpretation of the Bullfight Text," *A Companion*, 157.

40   For an account of Hemingway's relation to the Spanish and Cuban revolutions, as well his libertarian antipathy to government, see Kenneth Kinnamon, "Hemingway and Politics," in *The Cambridge Companion to Hemingway*, ed. Scott Donaldson (New York: Cambridge University Press, 1996), Ch. 8.
41   Hemingway, *Selected Letters*, 341.

Chapter 9

The Radical 1930s

Alan M. Wald

What Was New About the 1930s?

In retrospect, one might view the novel in the United States as dramatically transfigured by the momentous trauma of the Great Depression.
The unique compound of fear and hope associated with the 1930s
inflicted a searing brand on a generation of writers and intellectuals.
Yet the sequence of events that critic Edmund Wilson christened "The
American Earthquake" fashioned a hybrid breed of prose fiction – one
that amalgamated earlier trends in realism, naturalism, and modernism
into a serious literature accessible to more than just the elite classes.[1]
Techniques such as the use of a "hard-boiled" sensibility and stream
of consciousness interior monologues, certainly available before the
1930s, were blended into semi-documentary narratives. The 1930s
novel now holds a place in history in a manner analogous to the metamorphosis of modern poetry in the 1920s. That was when, represented
by the upper-class conservatism of Harvard-educated T. S. Eliot, the
category of high modernism with its characteristically difficult verses
and recondite allusions became permanently established. The parallel,
but less elite, founding of the depression-era novel was due to the advent
and growing ascendancy of a cohort of young fiction writers – plebeian,
not exclusively Anglo-American, open to literary experiments, sworn
to employ the tools of common experience, and emotionally bonded
to a desperate wager for social transformation in their lifetimes.

Certain of the archetypal youthful writers of the time, such as James T. Farrell, grew famous in the middle of the Great Depression, and their reputations have stayed fixed in that moment of literary history. Others, such as Richard Wright, initiated their careers brilliantly in the late 1930s and then attained sufficient momentum with fresh triumphs during the 1940s, so that their standing has remained pivotal to United States letters. A small number, such as Tillie Olsen, were rapidly whelmed as writers by the hard life and political commitments of the 1930s; they disappeared from view but were reclaimed in later cultural eras in a fashion that prompted new-sprung, retrospective readings of the genuine practice of the 1930s.[2] Many more, such as Saul Bellow and John Cheever, were simply young in the 1930s, and it is mainly literary historians who are cognizant of their almost-unrecognizable roots in the literary radicalization of the Great Depression.

A conventional literary survey of those novels which received foremost attention in the 1930s might accent the historic mutation in the novel's form and content principally by noting the stimulus of two or three prominent achievements.[3] After all, the prominent book reviews in the 1930s did not concern the work of neophytes but of successful authors who had written several youthful books in the 1920s and were now advancing into maturity.

In the early 1930s, John Dos Passos, who had published *One Man's Initiation* in 1920, *Three Soldiers* in 1921, and *Manhattan Transfer* in 1925, burst on the scene with his *USA* trilogy. The three tomes that comprised his magnum opus, *The 42nd Parallel* (1930), *1919* (1932), and *The Big Money* (1936), made a dazzling impression on the literary world with their collective protagonists, poetic explorations of history, and documentary techniques. Moreover, throughout the decade, John Steinbeck, whose first novel appeared in 1929, experienced a growing reputation. When *The Grapes of Wrath* won the Pulitzer Prize in 1939, the book seemed to summarize the social message of the decade. Steinbeck's triumph was instantaneously followed by Ernest Hemingway's masterwork, *For Whom the Bell Tolls* (1940). The martyrdom of Hemingway's middle-class hero, the Spanish civil war volunteer Robert Jordan, appeared to bring to a close the unique aura of the 1930s political radicalism on a note of social defeat. As a short-hand version of the 1930s, the trajectory of these novelistic achievements is suitable for popular consumption.

Yet the longer-lasting literary outcome of the social crisis of the 1930s might be more discerningly reasoned out through an examination the Great Depression's capacity to act upon the young – those literary aspirants without a book to their name. Searching for aesthetic tools by which to express their fantasies and fears, the new crop of writers faced an abundance of choices. They could draw upon recent experiments from the 1920s (such as the high modernists' sudden shifting of narrators, use of unusual punctuation, and frequent stream of consciousness); the classics studied in high school; and the growing mass culture that the Great Depression fostered and fed. Perhaps more than any previous generation, this cluster of novice writers felt free to construct hybrid literary identities with an unparalleled autonomy regarding choice of form and content. Even when they looked to earlier role models – from the socialist Upton Sinclair to avant-gardist James Joyce – the topsy-turvy terrain of the 1930s (with its social, political, and economic crises and its varied cultural responses) summoned novelists to place such earlier achievements in a new context. In the tumultuous political crisis, young writers from diverse regions and ethnic groups became bound together through the embracing of a sense of social commitment inflected by a radical, somewhat Marxist, sensibility.

This new sense of radical community emerged because the young writer was confronted by the 1930s social upheaval with certain exceptional and sweeping concerns. The most personally felt was economic. Although there was assuredly poverty and suffering in the United States of the 1920s, the stock market crash of 1929 produced substantial new unemployment and misery; by 1931 the collapsing economy had created a palpable terror of disaster throughout the population. This fear and insecurity led to political demoralization and even right-wing movements among some sections of the citizenry. As an antidote, the radical alternative – the angry demand for a government responsible to the needs of the people – became a growing obsession of writers and artists.

Another peculiar mark of the 1930s was the international predicament. The new reactionary movement of fascism had been on the march since the 1920s, but in the Great Depression fascism assumed a more menacing character. One of the achievements of the Left was to alert the United States population to the escalating jeopardy of Europe after Hitler came to power in 1933 and when Franco launched a war against the Spanish republican government in 1936. Radical artists saw in European fascism not only an expansionist threat but also a possible horrific future for the United States if a socialist alternative did not materialize. Into this picture the USSR sprang heroically for many writers as a utopia free of economic and racial injustice that was militantly devoted to anti-fascism.

These elements, economic catastrophe at home and the right-wing juggernaut abroad, combined to produce one of the most striking features of 1930s literature: a purposeful and direct exposure by fiction writers of ethnic prejudice and racism that was judged to be a key characteristic of an existing and potentially larger fascism fed by economic insecurity. Moreover, young writers were well aware that, in the United States, the growing 1930s mass culture of popular theater, pulp magazines, cartoons, radio, and film was corrupted by a sickening racism, anti-Semitism, and anti-immigrant prejudice. With only a few exceptions, such as Herman Melville and Mark Twain, the older high culture and middle-brow culture remained oblivious to, or complicit in, perpetuating a version of white supremacism. Accordingly, the "outing" of such bigotry that poisoned popular speech and beliefs was nearly a universal concern among the younger writers.

Politics and Literature

The new radical writing of the 1930s was not only inflected by multi-faceted attempts to find means to address the social crisis by the instrumentality of imaginative fiction; the writers themselves were also partisans of diverse kinds of active political commitment. For most on the Left, the major poles of attraction were the Communist movement and the New Deal, the domestic reform program led by President Franklin Delano Roosevelt that emphasized regulation of business and the creation of public works. In the early 1930s, radicalized writers such as Sherwood Anderson, Erskine Caldwell, and Theodore Dreiser commonly had to choose between the two loyalties. The Communists held that "the Roosevelt regime is not, as the liberals and Socialist party leaders claim, a progressive regime, but a government serving the interests of finance capital and moving toward the fascist suppression of the workers' movement."[4] Thus the Communist party counterpoised to New Deal liberalism the call for a "Soviet America" in addition to a cultural program urging "Proletarian Novels" along the lines of recent works by Agnes Smedley, Grace Lumpkin, and Michael Gold. This was the first time that pro-Communist ideologues, as a group, advocated novels that were aligned with the conjunctural Communist perspective.

Although such a policy had the potential to be constricting when interpreted narrowly, the championing of this "Proletarian Literature" corresponded with the general mood of young writers at the time and

189

left a memorable legacy of uneven works. Then, in 1935, the Communist International announced the innovative Popular Front policy, and a dramatic spurt in the strength of the Left came to pass. Radicals could now amalgamate their attraction to the USSR with a patriotic identification with the New Deal. Literary ideas evolved so that the political themes of the New Deal became acceptable alongside class struggle and anti-racist dramatizations, although there was always the pitfall that some reviewers in the Communist press would inadvertently invoke knee-jerk political criteria to praise or condemn. In the late 1930s, writers on the Left customarily called themselves "progressives" and "anti-fascists," and were advocates of a "People's Culture."[5]

What is significant, however, is how rarely the evolving doctrines promoting political leaders, critics, and organizations of the Left, such as the John Reed Club in the early 1930s and League of American Writers after 1935, determined the form and content of the novel. Criticism that appeared in leading Communist publications, such as the *Daily Worker*, would sometimes accuse books of being too obscure or individualistic, but creative writers nevertheless wrote what they had to write for psychological and aesthetic reasons, and also according to what publishers would accept. Moreover, the most widely-read novelists were already far too molded in their technique to make rapid transformations. Only a handful of established authors would consider joining a Leninist party; most simply made accommodations to the left-wing concerns that they shared. Some typical illustrations include Sinclair Lewis in his anti-fascist *It Can't Happen Here* (1935) and Ernest Hemingway in his proletarian *To Have and Have Not* (1937).

To be sure, the younger novelists of the early and mid-1930s were more actively involved in pro-Communist cultural debates than such already recognized authors as Lewis and Hemingway. Yet, the new generation, too, had emotional and intellectual foundations in the 1920s that lessened the likelihood of their art undergoing wholesale absorption by Communist ideology. This pre-depression legacy is evident in two obvious respects. Younger writers of the 1930s, like those of other generations, very frequently inaugurated their careers by recreating or reworking experiences of their childhood and youth; thus episodes of the 1920s became a prevailing subject of the work of writers first publishing in the early 1930s. Furthermore, the books garnering recognition at the moment that these same young people, adolescents in the 1920s, initially affirmed their literary sensibilities, were very often the writing that caused a sensation among the Lost Generation. That is, at the most impressionable moment, these future radical writers such as Robert Cantwell and Josephine Herbst, encountered the shocking inventions of James Joyce and Marcel Proust, the sardonic realism of Sinclair Lewis and H. L. Mencken, the popularization of hard-boiled language by Hemingway, and the experimentation with American speech of Gertrude Stein. Thus, the new writing of the early Great Depression might be looked upon as "The Thirties' Twenties."

Three Young Radicals

Perhaps the diverse means in which the 1930s transformed the novel in the United States at its roots can be best understood by profiling three of the young writers already mentioned who simultaneously launched their careers at the onset of the depression crisis – James T. Farrell (1904–1979), Tillie Olsen (1912 or 1913–2007), and Richard Wright (1908–1960). What is noteworthy about this triumvirate, and renders them sound representatives of the 1930s generation of novelists, is that they exemplify a new kind of literary producer. All are unabashedly from plebeian, ethnic minority backgrounds, and considerably identified with proletarian "little magazines" of the early depression.

Farrell was a first generation Irish American, born of a working-class family, although he was reared by lower-middle-class relatives. He remained in Chicago during his youth, and, after attending classes at the University of Chicago and briefly living in Paris, joined up with the radical literary movement in New York City in 1932. Tillie Olsen, born Tillie Lerner, was of a radical Russian Jewish family. She imbibed socialist consciousness from her youth in the mid-West and became an activist in the Young Communist League before she was out of her teens. Richard Wright was born into an African American family in Mississippi; after his family broke up, Wright lived in different cities of the South and relocated to Chicago at age twenty-one. Within a few years he was drawn to the John Reed Club and then the Communist party.

All three writers were attracted to the radical social movements of the 1930s, but their politics and the impact of the experiences on their literary careers were markedly different. Farrell was the most prominent figure early on, appearing frequently up until 1936 in the *New Masses*, *Daily Worker*, and the first (pro-Communist) *Partisan Review*. He was a featured speaker at the First American Writers Congress in 1935. Yet his early fame imparted to him an independence and authority, and he bristled at the efforts of any critics, Left, Right, or Center, to suggest how he might improve his writing – especially when they urged him to change his subject matter or use of language to mirror perceptions of characters. Within a short time he began to weigh in on left-wing literary debates, and showed little mercy in pointing to what he saw as the shortcomings of leading Communist critics, such as Mike Gold and Granville Hicks.

Farrell was also hard on writers, such as Clifford Odets and Jack Conroy, whose achievements he regarded as exaggerated by Communist publications. As Farrell's literary opinions became formulated into the estimation that he was more Marxist than the self-proclaimed Marxist critics, his political thinking evolved along comparable lines. In 1936 he issued a left-wing critique of Communist literary policy, *A Note on Literary Criticism*, which excoriated a "failure to realize the existence of pluralism in literature as literature and as part of the larger processes that go to make up society . . ."[6] Shortly thereafter he became known as a partisan of Leon Trotsky – the most vehement, and also the most credible, critic of the Communist party on the Left.

Notwithstanding, Farrell's *Young Lonigan* was rooted in experiences prior to these famous literary and political controversies. If his main character, William "Studs" Lonigan, exemplifies more the tragedy of the American working class than the heroic blossoming of that class into the agency of social revolution, it was not due to the Trotskyist politics he embraced a year after the Studs Lonigan trilogy was completed. Indeed, Tillie Olsen and Richard Wright, neither of whom shared his political trajectory, were as engaged as Farrell in fashioning in their writings workers and oppressed poor people who lacked the consciousness to change the world. Although Olsen may have intended her protagonist in *Yonnondio*, Mazie, to evolve in a revolutionary, pro-Communist direction, there seems little hope for any last minute reprieve on the part of Mazie's parents, Jim and Anna. Symptomatically, Olsen's work remained an incomplete manuscript inasmuch as its literary and political problems could not be resolved then or later.

Richard Wright assuredly dramatized an evolving political consciousness in *Uncle Tom's Children*, and there is a high point of interracial action in "Fire and Cloud," the penultimate novella in the volume. Yet this ideal outcome seems subverted by "Bright and Morning Star," the concluding story of betrayal by a white Communist (which was added to the collection in the 1940 edition). When Wright next turned to *Native Son* (1940), his protagonist, Bigger Thomas, was an African American Studs Lonigan who, even more than Farrell's character, was at the mercy of the lure of the society's decadent mass culture. Bigger's delusion that the route to survival can be found in the gangster's individualistic ethic of sacrificing all others and trusting no one, isolates him from potential allies and even suggests that he might become raw material for a Black fascist movement.

Farrell and Ordinary Experience

Rather than the idealization of working-class characters, *Young Lonigan* was consecrated to the new mission at the core of 1930s fiction: the drive to metamorphose the essence of United States literature by placing common experiences and ordinary, familiar people on center stage. These characters were to be laid open by recreating their consciousnesses on the page through the dramatization of their everyday experiences and thoughts; and these were expressed in their own ethnic and regional dialects. Without a doubt, there had been precursors in pioneering such methods in the earlier realist and naturalist writers such as Theodore Dreiser and Sherwood Anderson. Moreover, behind the technique of *Young Lonigan*'s stream of consciousness were Proust, Joyce, and especially Hemingway. In particular, Hemingway's adaptation of stream of consciousness to American speech, and his celebration of hard-boiled attitudes, were crucial to Farrell's more focused effort to present what appears to be a case study of an adolescent in a specific community. His criticism of *The Sun Also Rises* had been sharp: "Hemingway's realism is, by and large, one which deals with sensations . . . He has tended to reduce life to the effect that sights, scenes, and experiences make upon the nervous system; and he has avoided complicated types of response."[7] What Farrell postulated was missing in Hemingway's appropriation of hard-boiled subjectivity was the biography of the character's consciousness – its roots in childhood experiences that were in turn molded by the culture and community of specific ethnic groups and class configurations.

Farrell steadfastly denied that he was a naturalist in the prevailing understanding of the genre, frequently depicted as the promulgation of determinism; his work parallels and may even be seen as part of the "Proletarian Novel" tradition, but took inspiration from his own reading and experiences. If one counterpoises Farrell's Danny O'Neill Pentalogy (*A World I Never Made* [1936]; *No Star Is Lost* [1938]; *Father and Son* [1940]; *My Days of Anger* [1943]; and *The Face of Time* [1953]) to the Studs Lonigan Trilogy, it becomes clear that a combination of personal resolution and unique opportunities allow individuals from the same environment to seize the direction of their lives and liberate their consciousness from the shaping forces of economic compulsion and cultural bigotry. Moreover, Farrell's open embrace of classical Marxism, a philosophy based on the capacity of humanity to seize control of the productive forces to reform consciousness and institute economic justice, would also militate against the placing of the naturalist label on *Young Lonigan*. Yet such a qualification of Farrell's naturalism should not diminish the reader's appreciation of the brilliant deployment of aspects of naturalism in his work. *Young Lonigan* is in select ways a showcase for the naturalist literary tradition in Farrell's depiction of a war between biology and sentience, the powers of urban life and the resources of consciousness, and the impress of institutions and the temptation of the imagination.

Although Farrell makes occasional missteps in terms of language choices – sometimes words are used in the stream of consciousness that are unlikely to be available in Lonigan's world – the vision and environment are mostly refracted through the thoughts of an average boy in a typical environment of the time. Studs has features of a "type"; he is a lower-middle-class, Irish American, Catholic urban dweller. But not every person of that type is Studs. A significant contrast to the protagonist comes through Studs' rival, Weary Riley. Weary is larger than Studs and has many of the same aspirations to be a tough guy, break free of his family, escape the boredom of church, and define his masculinity through the conquest and domination of female bodies. Yet Weary evidently lacks Studs' conscience. This moral sense draws Studs back to religious ritual when he is frightened of his own impulses (as in the alarming scenes of incestuous desire with his sister), or when he is uncertain about the propriety of his behavior (as in his participation in the "gang shag" with Iris). Following both episodes, Studs performs a Catholic Act of Contrition.

Other characters in *Young Lonigan* yield even more intricate angles on the role of freedom and determinism in Farrell's imaginative world. The young Danny O'Neill is present in the novel, separated out from Studs' gang by the adjectives "goof" and "goofy," which are further used by Farrell to depict emotions that both attract and repel Studs. More striking in this first volume of the trilogy, however, is the "Tomboy" Helen Shires. Helen is portrayed in the traditionally ambiguous manner of the Tomboy character; she may well be a prototype of a lesbian, but here she is treated as a girl in early adolescence who is unhappy with restrictions of femininity and who seeks access to what is perceived as the wider male experience. Helen is a top athlete admired by Studs, although she is resented by Weary. The latter manages a collision with Helen in which he strikes her breasts, thus precipitating the legendary fight between Studs and Weary, which Studs effectively wins.

In the early chapters, Helen is treated as if she only wants to be a male, sharing in the boys' discussions about the local whorehouse and speculating on the thrill of joining Studs in getting a peak at what is going on inside. However, as Studs drifts further from his Indiana Avenue youth gang and more toward the older and more hard-boiled 58th Street gang, she begins to differentiate herself from him as well as from his heterosexist banter. Helen increasingly becomes the advocate of Lucy, whose infatuation with Studs is frustrated by his idealization of her to the point of self-paralysis. Then Helen wards off Studs' half-serious effort to seduce her, while making it clear that she is not attracted by the boy-obsessed lives of the other girls. Like Studs, Helen is in rebellion against the efforts of her family to socialize her into a particular role. Yet she contrasts with him in that her resistance and rebellion do not bring her under the sway of mass-culture romantic fantasies or "hard-boiled" gang culture. She wants to find her own way, although it is not clear that society will let her. Although a secondary character in *Young Lonigan*, Helen is an avatar of the 1930s spirit of rebellion against older customs – in this case, those promoting heteronormativity – that are seen by Farrell as retarding humanity from gaining control over the course of its social existence.

Olsen's "Other" Thirties

Tillie Olsen's notoriety and influence on the radical tradition of the Great Depression has a convoluted connection to that of Farrell. When one assesses 1930s fiction as it was encountered by readers, writers, and critics of the time, Farrell's work plainly epitomizes the new synthesis of hard-boiled, stream of consciousness, and Marxist-inflected writing that uniquely marked the era; the stamp of Farrell would be apparent in various ways in decades to come. In contrast, in the 1930s Olsen was a minor presence. A section of the manuscript later called *Yonnondio* was published in the Communist journal *Partisan Review* in 1934 to some acclaim; other sections, however, emerged unnoticed and the work had no palpable significance in literary history until a book-length volume of the unfinished manuscript was published in 1974. As a consequence of an immediate connection made by critics between the by-then vibrant movement of feminist literary criticism and the need for a usable past, before long *Yonnondio* became inscribed as a central work of the Great Depression. Indeed, in the subsequent decades, *Yonnondio* has received more notice than *Young Lonigan*. It is more commonly taught in colleges and universities, and for many students it is the main source of information on Great Depression literature, and even early-twentieth-century working-class life. Thus Olsen's role in creating today's vision of a 1930s tradition that shaped American literature is as significant as Farrell's yet began some decades later.

What *Yonnondio* adds to that tradition of 1930s radical literature is encapsulated by its title, a reference to a Walt Whitman poem lamenting the disappearing memory of Native American culture. In Olsen's recounting of the odyssey of a mid-Western family in the 1920s (with some anachronistic references to the 1930s), she has memorialized an area of life experience that would otherwise have vanished from remembrance. But what is special in this recreated world is not the commonplace proletarian environment of poverty, life in mining camps, migration, and so forth; other works such as Jack Conroy's *The Disinherited* (1933), Mike Gold's *Jews Without Money* (1930), and even *The Grapes of Wrath* conveyed that knowledge. The peerless bequest of *Yonnondio* lies more exactly in the delineation of women's work in a working-class family, along with the consequences of that labor on the consciousness of a declining mother and rising daughter. The story of Jim Holbrook, the father, is relatively undistinguished as subject matter; he battles to achieve his bread-winning responsibilities as a miner, sharecropper, sewer worker, and packinghouse laborer, but in each case he is beaten down by the social system. Jim is a soldier in a war with both the industrial system and, at times, nature. His personal qualities parallel those of Studs Lonigan; the material for compassion and intellectual development are evident in him, but they atrophy without sustenance.

What is singular is that the labors of Jim's wife, Anna Holbrook, are acutely enumerated as she strives as hard as Jim to carry out the necessary toil for survival – although, unlike Jim's efforts, her exertion is unpaid and usually unrecognized. In the first four chapters of *Yonnondio*, the only section of the manuscript that was satisfactorily completed in the 1930s, Anna and Mazie command nearly equal amounts of the text. Beyond Jim, a range of male characters provide backdrops to allow contrasts or provide insights. What is pronounced is the home labor that Anna accomplishes, day in and day out, in which Mazie naturally tries to emulate her.

In a strange reversal of subject matter for a novel of the proletarian school, Olsen's writing does not allow the reader to actually see Jim working; nor do we see Mazie's counterpart in the production process, Andy Kvaternick, who is said to replace his father, Chris Kvaternick, in the mines. The pattern of by-passing the representation of males at work is carried out in Chapter Three, in which Jim is said to be a tenant farmer but never depicted at toil. Only in the material starting in Chapter Five is the situation is modified – Jim is finally shown on the job. Yet this shift is not the central story because it occurs mainly after the horrendous scene in which Anna is raped by Jim and suffers a bloody miscarriage. Anna is then too ill to carry out her normal family duties, and the Holbrook household crumbles. Neighbors come into the home to carry out certain tasks, and Jim, in remorse and out of necessity, tries to do some basic domestic chores after work hours. What is pronounced in the narrative is a general descent into chaos and filth, along with incidents of physical injury.

After Chapter Five, themes about work are introduced in regard to both Jim and Anna. Although Jim's first urban labor in the sewers was barely described, outside his efforts to obtain his own protective clothing in order to save money, an unforgettable portrait of his suffering in the meatpacking plant is offered. Yet even here, what is most memorable is not Jim's own labor so much as that of the women in casings, the section of the factory where men refuse to work; the result of the rising temperature and unsafe conditions is a terrible accident that scalds the women. At the same time, Anna, in her desperation to recover her health and recoup some of the expenses of her illness, starts canning jelly in her home to augment the family income. Surprisingly, the final pages of the book depict Anna completing her arduous task and her youngest daughter, Bess, banging on the canning caps. There is, perhaps, a mild suggestion in these pages that women might enter the workforce and thereby create the foundations for independence and control. On the other hand, the reader has just witnessed the horrible episode in the casings room of the meat-packing plant, where the women are first super-exploited and then scalded. So Olsen leaves no illusions about the hardships ahead.

There is another property of Olsen's writing that goes beyond the unwavering, naturalistic style of Farrell, and yokes *Yonnondio* with other trends in the 1930s culture, especially the Southern gothic writing of William Faulkner. This is the presence and function in the manuscript of the two grotesque characters, Sheen McEvoy and Erina. Olsen's novel is unfinished, so it cannot be known whether the parallel figures and episodes were to be a dramatic juxtaposition or part of some larger pattern. Each of the grotesques – Sheen, a miner with his face blown off; Erina, a child brutally disfigured from birth – are credible. Yet they both push beyond the bounds of believability and enter the realm of the preternatural. The monstrous McEvoy is produced from the industrial culture of the mine; he is a middle-aged male victim of a mining accident, now driven to psychotic religious delusions by his outcast status. Erina, although her deformations are apparently congenital, has suffered increasingly through poverty and is covered with oozing sores. She too succumbs to religious delusions. Moreover, like Sheen, Erina does not just exist for Mazie in actual encounters in the dump but also enters her dreamworld of fears. Like McEvoy again, Erina threatens to hurl Mazie into the depths of the unknown – in McEvoy's case, it was down a mineshaft; in Erina's, off a cliff.

Thus the two economic environments, the rural mine and the urban industrial center, pose their particular threats to Mazie through symbolic "monsters." In the former, the threat is very specifically one of violent sexual abuse: not only does McEvoy kiss Mazie before trying to kill her, but Jim fears that Mazie has been raped, and the religious ranting of McEvoy associates his plan to commit a ritualistic murder of Mazie with his vision of feeding the needs of the mine which he imagines to be a childless woman desperate to give birth. There is a frightening pattern of association that the reader might see between McEvoy's sexualized assault on Mazie and her later traumatic responses to Anna's painful labor, rape and miscarriage.

The grotesque figure of Erina more precisely telescopes the dangers of the city and the deforming powers at work on the community of brutalized children. Whereas McEvoy haunts the mines, Erina wanders the dump, the area where children play and attempt to fulfill their imaginative and emotional needs by creating playhouses and toys from the garbage. It is in this wasteland that the child who names herself "Ginella" lives, too. Ginella, a sort of counterpart to Erina, is marked by a self-hatred that is based chiefly on abhorrence of her own Polish background – including her Polish birth-name, Gertrude – and a desire to substitute the glamour of the movies and popular culture. In contrast to the earlier threat to the female body that Mazie faced near the mine, she now faces in the dump the dual threats of the physical abuse of poverty (Erina) and cultural corruption of the spirit (Ginella).

Mazie is no longer so young as she was in the opening chapter by this time, however, and the urban environment is less isolated than the mining camp. Moreover, she now has a stronger sense of self thanks to the resuscitative experience she has undergone while living in the countryside and her encounter there with a character called Old Man Caldwell. A cultivated and compassionate man, Caldwell provides her not only with words of wisdom but also with a sense of the possibility of a different kind of self-determined adulthood from that she witnesses in the deteriorating life of her parents. Thus, the more mature Mazie escapes easily from the threat posed by Erina, and neither is she absorbed into the illusory world of Ginella – although it holds some fascination for her. Nevertheless, the corrosive effects of the culture of the city are powerful, particularly in the way that gender roles are systematically enforced through the family. Whatever Jim's special love for "Big Eyes" (his nickname for Mazie), he is undeviating in promulgating the theme that "girls" like Mazie have to behave differently from the boys, and are close in status to very small children.

The pastoral period portrayed in Chapter Three ultimately depicts the means by which the Holbrook family's security is undermined by the economics of the social institution of tenant farming, and then their helplessness in the face of the brutal winter storm. Yet the occurrences on the farm are free of the grotesque characters found in the mining community and the city. The only exception to the emotional therapy provided in this environment may occur when the terrifying memories of McEvoy are resurrected for Mazie by the pregnancy of Anna and birth of a new child. Even the death of Caldwell is softened in this setting; he is elderly, expiring of natural causes in the company of a devoted daughter, and so fully in control of his faculties that he can accept what is happening to him. The only "tragedy" in the countryside is in the symbolically loaded episode of the young chicks, which are roasted alive by accident. Jim finds the chicks during the terrible snow storm and leaves them in care of the family. Yet the family is too self-absorbed to pay attention while the chicks at first warm up in the oven and then are burned. Jim returns to discover the charred bodies, and goes into a rage.

Jim's subsequent, week-long disappearance from the house at the climax of the farm episode renders him complicit in the charge of being negligent. Indeed, survival depends on everyone playing his or her role. In the end, though, the sojourn in the country, free of human grotesques, is the time of happiness, health, and unimpeded wonder for Mazie. As a consequence, once she moves to the next location, where she will be dominated by the ugliness of city life – where horrors of industrial capitalism combine foully with nature in the sickening smell of the meatpacking plants – she retreats to fantasies that she is back in the country.

When Jim returns from his mysterious absence from the house he is pledged to carry out his family obligations and the Holbrooks then move to a third environment, where he devotes himself to a series of urban jobs. The triptych structure of the book – from mine, to farm, to city – serves the formal function of answering those readers who might regard the economic oppression as localized or linked to a particular occupation. Jim and the Holbrooks repeatedly try to better themselves by picking up and trying once more in new surroundings. But in each case society's labor system – both Jim's employment for wages and Anna's unpaid work – are just too much for them to handle. Jim has swings of hope and despair, but until the tentative closing passages he always comes back fighting and with new resolve. Anna's condition is generally one of steady deterioration; her labor is consistently home labor, although it increases with each child. She is less subject to the wild swings of optimism and dismay, but her body and mind have limits to their endurance. When her strength evaporates, due to exhaustion and then brutal miscarriage, her mental capacities disintegrate.

Initially Anna's automatic training in years of household labor sets in, and she tries to carry out her cleaning duties in spite of her physical incapacity. She takes Bessie to a medical clinic and the warning posters that she reads about the dangers of disease haunt her consciousness. Next Anna develops an obsession with picking dandelions that might be made into a food; she leads Mazie and the other children on a confused journey into the nicer neighborhoods of the city. Once there, Anna finds a park and seems to drift into an otherworldly state. She floats out of her "mother role" and into a mental world colored by the fantasies of her youth.

What ultimately saves Anna from complete catastrophe is a community of women – in particular Mrs. Kryckszi, who comes into the Holbrook home and carries out the necessary labor. It is possible that a parallel theme of collective salvation is in progress to rescue Jim from his victimization as worker, inasmuch as his new job has him functioning in a community of wage-slaves who are embattled by the speed-up system. Even Anna's surprising success at independent entrepreneurship carries a suggestion of some larger resolution; the jelly being canned by Anna, and under her control, recalls the frightening jelly face of Sheen McEvoy that had dominated Mazie's unconsciousness, especially when she was aware of her mother's powerlessness.

Nevertheless, the manuscript that survived to be published after nearly four decades is true to the larger ethos of the 1930s novel in the failure of its characters to establish any lasting personal or familial achievement within the boundaries of the fundamentally unstable social order.

Wright and Racial Protest

With her focus on the connections among gender, labor, and the family, Olsen's *Yonnondio* only treats in passing or by implication the issues of race and ethnicity. But the emergence of Richard Wright on the national scene in the 1930s transformed such subject matter into a major cultural theme in United States – Black Protest Literature. Wright in many respects revitalized the tradition launched by Frederick Douglass's 1945 *Narrative of the Life of Frederick Douglass*. Douglass had depicted racism as generated as a by-product of the slave system of the South, and had perhaps for a time succumbed to the hope that the abolition of one would lead to the disappearance of the other. In contrast, Wright's exposure of the post-slavery era suffers from no illusions about the capacity of racist ideology to detach itself from its point of origin and live on in new forms to assist domination. Wright's approach also contrasts with that of James T. Farrell, who shows the functions of anti-black and anti-Semitic prejudice within an Irish American culture that is subject to economic insecurity, a disaffection among young people, and the hypocrisy of the adult community. Wright's focus is on a generic "whiteness," founded in a region (the South) but transportable to new locales. In *Uncle Tom's Children* and later writings, Wright compares the force of such "whiteness" to a big white mountain, a fog, or a storm-like act of nature.

The novellas of *Uncle Tom's Children* are not as close to Farrell stylistically as Wright's first and posthumously published novel, *Lawd Today* (1963); nevertheless, the novellas resemble *Young Lonigan* in having many traits of a language experiment. Wright presents his characters in a variety of regional dialectics, differentiating between African American and Euro-American slang; interpolates songs; and presents many pages of dialog without auctorial intervention. The novellas are also, as in the work of Farrell and Olsen, a study in the formation of the subjectivity of the plebeian population and are based in pre-1930s experiences from a Great Depression perspective. Still, in his creative use of the novella form, Wright has alternatively chosen to display a sequence of episodes through a dramatic change of communities and characters that surpass the work of Farrell or Olsen. For example, there is an overall political and chronological development that follows the central characters in each novella with a richness and specificity that suggests a greater range in understanding personality types and inter-actions with the environment. Wright also has forceful foundation in cultural traditions such as the Bible and African American folk life that he combines with a sense of the dramatic that recalls pulp fiction and popular film. His symbolism, too, is richer in his use of buildings, animals, acts of nature, and suggestive groupings of characters. Finally, Wright brings more abundantly into view the specific problem of res-istance against overwhelming odds, and he even limns an alternative, interracial future, as well as its potential failures in his last two novellas of the book.

Whereas Farrell echoes Hemingway's hard-boiled perspective, and Olsen resurrects a theme from Whitman, the centrality of powerful physical and natural symbols in Wright seem to recall specifically the nineteenth-century American renaissance. One example is the devastating flood of biblical proportions in "Down by the Riverside," which poses a challenge to the mores of Jim Crow society and the ideals of Black religion. Another is Reverend Taylor's house in "Fire and Cloud," in which each room is filled with characters pressuring him for different responses. These are strategies familiar to readers of Melville and Hawthorne. His characters, too, recall the mid-nineteenth century "Romance" in that some (such as Sarah and Silas) seem driven by a predominating characteristic, while others (such as Mann) are more meditative. Even the doubtful resolutions of stories such as "Down by the Riverside," "Long Black Song," and "Bright and Morning Star" invoke the pondering uncertainties that haunt these gloomy predecessors.

At the same time, Wright is no fence-sitter; whatever reservations one has about what might lie ahead, passivity or inaction is ruled out in every story. Most often, one must capitulate and die, or one must fight back and die. Only in "Fire and Cloud" does aggressive action produce immediate progress, although the protest at the end is only an indeterminate beginning. In all these senses, Wright manages more successfully than most others of his generation to build upon and yet add to earlier traditions. Like Douglass, he understands the ironical function of Christian doctrine as a legitimator of repression, even as he recognizes its necessity for those who are oppressed as well as those who sympathize. Yet in the spirit of the 1930s, Wright also under-stands the necessity of shock in order to lay bare the broader and more involved complexities of a social system with endless capacity for absorbing resistance and creating new forms of domination.

Farrell may strike the reader as remarkable today in his brilliant revelations of the interaction between environment and character in creations such as Studs Lonigan, Weary Reilly, and Helen Shires. Olsen, in contrast, elicits admiration for her revelations of the physical and interior lives of Anna and Mazie. But Wright is most contemporary to the modern reader in the sheer and shocking power of *Uncle Tom's Children*. Wright's concealed or secret personal rage is disclosed by the fact that a white man is violently killed in three of the four novellas. Moreover, interracial sex and love are featured in two of the stories in ways that invert the stereotypes of the time; in "Long Black Song" an educated white man exploits a poor black woman, and in "Bright and Morning Star" a white, Southern, working-class woman expresses true love for a black Communist who is tortured to death.

Communism, in Wright's early work, emerges not only as an all-purpose synecdoche for resistance, as it did it Marxist novels of the early 1930s such as Grace Lumpkin's *To Make My Bread* (1932), but also as a utopian ideology flawed primarily by its questionable belief that faith in class unity can ultimately overcome ingrained white supremacist loyalties of white men. Elements in Wright that might be seen as crude agitprop are forgiven by readers and critics because of the power of his dramatic narrative as expressed in the style most characteristic of the 1930s. These include qualities of *Uncle Tom's Children* such as the broad accessibility of its language, shock of recognition in its human revelations, truth-telling about racial prejudice, and the formal experiments found in each episode.

Legacies

In the post-World War II era, a stunning reversal occurred in the political climate of the United States. Some novelists once associated with radicalism reacted violently against their past, most notably Ralph Ellison in *Invisible Man* (1952). Others simply used the setting of the Great Depression to comment sardonically on the irrelevance of the Left, as did Jose Antonio Villareal in *Pocho* (1959). A few, such as Jo Sinclair in *The Changelings* (1955), tried to forge new paths to rebellion. Additional writers meditated gloomily on the wasteland of a 1950s in which the signs of early social movements were barely vestigial, as Ann Petry in *The Narrows* (1953). Others, such as Irwin Shaw in *The*

Troubled Air (1951), commented brilliantly on the foibles of the Left without making concessions to McCarthyism. There was also a small number of writers who fought back in the name of older radical ideals, as did Willard Motley in *We Fished All Night* (1951), Howard Fast in *Spartacus* (1951), and Abraham Polonsky in *The World Above* (1953).

Although the tradition itself declined, novels continued to appear over the decades that referred back to earlier experiences and 1930s-based radical culture. E. L. Doctorow's *The Book of Daniel* (1971) and K. B. Gilden's *Between the Hills and the Sea* (1971) are just a few of the extraordinary works rooted in the radical 1930s and its legacy. Yet American literature as a whole marched forward in new directions during and after the cold war. By the century's end, the specific impress of the memory and traditions of Great Depression radicalism existed among smaller and smaller numbers of readers and scholars, even though its impact on the novel form had been monumental and indelible.

Notes

1   This was the title that Wilson used for his 1958 volume, *The American Earthquake: A Documentary of the Jazz Age, the Great Depression, and the New Deal*; some of the material had appeared earlier under the titles *The American Jitters* (1932) and *Travels in Two Democracies* (1936).

2   The rediscovery of Olsen was part of the rise of feminist literary studies that re-formulated the study of the 1930s novel most famously in Paula Rabinowitz's *Labor and Desire: Women's Revolutionary Fiction in Depression America* (1991).

3   For a traditional overview, see Robert E. Spiller, Willard Thorp, Johnson, Thomas H., Henry Seidel Canby, and Richard M. Ludwig, *Literary History of the United States* (originally 1946; revised 1963).

4   Irving Howe and Lewis Coser, *The American Communist Party: A Critical History* (New York: Praeger, 1962), 232.

5   For an overview of this development, see Harvey Klehr, *The Heyday of American Communism: The Depression Decade* (1984). For a more sympathetic interpretation, see Michael Denning, *The Cultural Front: The Laboring of American Culture in the Twentieth Century* (1997).

6   James T. Farrell, *A Note on Literary Criticism* (New York: Columbia University Press, [1936] 1992), 201.

7   James T. Farrell, "*The Sun Also Rises,*" in Carlos Baker, ed., *Ernest Hemingway: Critiques of Four Major Novels* (New York: Charles Scribner's Sons, 1962), 6.

Chapter 10

Racial Uplift and the Politics of African American Fiction

Gene Andrew Jarrett

In the postbellum nineteenth century, the federal program known as Reconstruction deployed troops in the South in order to uphold the enfranchisement of blacks and thereby foster a more racially equitable, "New" South. Many whites, especially those who were born in the "Old" South and who demanded black subservience to whites, reacted to Reconstruction with disgust and anger. Coterminous with this response, congressmen passed the Compromise of 1877. In this act, the Republican Party agreed to withdraw the federal army from the South in exchange for the Democrats' acceptance of a Republican, Rutherford B. Hayes, as the nineteenth president of the country. The racial consequences of these concessions were remarkable. Over four million former slaves were left unprotected from violent white supremacists and Jim Crow segregation; the rate of blacks being lynched, among other kinds of racial terror, skyrocketed; the Republicans abandoned their fight for black civil rights; and blacks lost their power in Congress. For these reasons, this unfortunate period, from Reconstruction through the Harlem Renaissance, has been called the "Nadir," the "Dark Ages of Recent American History," and the "Decades of Disappointment."[1]

Many scholars have examined the formation of African American culture, and the idea of the "New Negro" in particular, against the backdrop of this well-known racial-political history of postbellum America.[2] They have shown that black artists and intellectuals told the compelling story of the Negro's symbolic transition from Old to New in order to overcome the prevailing theme of mainstream popular culture that blacks were inferior to whites, and thus were stereotyped as unassimilable in American "civilization." Portrayals of blacks in various contexts, ranging from literature and theater to illustrations and speeches, sought to prove that blacks, as a race, could be uplifted in moral, intellectual, and cultural ways. Such representations hoped to counteract the widespread impression that blacks were ultimately unworthy of political enfranchisement.

This essay considers how black artists and intellectuals, in response to circumstances such as Reconstruction, for example, used aesthetic–cultural expression, namely, fiction, to understand or facilitate political action.[3] I want to argue that the long-standing and specific political correlation between black communities and racial uplift ideology has translated into special rhetorical, formal, and thematic features in African American fiction. In his monumental 1996 book, *Uplifting the Race*, Kevin K. Gaines elaborates the nature of this political correlation: uplift "represented the struggle for a positive black identity in a deeply racist society, turning the pejorative designation of race into a source of dignity and self-affirmation through an ideology of class differentiation, self-help, and interdependence." African American fiction played a remarkable role in capturing the ideological and political mission of racial uplift, namely, fulfilling the hope that "unsympathetic whites would relent and recognize the humanity of middle-class African Americans, and their potential for the citizenship rights black men had possessed during Reconstruction."[4] At the turn of the twentieth century, the rhetoric and stories of racial uplift have consistently distinguished the political value and intentions of African American fiction.

For this reason, I turn to racial uplift as an organizing principle of African American fiction from 1900 to 1950. I historicize and examine this principle in four broad strokes: its formal and thematic entrenchment in African American fiction at the turn of the twentieth century; black writers' continued adoption, but also critique and revision, of it during the Harlem Renaissance; its dismissal, especially by Richard Wright and his generation, during the post-Renaissance era of the 1930s and 1940s; and, finally, its reincarnation in the postwar 1940s, captured in the celebration of black writers as American writers if they eliminated racial representation entirely or subordinated its traditional racial-political themes to more universal aspects of human existence and interpersonal encounters.

More specifically, what is readily apparent, especially in the literature between and including Reconstruction and the Harlem Renaissance, is the preponderance of themes related to Booker T. Washington and his institute for industrial education, the so-called Tuskegee Machine; the black elite and its routine intellectual-cum-political meetings or conferences; the nature and implications of blacks passing for white; the historical connection between racial inheritance and financial inheritance; and the threat of racial uplift to white supremacy. I hope to show the consistency of philosophical opinions black writers held on the value and limitations of racial uplift, along with the historical patterns in their literary expressions of these opinions.

This paradigm of the politics of African American fiction changed after the Harlem Renaissance, when "politics" assumed a more radical, if Marxist and Communist, edge during the age of Richard Wright. Wright's rise to deanship of the so-called Chicago Renaissance was a response to the racial uplift ideology of the Harlem Renaissance, which he felt was embodied by Alain Locke, whom he believed catered to the black middle-class and to white mainstream interests. Thus, in his fiction, Wright represented blacks in ways that deviated from the elite, respectable figures that had come, by his era, to characterize the pro-tagonists of canonical African American fiction. Reviewers of Wright's fiction and his generation regarded such representations as realistic, but they created several critical, commercial, and canonical consequences that overshadowed the literary complexity and originality of contem-poraneous black authors, who worried about being pigeonholed. Indeed, complaints that Wright's "school" pigeonholed African Ameri-can literary expression coincided with the prevailing insistence that, according to Sterling Brown, Arthur P. Davis, and Ulysses Lee, the edi-tors of *The Negro Caravan* (1941), the "bonds of literary tradition seem to be stronger than race" for African American writers.[5] Racial uplift ideology thus came to refer to how black writers could be uplifted in professional terms, not to the level of American civilization (for, that was no longer really up for debate), but rather to the level of American literature, where they could be treated as equal to their fellow white writers.

I must state here that, clearly, I do not consider 1900 and 1950 the ideal bookends for thinking about the ideological tradition of racial uplift in African American fiction. While convenient historical limits for the essays included in this volume, they are too arbitrary to represent the beginning and end of this tradition during the century after slavery. A more accurate starting-point is the early 1890s, when the canonical texts of black intellectual discourse were beginning to be published.

Literature, in general, enabled blacks to explore and implement racial uplift. Black periodicals were a major venue for such literature, as were books, obviously.[6] The emphasis of *Colored American Magazine*, *Voice of the Negro*, and *Horizon*, for example, on how to capitalize on the United States literary marketplace to achieve racial goals marked a decided, postbellum turn of black intellectual discourse away from the abolitionist rhetoric found in antebellum periodicals like *Anglo-African Magazine*, *Freedom's Journal*, *National Reformer*, *Mirror of Liberty*, and *Douglass' Monthly*. This turn comprised a growing black intellectual focus on the responsibility of African American fiction to racial uplift, and the kind of forms and themes that could best facilitate the expression and impact of this doctrine.[7]

Racial uplift compelled some editors of black periodicals to publish literature that alluded to, say, black social marginalization, economic disfranchisement, and political disempowerment. Other editors did not place as much emphasis on these themes, and published, instead, literature that more formally – that is, through a numinous writing style – implied the collective, racial progress of black writers in the realm of letters.[8] Such ideas were largely consistent, at the turn of the twentieth century, with what Amy L. Blair calls a "peculiarly American," but mostly white middle-class, sensibility, a "fixation on and idealization of upward mobility."[9]

Black writers understood the central role of their literature in espousing racial uplift, which demanded at least a respectable writing style (which excluded dialect) and, as I shall now show, themes regarding the civilization of blacks in the postbellum New World.[10] At the same time, and especially in the pages of black periodicals, this literature had to help advance the political (that is, activist) cause of the black intelligentsia; to mobilize black readers to commit to serious thought or social action; and to educate blacks who could not read but still participated in reading societies and thus acquired information at second hand. Pauline Hopkins, as I shall soon discuss, emphasized this theme of reading (and political) societies in her fiction, while encouraging, in her editorial capacity at the *Colored American Magazine*, the involvement of black writers in racial uplift. In this latter regard, they should "develop the men and women who will faithfully portray the inmost thoughts and feelings of the Negro with all the fire and romance which lie dormant in our history, and, as yet, unrecognized by writers of the Anglo-Saxon race."[11] She applied this mantra to her fiction. According to Hazel V. Carby, "Hopkins regarded fiction as a particularly effective vehicle of instruction as well as entertainment. Fiction, Hopkins thought, could reach the many classes of citizens who never read history or biography, and thus she created fictional histories with a pedagogic function: narratives of the relations between the races that challenged racist ideologies."[12] Similar to antebellum domestic novels, Hopkins's magazine fiction featured lurid details intended to elicit intense curiosity and emotion from its readers. In retrospect, her fiction demonstrated how the sensational black dime novels and story papers of her era riveted readers in order to deliver an important social message while overcoming the narrative discontinuities that resulted from serializing a story.

Likewise, Dunbar realized that fiction was a popular and effective medium for the development and sustenance of racial uplift discourse. As one of the most prodigious black fiction writers of his generation, he wrote or published more than one hundred short stories between 1890 and 1905.[13] Quite a few of these stories focus on the strengths and weaknesses of black electoral politics, and its relationship to racial uplift.[14] Consistent with his emphasis on racial uplift in his essays, these stories further illustrate the extent of Dunbar's interest in the black political issues and debates of his era.[15] At the turn of the twentieth century, novels were just as convenient as the short story for black writers to explore the meaning of racial uplift. Despite their length and complexity, most of these novels have one thing in common: a brief yet informative scene in which the characters debate over racial uplift, progress, or politics. These scenes represent moments when political didacticism, the kind found in speeches and essays, and literary exigencies, such as moving the story along, collide. Sometimes these moments seem out of place, and the story slows down to a crawl. However, not only do these sections lubricate the turn of the plot in a certain direction, but, as in Dunbar's short stories, they also indicate the author's awareness of the political issues, debates, and actions stimulating both black and white communities in the real world.

Two 1899 novels, Sutton Griggs's *Imperium in Imperio: A Study of the Negro Race Problem* and Frances E. W. Harper's *Iola Leroy: Or, Shadows Uplifted*, stand out for their depiction of black elites in racial uplift activism. Historically, this class of individuals "made uplift the basis for a racialized elite identity claiming Negro improvement through class stratification as race progress, which entailed an attenuated conception of bourgeois qualifications for rights and citizenship."[16] Racial uplift discourse, as articulated by the special, compartmentalized scenes in Griggs's and Harper's novels, appears in political speeches delivered before an intellectual audience, or in political debate between intellectuals.

In particular, the portrayals of the Imperium speeches recall the equally poignant reprint in *Up from Slavery* of Washington's 1895 address at the Cotton States and International Exposition address in Atlanta, Georgia. At this event, Washington's speech succeeded in amazing both white philanthropists and black leaders (who, though, were consistently more skeptical than whites) with his oratory. *Up from Slavery* succeeds in capturing this appeal and broadening its base of political support by transcribing the eloquent speech in the elegant prose of his autobiography. Indeed, some readers admitted to crying while reading *Up from Slavery*, while others claimed that it was as powerful as the Holy Bible.[17]

When juxtaposed, *Imperium in Imperio* and *Up from Slavery*, we can see, similarly climax when racial uplift discourse is most clearly and directly expressed through the trope of speech. *Imperium in Imperio* focuses on an underground network of racial uplift ideologues, led by the president of the Imperium, Bernard Belgrade, against whom Belton Piedmont, his adviser, competes for the Imperium's leadership. Both men deliver speeches that illustrate two philosophical extremes: political militancy and conservative assimilationism. By investing the written word with an oratorical quality, Griggs's novel captures "the aesthetic dilemmas of his predecessors in their attempts to sound an authentic voice through the strategies of nineteenth-century popular fiction."[18] In the 1890s, they typify the tendency of African American fiction to incorporate the special scenes of historical realism, rhetorical devices, and political debate in order to facilitate its program of racial uplift.

In the early twentieth century, these special scenes continued to be a staple in African American fiction. In her novel, *Contending Forces*, about the relationship between racial genealogy and the inheritance of wealth, Pauline Hopkins deploys scenes of reading and political societies to punctuate certain political themes and views. For example, the sewing-circle, depicted in Chapter Eight, seeks to contradict an idea presented by Arthur Lewis, the principal of a black industrial institution in Louisiana, that "women should be seen and not heard, where politics is under discussion."[19] In vogue among Boston's black middle-class, the sewing-circle indeed enabled influential black women to discuss politics. More broadly, the sewing-circle and the meeting of the American Colored League serve two roles in *Contending Forces*. First, they allow Hopkins to isolate the political discussions of racial uplift from the novel's narrative exigencies. Secondly, and almost paradoxically, Hopkins subtly interweaves the very plot of Sappho Clark's (or the heroine's) life in order to show that, on the one hand, white male predators of black women and, on the other hand, the rationale for the enslavement and the postbellum, continued oppression of blacks, both work to undermine black women's moral claims to virtue and their claims to social and political power.

In his 1901 novel, *The Marrow of Tradition*, Charles W. Chesnutt focuses on the political disempowerment of blacks from a different angle to reveal the strategy and harm of racism. To do so, he refers to actual history in order to discuss the politics and problems of racial uplift. Set in a Southern town called Wellington, the novel recreates the build-up to whites' massacre of blacks in Wilmington, North Carolina, in November 1898, which Chesnutt investigated in the aftermath, and which, due to the white media bias across the country, deserved, he felt, a more accurate, albeit literary, historiography.[20] For our purpose here, the story depicts the extent to which the socioeconomic and political visibility of racial uplift, personified by the black middle class, threatened white supremacy.

This specific storyline of *The Marrow of Tradition* enables Chesnutt to touch on a host of important issues and events that were also very real concerns in the New South during the build-up to the riots. They include the disagreements among whites in the Republican and Democratic parties on the nature and implications of black political growth; the vitriol and violence of white supremacists as they sought to intimidate white sympathizers with, and black leaders of, racial uplift; the Southern adoption of such discriminatory schemes as the "grandfather clause," which restricted suffrage to citizens, particularly whites, whose fathers and grandfathers could legally vote during the era of slavery; and the differences in racial-political activism between the middle-class and lower-, planter-class segments of white society. All of these were mechanisms by which whites coped with the extent that racial uplift, according to Bryan Wagner, "reconfigured the visual field of [Wellington] by initiating changes in local architecture, neighborhood demographics, and sidewalk etiquette." Such reconfiguration damaged "the epistemology of white supremacy," and hence, at the same time, underwrote "a crisis in white identity."[21] Racial uplift thus should be regarded as a field of power relations, that is, a field where black intellectuals defined their position in the race against other, if lesser, blacks; but also a field in which the intellectuals had to define and assert their claims to civilization in the face of whites' sense of entitlement, and their consistent resort to hostility and violence to secure their social privilege.

The adversarial role of whites was a theme in racial uplift fiction after its golden age in the 1890s. Indeed, during the Harlem Renaissance, black authors of novels about racial uplift tended to echo Du Bois's side of the debate with Alain Locke when they asserted that blacks interested in uplift face several pitfalls in trying to meet the expectations of whites. What is more, these novelists took this argument one step further by focusing on the role of such black conformity in the problems afflicting the practice of racial uplift. Through this line of reasoning, black authors questioned not so much the theoretical and political value of racial uplift as the potential failures and hypocrisies in how some blacks and whites practiced it.

Certain novels published before the Harlem Renaissance cast a critical eye toward racial uplift, but in a special way – through the theme of passing. As Werner Sollors explains, passing in general refers to a host of ways that one or more people cross "any line that divides social groups," but it usually pertains, in the nineteenth and the first half of the twentieth century, to blacks racially passing for whites in "modern social systems in which, as a primary condition, social and geographic mobility prevailed, especially in environments such as cities or crowds that provided anonymity to individuals, permitting them to resort to imaginative role-playing in their self-representation."[22] Blacks who intended to pass for white – that is, those who could manipulate their appearance and behavior enough to do so – exploited the social performativity and ambiguity of racial identity to achieve two main things, as long as their original identities were not discovered: the social privileges and the material, economic benefits enjoyed by white society; and the protection from racist violence and discrimination that members of this society inflicted on blacks.[23]

Implicitly, racial passing critiqued the black solidarity of racial uplift. The long-term program of racial uplift, a program that worked gradually through the cultural and moral influence of whites and through the political process of social activism, public policy, and governmental intervention, could not match the attractive immediacy with which racial passing afforded blacks. It must be stated, though, that passing was also an ultimately more dangerous route toward individual freedom; indeed, it was a criminal offense incurring great punishment if discovered. But that was a risk countless of blacks were willing to take.

It was the barrage of racist treatment that compels the unnamed protagonist of James Weldon Johnson's novel, *The Autobiography of an Ex-Coloured Man*, to pass for white. First published anonymously in 1912 and then under Johnson's name in 1927, *The Autobiography of an Ex-Coloured Man* follows the precedent form of the racial uplift novel. It incorporates a climactic scene in which a debate between various parties was by turns "miscellaneous," "drifted toward politics," then, "as a natural sequence, turned upon the Negro question," particularly whether whites are truly superior to blacks.[24] In the wake of this conversation, while spending his first time in a Southern black community, the protagonist remarks that he has a greater appreciation for, because he tries to identify with, racial uplift literature.[25]

The genre of racial uplift literature coincides with the protagonist's optimistic view of his own life as a person publicly identified as black, and of African America, which continues to overcome the social, economic, and institutional inequities that hinder its collective advancement. Upon fathering the two children of his white wife, however, to whom he discloses his racial identity but who soon dies with his secret, he chooses to pass for a white man in order to spare them the stigma of being black. The protagonist appreciates race men, especially Booker T. Washington, "who are publicly fighting the cause of their race," "who are making history and a race." But his admittedly "small and selfish" act to maintain his status as a white man reflects a strong indictment of the limitations of racial uplift ideologues: "these men have the eternal principles of right on their side, and they will be victors even though they should go down in defeat."[26] Put more pessimistically, their theoretical victory in the ethical world could not guarantee a practical victory in the political world.

During the Harlem Renaissance, black intellectuals echoed, more generally, the sentiments of the narrator of *The Autobiography of an Ex-Coloured Man*, namely, that the success or failure of racial uplift is intimately tied to how black leaders, especially Washington, negotiated their relationship with white political leaders, patrons, and philanthropists. Indeed, the debate at the turn of the century over Washington's philosophy of racial uplift was for a long time afterward the subject of much partisanship within the black intellectual community. It turns out, however, that the storied philosophical distance separating Washington and Du Bois is misleading. Indeed, the substance of Washington's appeals, namely, the need for the political alliance of white patrons and black leaders, did not pose a problem for Du Bois.[27] However, the obsequious nature of Washington's pleas, as well as their monopolization of the philanthropic resources of white corporate capitalism, offended and frustrated Du Bois. What is more, Pauline Hopkins likewise experienced first-hand the political power of Washington when she was dismissed as he assumed control of the periodical she long edited, *Colored American Magazine*, and then directed it to address more white readers, a significant portion of whom did not aggressively support its politics of black solidarity. In this situation, Washington's commitment to the racial-supremacist sensibility of white patronage undermined progress of black culture and politics, as Hopkins saw it.[28]

Writers of the Harlem Renaissance, including Nella Larsen, recognized and critiqued this misstep in Washington's political philosophy. In her 1928 novel, *Quicksand*, we learn that the light-skinned black protagonist of African American and Danish ancestry, Helga Crane, begins a remarkable journey in her life: she leaves her teaching post at a southern institution similar to Alabama's Tuskegee Institute; she likewise abandons her well-to-do, black middle-class fiancé; and she proceeds to move from the South to Chicago, Harlem, Copenhagen, and then finally to Alabama as she struggles with the demands of work, love, marriage, and motherhood.

Quicksand is one of several Harlem Renaissance novels that expose the pitfalls of white involvement in racial uplift. These novels are consistent with studies that show that white patronage and philanthropy had maintained white supremacy, treated blacks in racist ways, and perpetuated the idea that blacks were inherently inferior and thus always in need of elevation or civilization. By definition, patronage signified the support of a cultural idea through the actual funding of individual artists, artistic groups, or cultural institutions, while philanthropy entailed a more long-term, humanitarian focus. In any case, however, a condescending relationship formed between patron and client, donor and recipient. And during the Harlem Renaissance, such power relationships were just as often sexual as they were racial.[29]

Jessie Fauset's 1924 novel, *There is Confusion*, for example, closes with a stinging indictment of this problematic aspect of white philanthropy. Written in response to T. S. Stribling's 1922 novel, *Birthright*, whose story of a light-skinned, mixed-race, Harvard-educated young man from "Niggertown," Tennessee, who ends up rejecting his race captures for Fauset the tendency of Anglo-American literature to misrepresent the Negro; *There is Confusion* seeks to portray, in relatively accurate terms, how Philadelphia's black middle class embraces racial heritage and kinship and how it struggles with the legacy and current realities of racism.[30] In Fauset's novel, we encounter respectable black characters who are self-made and upstanding, aspiring artists and professionals, and patriots in World War One. The novel concludes that even when familial connections justify whites' financial support, *vis-à-vis* racial uplifting, of their mixed-race progeny, this support can indirectly preserve the status quo of uneven power relations between whites and blacks.

In *The Walls of Jericho* (1928), Rudolph Fisher similarly exposes the problem of white patronage and philanthropy in the program of racial uplift. In a central section, entitled "Uplift," however, he satirizes the very scene of the Harlem Renaissance – the trope of the club, which appeared in several novels of the era – to illustrate the specific ways that whites, along with blacks, have become "professional uplifters," or experts in exploiting the program for their own advantage.[31] The novel also advances our understanding of racial uplift, particularly of what is at stake in the program's incorporation of white patronage and philanthropy. By the end of the novel, readers are presented with a profound image of what Phillip Brian Harper calls "a united and socially-solidified black community," a utopianism which "is arguably essential to the viability of any progressive political vision."[32] During the Harlem Renaissance, however, the symbolic failure of Marcus Garvey's and Hubert H. Harrison's organizations for a racial nation-state, with its own independent political and economic infrastructure, prophesied that such a vision would be nearly impossible to realize.

The year of 1929, when the American stock market crashed and the Great Depression began, underscored the political and economic improbability of racial uplift. Indeed, the country suffered unprecedented unemployment, economic weakness, consumer debt, and poverty. African Americans bore the brunt of this misery. No group of farmers was more impoverished than black farm tenants and wage laborers. No group of urban laborers was more unemployed or underpaid than black workers. The Great Depression exacerbated the racial discrimination African Americans had historically experienced in social, institutional, and governmental contexts. The New Deal (1933–8) sought to counteract the Great Depression by establishing various domestic programs, including the Public Works Administration and Works Progress Administration. Nevertheless, the congressional under-representation of African Americans, the racially biased legislation and distribution of funds and services for the poor, and the social intimidation of the African American poor further burdened the African American struggle for jobs and means of subsistence. Between 1920 and 1930, more than one million black people had migrated from the rural South, congesting the urban North and falling victim to the Great Depression.

Such socioeconomic problems affected African American culture. The Great Depression undercut the patronage of African American performances and the philanthropy of African American culture, effectively ending the commercialism of the Harlem Renaissance, which subsidized black cultural production with white patronage and philanthropy, but which also ended the performative culture of primitivism or exoticism that restricted the creative freedom of black artists. The imminent decline of this movement, however, did not cause a longstanding depression in African American political and cultural activities. In 1936, the National Negro Congress initiated a "Negro People's Front," according to Bill V. Mullen, which was "an auxiliary to the Popular Front meant to promote a synthesis of communism and black cultural and political work."[33] The larger Popular Front had already planted in American society a "cultural apparatus," consisting of "the organizations and *milieux* in which artistic, intellectual and scientific work goes on, and of the means by which such work is made available to circles, publics, and masses. In the cultural apparatus art, science, and learning, entertainment, malarkey and information are produced and distributed." Despite the threat of its populist integrationism to subsume specific issues of racial discrimination, prejudice, and oppression in the United States, this "cultural front," this "often unstable alliance of cultural figures with distinct alignments: modernist, émigré, or plebeian," enhanced *Wright's* literary imagination and productivity.[34]

Two *Daily Worker* articles in particular capture an approach to African American fiction that would be associated with Richard Wright. In "Negro Writers Launch Literary Quarterly" (1937), Wright urges African American writers "to render their race in social and realistic terms," with particular attention to "problems such as nationalism in literature, perspective, the relation of the Negro writer to politics and social movements."[35] And in another article, "New Negro Pamphlet Stresses Need for U.S. People's Front" (1937), Wright describes a "penny-pamphlet, 'The Road to Liberation for the Negro People,' . . . a short statement by 16 leading Negro Communists summarizing from a Marxist point of view the Negroes' position in the United States today."[36] Published four months before and one month after the inaugural release of *New Challenge*, respectively, these two articles symbolize the philosophical nexus of aesthetics and racial politics within which Wright, among other writers, conceived of avant-garde African American literature as a radical revision of the Harlem Renaissance.

The emergence of *New Challenge*, alongside other magazines such as Chicago's *Defender* and *Negro Story*, reflected the impact of radicalism on African American literary experimentations with racial realism, and therefore encouraged an analysis of how racial uplift has long implied social, cultural, and economic wedges between the intellectual and the folk, or what eventually, in the modern era, came to be called the masses.[37]

The chief editors of the magazine, Dorothy West and Marian Minus, were previously in charge of the monthly *Challenge*, which had run from March 1934 until April 1937 and had been a major forum for several writers of the Harlem Renaissance, including Langston Hughes, Zora Neale Hurston, and Countee Cullen. The spin-off, *New Challenge*, marketed the newer generation of African American writers. The title change, the cancellation of *Challenge*, the transfer of West's and Minus's editorial responsibilities to the new magazine, the addition of Wright as associate editor, the well-publicized mission of the new magazine – all of these factors combined to make the inaugural edition of *New Challenge* a remarkable event in African American literary history.

The mission of *New Challenge* asserted the aesthetic and racial-political salience of New Negro radicalism. In the first editorial of the magazine, West, speaking on behalf of Minus and Wright, states that "the realistic depiction of life . . . should not be *in vacuo* but placed within a definite social context." They also go on, implicitly, to distinguish the symbolism of the magazine from that of *The Survey Graphic Number* twelve years earlier, which helped to usher in the Harlem Renaissance:

> We are not attempting to re-stage the "revolt" and "renaissance" which grew unsteadily and upon false foundations ten years ago. A literary movement among Negroes . . . should . . . be built upon the writer's placing his material in the proper perspective with regard to the life of the Negro masses. For that reason we want to indicate, though examples in our pages, the great fertility of folk material as a source of creative material.[38]

Of all the essays included in the first issue of *New Challenge*, Wright's essay, "Blueprint for Negro Writing," best elaborates the magazine's mission. Part of this reputation resulted from the fact that Wright derived the thesis and logic of the essay mostly from his conversations with members of Chicago's South Side Writers' Group, which he organized in 1936. The members included Marian Minus, Arna Bontemps, Margaret Walker, Frank Marshall Davis, Edward Bland, Russell Marshall, Robert Davis, and Theodore Ward, all of whom associated further with Fern Gayden, Dorothy Sutton, Julius Weil, and Fenton Johnson. These writers constituted the avant-garde of African American literature and members of the Chicago Renaissance.[39]

During the Second World War, however, no African American novelist could parallel Wright in stature and influence. *Uncle Tom's Children* in 1938, *Native Son* in 1940, and *Black Boy* in 1945 had deepened his foothold in the American cultural marketplace. Several literary awards, wide critical acclaim, and extraordinary sales legitimated him as one of the greatest novelists in the United States.

Several African American writers openly acknowledged and embraced Wright's importance to their own work and to the tradition as a whole. In the early part of his career Ellison regarded Wright a literary advisor and hailed *Native Son* as American literature of the first order and the starkest contrast from the African American fiction of both the 1920s and the 1930s. Baldwin owned a similar early relationship with Wright.[40] Himes, too, appreciated Wright for creating opportunities for African American writers in the literary marketplace and for opening lines of access between African American writers and the masses.[41] In his reviews of *Uncle Tom's Children* and *Native Son*, Locke also recognized the potential of Wright's "stark contemporary realism" in these very terms.[42]

However, several black writers faced the daunting critical, commercial, and canonical consequences of Wright's popularity. Complaints that Wright's school pigeonholed African American literary expression coincided with the prevailing insistence that the formal or thematic similarities between literary texts "seem to be stronger than race" for black writers. In reaction to Wright's celebrity, a critical camp formed with the hope of performing the kind of racial desegregation of American literature that Wright and his school allegedly hindered. Instead of appreciating Wrightean African American fiction, which reflected such radical doctrines as proletarianism, Marxism, and communism, some black writers saw it as a professional handicap.

A corollary of this consideration was the belief that the racial desegregation of American literature required the avoidance of the dominant genre of African American fiction at the time: racial realism. Racial realism comprises black protagonists alongside certain historical themes, cultural geographies, political discourses, or perspectives defined by race. To some critics, this approach bespoke the immaturity of black authors who could not think beyond the so-called Negro Problem. Purportedly characterized by propaganda and didacticism, and informed by racial hypersensitivity, it spawned, some argued, the shortsighted and dangerous expectation among American readers that black authors could not help but write about race and racism.[43] In the postwar 1940s, Ann Petry's *Country Place* (1947), Zora Neale Hurston's *Seraph on the Suwanee* (1947), Willard Motley's *Knock on Any Door* (1947), and Yerby's *The Foxes of Harrow* (1946), *The Vixens* (1947), *The Golden Hawk* (1948), and *Pride's Castle* (1949) demonstrated that the avoidance of racial realism in African American fiction could make an author's own racial identity incidental. This idea proved favorable to black aspirations toward the nationality and popularity that overcame racial stigma, and thus became a reincarnation, though on the literary-professional level, of the racial uplift program.

Not all black writers were willing to avoid racial realism, however. In a 1961 interview published in *December*, Ralph Ellison was asked what seemed to be a straightforward question about the early part of his literary career: "Did you think you might write stories in which Negroes did not appear?" Ellison's elaborately autobiographical and theoretical answer reveals that the question actually was not so straightforward:

> No, there was never a time when I thought of writing fiction in which only Negroes appeared, or in which only whites appeared. And yet from the very beginning I wanted to write about American Negro experience and I suspected that what was important, what made the difference, lay in the perspective from which it was viewed . . . Unfortunately, many Negroes have been trying to define their own predicament in exclusively sociological terms, a situation I consider quite short-sighted.[44]

Ellison participates in a wider postwar critique of Wright's fictive practice, evident in his reservations regarding the "overemphasis of the sociological approach." However, he refuses to follow in the footsteps of black writers who sought entirely to avoid racial realism. The benefits of writing directly on the "American Negro experience," according to Ellison, outweighed those of eliminating this experience in order to demonstrate one's Americannness. Rather, Ellison contends, the literature should prove its Americanness *through* depictions of the black experience.

Critic and novelist Lloyd L. Brown is even blunter than Ellison about the problems of avoiding racial realism. In "Which Way for the Negro Writer?", an essay serialized in the March and April 1951 issues of *Masses and Mainstream*, Brown argues that the abandonment of "racial material" for "universal perspectives" and "global points of view" only perpetuates the ideas and values of "the white ruling class," "American imperialism," and the "melting pot" paradigm by which "all so-called inferior cultures must be re-molded to conform to the Anglo-Saxon ideal." The black avoidance of racial realism and gravitation toward aesthetic universalism reflected, he felt, the self-destructive internalization of antiblack racism.[45] Brown's complaint that African American literature "has not been Negro enough – that is, it has not fully reflected the real life and character of the people" – anticipates the Black Arts Movement of the 1960s and 1970s, with its call for black authors to remain dedicated to racial realism for the sake of black cultural nationalism and political action.[46]

Nonetheless, if Wright was the first great Negro novelist, then another group had succeeded in coming of age by, in a sense, emancipating themselves from Wright's school. Indeed, it was said that the American cultural nationalist "coming of age" of the Negro novelist predetermined the coming of age of the American novelist. Albert Halper said in 1929 that "editors and other folk seem to believe that out of the negro will come the great American Novel, the epic poem of America."[47] In the two subsequent decades, the prime candidates for this mantle of greatness were, by most accounts, Wright's *Native Son* (1940) and Ralph Ellison's *Invisible Man* (1952).

The postwar circumstances of racial integration in the United States, for example, stimulated what Houston Baker Jr. has called the "integrationist poetics" of African American literature.[48] In 1941, after certain African American intellectual and political demands, president Franklin Roosevelt issued an executive order establishing the Fair Employment Practices Committee. The goal was to indict war manufacturers and other governmental industries for evidence of racial discrimination in hiring practices. Seven years later, new president Harry Truman signed a similar executive order barring racial segregation in the armed forces and civil service. In the intervening years, other federal and judicial policies enforced desegregation in interstate transportation, housing, and schools. Statutes prohibiting interracial marriage and endorsing white primaries and electoral poll taxes were also being overturned. Racial progress continued in other cultural arenas, such as major league baseball, in which Jackie Robinson became the first African American player in 1947.

The racial desegregation of American literature, whereby texts authored by African Americans and Anglo-Americans shared the national literary tradition, supposedly reflected the racial desegregation occurring in the living human world. Racial desegregation, of course, could not totally overcome the social, cultural, political, economic, and institutional entrenchment of anti-black racism in the United States. Nonetheless, the discourse and law of racial desegregation enforced at the federal and judicial levels rippled through society, institutions, and eventually African American culture.

Northern and liberal southern publishers and periodicals were becoming more progressive by featuring African American reporters, writers, and editors, in contrast to the state of the publishing industries in the late nineteenth century. These African American industries were reaching a coming of age as well. Writing in 1950, for example, Era Bell Thompson smiled on the great progress in publishing and journalism. Black and white abolitionists had worked side by side in the antebellum years, T. Thomas Fortune became assistant editor of the New York *Evening Sun* in the 1880s, Charles Chesnutt was publishing stories at the time in such periodicals as *Atlantic Monthly*, and in the early twentieth century William Stanley Braithwaite worked as a critic for the Boston *Evening Transcript*. "Today," Thompson exclaims, "it is quite common in the North for the larger white dailies to employ a Negro reporter and even some of the more liberal Southern papers are following suit . . . Negro journalism has at last come of age."[49]

Against this contextual backdrop, critics had come to appreciate certain African American authors ranging from former participants in the Harlem Renaissance to those in Wright's generation for producing literature that viewed race and racism as incidental in the world of human interaction. Critics described literary works such as Jean Toomer's *Cane* (1923), Langston Hughes's *Not Without Laughter* (1930), Countee Cullen's *One Way To Heaven* (1932), Hurston's *Jonah's Gourd Vine* (1934) and *Their Eyes Were Watching God* (1937), William Attaway's *Let Me Breathe Thunder* (1939), Adam Clayton Powells's *Picketing Hell* (1942), Lewis Caldwell's *The Policy King* (1945), George Henderson's *Jule* (1946), Alden Bland's *Behold a Cry* (1947), Ann Petry's *The Street* (1946), and Dorothy West's *Living Is Easy* (1948) as examples of African American aspiration toward the kinds of acculturation and socioeconomic mobility that appealed to American society as a whole.[50]

The critical insistence on defining Negro writers as American writers and Negro writing as American literature characterized *The Negro Caravan* (1941), an anthology edited by poet Sterling Brown and critics Arthur P. Davis and Ulysses Lee. Designed to supersede previous anthologies by being "more comprehensive in scope" and "a more accurate and revealing story of the Negro writer than has even been told before," *The Negro Caravan* spans over one thousand pages and includes selections of short stories, novels, poetry, folk literature, drama, speeches, pamphlets, letters, biography, and essays. The anthology resists the notion that African American literature historically clusters into aesthetic movements or a "unique cultural pattern" such as the kind typifying Wright's era. Rather, "Negro writers have adopted the literary traditions that seemed useful for their purposes," namely those developed by Anglo-European and Anglo-American writers. Thus the notion of "Negro literature" is at once inaccurate and ambiguous.[51]

Reorienting the African American literary tradition on a cultural–nationalist map, the editors of *The Negro Caravan* echo almost verbatim Countee Cullen's foreword to *Caroling Dusk: An Anthology of Verse by Negro Poets* (1927). African American writers, Cullen asserts, do not automatically think, feel, or write the same way by virtue of common racial ancestry. Inaccurately classifying African American authors and their literary works in terms of race rather than national culture, "Negro literature" has existed in an aesthetic and cultural "alcove" apart from American literature. The editors of *The Negro Caravan* likewise "consider Negro writers to be American writers, and literature by American Negroes to be a segment of American literature."[52]

Likeminded critics of the 1940s perceived racial identification in paratexts and racial realism in texts as the bane of African American existence. E. M. Forster's review of *Knock on Any Door* wondered aloud about the novel's author, Willard Motley: "Is it true that he is a Negro? How incredible, how very nice, for there is no inkling of it in his writing."[53] The novel's avoidance of racial realism made Motley's racial identity a bonus. On theoretical and practical levels, such literature rendered moot the necessity to racially desegregate American literature. By the 1950s, there was no longer a need to judge a book by its author's skin color.

Notes

1 Barbara McCaskill and Caroline Gebhard, Introduction, in *Post-Bellum, Pre-Harlem: African American Literature and Culture, 1877–1919*, ed. McCaskill and Gebhard (New York: New York University Press, 2006), 1–14; 1.

2 Scholars have long retold this story. For example, see Henry Louis Gates Jr., "The Trope of a New Negro and the Reconstruction of the Image of the Black," *Representations* 24 (Fall 1988); Wilson Jeremiah Moses, *The Golden Age of Black Nationalism, 1850–1925* (New York: Oxford University Press, 1988); George Hutchinson, *The Harlem Renaissance in Black and White* (Cambridge, MA.: Belknap Press of Harvard University Press, 1995); Jon Michael Spencer, *The New Negroes and Their Music: The Success of the Harlem Renaissance* (Knoxville: University of Tennessee Press, 1997); J. Martin Favor, *Authentic Blackness: The Folk in the New Negro Renaissance* (Durham, NC: Duke University Press, 1999); William J. Maxwell, *New Negro, Old Left: African-American Writing and Communism between the Wars* (New York, NY: Columbia University Press, 1999); Anne Elizabeth Carroll, *Word, Image, and the New Negro: Representation and Identity in the Harlem Renaissance* (Bloomington: Indiana University Press, 2005); Rebecca Carroll, ed., *Uncle Tom or New Negro: African Americans Reflect on Booker T. Washington and* Up

from Slavery *100 Years Later* (New York: Broadway Books/Harlem Moon, 2006); Marlon Ross, *Manning the Race: Reforming Black Men in the Jim Crow Era* (New York: New York University Press, 2004); Martha Jane Nadell, *Enter the New Negroes: Images of Race in American Culture* (Cambridge, MA: Harvard University Press, 2004); and Barbara Foley, *Spectres of 1919: Class and Nation in the Making of the New Negro* (Urbana: University of Illinois Press, 2003).

3 Barbara McCaskill and Caroline Gebhard rightly assert that "high aesthetic experimentation and political dynamism" of blacks bolstered "the vocal press and spiritual institutions they had organized during slavery," erected "new educational institutions," and forged "networks of political and social leadership to resist both the illegal and legal violence aimed at keeping them from full and equal participation in the nation's life" (Introduction, 2, in *Post-Bellum, Pre-Harlem*).

4 Kevin Gaines, *Uplifting the Race: Black Leadership, Politics, and Culture in the Twentieth Century* (Chapel Hill and London: The University of North Carolina Press, 1996), 3.

5 Sterling Brown, Arthur Paul Davis, and Ulysses Lee, eds., *The Negro Caravan* (New York: The Dryden Press, 1941), 6–7.

6 A few of the best critical and bibliographic scholarship addressing this issue include Abby Arthur Johnson and Ronald Maberry Johnson, *Propaganda and Aesthetics: The Literary Politics of Afro-American Magazines in the Twentieth Century* (Amherst: The University of Massachusetts Press, 1979); Carolyn Fowler, *Black Arts and Black Aesthetics: A Bibliography* (Georgia: First World, 1981); "Aesthetics" in Lynn Moody Igoe, *250 Years of Afro-American Art: An Annotated Bibliography* (New York and London: R. R. Bowker Company, 1981), 233–9.

7 Kenneth W. Warren, *So Black and Blue: Ralph Ellison and the Occasion of Criticism* (Chicago: University of Chicago Press, 2003), 33–4.

8 Sigrid Anderson Cordell, " 'The Case Was Very Black Against' Her: Pauline Hopkins and the Politics of Racial Ambiguity at the Colored American Magazine," *American Periodicals: A Journal of History, Criticism, and Bibliography* 16.1 (2006), 52–73; 56.

9 Amy L. Blair, "Misreading the House of Mirth," *American Literature: A Journal of Literary History, Criticism, and Bibliography* 76.1 (2004), 149–75; 150, 151.

10 For many black intellectuals, African American literature written in dialect, such as the writings of Paul Laurence Dunbar, bore the linguistic stigma of minstrelsy. For example, an article in *A. M. E. Church Review* 13 (October 1896) worried that, in the wake of William Howells's 1896 review of Dunbar's *Majors and Minors*, "titillated" editors "with the commercial side well developed will besiege [Dunbar] for a copy in a 'minor' [or allegedly black dialect] view" (H. T. Kealing, Review of *Majors and Minors*, *A.M.E. Church Review* 13 [October 1896], 256).

11 Pauline Hopkins quoted in Johnson and Johnson, *Propaganda and Aesthetics*, 7.

12 Hazel V. Carby, Introduction, in *The Magazine Novels of Pauline Hopkins*, ed. Carby (New York: Oxford University Press, 1988), xxix–xlx; xxxiv–v.

13 Dunbar's collected stories include *Folks from Dixie* (1898), *The Strength of Gideon and Other Stories* (1900), *In Old Plantation Days* (1903), and *The Heart of Happy Hollow* (1904). Dunbar also wrote stories that did not appear in these collections, that were published either in periodicals or went unpublished. See Gene Andrew Jarrett and Thomas Lewis Morgan, Introduction, in *The Complete Stories of Paul Laurence Dunbar*, ed. Jarrett and Morgan (Athens: Ohio University Press, 2005), xv–xlv.

14 In total, Dunbar's political short stories include "The Trial Sermons on Bull-Skin," "Aunt Mandy's Investment," and "At Shaft 11" in *Folks from Dixie*; "The Ingrate," "One Man's Fortunes," "Mr. Cornelius Johnson, Office-Seeker," "A Mess of Pottage," "The Finding of Zach," and "A Council of State" in *The Strength of Gideon and Other Stories*; "A Judgment of Paris" in *In Old Plantation Days*; and "The Scapegoat," "One Christmas at Shiloh," "The Mission of Mr. Scatters," and "Cahoots" in *The Heart of Happy Hollow*.

15 See Dunbar's essays, "England as seen by a Black Man," *The Independent* 48 (16 September 1897); "Recession Never," *Toledo, Ohio, Journal* (18 December 1898); "The Negroes of the Tenderloin," *Columbus Dispatch [Ohio]* (19 December 1898).

16 Gaines, *Uplifting the Race*, xv.

17 Louis Harlan, Introduction, *Up from Slavery*, by Booker T. Washington (New York: Penguin, 1986), vii–xlviii; xx, xli. Noteworthy is that the biblical qualities conveyed in Washington's prose justifies its link, at least on this rhetorical ground, with Du Bois's *The Souls of Black Folk*.

18 *The Oxford Companion to African American Literature*, ed. William L. Andrews, Frances Smith Foster, and Trudier Harris (New York and Oxford: Oxford University Press, 1997), 328.

19 Pauline E. Hopkins, *Contending Forces; a Romance Illustrative of Negro Life North and South* (New York: AMS Press, 1971), 126.

20 For more information about Chesnutt's travel to the Wilmington site and his response, see Bryan Wagner, "Charles Chesnutt and the Epistemology of Racial Violence," in *American Literature: A Journal of Literary History, Criticism, and Bibliography* (2001), 311–37; and Jae H. Roe, "Keeping an 'Old Wound' Alive: *The Marrow of Tradition* and the Legacy of Wilmington," *African American Review* 33.2 (1999), 231–43.

21 Wagner, "Charles Chesnutt and the Epistemology of Racial Violence," 213.

22 Werner Sollors, *Neither Black nor White Yet Both: Thematic Explorations of Interracial Literature* (New York: Oxford University Press, 1997), 247–8.

23 On the other hand, as Werner Sollors and Julie Cary Nerad note, there have been occasions when blacks did not intend to pass; they inadvertently passed in situations where people had mistaken them for whites, or they involuntarily passed because, for example, they were too young

to understand the complex issue of racial identity. See Sollors, *Neither Black Nor White Yet Both*, 250. Also see Julie Cary Nerad, "Slippery Language and False Dilemmas: The Passing Novels of Child, Howells, and Harper," *American Literature* (December 2003) 75.4, 813–41.

24   James Weldon Johnson, *The Autobiography of an Ex-Coloured Man* (New York: Vintage Books, 1989), 158.

25   Ibid., *Autobiography*, 168.

26   Ibid., *Autobiography*, 211.

27   Reed, *W.E.B. Du Bois and American Political Thought*, 62–3.

28   For more information about Hopkins's dismissal from *Colored American Magazine*, see Cordell, " 'The Case Was Very Black Against' Her," 57–61.

29   For more information about the sexuality and power dynamics of patronage, see Chapter 5 of Ross, *Manning the Race*.

30   After reading Stribling's novel about Niggertown, Tennessee, Fauset lamented that "Nella Larsen and Walter White were affected just as I was. We could do it better." She went on to say that "here is an audience wanting to hear the truth about us. Let us who are better qualified to present that truth than any white writer, try to do so" (Fauset quoted in Thadious Davis, Foreword, in *There Is Confusion*, by Jessie Redmon Fauset [Boston: Northeastern University Press, 1989], v–xxvi; xxii).

31   Rudolph Fisher, *The Walls of Jericho* (Ann Arbor, MI.: University of Michigan Press, 1994), 73. Other Harlem Renaissance, African American novels that include such major club scenes are Claude McKay's *Home to Harlem* (1928) and Wallace Thurman's *The Blacker the* Berry (1929).

32   Phillip Brian Harper, "Passing for What? Racial Masquerade and the Demands of Upward Mobility," *Callaloo: A Journal of African-American and African Arts and Letters* 21.2 (1998), 381–97; 395.

33   Bill V. Mullen, *Popular Fronts: Chicago and African-American Cultural Politics, 1935–46* (Urbana and Chicago: University of Illinois Press, 1999), 4.

34   Michael Denning, *The Cultural Front: The Laboring of American Culture in the Twentieth-Century* (London, New York: Verso, 1996), 38, 62.

35   Richard Wright, "Negro Writers Launch Literary Quarterly," *Daily Worker* (8 June 1937), 7.

36   Richard Wright, "New Negro Pamphlet Stresses Need for U.S. People's Front," *Daily Worker* (25 October 1937), 3.

37   For more information about the importance of the radicalism and African American literature of *Defender* and *Negro Story* to the cultural front, see Mullen, *Popular Fronts*, 44–74, 106–25.

38   Dorothy West, "Dear Reader," *Challenge* (March 1934), 3.

39   According to one of the members of this group, Margaret Walker, in her biography of Wright:

> At least five or six members of the South Side Writers' Group contributed to "Blueprint for Negro Writing": Wright and myself, and possibly Ted Ward,

> Ed Bland, Russell Marshall, and Frank Marshall Davis. What Wright did was take ideas and suggestions from four or five drafts by others and rewrite them in definite Marxist terms, incorporating strong black nationalist sentiments and some cogent expressions on techniques and the craft of writing. He published it as his own, and I remember my surprise on seeing the printed piece. (355–6 n.18)

Margaret Walker, *Richard Wright: Daemonic Genius* (New York: Amistad, 1988).

40 For information about Ellison's regard of Wright as a mentor, see Ralph Ellison, "That Same Pain, That Same Pleasure: An Interview," in *Shadow and Act* (New York: Vintage International, 1995), 15. Ellison discussed *Native Son* in "Recent Negro Fiction," *New Masses* 40 (5 August 1941): 22–6, and "Richard Wright and Recent Negro Fiction," *Directions* 4 (Summer 1941): 12–13. For Baldwin's description of his own relationship with Wright, see James Baldwin, "Alas, Poor Richard," in *Nobody Knows My Name* (New York: Vintage, 1993), 190.

41 Chester B. Himes, quoted in Michael Fabre and Robert E. Skinner, eds, *Conversations with Chester Himes* (Jackson, MS: University Press of Mississippi, 1995), 49–50.

42 Alain Locke, "Of Native Sons: Real and Otherwise," in *The Critical Temper of Alain Locke: A Selection of His Essays on Art and Culture*, ed. Jeffrey C. Stewart (New York: Garland Publishing, 1983), 299. For Locke's complete retrospective reviews and contexts of *Uncle Tom's Children* and *Native Son*, see Locke, "The Negro: 'New' or Newer" and "Of Native Sons."

43 See the special *Phylon* issue (Fourth Quarter, 1950) for the topics of sermonizing and propaganda in African American literature, the professional handicap of racial realism, the black writer's inability to think outside the Negro Problem, and the black writer's hypersensitivity and immaturity.

44 Ralph Ellison, "That Same Pain, That Same Pleasure: An Interview," In *Shadow and Act* (New York: Vintage International, 1995), 24–44; 16.

45 Lloyd L. Brown, "Which Way for the Negro Writer?" *Masses and Mainstream* 4.3 (March 1951), 60–1.

46 Lloyd L. Brown, "Which Way for the Negro Writer?: II," *Masses and Mainstream* 4.4 (April 1951), 54.

47 Albert Halper quoted in Charles Scruggs, *The Sage in Harlem: H. L. Mencken and the Black Writers of the 1920s* (Baltimore: Johns Hopkins University Press, 1984), 143.

48 Houston A. Baker, *Blues, Ideology, and Afro-American Literature: A Vernacular Theory* (Chicago: University of Chicago Press, 1984), 69.

49 Era Bell Thompson, "Negro Publications and the Writer," *Phylon* 11.4 (Fourth Quarter, 1950), 306.

50 See Lawrence P. Jackson, "The Birth of the Critic: The Literary Friendship of Ralph Ellison and Richard Wright." *American Literature* 72.2 (June

2000), 321–55; 342, for Hughes. Langston Hughes and Editors, "Some Practical Observations: A Colloquy," *Phylon* 11.4 (Fourth Quarter, 1950), 311, for Petry and West. Nick Aaron Ford, "A Blurprint for Negro Authors." Phylon 11.4 (Fourth Quarter, 1950), 374–7; 376, for Cullen and Hurston. Alain Locke, "Self-Criticism," Phylon 11.4 (Fourth Quarter, 1950), 391–2; 392, for Toomer. Also see Hugh Morris Gloster, *Negro Voices in American Fiction* (Chapel Hill: University of North Carolina Press, 1948), 250, for Attaway. Carl Milton Charles, *The Negro Novelist* (Plainview; NY: Books for Libraries Press, 1953), 115, for West, Caldwell, Henderson, Powells, and Bland.

51 Brown et al., Introduction, *The Negro Caravan*, v, 15, 144.
52 Ibid., 7.
53 E. M. Forster, "[Review of Willard Motley's *Knock on Any Door*]," *The New York Times Book Review* (19 June 1949), 35.

Chapter 11

The Modernism of Southern Literature

Florence Dore

About two-thirds of the way through Faulkner's 1936 masterpiece *Absalom, Absalom!* Quentin Compson explains to his friend Shreve that Thomas Sutpen's dynastic "design" (196) originated at the moment a black butler sent him to the back door of a rich white plantation owner's house. Sutpen is a poor white boy, and he has come to the front door because he is unaware of his economic status. When the "innocent" Sutpen approaches the front door of the "big house" (185) with a message for the owner, a servant described as a "monkey nigger" tells him "never to come to that front door again but to go around to the back" (188). Faulkner scholar Carolyn Porter describes this as Sutpen's "crisis" (180), and indeed Quentin tells Shreve that being barred entry at the front door "dissolves" Sutpen and sends him back in time: "before the monkey nigger who came to the door had finished saying what he did, [Sutpen] seemed to kind of dissolve and a part of him turn and rush back through the two years they had lived there" (186). Faulkner portrays Sutpen's move back in time, significantly, as repetitious, "like when you pass through a room fast and look at all the objects in it and you turn and go back through the room again and look at all the objects from the other side" (186). Sutpen's "crisis" both returns him to his proper place at the back door, then, and returns him "back through" time; it forces him to repeat earlier events with the new knowledge of his class inferiority. This is a key moment in *Absalom, Absalom!*: it reveals class as the motive for Sutpen's "design" and thus to some extent explains something basic about

Absalom, Absalom! generally. The narrator's use of the racial epithet in this scene therefore seems crucial, but for some reason it has received relatively little attention. The two most influential readings of Sutpen at the door focus on the issue of his sexual development. In John T. Irwin's foundational psychoanalytic reading, for example, he argues that when Sutpen is sent to the back door, he "rejects his father as model and adopts the plantation owner as surrogate father, as his model for what a man should be" (98). Revising Irwin, Porter aptly observes that in aligning Sutpen's experience of class inferiority to his sexual development, "Faulkner binds the dream of equality to the regime of patriarchy" (180). Why does the racist figure of the "monkey nigger" emerge at the moment Sutpen develops from boy to man, and from poor to potentially wealthy? What is the role of race in this twentieth-century Southern narrative of upward mobility, and what does repetition have to do with it?

Sutpen's crisis at the door is a defining scene in one of the foundational documents of Southern literature, but we find the same trope in one of the most important novels in the African American tradition as well, Richard Wright's *Native Son* (1940). At the beginning of Wright's novel Bigger Thomas finds himself in crisis, like Sutpen, at the front door of a rich white man's house, this time in Chicago. Standing outside, Bigger is "filled" with "fear and emptiness" (44) as he wonders, "Would they expect him to come in the front way or the back?" (44). Bigger's "emptiness" here echoes Sutpen's dissolution, and, as we will see in more detail below, *Native Son* produces a dissolving, repeating Bigger whose manhood, like Sutpen's, is linked to a narrative of class mobility that begins at a white man's front door. Although Bigger clearly resembles Sutpen, however, critics have preferred to think of *Absalom, Absalom!* as a great "Southern" novel and *Native Son* as a great "black" one; and studies of the two novels have therefore rarely overlapped. Both Faulkner and Wright were born in Mississippi, and Wright's novel was published just four years after *Absalom, Absalom!*, yet it is Sutpen's crisis, not Bigger's, that defines Southern literature. Why should this be? There are significant differences, of course, between Faulkner's portrayal of an identity crisis at the front door and Wright's. Supten is white, after all, and Bigger is black. And whereas a "monkey nigger" bars Sutpen at the white man's door, in Wright's novel "Bigger," a character whose name echoes the epithet given to the Faulknerian servant, is allowed passage through by a white woman. Still, given the similarities, it is a little curious that the relation between Bigger and Sutpen has received so little attention.

It turns out that Southern literature is a modern category, and this fact in large part explains the diverging critical paths of *Absalom, Absalom!* and *Native Son*. In a purely chronological sense, Southern literature is modern in that people did not begin to think of the literature that term now describes as forming a distinct field until the early decades of the twentieth century. In 1930, in particular, a group of Southern intellectuals who identified themselves as "the Agrarians" wrote an infamously racist tirade against modern industry called *I'll Take My Stand*, and the movement this book heralded inaugurated the field of Southern letters. But Southern literature is also modern philosophically, in the sense that it emerged as part of a broader resistance to modernity. In their influential accounts of modernism, Walter Benn Michaels and Marianna Torgovnick have each identified this resistance – Michaels in "nativism" and Torgovnick in "primitivism" – as defining the modernist aesthetic. Think of the famous line in T. S. Eliot's "The Waste Land," "These fragments I have shored against my ruins," where "fragments" constitute a protection against modernity's "ruins." Like Eliot's "fragments," Southern literature was part of a salvaging of American culture in the midst of what was perceived as its "ruin." The Agrarians argued that the South's defeat in the Civil War had relegated the region to what we might describe as the "back door" of American culture, and their task as they saw it was to bring the South back into prominence. As part of their defense of the South, the authors of *I'll Take My Stand* point to a destructive "progressive principle" in the modern moment: "the American progressive principle has developed into a pure industrialism without any check from a Southern minority" (22). Like the contemporaneous nativism, on one hand, and primitivism on the other, Agrarianism typifies an early-twentieth-century sense that the "progressive" forces of modernity – industry, urbanism – were destroying culture. What follows is an attempt to understand the relation between Southern literature's historical origin as modern and Southern literature written during the modernist era. In particular, I am going to suggest that the literature exposes the racist subtext of the history; the literature helps us to clarify, in particular, the relation between the Agrarian construal of a "Southern minority" and the newly liberated black American "minority."

In contrast to Southern letters, African American literature enjoyed a relatively positive relation to modernity. In a dissertation on Southern literature, Caren Lambert observes that critics have construed African American literature as "a primarily male, Northern, urban tradition," and she cites modernist literary movements – "the Harlem Renaissance, the naturalism of Richard Wright, and the nationalist Black Aesthetic of the 1960's" – as foundational in the creation of that influential "paradigm" (10). African American literature can be described as a "modern" creation as well, but as an urban field, it was an element in the "progressivism" that inspired Agrarian resistance. The anti-modern stance expressed by the Agrarians not only gave rise to the field of Southern literature, then, it was also explicitly hostile to the urban and "progressive" ideals that helped valorize African American litera-ture. In other words, as a black novel, *Native Son* was also a modern novel, and both of these features – its blackness and its modernity – disqualified it as Southern. In what follows, we will examine what this historical definition of Southern literature means for the two authors who can be said to have defined Southern literature from a literary point of view: William Faulkner and Flannery O'Connor. If the Agrarians gave the field its historical contours, Faulkner and O'Connor undeni-ably gave it its literary character, and close textual examination of some of the key fiction – Faulkner's *Absalom, Absalom!* and O'Connor's *Wise Blood* and "The Artificial Nigger" – turns up an intriguing tension between the historical, racist field to which the Agrarians gave rise and the aesthetic field generated by the fiction they canonized. Faulkner and O'Connor may be "Southern," but as we shall see, their fiction aligns them more closely with Wright than with the Agrarians.

In his *Inventing Southern Literature*, Michael Kreyling – current South-ern literature scholar at Vanderbilt University, home of the Agrarian movement – has demonstrated that most Southern literature antho-logies emerged after 1930, and he argues convincingly that the canon was thus in large part "invented" by the Agrarians. Because the editors of these anthologies placed more "value" on Southern culture produced in the twentieth century, Kreyling argues, the "Agrarian interpreta-tion of southern history and culture" came to define all of Southern literature, past and present, even "project[ing]" its "shaping influence into the past" (63). This Agrarian "interpretation" involved the view that modern race relations were, like modern industry, detrimental to American culture. In particular, the authors of *I'll Take My Stand* con-spicuously locate the origin of modern social upheaval at the end of slavery. In "Reconstructed but Unregenerate," the first essay of the book, John Crowe Ransom puts it this way:

> Then the North and the South fought, and the consequences were disastrous to both. The Northern temper was one of jubilation and expansiveness, and now it was no longer shackled by the weight of

the conservative Southern tradition. Industrialism, the latest form of pioneering and the worst, presently overtook the North, and in due time has now produced our present civilization. (15)

Ransom neglects to mention the end of slavery as one of these "consequences," but the implication of this glaring omission – along with the claim that the defeat of the South was "disastrous" – is clear: a return to the "conservative Southern tradition" would constitute a return to clearer racial stratification.

The most explicit comment on race in *I'll Take My Stand* comes from Robert Penn Warren in his essay, "The Briar Patch." Warren argues that the "small town and farm" is where the Southern black "chiefly belongs," because it is there he is "likely to find in agricultural and domestic pursuits the happiness that his good nature and easy ways incline him to as an ordinary function of his being" (260–1). He con-cludes with the biblical invocation of peace under the "vine and fig tree" at the end of days: "Let the Negro sit beneath his own vine and fig tree" (264). Intriguingly, Warren's valorization of nature in the South involved a temporal assertion: a movement back in time is a move-ment towards racial segregation at the end of time. Although its biblical origin refers to the end of time, that is, the place beneath the "vine and fig tree" would also return Americans to an earlier moment in which "trees" would be segregated so that the "Negro" would have "his own." The Agrarian nostalgia for a more "natural" moment was also nostalgia for a whiter moment, and Warren's essay thus contains the implication that the racial stratification of the pre-Civil War South is natural. In defending what they identify as a "Southern way of life" against "the American or prevailing way" (xix), then, the Agrarians were calling for a retreat from industry, but they were also calling for a flight from the racially ambiguous present in particular. This return to the past, moreover, was conceived as the preservation of a "minority" identity in the face of a mixed – and therefore black – majority. Southern literature came out of this "interpretation," to quote Kreyling, and so it makes sense that critics have taken Wright – as well as Zora Neale Hurston and Ralph Ellison, both also born in the South – as African American rather than as Southern authors. It is a rather strange, after all, to situate Wright in a field that originated as a negative response to the discourses that canonized him. But from another point of view, the scene we are considering in *Absalom, Absalom!* defines class crisis at a white man's front door as an archetypal Southern trope, and so it is also a bit odd not to consider Wright, a

Southern author who takes up this trope, in relation to the Southern tradition.

What does it mean to describe *Native Son* as an example of Southern literature? Does it suggest that the field dissolves, like Sutpen himself, just as it comes into prominence? Demonstrating the relevance of *Native Son* to Southern literature might seem at first to provide evidence for such a claim. The retroactive recognition that Bigger is a Sutpen figure surely denies the whiteness of the field, as does the acknowledgment that a black author fits into it. On this view, it would be the presence of black bodies – Bigger's and Wright's – that undoes the field, since this presence invalidates the racist "interpretation" that created Southern literature. We might be tempted to conclude from this that Southern literature is anachronistic and that we should study something else instead. Indeed, the current critical wave called "global South" studies exemplifies this logic. In broadening the field of Southern literature beyond its geographic borders, scholars of the "global South" mean to suggest that regional designations are not essential but rather arbitrary and open to redefinition. Lambert usefully contrasts this international approach to the study of America's South with what she calls "intra-national regionalism," the well-established concept of regional iden-tity from which the Agrarians took their notion of the South. Lambert points out that this theoretically deterministic version of regionalism "assumes that each region generates a culture that is true to place," and construes nature in a given region as "largely determin[ing]" its culture (3). A special issue of the journal *American Literature* – entitled *Global Contexts, Local Literatures: The New Southern Studies* (November 2006) – advances an international South in comparative essays about the US South in relation to Haitian, Latino, and "underprivileged global South" cultures. The volume thus eschews the deterministic idea of region by delineating a South not bound by the borders of the United States. The editors of *Global Contexts* indeed seek to redefine Southern literature by examining the South as what they call a "construction of border crossings." Studying Southern literature comparatively, they imply, recreates the region, clarifies that its identity is constructed rather than natural.

The textual analyses that comprise the remainder of this chapter are informed, similarly, by an idea of the region as constructed, and so this analysis of Southern literature follows the same theoretical trends that inspired "global South" studies. But rather than provide a global con-text for Southern authors, I am going to demonstrate that Faulkner and O'Connor have already accomplished the theoretical task of unmooring

Southern literature from a naturally defined, essential region by engaging in aesthetic practices. Whereas scholars of the "global South" de-essentialize the South by making Southern literature comparative, Faulkner and O'Connor do so in the creation of various metaphorical equations: in their work black becomes white; American becomes Canadian, Haitian, and Arab; and "Southern" comes to designate all of these "crossed" identities. Faulkner's use of the figure of the "monkey nigger" – and, as we shall see, O'Connor's postwar reconfiguration of it – exemplifies a dissolving impulse in Southern letters that collapses not only white identity, but regional and national identity as well. In their fiction, Faulkner and O'Connor create a dissolving field that produces precisely the sort of mixture the Agrarians saw as a troubling consequence of modern progress. Consequently, so these authors imply, for Southerners to engage in writing fiction is to undo one of the defining features of Southern identity. It makes sense, then, to argue that the presence of black or brown bodies is important to a redefinition of Southern literature. But Faulkner and O'Connor also raise theoretical questions about the reliability of bodies in the first place: Sutpen's, for example, hardly delineates race, region, or nation as clearly distinct – that is, in the way the Agrarians would hope. As we shall see, moreover, Wright's novel produces unreliable bodies as well, and so it is his aesthetic engagement in the question of black identity, as much as his identity as a black author, that contributes to the historical redefinition of Southern literature as a paradigmatically interracial field.

Returning to our query about the significance of the "monkey nigger" barring Sutpen's entry, we might now consider whether the figure refers not just to the butler, but to Sutpen himself. Whereas Irwin and Porter focus on Sutpen's crisis to examine how gender and class are formed, another dissertation on Southern literature, by Kimberley Magowan (1999), shows that the "monkey nigger" indicates that whiteness is established at the front door as well. Magowan observes that when Sutpen "dissolves," he dissolves into the black butler in particular, and hence, she reasons, his " 'design' of upward mobility" is "as much of an effort to escape blackness as to escape poverty" (15). Magowan's reading clarifies that the critical attention given to Sutpen's identification with the white planter has obscured his prior identification with the black butler, and in the novel, indeed, as Sutpen stands at the door, he melts into the butler:

> the nigger was just another balloon face slick and distended with that
> mellow loud and terrible laughing so that he did not dare to burst it,

looking down at him from within that half closed door during that instant in which, before he knew it, something in him had escaped and – he unable to close the eyes of it – was looking out from within that balloon face. (189)

Here, "something" in Sutpen "escapes" and "looks out" from the "balloon face," and, as Magowan aptly argues, Sutpen takes on the black Butler's point of view at this moment, then "discards it, to adopt instead the vision of the master" (14). This reading helps to clarify that for Faulkner, the social fluidity indicated by confusion about front doors signifies a racial proximity that threatens to "dissolve" whiteness itself, and in *Absalom, Absalom!* this proximity is expressed in an equation between black men and monkeys that ensnares white boys in its substitutive logic.

But why should this proximity be expressed in the figure of a monkey? In *The Signifying Monkey*, Henry Louis Gates famously recast the "racist image of the black as simianlike" as a "signifying monkey," a version of an originary trickster monkey in African myth that has the ability to proliferate meanings beyond its racist intentions (1988: 52). Gates reclaims the racist figure to argue that "signifying" is a black practice, but the easy association between Sutpen and Bigger suggests that it is as much a Southern as an African American literary trait. There are ambivalent figures strewn throughout Southern texts – black and white – that take up the terminology of racism only to turn it on its head. In Gates' terms, then, we might say that the dissolution Sutpen experiences in the presence of the monkey both leads to an inevitable collapse between Sutpen and black men and figures, precisely, the power of literature to "signify," to collapse white men into black ones. In early-twentieth-century America, moreover, the racist trope of the monkey took on a new layer of meaning in the highly visible 1925 Scopes Trial, popularly known as the "monkey trial." The figure of the monkey, yoked since the mid-1800s to the modern scientific discourse of Darwinian evolution, became a national obsession with the eruption of *State v. Scopes* in 1925. In her reading of the 1961 film *Inherit the Wind* – a remake of the play by the same name, which dramatizes the Scopes trial – Marjorie Garber notes the trial's extraordinary publicity, and observes that its dominance in American culture came from "the very intensity of media coverage, and, quite specifically, from the convergence of radio, movie camera, still photography, print reporting, and commercial advertising" (122). In teaching his students that man is descended from monkeys, John Scopes violated a Tennessee bill that declared it "unlawful for any teacher in the Universities, Normals, and other public schools of Tennessee, which are supported in whole or in part by the public school funds of the State, to teach any theory that denies the story of the Divine Creation of man as taught in the Bible, and to teach instead that man has descended from animals" (quoted in de Camp 2).

Following Gates, we might say that the monkey redefined in terms of evolution provided Faulkner with a new way to "signify" – to redefine the racist trope by inserting it into an aesthetic field that would unmoor it. There are versions of "the monkey nigger" in O'Connor, as well, and for both authors it enables the suggestion that sexual and class mobility are versions of the advancement of the species from "monkeys" to white men. The conflation, for example, of the black butler with a monkey in *Absalom, Absalom!* is infused with a Darwinian logic that both pushes blacks back in the evolutionary chain and makes of the butler a kind of phantom third father, effectively blackening Sutpen himself. The scene at the door in *Absalom, Absalom!* thus constellates three discourses of progressive ascent – sexual development, class mobility, and the evolution of the species – to construe white male identity as predicated on a prior blackness.

Faulkner depicts a racist modern America in revealing this dimension of the resistance to post-Civil-War economic mobility. In particular, in *Absalom, Absalom!* racism generates narratives that prefer repetition to progress, since progress implies mutability. Sutpen's return to the back door – a version of this repetition, his return through time – symbolizes his "return" to the origin of man. Sutpen's collapse backward into the "monkey nigger" at the door indicates that evolutionary ascent could just as easily lead the other way, and that embracing modern discourses of progress like Darwinian evolution means reverting to a moment in the development of the species when whiteness was not distinct from blackness. This logic clarifies the relation between Sutpen's white son, Henry, and Henry's spurned black half-brother Charles Bon. Before Henry knows who Bon is, Henry emulates him, and Mr Compson describes this emulation as an "aping." Bon is "the mentor," Mr Compson says, "whose clothing and walk and speech [Henry] had tried to ape along with his attitude toward women and his ideas of honor and pride too" (88). Henry is "the country boy born and bred . . . who aped his clothing and manner and . . . his very manner of living" (76). Henry's imitation of Bon is an "aping," and so it renders Henry a symbolic "ape"; he becomes an ape, that is, in imitating an ape, and he does this to imitate Bon. In the implied parallel, Henry imitates an ape and Bon, Bon is likened to an ape. Like the black butler, Bon's blackness equates him with monkeys, and this collapses him, too, back in time to the origin of man. But Bon is also a Sutpen, and indeed he is Henry's older half-brother. When Sutpen discovers that Bon is black, he literally repeats himself by starting his dynasty again, the second time with a white woman. This is an ironic gesture, however, since repetition is return. Return is, as we have seen, a return to a time before whiteness seemed distinct, and so the "ascent" from blackness is also descent into it.

The presence of half-siblings indicates repetitive time in *Absalom, Absalom!*, and repetition indicates the quest for white purity that begins with the recognition of a collapse into blackness. Although Henry "apes" Bon, then – repeats him – Henry already embodies Sutpen's repetition of Bon. Henry's "aping" is thus superfluous, and we might read his imitation, his enactment of Bon's "ape" status, as an obscuring of Henry's actual proximity to apes. If Henry must imitate Bon, in other words, then he is not already Bon, and so the imitation inserts a difference where there is not one. Towards the end of the novel, the association between Henry's collapse into blackness and Sutpen's is rendered explicit. Bon explains that when Sutpen sends him a message via Henry, Henry becomes a version of the "monkey nigger" who tells Sutpen to go to the back door: "But he didn't tell me. He just told you, sent me a message like you send a command by a nigger servant to a beggar or a tramp" (272). Henry's imitation of Bon thus resembles Sutpen's "imitation" of the white plantation owner: Sutpen disturbingly "dissolves" into a "monkey nigger" and then covers over that interracial merging in becoming the rich white man. Similarly, Henry's secret blood relation to his black half-brother disturbingly indicates a merging with Bon, and his imitation covers this over. With these collapses in mind, we should recall that the Agrarians actively claimed Faulkner as one of their own "minority" and yet ignored Wright, Faulkner's fellow Mississipian. In Warren's 1966 introduction to critical essays on Faulkner, he argued that Faulkner's regional identity allowed him to take his "locality as a vantage point from which to criticize modernity for its defective view" (2). Surely the "native" in Wright's title *Native Son* offers a wholly different idea of "nativism" than the movement that inspired Warren's idea of the South. But so does Faulkner: if Sutpen is the South's "native son," then the Agrarian claim on Faulkner is entirely ironic.

Repetition is a key feature of Faulkner's fiction and, as we shall see, of O'Connor's as well, but it is also a paradigmatically modernist tool. Recall, for example, the last line of F. Scott Fitzgerald's classic, *The Great Gatsby* (1925), which figures forward progress as repetition of the past: "So we beat on, boats against the current, borne back ceaselessly into the past" (180). The Southern authors' preoccupation with repetition clarifies that this feature of American modernism indicates racial anxiety. Like Sutpen, Gatsby finds himself at a front door, and Faulkner's novel thus glosses Gatsby's class aspirations as thwarted because of the possibility of racial collapse they imply. Towards the end Fitzgerald's novel, Tom Buchanan insults Gatsby by figuratively sending him, too, to Daisy's "back door." When Gatsby tells Tom that he and Daisy have been in love for years, Tom "explode[s]": "I'll be damned if I see how you got within a mile of her unless you brought the groceries to the back door" (131). Gatsby has been "within a mile" of Daisy; in fact, while he was in the army, he got inside Daisy's house through the front door. Gatsby's move through the front thus seems at first glance to contrast Sutpen's relegation to the back. But Tom's insult works to align Gatsby with Sutpen, since Gatsby is only allowed through Daisy's front door because of the "cloak of his uniform" (149). Gatsby's army uniform, that is, disguises his class, and Tom's revelation – he easily wins Daisy back from Gatsby by exposing Gatsby's inferior class status – suggests that Gatsby actually belongs, like Sutpen, at the back door. Gatsby's failure to win Daisy turns out to be a failure to move into her class, and so Tom's comment suggests that Gatsby's entry at the front should have been blocked just as Sutpen's was. At the moment Tom insults Gatsby, that is, it becomes clear that Gatsby has belonged at her back door with the groceries all along. Gatsby is thus "borne back" to the back door, and we can read Tom's insult as a version of the call to repetition with which the novel ends.

In *Our America: Nativism, Modernism, and Pluralism* (1995), arguably the most influential account of American modernism of the past twenty years, Michaels argues that Tom's "diatribe" in this scene "begins by attacking Gatsby and ends by predicting 'intermarriage between black and white'" (25). In Michaels's reading, Gatsby embodies the ethnic threat to American identity, and this threat makes him a little black: "For Tom as for [racial supremacist] Stoddard, Gatsby . . . isn't quite white, and Tom's identification with him as in some sense black suggests the power of the expanded notion of the alien" (25). Tom's racist prediction about the interracial future, which Michaels identifies as a key expression of nativism, bears a striking resemblance to Shreve's at the end of *Absalom, Absalom!* By the end of the novel, Shreve, Quentin's Canadian college roommate, has all but taken over as narrator of Quentin's quintessentially Southern story. In Shreve's version, the future holds a racial melding in which white identity will indeed be utterly dissolved:

> I think that in time the Jim Bonds are going to conquer the western hemisphere. Of course it won't quite be in our time and of course as they spread toward the poles they will bleach out again like the rabbits and the birds do, so they won't show up so sharp against the snow. But it will still be Jim Bond; and so in a few thousand years, I who regard you will have sprung from the loins of African kings. (302)

Shreve's prediction about the racially mixed future, which he delivers without any trace of the hysteria that characterizes Tom Buchanan's, clarifies the relation in *The Great Gatsby* between repetition and class mobility: *The Great Gatsby* repeats in order to eschew the possibility of racial mixture that Gatsby's mutability implies. In other words, Faulkner's novel clarifies that Gatsby's social mobility is a racial mobility, and that *The Great Gatsby's* progressive discourse of ascent, like *Absalom, Absalom!*'s, collapses into repetition in order to avoid the taint of mutability. On this view, we might say that in addition to revealing the racist logic in an American modernist classic like *The Great Gatsby*, Faulkner's novel also construes the Agrarian call for a return to "Southern ways" as a version of the repetition we find at the end of Fitzgerald's novel. *Absalom, Absalom!* thus uncovers what appears to be an unconscious thwarting impulse in the American modernist aesthetic – something we might identify as its Agrarian shadow.

Returning to our reading of repetition in *Absalom, Absalom!* with Gatsby in mind, we can see how Faulkner construes the Agrarian call for a return to "Southern ways" as a sort of shadow version of American progressivism. For Sutpen's dynasty to be white, he has to repeat himself rather than to advance in time, and this is the meaning of Henry's relation to Bon: Henry's whiteness indicates Sutpen's refusal not only of blackness, but of temporal continuation as well. Henry does not so much advance Sutpen's design as repeat his first attempt at creating it, and so in *Absalom, Absalom!* the impulse toward white purity is like the Agrarian call to retreat from progress. As we have seen, the reference to the "monkey nigger" suggests that Sutpen's class mobility is also an evolutionary mobility: a progression out of an origin figured as bestial (Magowan observes that that when Sutpen imagines being seen by the white plantation owner in this moment, he conjures an image of his own family as "cattle" [190] – or so Mr Compson surmises). Sutpen's collapse into the "monkey" suggests that his ascent is at the same time a descent, and that his social mobility implies a worrisome racial mutability. In addition to clarifying something about Gatsby, then, Sutpen's collapse backward in time to the origin of man also reveals the worry underlying Warren's assertion between race and time: hardly a retreat to segregation, the temporal move back to nature is actually a leap forward – a move into a present moment defined by science as racially undistinguished. Quentin explains that Sutpen goes to the front door in the first place because he is backward; he describes Sutpen, that is, as "innocent" – not "conscious" (185) of his class inferiority – and this "innocence" is aligned with Sutpen's backward country nature. But "innocence" of the difference between front and back doors surely also indicates the social disarray of a world in which class distinction has become invisible. In other words, Sutpen's "innocence" locates him in a world that resembles Gatsby's, a world of class mobility and social fluidity – the modern world, it seems, the world that Warren called "defective." Sutpen's backward innocence might thus be understood as a metaphorical inversion of his modern status, and his collapse backward into the ape can be understood as indicating that he has advanced into the modern world as redefined by Darwin, a world to which Shreve clearly nods in his prediction. Sutpen's repetition of Bon in Henry, similarly, puts Sutpen in a chaotic temporal moment in which the preservation of white purity removes him from a modern progressive world where difference is not clear. Sutpen's ultimate failure in the novel can thus be read as Faulkner's way of suggesting that modern progress cannot be evaded. Insofar as *Absalom, Absalom!* is the great Southern novel, then, Faulkner utterly unravels Agrarianism even as he advances its cause.

Flannery O'Connor's 1950's fiction produces a strikingly similar logic, but in her work, which emerged in the midst of a general national consensus that Jim Crow's days were numbered, the impulse toward white purity aborts rather than initiates narratives of development. In *Absalom, Absalom!*, Sutpen's collapse with the monkey energizes Sutpen, sends him forward, if repetitively, in his upwardly mobile narrative. In O'Connor's fiction, by contrast, there is nowhere to go but down, and this trajectory exposes the quest for white purity as a form of suicide. It seems relevant that the authors were writing at distinct moments in the history of Civil Rights. Like Faulkner, O'Connor portrays the white anxiety about collapsing into blackness to reveal something about the broader American impulse towards segregation, but by the time she was writing, segregation was becoming legally anachronistic. In her work, then, white purity is futile, and she represents the repetition her characters employ to achieve it as an expression of postwar pathology. In the short story "The Artificial Nigger," ([1962] 1971) for example, a young white boy, Nelson, becomes sexually aroused while staring at a black woman's breast. This scene of Nelson's arousal prompts his racist grandfather, Mr Head, to call Nelson a "chim-pan-zee" (263), and moments later the narrator repeats this racial slur but appends it to the old white man himself: in the repetition it is Mr Head who is "an old monkey" (264). As with Faulkner's portrayal of narrators who describe imitation as an "aping," O'Connor creates a narrator who invokes monkeys to signal a white anxiety about collapsing back into the racially mixed origin of man. Like Faulkner, O'Connor constructs this collapse into the past as a version of collapse in a racially mixed, socially fluid present; like Faulkner as well, O'Connor portrays repetition as the way out of the dangerously fluid present. In "The Artificial Nigger," this repetition becomes psychological damage, and the desire for whiteness is for O'Connor the object of biting satire.

In the story, Nelson looks exactly like his grandfather, Mr Head, and O'Connor's narrator presents this as repetition. In O'Connor, this repetition emerges as a neurotic way to reconfigure genetic pro-gression. As the narrator observes, Nelson's physical similarity to his grandfather alters their genealogical ordering, and hence seems to alter time: "They were grandfather and grandson but they looked enough alike to be brothers and brothers not too far apart in age" (251). Their identical status at points even reverses time, so that grandson becomes grandfather, and the grandfather appears as the youth: "Mr Head had a youthful expression by daylight, while the boy's look was ancient" (251). At a key moment in the story, the ironically named Mr Head expresses this temporal reversal when he denies his blood relation to Nelson. The two have come to Atlanta from their insular white town in the country, and on their trip Nelson accidentally knocks a white woman down in the street. When a crowd gathers, Mr Head claims, "This is not my boy . . . I never seen him before" (265). The crowd recoils, as we are told, from "a man who would deny his own image and likeness" (265). We might read the denial of Nelson's "likeness" as another version of his physical similarity to his grandfather. As we have seen, Nelson physically repeats his grandfather, and this repetition substitutes for a genealogical relation. Repetition replaces and thus denies "likeness," since "likeness" implies difference: Nelson and his grandfather have the same face, not two faces "like" each other. Repetition is meant to erase this difference, and Mr Head's denial of "likeness" might thus be read paradoxically, as another affirmation that he and Nelson are identical.

The erasure of difference between Nelson and his grandfather is motivated by a worry about what the narrator presents as the threat of a black majority in the city. In Atlanta, which Mr Head describes as "full of niggers" (252), Nelson and Mr Head find themselves in the minority, entirely surrounded by blackness: black "eyes in black faces were watching them from every direction" (260). Nelson becomes sexually aroused by one of these "black faces": "drinking in every detail" of a black woman who gives him directions, Nelson wants to "look down and down into her eyes while she [holds] him tighter and tighter" and to "feel her breath on his face" (262). The suggestion that Nelson might penetrate this woman raises the possibility that the surrounding blackness might penetrate Nelson and Mr Head by blackening their bloodline. Mr Head chastises his grandson here, and it is in expressing his prohibition against interracial sex that he likens Nelson to a monkey: "And standing there grinning like a chim-pan-zee while a nigger woman gives you direction" (263). As Porter and Irwin make clear, Faulkner portrays Sutpen's "crisis" at the moment of his sexual maturity; when he approaches the front door, he is "thirteen or fourteen, he didn't know which" (*Absalom, Absalom!*: 185). O'Connor's portrayal of Nelson's arousal locates him similarly on the brink of manhood, and like Sutpen, Nelson collapses into a monkey at the moment he becomes a man. Nelson's collapse, like Sutpen's, indicates a worry that descent is an aspect of sexual ascent, and as with Sutpen's narrative, Nelson's too exposes this as a worry about the end of whiteness. In O'Connor as in Faulkner, then, the discourse of sexual ascent overlaps past and future, and, like Sutpen, Nelson is collapsed into the past origin of man to cover over the fact of his presence in a modern – and in his case explicitly black – city. O'Connor portrays this narrative of manhood as thwarted by repetition as well: it is just after he calls Nelson a "chim-pan-zee" that we find Mr Head "hunched like an old monkey on a garbage can lid" (264). Mr Head becomes a monkey after accusing Nelson of being one, and we can read this repetition as covering over the worry that he already is one.

In *Absalom, Absalom!* it is Sutpen's dynasty that is threatened by Bon's black blood, but Shreve's comment at the end of the novel suggests that future racial intermingling will retroactively blacken all of humanity: "in a few thousand years," he tells Quentin, "I who regard you will have sprung from the loins of African kings." In "The Artificial Nigger," the avoidance of future racial intermingling – such as that which would result from Nelson's unchecked arousal – is portrayed as a futile way to avert an accomplished past fact. It turns out that Nelson was born in Atlanta, the place where he and his grandfather are surrounded by "black faces," because his now dead mother ran off to the city "and returned after an interval with Nelson" (251). Nelson's father, entirely absent from the story, exists in what the narrator describes here as an "interval" – a foreclosed moment during which Nelson's mother is absent from Mr Head's white house. The suggestion is that Nelson's father lives in a city where whites become aroused by blacks, and that Nelson is the result of just such a union. Nelson emerged from a break in the white genealogical line originating in his grandfather, that is, and the logic that makes Mr Head reflect his grandson might thus be seen as a futile attempt to deny this "interval" by imitating it. In other words, reflection indicates a temporal break rather than progression: their identical faces conflate Mr Head and Nelson temporally and thus avert a sequential relation that would arrange them along generational lines. The assertion of the temporal break between Mr Head and Nelson suggests that genealogy can be seen as a series of breaks, and that broken reflection replaces linear "likeness" in genealogical relations generally. This would keep Mr Head at a safe genetic distance from the "interval" that has led to Nelson's black blood. Mr Head's prohibition of Nelson's sexuality thus falsely casts racial mixture as a future problem, one that might still be prohibited if he can compel his grandson not to progress. But the narrator has already exposed Nelson's potential black origin, creating the distinct sense that it is too late. O'Connor produces a narrative perspective, then, that resembles Shreve's. Shreve, a Canadian who can nonetheless narrate a Southern story, might be thought of as Faulkner's way of creating an outside in the Southern story of repetition. O'Connor's narrator, similarly, exists inside and yet out of her narrative: her repetitive narrator casts doubt on its own characters' impulse to repeat.

Kreyling identifies Thomas Daniel Young et al.'s 1952 anthology, *The Literature of the South*, as one of the most influential of the Southern anthologies. Declaring the South's "hegemony" (vi) in American letters, the editors make this pronouncement in their Introduction: "The South's leadership during the last twenty-five years is now generally recognized, and it has become accepted usage to speak of the 'Southern literary renaissance'" (vi). One of O'Connor's stories – "Everything that Rises Must Converge" – appeared in *The Literature of the South*, and in the same year, she published her first novel *Wise Blood* (1952). The novel is devoted to lampooning the racial politics that, as we have seen, inspired the anthologizers to make these sorts of claims about Southern hegemony. *Wise Blood* centrally concerns the relation between a "dried yellow" (98) prehistoric man and two disturbed white men, Enoch Emory and Hazel Motes. When Enoch steals the prehistoric man from a museum to deliver it to Hazel, Enoch complains that in committing the crime he has "risked" his "skin": "He couldn't understand at all why he had let himself risk his skin for a dead, shriveled-up part-nigger dwarf" (176). Although the "risk" Enoch describes is literally the risk he takes in stealing the mummy, the suggestion throughout the novel is that the mummy itself might blacken both Enoch and Hazel. Like Nelson, Hazel Motes is a spurned grandson who physically repeats the grandfather who denies him. Hazel's grandfather, we are told, "had a particular disrespect for him because his own face was repeated almost exactly in the child's and seemed to mock him" (22). The prehistoric man's "shrunken" status is a version of this repetitious logic. Hazel first sees the prehistoric man on display in the museum at the center of the zoo:

> The two of them stood there, Enoch rigid and Hazel Motes bent slightly forward. There were three bowls and a row of blunt weapons and a man in the case. It was the man Enoch was looking at. He was about three feet long. He was naked and a dried yellow color and his eyes were drawn almost shut as if a giant block of steel were falling down on top of him. (98)

There is a "typewritten card at the man's foot" (98) that Enoch explains to Hazel: "It says he was once as tall as you or me. Some A-rabs did it to him in six months" (98). Nelson becomes older than his grandfather in reflecting his face, but in the case of the prehistoric man, repetition becomes division: rather than repeating himself in his grandson, that is, the prehistoric man simply becomes his own grandson. The prehistoric man does not begin as a child and develop into a larger adult, beginning "three feet tall" and becoming "as tall as you or me." Instead, this human has gone the other way: "as tall as you or me" to his current shrunken size. Like Hazel and Nelson, identical to their grandfathers only smaller, the prehistoric man is an identical but smaller version of himself. The prehistoric man's shrunken status is thus like Hazel's repetition of his grandfather: both redefine the filial blood relation as repetition, and so both reinforce the idea of a generational break that would preserve whiteness. In the logic that O'Connor sketches out, then, the "shrunken" yellow man indicates a panicked version of procreation: rather than creating new, different people – people in one's "likeness" – the characters in this world fantasize about shrinking themselves to eradicate difference entirely. The suggestion that "A-rabs" shrunk the "yellow" man, moreover, redoubles the threat that the shrinking guards against: Arab identity is conflated with blackness, and O'Connor thus suggests that what is at stake for a character like Enoch or Hazel in the preservation of whiteness is nothing less than national identity itself. We might thus read O'Connor's narrator as creating an idea that leads more easily to a global than to an Agrarian conception of the South. The xenophobic worry this narrator sketches out, that is, implies a knowledge of evolution that renders absurd the characters' desperate claims to racial, regional, and national distinction.

The "risk" this "yellow" man poses to white "skin," moreover, emerges in Enoch's equally absurd relation to monkeys. Towards the end of the novel, Enoch steals a gorilla suit, and to describe his elation, the narrator inhabits his deranged point of view to mock it: "No gorilla in existence, whether in the jungles of Africa or California, or in New York City in the finest apartment in the world, was happier at that moment than this one, whose god had finally rewarded it" (198). Enoch expresses a humorously literal version of the logic that collapses Nelson and Henry into apes: the "yellow" prehistoric man presents a "risk" to his "skin" in the sense that he indicates man's black, Arab origin, and this threat leads him to become the "part-nigger dwarf" he fears he already is. O'Connor represents this racism as ridiculous, and as an aspect of this, she presents him as competitive with the monkeys at the zoo: "'If I had a ass like that,' he said prudishly, 'I'd sit on it. I wouldn't be exposing it to all these people come to this park'" (94). Enoch's outrage at the monkeys' impropriety distances him from them, but in the process of distancing, he imagines he is one of them: "If I had a ass like that . . . I'd sit on it." This scene collapses Enoch into the monkeys in two ways: not only does Enoch imagine the monkey "ass" is his, but his need to distinguish himself from the monkeys calls attention to his likeness to them. Here is an allegorical – and hilarious – version of the logic we have been examining: like Sutpen and Mr Head, Enoch's worry that he is a monkey leads to an imitation of one, and this imitation is clearly a way to ward off the "risk" to his "skin" posed by the prehistoric man. That O'Connor surely means us to laugh at such a character suggests that, like Faulkner's, her fiction creates a space outside in the field that includes her as its own.

Wise Blood was published two years before the landmark desegregation case *Brown v. Board of Education*, and O'Connor's novel centrally

concerns the desire for racial segregation that *Brown* was installed to
end. In *Wise Blood*, indeed, keeping white and black spaces separate
is depicted as a ridiculous hope held by psychologically damaged
Southerners. When Hazel first arrives in the city, he feels the need
for a "private" space in the racially mixed crowd, and he seeks it in
the bathroom, which is guarded by a sign reading "MEN'S TOILET.
WHITE" (30). "Privacy" is thus associated with whiteness, and towards
the end of *Wise Blood*, it becomes clear that his car is similarly a pro-
tected white space. Like the room guarded by the sign, the narrator
describes Hazel's car as "private": it is "something that moved fast, in
privacy, to the place you wanted to be" (186). Before Hazel buys his car,
he crosses a city street against the light, and a policeman chastises him:
"Red is to stop, green is to go – men and women, white folks and
niggers, all go on the same light" (45). Outside the car, then, Hazel is
not distinguishable by his whiteness – "all go on the same light" – and
the guarantees promised by the bathroom sign evaporate. But from
the beginning, the "white" bathroom is in fact "colored": "The walls
of this room had once been a bright cheerful yellow but now they
were nearly green" (30). And although Hazel seeks "privacy" in the
bathroom, he finds instead bodily exposures: "drawing of the parts of
the body of both men and women" (30). In *Wise Blood*, the "MEN'S
TOILET. WHITE" sign is thus cast as a futile retroactive attempt to
prevent a racial intermingling that already exists.

O'Connor portrays Hazel's apartment as similarly failing to remain
white. When Enoch brings Hazel the prehistoric man, Sabbath Hawks,
the woman who has moved in with Hazel, immediately enacts the role
of mother, and she construes Hazel as the father and the mummy
as their baby in an interracial nuclear family. Rocking the "yellow"
prehistoric man in "her arm," Sabbath weirdly coos, "who's your
mamma and daddy?" (185). It is as if in becoming the prehistoric man's
parents, they simultaneously avert the suggestion of a "yellow" origin
and create the interracial future they thus seek to prevent. This same
collapse occurs towards the end of the novel when Hazel breaks the
prehistoric man against the wall and then throws him outside the door.
As he argues with Sabbath, Hazel begins to cough: ". . . he was stopped
by a cough. It was not much of a cough – it sounded like a little yell
for help at the bottom of a canyon – but the color and the expression
drained out of his face until it was as straight and blank as the rain
falling down behind him" (189).

As Hazel coughs, he whitens: "the color and the expression drained
out of his face," and this blanching appears at first to symbolize the

successful ejection of the black prehistoric man from the white space: as the "part-nigger" exits the room, that is, the color "drains" out of Hazel's face. But this draining process – this whitening – paradoxically blackens Hazel: "the color and the expression drained out of his face until it was a straight and blank as the rain falling down behind him." Like the prehistoric man, in the rain outside the white space, Hazel's "color" is gone. At the very moment his color "drains," however, Hazel's face becomes the rain, "straight and blank." Hazel thus becomes the outside into which he has just thrown the "part-nigger" baby in order to whiten his space, and, as the rain outside, he comes to contain the originary black figure. Just as construing the "yellow" man as a baby both removes him from his originary status and produces the mixed future this removal is meant to avert, throwing him out of the door paradoxically puts him inside the white space from which the throwing is meant to expel him. In *Wise Blood*, then, it is precisely the ejection of blackness that locates it "inside" whiteness. Similarly, in *Absalom, Absalom!* Sutpen's design will, he hopes, differentiate him from the black butler, and the racial epithet used to describe him is meant to serve this purpose. As we have seen, however, the "monkey nigger" fails as a barrier and in the end puts the rejected blackness inside Sutpen. Hazel's "blanching," moreover, is like Sutpen's identification with the white planter: both occur at precisely the point where white cannot be distinguished from black. Whereas for Sutpen the moment of collapse begins his narrative of ascent, for Hazel it precipitates death, and so Hazel rewrites Sutpen's identification, we might say, as a sickening. Hazel's blanching accompanies what turns out to be a lethal cough, after all, and O'Connor's novel ends with the point that the ideas behind the Agrarian retreat from "progressivism" have failed to prevent urban racial mixture. The quest for white purity, it seems, is a version of suicide.

The resistance to a mixed-race future – envisioned by Shreve on the one hand and Tom Buchanan on the other – seems a facet of the racist logic we have been examining, but it emerges again in Wright's antiracist novel, *Native Son*. In spite of *Native Son*'s reception as an urban, hence essentially modern text, that is, its narrator portrays Bigger Thomas as, like Sutpen, subject to dissolution and repetition at the brink of his manhood. Wright's portrayal of interracial futures surprisingly generates the repetitive narrative that we have identified as avoiding progression to avoid blackness. In particular, the narrator presents the possibility of a literal interracial future – one that for Shreve and Tom is largely imaginary – only to remove it. In *Native Son*, the young black man Bigger takes a job as a driver for the Daltons, a rich white family. His job requires Bigger to live with the Daltons, and on the first night of his stay he accidentally kills the daughter Mary. Bigger is about to have sex with Mary when her blind mother enters the room. To conceal his presence, Bigger puts a pillow over Mary's face so that her mother will not hear her drunken moans. Mary suffocates and dies. Bigger shoves Mary's body into the family furnace so that the evidence of his "crime" will burn away, and, in one of the more grue-some scenes in American modernism, Bigger cuts off Mary's head to fit her body entirely in. Like Sutpen, Bigger goes to a rich white man's house to better his economic circumstances, and like Sutpen, this occurs at the moment Bigger becomes a man: he goes to the Dalton house in order to support and thus become the man of his fatherless birth family. Almost immediately after he is allowed into the Dalton home, he finds himself drunk and in bed with the daughter of the house, Mary, and his sexual ascent comes close to what is portrayed as its culmination. But the sexual intercourse is significantly blocked: at the moment Bigger places his "fingers" on Mary's breasts (97), Mary's blind mother comes into the room, and her presence stops the encounter. We might read the moment Mrs Dalton comes into the room as a sym-bolic expulsion of Bigger from Mary's body, and thus as an ejection from the white man's house generally. Like Tom's insult, Mrs Dalton's entry into the room sends Bigger back, like Gatsby, to a metaphorical back door. Like Sutpen's, moreover, Bigger's expulsion is accompanied by collapse. Mary's body disappears out of the house through the chim-ney, and so it is Mary's body, not Bigger's, that is literally – and com-pletely – ejected. Bigger's metaphorical expulsion, then, is a version of Mary's. Later in the novel, as well, Bigger dreams that Mary's decap-itated head is his own: "It was his *own* head – his own head lying with black face and half-closed eyes and lips parted with white teeth show-ing and hair with blood" (189). We might say that Bigger and Mary become versions of each other instead of having sex, and that at his ascent to manhood, the narrator replaces the biological repro-duction of others with this more palatable dissolution into that other. Whereas Sutpen becomes black at this moment, Bigger becomes a white woman, and Wright's text thus clarifies that if modernist return is recu-perative, it is also quite clearly emasculating.

Bigger's collapse into a racial other, like Sutpen's, is portrayed as a move backward in time. Just as he merges with Mary, that is, Bigger also merges with her mother. When Mrs Dalton comes upon the sexual scene between Bigger and Mary, the narrator describes her as a "white blur . . . standing by the door, silent, ghostlike" (97). Later, Bigger hallucinates the "white blur" (102) as he lifts Mary's body to put it into the trunk, and he remembers Mrs Dalton as a "white blur" approaching him in Mary's room twice more in the novel (125, 494). Like Mrs. Dalton's "blurry," transparent body, Bigger's is "blurry" as well. When Mary and her white Communist boyfriend Jan take Bigger out for a drive, they stare at him, and the narrator describes this as excruciating for Bigger. As the narrator explains, Bigger feels he has "no physical existence," that he is "transparent" (76). They are both "blurs," then, both physically insubstantial, and thus they seem metaphorically aligned. Early on in the novel, as well, the narrator associates them in construing both as blind: "He had the feeling that talking to a blind person was like talking to someone whom he himself could scarcely see" (69). Here, we might say, is another collapse: rather than render vivid the racial intermingling that would locate Bigger in the modern, Gatsby-like world that has allowed him into Mary's bed, the narrator collapses Bigger into Mrs Dalton – into a past version of Mary. Like the "monkey-nigger" in *Absalom, Absalom!*, it seems, Mrs Dalton is a site of temporal collapse that indicates a racial prohibition in the present. Instead of having sex with Mary, Bigger becomes her mother, and this puts Bigger at a moment before Mary's birth, a moment of clearer racial stratification. Mary's death might thus be read as a racist fantasy, a sign that Bigger has been resituated in a world that has not advanced to the point where a man whose name rhymes with "nigger" might be given access to front doors. The name "Bigger" implies ascent, progress: being "bigger" should put him ahead. But Bigger's name also negates the ascent it implies in collapsing, precisely, into the epithet it repeats. We can thus read Wright's depiction of interracial sex as stuttering at the moment of its inception, and in *Native Son*, no less than in *Absalom, Absalom!* or *Wise Blood*, we can discern the racist Agrarian impulse shadowing modernist narratives of progress.

Is Southern literature racist? If all of these authors – even Wright – reproduce the repetitious logic that opposes progress, do they simply advance Agrarian racism? I have been suggesting that the fiction of Faulkner and O'Connor alters the category "Southern literature" specifically by challenging its racist origins. As I hope is now clear, *Native Son* recasts Southern literature as well, and not only because it was written by an African American author. Like Faulkner and O'Connor, even as Wright reproduces repetition in his narrative, he creates a critical outside perspective that undermines it. In O'Connor, the creation of an ironic narrator who presents her characters' repetition as pathological produces this inside-out perspective; in Faulkner, the portrayal of a narrator as geographic outsider accomplishes the same task. Like O'Connor's narrator, whose satirical tone indicates a distance from her repetitious characters, Wright's narrator also maintains a certain detachment, casting Bigger as an object of distant study. Such a narrator – the objective observer of scientific realities – is a classic feature of the naturalist novel, the genre with which critics most often associate Wright's work. In *Native Son*, this perspective is clearest in the moments where the narrator inhabits Bigger's limited consciousness and exposes it as limited: Mary tries to talk to Bigger, " 'I'm on your side,' " she says; Bigger thinks, "Now, what did *that* mean? She was on *his* side. What side was he on? Did she mean that she liked colored people?" (64). When the narrator explains that the "only thing" Bigger gleans from his conversation with Mary is a hope "that she would not make him lose his job" (65), he produces a perspective beyond that limitation – one which narrator and reader are meant to share – in which Bigger's response appears as a disturbing focus on immediate circumstances to the exclusion of his larger political interests. Wright thus produces a perspective beyond the racist repetition that Bigger enacts. O'Connor's satirizing narrator seems a version of the naturalist observer we find in Wright, and we might go so far as to describe both authors, distinct as they are, as similarly influenced by the scientific discourse of progress that their characters' repetitions oppose. In any case, in Faulkner, O'Connor, and Wright alike, the depiction of the critical view of repetition along with that repetition offers a fictional space outside of the racism that generated it.

All of the Southern modernists we have been examining to some degree thus reiterate Agrarian assumptions, but they also create the possibility for a repudiation of them, not just narratively but structurally and rhetorically as well. Returning to the Agrarian construal of a Southern "minority," we might now see with more precision the irony in the use of this term: the idea of a Southern "minority," that is, is a failed attempt to eject African Americans, even from the "space" of the word "minority." But to be the "Southern minority" is to be black, it seems, and as the authors we have been examining forcefully demonstrate, the sort of ejection enacted by the appropriation of the term "minority" – like the "blanching" Hazel's face, the epithet meant to preserve Sutpen's whiteness, or the substitution of Mary for Bigger – in the end only dissolves the racial clarity it was meant to preserve. Bringing Wright into the "space" of Southern literature, then, helps us to redefine it as an interracial field, one that distinguishes itself, precisely, by its tendency to explicate a modern resistance to racial heterogeneity.

Acknowledgments

I wish to thank Dorothy Hale, Kim Magowan, Deak Nabers, and Benj Widiss for their engaged, unbelievably smart readings of early drafts of this chapter.

References

DeCamp, Sprague 1968: *The Great Monkey Trial*. Garden City: Doubleday.

Faulkner, William [1936] 1990: *Absalom, Absalom!* New York: Vintage Books.

Fitzgerald, F. Scott [1925] 2004: *The Great Gatsby*. New York: Scribner.

Gates, Henry Louis 1988: *The Signifying Monkey: A Theory of Afro-American Literary Criticism*. New York: Oxford University Press.

Irwin, John T. 1975: *Doubling and Incest/Repetition and Revenge: A Speculative Reading of Faulkner*. Baltimore: Johns Hopkins University Press.

Kreyling, Michael 1998: *Inventing Southern Literature*. Jackson: University Press of Mississippi.

Lambert, Caren 2000: Haunting and Conjuring: Absence and Metamorphosis in Constructions of United States Southern Regional Identity, 1782–1941. PhD dissertation, University of California at Berkeley.

McKee, Kathryn and Annette Trefzer (eds.) 2006: *Global Contexts, Local Literatures: The New Southern Studies. American Literature* 78.4 (December).

Magowan, Kimberley Iris 2000: Strange Bedfellows: Incest and Miscegenation in Thomas Dixon, William Faulkner, Ralph Ellison, and John Sayles. PhD dissertation, University of California, Berkeley.

Michaels, Walter Benn 1995: *Our America: Nativism, Modernism, and Pluralism*. Durham: Duke University Press.

O'Connor, Flannery [1952] 1979: *Wise Blood*. New York: Farrar, Strauss, and Giroux.

O'Connor, Flannery [1962] 1971: The Artificial Nigger. *The Complete Stories*. New York: Farrar, 249–71.

Porter, Carolyn 1995: *Absalom, Absalom!*: (Un)Making the Father. *Cambridge Companion to Faulkner*. Ed. Philip M. Weinstein. Cambridge: Cambridge University Press, 168–96.

Twelve Southerners [1930] 1962: *I'll Take My Stand: The South and the Agrarian Tradition*. New York: Harper-Torchbook.

Torgovnick, Marianna 1990: *Gone Primitive: Savage Intellectuals, Modern Lives*. Chicago: University of Chicago Press.

Warren, Robert Penn 1966: Introduction: Faulkner: Past and Present. *Faulkner: A Collection of Critical Essays*. Ed. Robert Penn Warren. Englewood Cliffs: Prentice-Hall, 1–22.

Wright, Richard [1940] 1993: *Native Son*. New York: Harper Collins.

Young, Thomas Daniel, Floyd C. Watkins, and Richard Croom Beatty (eds.) 1952: *The Literature of the South*. Glenview: Scott, Foresman.

Chapter 12

Cosmopolis

Mary Esteve

Whether attracted to or disturbed by the emergence in the United States of big, modern cities, particularly New York and Chicago, twentieth-century fiction writers joined sociologists and other urban professionals in examining the empirical realities of – and thus shaping the discursive truths about – the American cosmopolis. The renowned Chicago School sociologist Louis Wirth observed in his classic 1938 essay, "Urbanism as a Way of Life," that urbanism no longer pertained merely to actual city dwellers, but informed all of modern society: "The city is not only increasingly the dwelling place and the workshop of modern man, but it is the initiating and controlling center of economic, political, and cultural life that has drawn the most remote communities of the world into its orbit and woven diverse areas, peoples, and activities into a cosmos" (60–1).

By "cosmos" Wirth has in mind the core–periphery structure of modern societies in general, brought about by historical patterns of imperialism, and giving rise to asymmetrical relations between dominant cultural centers and marginal outlying regions. But later in the essay he suggests that American culture is especially marked by cosmopolitan tendencies:

> Never before have such large masses of people of diverse traits as we find in our cities been thrown together into such close physical con-
> tact as in the great cities of America . . . [which] comprise a motley of
> peoples and cultures of highly differentiated modes of life [and] between

which there often is only the faintest communication, the greatest indifference, the broadest tolerance, occasionally bitter strife, but always the sharpest contrast. (Wirth [1938] 1964: 79)

Combining Georg Simmel's theory of urban mentality with social science's materialist positivism, what emerges from Wirth's sociological picture is an argument about urban modernity that comprises two distinct yet intimately intertwined strands of phenomena: on one hand, the city's concentrated powers give general shape to modernity's political, economic, and social spheres; on the other hand, the city itself is the site of heightened and potentially destabilizing heterogeneity. Generality and heterogeneity, Wirth implies, inhering as they do in both mental and material dimensions of city life, provide the heuristic skeleton, the conceptual framework, for understanding the American cosmopolis.

American writers of realist, naturalist, and modernist fiction of the first half of the twentieth century actively participated in the thickening of Wirth's description and argument. Not until 2003 did a major American writer, Don DeLillo, use the title *Cosmopolis*, but it could well have been affixed to many works of fiction appearing between 1900 and 1950, including Theodore Dreiser's *Sister Carrie* (1900), John Dos Passos's *Manhattan Transfer* (1925), Janet Flanner's *The Cubical City* (1926), Henry Roth's *Call It Sleep* (1934), F. Scott Fitzgerald's *The Great Gatsby* (1925), perhaps even Edith Wharton's *The House of Mirth* (1905), Abraham Cahan's *The Rise of David Levinsky* (1917), and Richard Wright's *Native Son* (1940).[1] DeLillo's novel of 209 pages might best be understood as a compressed, postmodern version of these much more voluminous predecessors. Indeed, due to the way DeLillo distills and crystallizes some of the most prominent concerns of these earlier writers, a brief look at his novel will help to identify the parameters they set for representing the sociopolitical and aesthetic dimensions of modernity's cosmopolitan condition, as well as to firm up important distinctions between their representational modes and postmodern alternatives.

Near the end of *Cosmopolis*, as the protagonist Eric Michael Packer experiences his own fatal demise, he asks himself, "How do we know the wall we're looking at is white? What is white?" (206). In isolation these questions seem purely epistemological and ontological; in the context of the narrative, they become historically and anthropologically loaded, related by way of dialectical contrast to the veritable galaxy of ethnic and racial markers surrounding the protagonist. The questions are posed at the end of his all-day vehicular crawl through Manhattan traffic in a notably white and fortressed stretch-limousine. Over the course of this day he has encountered ethnicized – more precisely, ethno-nationalized – particulars at every turn: Greek and Ethiopian restaurants, Czech weaponry, a Chinese currency analyst, Swedish tourists, an Israeli bank, a Spanish-speaking waiter, a Russian media conglomerate, South Asian taxi drivers, a Slavic economic theorist, a rapper who combines ancient Sufi music with lyrics in Punjabi, Urdu, and "black-swagger English" (133). The quantity and indeed shallowness of these identity markers point to the trawling nature of Eric's consciousness and to DeLillo's sense of the postmodern condition of New York. They function more like brand names or clothing labels – simultaneously distinctive and trivial – than indices of deeply experienced cultures or even geographically stabilized origins. They also secure Eric's self-definition and social status. Conspicuously WASP American, Eric considers himself a "world citizen with a New York pair of balls" (26). He is a billionaire assets manager with an insatiable heterosexual appetite and a shark tank in his penthouse. He leads an appropriately hyper-transactional life, having sexual, social, and business contact throughout the day with consorts of all ethno-racial hues and national stripes. DeLillo thus suggests none too subtly the predatory nature of a global finance-capitalist system whose coordinates are diverse and worldly, but whose axes of power and definition remain WASP American, fueled by WASP American institutions, and manipulated by WASP American desire. Such is the general structure of the cosmopolis, the "initiating and controlling center," to recall Wirth, but now transmogrified into a socio-economic monstrosity.

The novel makes the status of Eric's whiteness within a heterogeneous cosmopolis profoundly ambiguous. On the one hand, Eric drains the cosmopolis of its ethno-national colors by absorbing them into his own high-stakes financial scheme, namely, his all-or-nothing gamble with the Japanese yen, which he makes after abandoning old-fashioned stocks forecasting for an obsession with "techniques of charting that predicted the movements of money itself" (75). On the other hand, Eric navigates the cosmopolitan terrain by fortressing himself against its ethno-national particulars. When he encounters a violent anti-globalization protest by "people from forty countries" (93) he considers it mere spectacle, a "fantasy generated by the market" (90), which he watches on multiple screens inside his limo, while his chauffeur drives him through it. Earlier in the century writers often created a sense of empirical reality by referencing the modern city's mechanisms of display and spectacle – the plate glass of restaurants and department stores in *Sister Carrie*, the Statue of Liberty in *Call It Sleep*, the skyscraper in *Manhattan Transfer*, the rise of theatricality as a social phenomenon in *The House of Mirth*, and of theater districts like Broadway in *The Cubical City*. But in DeLillo's hands spectacle detaches itself from its empirical referent: Eric views the protest as mere "fantasy." This detachment reaches the extremity of specular self-abstraction when Eric manages to witness his own death as a disembodied simulacrum, thanks to an electron camera embedded in his wristwatch whose crystal doubly functions as a screen. Producing and consuming experience as simulacral spectacle, amid a swirl of ethno-national particles, Eric has effectively hollowed out himself and the cosmopolis even before the assassin strikes.

For the present discussion, what is more important than DeLillo's apocalyptic plot is his characterization of Eric as de-interiorized "world citizen." His performance both of WASP financial wizard and disembodied witness to his own execution makes him a parody of liberalism's cosmopolitan ideal. In her overview of the idea of cosmopolitanism Amanda Anderson explains that it "endorses reflective distance from one's cultural affiliations, a broad understanding of other cultures and customs, and a belief in universal humanity." In Greek and Roman antiquity such "detachment was defined against the restricted perspective and interests of the polis. In the Enlightenment it was defined against the constricting allegiances of religion, class, and the state" (267). Functioning then as a regulatory ideal, cosmopolitanism, I would add, was deeply bound up with Kantian liberalism's universal principles of equality, self respect, and liberty, thus with institutions of justice and socially contracted consent. For the past century it has been "defined against those parochialisms emanating from extreme allegiances to nation, race, and ethnos" (267). As a subjective disposition, then, or a characterological feature, cosmopolitan detachment becomes central to liberalism's claims about the viability and value of abstract universalism as a foundational ethical principle. It is thus antithetical to Eric Packer's highly idiosyncratic, personalized approach to financial gambling as well as to his self-witnessing a disembodied simulacrum. The cosmopolitan mode of detachment is more abstract than the former and less cosmic than the latter. Eric does not so much fail this ideal as mask its inoperative absence, its obliteration as a condition of possibility. That is, in *Cosmopolis* the self-respect that undergirds the cosmopolitan ideal gives way to narcissistic self-specularization. As a WASP American who either absorbs or blocks out the cosmopolis's heterogeneous particulars, who both holds the general market structure hostage to his own pet project and hyper-realistically renders himself a simulacral observer of a simulacral cosmopolis, Eric effectively negates self-reflective detachment by way of self-serving simulation.

More to the point, DeLillo performs this negation by way of meta-phorical substitution. That is, the author himself – not merely a deluded protagonist – flirts with cosmic supernaturalism as a truth claim to solve the narratological problem of what to him is postmodernity's unreality. For he creates a protagonist who, seemingly literally, has the capacity to anticipate events before they happen. Eric and a cohort watch on screen how Eric "recoiled in shock" before – rather than after – a bomb explodes (95). Further defying causal realism, DeLillo has Eric see the morgue vaults and the corpse's (his) identification tag on his wrist-watch screen before his death occurs. He has Eric think, "O shit I'm dead," while envisioning "liv[ing] outside the given limits, in a chip, on a disk, as data, in whirl, in radiant spin, a consciousness saved from void" (206). And yet DeLillo also has Eric wait for the assassin's bullet: "He is dead inside the crystal of his watch but still alive in original space, waiting for the shot to sound" (209). In DeLillo's hands, hyper-realism's central conceit – the screen and its image – no longer merely implies that the medium is the message; it now has the cosmic power to reverse causal sequence.

For American writers of urban fiction and other social profes-sionals in the first half of the twentieth century, postmodern hyper-realism was not discursively available (though Nathanael West's novel about Hollywood, *The Day of the Locust* [1939], arguably anticipates Guy Debord's and Baudrillard's theories of spectacle). Nor, it appears, was cosmic supernaturalism a satisfying solution to the problem of representing modernity's strangeness. In *Sister Carrie* Dreiser per-haps comes closest to DeLillo's supernaturalism when he describes Carrie as "the victim of the city's hypnotic influence, the subject of the mesmeric operations of super-intelligible forces," before launch-ing into a full-blown meditation on the cosmic conditions of the universe:

> We have heard of the strange power of Niagara, the contemplation of whose rushing flood leads to thoughts of dissolution. We have heard of the influence of the hypnotic ball, a scientific fact. Man is too intimate with the drag of unexplainable, invisible forces to doubt longer that the human mind is colored, moved, swept on by things which neither resound nor speak. The waters of the sea are not the only things which the moon sways. All that the individual imagines in contemplating a dazzling, alluring, or disturbing spectacle is created more by the spectacle than the mind observing it . . . We are, after all, more passive than active,

> more mirrors than engines, and the origin of human action has neither yet been measured nor calculated. (78)

Dreiser thus commits what by 1906 was known among sociologists as "the social forces error," that is, resorting to metaphysical, "extra-experiential" explanation for social behavior (Ross 1991:347). But what is notable about Dreiser's purple philosophizing is that the formal nature of his authorial intrusion renders the metacommentary narratologically inert. His "invisible forces" never quite intervene or create empirically inexplicable situations, leaving the novel's normative illusion of reality intact.

Similarly, though in a linguistic and more self-consciously modernist register, Dos Passos can be seen both to yearn for and dread the cosmic. In his self-described effort to "make the narrative stand up off the page," to achieve the "simultaneity" of visual cubists and montage artists (1988: 239), Dos Passos reaches for a cosmos in which language is detached from its referential function. Throughout *Manhattan Transfer* he brings attention to the materiality of language. His technique of eliminating space between words – for instance, he writes of the "dollarproud eyes" and "dollarbland smile" of a man's image advertising "nickelbright" razors at a "yellowpainted drugstore" (10–11) – suggests that speech itself is speedier in the twentieth-century city. Similarly, one character "feel[s]" another character's "words press against her body," suggesting that city speech is tactile (202). The main character, Jimmy Herf, also feels "pockmarked with print" and, though a journalist, he loses his "faith in words" (354, 366). At one point he seems to look at, rather than to read, the newspaper: "The print swam and spread like Japanese flowers. Then it was sharp again, orderly, running in a smooth black and white paste over his orderly black and white brain" (369).

Yet despite such hostility to normative modes of communication, Jimmy does clearly process the meaning of words. As he leaves the diner where he has been looking at the newspaper, he contemplates the article's content, its description of the arrest of two criminals: "He felt vaguely sorry that [they] had been arrested . . . He had looked forward to reading their exploits every day in the papers" (370). Indeed, Dos Passos ultimately demonstrates that however imbued with materiality, words and letters cannot be detached from their semiotic systems. This is vividly dramatized when Dos Passos describes the behavior of people in a sandwich shop: "Some turn their backs on the counter and eat looking out through the glass partition and the sign ʜᴄɴᴜʟ ᴇɴɪʟɴᴇᴇʀG at the jostling crowds" (314). The fact that in the text the *order* of the letters are reversed but the *letters* themselves are not flipped – which is how one would actually see stencilled letters on glass – emblematizes the difficulty of taking the meaning out of linguistic materiality, indeed of severing the link between sign and referent.

More generally, then, what might be called the cosmopolitan ordeal for writers of the first half of the twentieth century combined the recognition of actual urban phenomena with the imagination of viable modes of self-reflective detachment. As a discursive project it further entailed developing strategies of discernment which could disclose the means through which persons and institutions succeeded, like Eric Packer, in masking (wittingly or not) parochial allegiances. Or conversely, it entailed registering a persistent commitment to the ethical ideal of abstract principle and universal humanity in the face of the era's strong attraction to ideological naturalism, ethnic pluralism, and evolutionary or utilitarian ethics. While DeLillo's novel does not so much discern as enact a full-blown ideological naturalism in its negation of the cosmopolitan ideal, the work of fiction writers of the earlier era, however dim their view of actual urban conditions, generally offered more promising pictures of this ideal's functional presence. This is the case even with novelists who frame their narratives as exemplifications of urban modernity's dehumanizing tendencies or patterns – such as the expansive nature of desire in a market economy in *Sister Carrie*; the uses and abuses of self-fashioning in a culture of consumption in *The Great Gatsby* and *The House of Mirth*; and the methods and agonies of self-alienation in James's "The Jolly Corner" (1908) and *Manhattan Transfer*. As one may deduce from these texts, New York and Chicago most frequently provided the stage and vivid phenomena for testing out cosmopolitan formulations and commitments. By 1890 the latter had become second in size and economic clout only to the former, owing in large part to the development of its railroad system and concomitant industrial growth. Magnets for laborers, immigrants, journalists, sociologists, social climbers, and the industrial and cultural elite, New York and Chicago supplied the fiction writer with an abundant and varied cast of characters.

In everyday parlance, the term "cosmopolitan" was often a synonym for the modern person of culture and good taste, such as when Wirth in the same essay cited above (1938) notes that the "fact" of "heightened mobility" in the city "helps to account . . . for the sophistication and cosmopolitanism of the urbanite" (75). At the turn of the century Theodore Roosevelt denigrated this rootless and "flaccid habit of mind" as violating the standards of true Americanism (20). Cosmopolitanism could also connote sexual promiscuity and moral laxity, such as when Dreiser prophesies the alternate fates of the single girl who has left the country for the city: "Either she falls into saving hands and becomes better, or she rapidly assumes the cosmopolitan standard of virtue and becomes worse" (*Sister Carrie* 3–4). The elements of flexibility and openness that informed these connotations also informed the cosmopolitan intelligence that more self-consciously applied itself to urban aesthetic and anthropological projects.[2] They inform, for instance, Dreiser's account in *The Color of a Great City* (1923) of the ethnic variety of turn-of-the-century New York:

> From all parts of the world they are pouring into New York: Greeks from Athens and the realms of Sparta and Macedonia, living six, seven, eight, nine, ten, eleven, twelve, in one room . . . Jews from Russia, Poland, Hungary, the Balkans, crowding the East Side and the inlying sections of Brooklyn, and huddling together in thick, gummy streets, singing in street crowds around ballad-mongers of the woes of their native land, seeking with a kind of divine, poetic flare a modicum of that material comfort which their natures so greatly crave, which their previous condition for at least fifteen hundred years has scarcely warranted; Italians from Sicily and the warmer vales of the South, crowding into great sections of their own, all hungry for a taste of New York; Germans, Hungarians, French, Polish, Swedish, Armenians, all with sections of their own and all alive to the joys of the city, and how eager to live – great gold and scarlet streets throbbing with the thoughts of them! (7)

While Dreiser's recognition and obvious enjoyment of New York's ethnic populations reflect his attachment to this urban reality, his pluralistic embrace detaches him from any particular affiliation. And while his status as professional social observer means that Dreiser cannot help but exploit his material for his own financial gain, by providing details of the various ethnic groups' sensibility, conduct, and history, he implies that ethnic identity is no flimsy label. Rather, it comes attached to long-lived and historically shaped experiences that resist full absorption into his cosmopolitan picture. Further, here as throughout the collection of sketches, Dreiser delights in the spectacle of his material: he studies the city's "bums" for the "interesting and amazing spectacle they present" (39); he writes about the "spectacle" of a neighborhood fire that "the people are gazing [at] in terror and intense satisfaction," as well as the firemen themselves who in their heroic performance find it "exhilarating thus to be gazed at" (60–1); he describes how as a boy he "was forever arrested by the spectacle of [the] great freight trains, yellow, white, red, blue, [and] green" (68).

But for Dreiser spectacle is not exactly specular fantasy as it is for DeLillo; rather, it is an aesthetic quality generated by the actual details of everyday modernity and available for appreciation by observers such as Dreiser who are predisposed to find "beauty" in "variation" and "vital instability" (168). The obviously metaphorical allusion to throbbing "gold and scarlet streets" does not attempt to substitute a simulacral self for a reflective self; rather it reveals the reflective self on a flight of recognizably poetic fancy.

In a similar manner, but one less prone to poetic sentimentality, Chicago School sociologists such as Robert Park, Ernest Burgess, and W. I. Thomas, cultivated an engaged yet neutral perspective on their objects of investigation. They accomplished this primarily by developing a scientific–naturalist approach, often by envisioning the city as an ecological or physiological system. In his essay, "The Growth of the City," Burgess likens the process of zone "expansion" and "invasion" to the process of "*succession* . . . which has been studied in detail in plant ecology" (50), while later describing urban growth as "a resultant of organization and disorganization analogous to the anabolic and katabolic processes of metabolism in the body" (53). These naturalizing metaphors helped sociologists to sidestep morally charged debates about emerging urban phenomena – such as the rootlessness of hobos populating the fringes of business districts, the disruptiveness of juvenile delinquents and gangs, or the trend that Thomas, like Dreiser, was particularly engaged in studying of young, unmarried women moving from the country to the city. However, some contemporary critics have argued that early twentieth-century naturalist sociology tended also to diminish the role of human agency in determining humanity's destiny by downplaying historical change.[3] Such critiques suggest that efforts at scientific neutrality either implicated themselves in evolutionary, if not Darwinistic, ideology or compromised their positivist projects by interpreting general patterns of behavior as universal laws. Yet these critiques scant the role this mode of sociology could play both in developing the liberal ethos of tolerance and in bolstering a liberal vision of human agency. For not only was empirical knowledge power, but the detached disposition that was requisite to acquiring such knowledge held the potential of being keyed to abstract ethical principles of equality and justice.[4] As a discipline, then, twentieth-century sociology can be seen to contribute importantly to the development of a cosmopolitan consciousness.

A combination of observational neutrality and principled, liberal–progressive indignation is visible in the era's muckraking discourse, such as Lincoln Steffens's *The Shame of the Cities* (1903). As a journalist, Steffens aspired to documentary or naturalistic neutrality as he sought to expose the way municipal operatives betrayed, in their corrupt practices of boodle and graft, American principles of good government. Yet he also lambasted the citizenry for letting politicians "boss the party and turn our municipal democracies into autocracies and our republican nation into a plutocracy" (7–8). While literary critic Christopher Wilson has shown how Steffens came to view journalism itself, including his own, as complicit with the public failure to maintain purity of purpose, what nevertheless remains central to Steffens's project is an ethos guided by the cosmopolitan ideal. The key term for Steffens is *shame*, after all, not guilt. Where the latter connotes an irreversibly fallen and corrupted state, the former connotes the possibility of reform. This possibility, at least, animated Steffens's declared purpose for accusing St Louis citizens of "civic shamelessness"; he hoped to provoke them to reclaim their "pride," which "implied a faith that there was self-respect to be touched and shame to be moved" (12, 14). For Steffens, who studied ethics in Germany, the American city made palpable the promise, however sullied, "of our democratic institutions and our republican form of government, of our grand Constitution and our just laws" (7). In other words, within the cosmopolis's general structure remained the potential for its being not only "the initiating and controlling center" of modern life, but also a platform for practicing and legitimizing commitments to abstract ethical principles.

Even a novel as devoted to portraying the anti-democratic, predatory world of New York's leisure class as *The House of Mirth* allows ethical–liberal principles some circulation. More specifically, these principles inform Wharton's depiction of work in the way she contrasts Lily Bart's project of self-fashioning, which resembles a kind of artisanal labor, to the wage-earning girls' production of hats. Lily complains more than once that her income is not "regular" or "fixed," and that even her maid has the advantage of "receiv[ing] her wages more regularly" (32, 24). The problem with Lily's work as self- and society-enhancer is primarily its obsolescence; opportunities are few and her skills lack transferability. Trapped in high-society's Darwinistic logic, where she is only valuable when successful, the scene of her spectacular *tableau vivant* – which figures both her triumph and self-ruination – reveals a sort of glass ceiling limiting her advancement and spelling her doom. By contrast, the girls she briefly works with embody a less specialized and more interchangeable, indeed dispensable, mode of occupational practice. As the wage-earner came to replace the independent artisan, this new status as permanent employee need not, as historian Lawrence Glickman has shown, be experienced as demeaning wage-slavery: "In coming to accept the necessity of wages, then, workers also redefined wage earning to make it consistent with their vision of a just world . . . The linchpin of this transformation was the demand for a 'living wage,' usually defined as remuneration commensurate with a worker's needs as citizen, breadwinner, and consumer" (2–3).

In *The House of Mirth* Lily may well denigrate the millinery wage-earners as "sallow," "dull and colourless," as "an underworld of toilers" who parasitically "lived on [the] vanity and self-indulgence" of high-society, but Wharton as narrator remarks that they themselves do not show "any actual signs of want" and that they are "fairly well clothed and well paid" (219, 223). Miss Kilroy, for example, the girl who approaches Lily after Lily has been reprimanded by the forewoman Miss Haines for sewing on spangles crookedly, exhibits the wage-earner's sense of dignity and self-respect when, commiserating with Lily, she complains that "Miss Haines didn't act fair" (224). Knowing what fair treatment entails, and expecting it not only for herself but also her co-workers, Miss Kilroy exemplifies the consciousness of class unity that labor leaders envisioned, linking, as Glickman puts it, "all workers by virtue of their status as wage earners, rather than on the basis of craft or ethnicity" (5). Diminishing the power of guild or ethnic allegiances by imagining their identity more functionally, even non-worldly wage-earners could align themselves with the cosmopolitan ideal of detachment.

Social analysts and literary writers who explored urban phenomena did so in a cultural climate that was not entirely hospitable to the nation's urbanizing trends. By 1920 census data showed that urban Americans outnumbered rural Americans. Increasing industrialization was an obvious factor, as was the ongoing mass influx of immigrants. Legislation restricting immigration in 1917, 1920, and 1924 was but one indication of Americans' concern over the largely one-directional transnational flows of population that accelerated and intensified urban growth, contributing to what some considered the ethnic "mongrelization" of American culture. The internal migration of blacks from the South to northern cities was another contributing factor. At the same time, public-culture workers took pains to align the nation's urban identity with Anglo-American whiteness emblematically. As early as 1893 the Chicago World's Fair furnished the nation with a grandiose icon that combined urban modernity and whiteness when its public relations managers dubbed the fairgrounds "White City," drawing on the white, classically inspired architecture of the exposition halls. As historian Peter Hales comments, "the American urban elite quickly agreed that the Exposition would provide an opportunity to create the ideal city and realize their grand scheme: an urban environment based on concepts of planning, order, monumentality, and symbolic historicism" (1984: 134).

Hence the cosmopolitan flourish of the Exposition's president, T. W. Palmer, as he invited "the commingling of our people from East, West, North, and South, from farm and factory." His hope was that "our people" shall "learn to realize that all are of one blood, speak the same language, worship one God, and salute one flag," even as it helps to "bring nations closer to one another, and thus promote civilization" (quoted in Miles 1892: 25). While recognized even at the time by race activists such as Frederick Douglass and Ida B. Wells (Barnett) as an illusory and, especially to black citizens, hostile symbol of the nation's racial homogeneity, White City could draw on a centuries-long mythos of the New World as a city upon a hill into which all those who accepted its covenant might enter and thereby become both American (and, by implication, Christian) and world citizens – a species of cosmopolitanism that possessed the sheen of universal inclusiveness yet, like DeLillo's Eric, threatened either to absorb and thereby erase the value and meaning of the populace's differences or actually to fortress itself against them, excluding non-Christian, non-white elements from the national project. The temporal proximity of the Chicago World's Fair and *Plessy v. Ferguson* (the 1896 Supreme Court case that effectively legalized racial segregation) indicates the racially troubled state of the nation at the dawn of the twentieth century. All the more striking, then, that in this political and cultural climate certain black intellectuals and race activists, rather than rejecting cosmopolitanism as false and pernicious, developed alternative versions of it.

Harlem emerged in the early decades of the twentieth century as "Black Manhattan," to borrow James Weldon Johnson's appellation, as a "city within a city" with a "world-wide reputation" (147, 160). It thus became the geographical and iconic counterpart to Chicago's White City and the center of black cosmopolitanism. Perhaps most prominent and provocative in this milieu were W. E. B. Du Bois and Alain Locke. As Ross Posnock argues (1998), their unabashed appreciation of the white world's putatively elitist, highbrow aestheticism and their insistence on the absurdity of anybody claiming proprietary rights to cultural forms effected a deracialization of taste and a deracination of aesthetic value (10). Aesthetic experience was understood as a form "of freedom founded on release from particularity, from preordained identity" (14). Given the current conditions of disfranchisement and discrimination, Du Bois and Locke hardly wanted to deny the legitimacy of advancing black causes, both political and cultural; nevertheless they affirmed detachment from the prevailing model of the organic and essentialist black intellectual and aspired to replace socio-legal boundaries with " 'limitless' interchange" (11). By the mid-century Ralph Ellison in *Invisible Man* (1952) could lampoon public culture's obsession with urban–national whiteness when his protagonist, having migrated to New York, goes to work in the Liberty Paints factory whose main product is the dazzlingly white paint for government buildings in the nation's capital. One might argue that on the eve of *Brown v. Board of Education* (the 1954 Supreme Court case that disabled racial segregation in schools, effectively striking down *Plessy*), it is the mitigation, rather than aggravation, of racist culture that enabled Ellison to satirize, rather than more militantly protest, public icons of whiteness.

However, for first- and second-generation ethnic immigrants, who arrived largely from eastern, central-eastern, and southern countries of Europe, iconographic whiteness still played into the vision of what they could more or less become. As Matthew Frye Jacobson and other historians have shown, the odyssey of ethno-racial transformation into white, Caucasian, and/or Anglo-Saxon Americans was uneven and shifty (and largely facilitated by the contrasting presence of African Americans whose racial inertness was a foregone conclusion). Immigrants of Jewish descent were particularly susceptible to fluctuating ethno-racialist views. Yet "despite the transnational history of anti-Semitism . . . 'Hebrews' nonetheless traveled the path of other white races through the historic vicissitudes from white, to non-Anglo-Saxon, to Caucasian" over the nineteenth century, and "from Semite or Hebrew to Caucasian" over the first half of the twentieth century (Jacobson 1998: 126). The status of Jewishness was often central to debates about assimilation and cultural pluralism during this era. In the 1910s and 1920s the social philosopher Horace Kallen advanced the argument of cultural pluralism as a polemical counterforce against the ideology of the melting pot and 100 percent Americanism which had come to dominate national discourse. David Hollinger (1995) describes how he "defended the right of immigrants to resist assimilation and to maintain cohesive communities devoted to the perpetuation of ancestral religious, linguistic, and social practices" (92–3). But if Kallen advanced a "protoseparatist extreme" (93), others such as Randolph Bourne saw the nation's immigrant populations as providing the grounds for "dynamic mixing," which enabled a more flexible, transformative, and anti-parochial form of cosmopolitanism (94). Immigrant fiction of the era was thus framed by the interlocking paradigms of assimilationism, pluralism, and cosmopolitanism. The latter proved best able to envision identity as a function not of one's inherited traits but of one's actions and chosen values.

Perhaps no work of immigrant fiction makes such dramatically concentrated use of white iconography as Anzia Yezierska's short story, "The Lost 'Beautifulness'" ([1920] 1997). It tells of the devastating demise of Hanneh Hayyeh, a poor Russian Jewish immigrant in New York, who finally saves enough money to fulfill her passionate "ambition to have a white-painted kitchen exactly like that" of the wealthy Mrs Preston, the "Anglo-Saxon" whose silks and linens Hanneh Hayyeh launders (43, 50). This passion for a white kitchen is bound up with her sense of becoming American, for she envisions now being able "to invite all the grandest friends" that her "idolized" son has made in the US military. "So long my Aby is with America," she says, "I want to make myself for an American" (45). Mrs. Preston encourages this identification by blithely praising her as "an artist laundress" who expresses her "love for the beautiful" in washing things white "just as a painter paints it in a picture" (49). Beholding the spectacle of her newly painted kitchen, even Hanneh Hayyeh's immigrant neighbors encourage the link between whiteness aesthetics and social belonging. As one exclaims, "What a whiteness! And what a cleanliness! It tears out the eyes from the head! Such a tenant the landlord ought to give out a medal or let down the rent free" (48). Far from being reduced, however, the rent is increased by the landlord, a fellow Jew (though in naming him Rosenblatt, Yezierska aligns him with the historically more assimilated German Jews).

When Hanneh Hayyeh takes the landlord to court, seeking "justice" in the form of rent control, she mistakenly presumes that the nation's vaunted "democracy" (57) – that is, its universalist commitment to equality before the law – translates unimpeded into protection for the economically underprivileged. When the court decides in the landlord's favor, she is crushed: "hair disheveled, clothes awry, the nails of her fingers dug into her scalp, [she] stared with the glazed, impotent stare of a madwoman" (59). Her subsequent action indicates that she rejects not only the court's decision but the institution of law itself, for she seeks "vengeance" by destroying the kitchen with an axe, including her own possessions (60). Yezierska thus offers two contrasting critiques of cosmopolitan culture. On the one hand she questions ethnic immigrants' eager internalization of Anglo-Saxon values in their bid for Americanization, succinctly and bitterly ironized first by Mrs Preston's flattery and then by her similarly blithe but now insulting offer of money to cover the rent increase. Yezierska plants the suspicion that Mrs Preston's verbal and financial charity is a function of the severe asymmetry of their employer–employee relation – the Anglo-Saxon need not worry that the immigrant Jew will ever command enough power or attention or even common sense to rival her own clean white world. On the other hand, Yezierska questions the violent rejection of the nation's political values of justice and equality, however white or Anglo-Saxon they may appear, and however imperfectly they may be realized. Hanneh Hayyeh herself admits that along with the kitchen, "it was her own soul she had killed" (60). The problem of Hanneh Hayyeh is that she does not yet have the appropriate affective and cognitive mechanisms in place to bridge the gap between her own Old World experience and her New World ideals and expectations.

A novel that develops a more complicated picture of WASP–Jewish relations is Flanner's *The Cubical City*. Her representation of the Jew is different from most other white novelists. When ethnic or immigrant Jews appear at all in their narratives, they are usually two-dimensional if not caricatures, such as Zerkow the obsessive miser in Norris's *McTeague* (1899) and Rosedale the wealthy parvenu in Wharton's *The House of Mirth*. Or their Jewishness might be cryptically embedded, as with Gatsby's familial origins and Spencer Brydon's spectral alter-ego in "The Jolly Corner."[5] Flanner, however, not only makes her WASP protagonist Delia Poole's counterpart visibly and self-consciously Jewish, but more important, she has Delia herself contemplate his Jewishness. In a literary-historical sense, Flanner's Delia picks up where Dreiser's Carrie leaves off. Like Carrie, the beautifully blond Delia hails from the Midwest, although by the time the novel's action begins, she's a cosmopolitan sophisticate. Indeed, she seems a born cosmopolitan, driven by her "glands" (Flanner [1926] 1974: 300) to leave the cubical town that her realtor father has helped to develop and to indulge her promiscuous sexual appetites in Manhattan. Like Carrie, she's in the theater business, but as a highly successful set designer, not an actress. Also like Carrie, her paramours adore her; and her paramount paramour adores her whiteness: "The moons at night are white, white, Delia," Paul gushes, "oh, whiter than anything – except your face" (79). But where Carrie's employers have minimal presence, Delia's employer, the theater owner-producer Goldstein, has important narrative functions. For one thing, he protects her financial autonomy and security by engaging her contractually, and by holding her to her contracts when she is tempted, against her own good sense, to follow Paul to the Philippines. (Where cosmopolitanism thrives, Flanner hints, economic imperialism is sure to be active.)

For another thing, Goldstein never forgets and never lets Delia forget that he "had come from the slavery of an East Side apple-cart to set up their final magnificence on Broadway" (96). Together they will eventually "stage an enormous spectacle," with the "biggest cast and payroll ever seen in New York" (128). As though also never to allow them to forget the ethno-racial truths defining his Jewishness, he has his office walls decorated in what to Delia "looked like epidermal colors":

> There was an occasional black satin slit for hot skins, some brown for island shades, Manchu yellows like strips from a Chinaman's back, slivers of blue as if it would seem (though it was not likely) that among theatrical literature either Goldstein or Bennie [his assistant] had read of antique fighting Britons, painted and bright. Slashes of white varied this mixture, white like the arms of blonds with scarlet lines for their broad lips. The wall looked like a long background of carnal tints and here and there the priceless silk sagged as skin does when it drops away from maturing bones. (106–7)

These metaphors of skin and flesh tone anticipate DeLillo's thin ethno-national labels. But where DeLillo keeps his ethnic particulars suspended in hyper-real abstraction, Flanner eventually equips Goldstein, the novel's central ethnic subject, with deeply interiorized pathos. Doggedly and agonizingly in love with Delia, Goldstein reveals a kind of abject version of Du Boisian double-consciousness when he simultaneously declares his love for her and recognizes, upon her refusal of his marriage proposal, that Delia, along with the rest of Anglo-American society, finds his Jewishness loathsome:

> He relaxed, inch by inch, into the lounge. His fingers uncurled. His palms dropped open. "Goldstein! What a name! I don't blame you. I could only understand you a little better if it was Finklebein or Schlossenger. My God," he screamed, "aren't our noses enough? Why did we have to get such names? Ain't the hooked beak sufficient to give the world a laugh? What woman with a Christian name wants to swap it for 'Pleased-to-meet-you,-Mrs.-Baumgartner.' 'Jews not allowed in this apartment house.' Oh sure not. Tie your motor cars and your Jews out

on the sidewalk where they belong. The land of the free and the home of the brave. Huh!" (394)

Delia is "embarrassed" and "humiliated" but nevertheless sincerely unable to love him even if his "name could be anything in the alphabet" (394, 396). Yet his outburst jolts her into reflecting on his social plight and the historical circumstances that inform his self-loathing:

> From the Palestine hills to Riverside Drive, from the Rose of Sharon to Schmalski's Delicatessen on Avenue A, – this had been their new wilderness, via pogroms, inquisitions, restricted privileges and unrestricted hate, a two thousand year journey of beards, sheidles, insults and special caps, of new European nomenclature and fearful Atlantic immigration, wanderers on the cruel earth, a people spat on, reviled, burned at the stake until their talent for capitalism finally calmed the Christian heart and a gold standard sweetened the cross of Jesus at last. (395–6)

Flanner suggests that no matter what Goldstein *does*, to himself as much as others, he is first and foremost a Jew. However aware of history's construction of his ethno-racial plight, he remains overwhelmed by the psychological and emotional experience of being Jewish, and thus willy-nilly constitutes a sliver of Kallen's pluralistic pie.

By contrast, Delia's Anglo-Saxon white beauty is less a self-defining feature than a circumstantial opportunity that she exploits. It opens doors to attractive, wealthy men and to an attractive, well-paying career. And while she is neither ideologically nor psychologically attached to her WASP attributes, they do enable the self-defining actions with which Delia is preoccupied, namely sexual adventure and theater design. Exemplifying both a detachment from her inherited identity and an awareness of the era's ethno-racial realities, Delia recalls how, returning from a "grand continental tour" of Europe, she "contentedly enter[ed] the bay of Manhattan like all the other immigrants surrounding her, her handsome yellow head wrapped in a striped peasant scarf" (80). Delia the cosmopolite through and through, is at ease with this temporary identification with the ethnic and economic alien. She arrives at her identity by reiterating her beliefs and practices, rather than, as Walter Benn Michaels describes the imperative of early twentieth-century pluralism and nativism alike, "*deriving* one's beliefs and practices *from* one's cultural identity" (1995: 16). Delia ends up sexually thwarted, having to accept marriage after her promiscuity becomes public and threatens to ruin her altogether. Nevertheless, Flanner dramatizes how Delia's self-reflective detachment facilitates and intensifies her engagement with the cosmopolis, even as it releases her from predetermined attachments. Sexual promiscuity and stagecraft thus become Flanner's discursive vehicles for figuring identity apart from ethnicity, for aligning it with practice instead of inheritance. Further, in her attention to the modern institution of contract, Flanner articulates the promise of autonomous and consensual cosmopolitan life, even as she critically points out the ways in which social circumstances and habits of mind limit opportunities for signing on the dotted line.

Like Flanner, Jewish writers of the era more often than not portrayed ethno-racial awareness as an inevitably central feature of urban Jews' lives. For Cahan's David Levinsky, for example, his self-consciousness as a Jew prevents him, just as nativist ideologues could only hope, from feeling fully American. Despite the fact that his career, from peddler to captain of the garment industry, embodies the Horatio Alger mythos, replete with American can-do spirit, Levinsky is plagued by the intractable fact of his foreign birth: "That I was not born in America was something like a physical defect" (1960: 291). Yet however psychically scarred the immigrant *character* is the immigrant *author* need not be. As Phillip Barrish (2001) argues, "Reading Cahan's work, for example, helps to suggest how an intimate knowledge of Eastern-European Jewish immigrant life could enable an immigrant to figure as a 'natural' expert, while, conversely, his status as self-consciously analytic could simultaneously help him to seem culturally and intellectually distinct from the immigrant world his writing elaborated" (2001: 78). Such distinction registers, I would add, a mode of self-reflective detachment, a cosmopolitan consciousness that places Cahan in the company of his contemporary WASP social professionals.

Perhaps no Jewish writer thematizes this double relation to ethnic experience so dramatically as Henry Roth in *Call It Sleep* (1934). Narratologically, Roth builds this drama by alternating between a focalized but nevertheless distinctly third-person perspective and an intimate psycho-narration of David the protagonist's experiences. Moreover, David is a young boy, whose deeply inward, sensitive, and seemingly trauma-driven nature effectively exempts him from cosmopolitan duties. He may wander about the streets of the Lower East Side and Brownsville, absorbing its shocks like a modernist flaneur, but when lost, he is genuinely and desperately lost, unable even to name the street his family lives on and requiring rescue by the police and his mother. Likewise, the shocks he sustains are not pleasantly aesthetic but painfully daunting – indeed nearly fatal when he not once but twice engages the trolley line's third rail. Detachment he certainly exhibits, but of a self-evacuating, not self-reflecting, kind.

In the novel's deservedly famous penultimate chapter, in which the heterogeneous, polyglot populace gathers around the stricken boy, Roth discloses how ethnic immigrants doubly function as slices of Kallen's pluralistic vision and as keepers of cosmopolitan peace. Literally these immigrants make a lot of noise, as Roth portrays their cacophony of heavily accented, grammatically poor, dialogue in English. But within this "confused, paralyzed, babbling" speech environment, these immigrants also manage to communicate intelligibly enough to locate a wooden broom and to remove David from the tracks (421). They also exchange opinions on the trolley company's possible culpability and whether someone should sue. In other words, they exhibit all the signs of being sufficiently detached from their particular ethno-racial and linguistic allegiances to focus on restoring the boy's physical order and maintaining the municipality's public order.

Roth vividly reveals the dual logic of the modern cosmopolis: though categorically distinct, heterogeneity and generality need not be mutually exclusive. Further, generality need not be understood as merely a cover for white or nativist ideology, perpetuating Anglo-Saxon privilege and prestige. Rather, generality may be the manifestation, however imperfect, of universal ideals and liberal principles as basic as communication and as lofty as equitable justice. As David's Aunt Bertha reminds his mother, pogroms take place in Russia, not in "this land." And apart from the occasional Hanneh Hayyeh in their new cosmos, they need not fear the "peasant looking for [his enemy] with an ax" in hand (154). In bringing both everyday urban detail and heightened drama to his representation of the cosmopolitan ordeal, Roth, like other writers discussed in this chapter, manages to convey the twin senses of deeply lived life and deeply held principle. It is perhaps the mark – if one will pardon the infelicitous phrase – of the urban pre-postmodernist to keep a cosmopolitanism comprised both of generality and heterogeneity, of abstract universality and concrete particularity, in play. A postmodernist such as DeLillo might view his predecessors as naïve and simplistic in their commitments to such categorical distinctions, and therefore himself opt to erase these distinctions by asserting the truth of the simulacrum and by doing away with subjective interiority and referential and causal logic. But as we saw, DeLillo's postmodern options end up reinforcing a much more cosmic or fantastic cosmopolitan logic. However familiar and even normative the earlier writers' representational approaches to the cosmopolis may be, they have the virtue of being believable.

Notes

1 The French writer Paul Bourget used the title in 1893.
2 For a broader discussion of conventional usage of the term "cosmopolitan," see Berman (2001: 28 ff).
3 See Higham (1984: 243); Ross (1991: 353–5).
4 Higham explains:

> In the late 1920's [*sic*], when Park and his University of Chicago colleague Louis Wirth developed the first courses concerned solely with racial and ethnic relations, they opened a scholarly counter-offensive against the Anglo-Saxon racists and 100 per cent Americans of the day. The latter insisted that the Negro and the immigrant comprised a single problem. The sociologists in effect agreed, but rejected an ethnocentric framework for explaining the problem. Against nationalists, pluralists, and racists, they raised the banner of social science and inscribed on it the old faith that all men are basically alike. (218)

5 Jacobson notes the passage in *The American Scene* (1907) where James visits Ellis Island, paying particular attention to the Jewish arrivals, and "ventured that the sight would bring 'a new chill in [the] heart' of any long-standing American, as if he had 'seen a ghost in his supposedly safe old house'" (172). Considering the autobiographical similarity between James and Spencer Brydon the protagonist of "The Jolly Corner," along with the way the story dilates on ghostliness – where the spectral figure is no longer a Jew but now Brydon's maimed, capitalist alter-ego haunting the house of his birth – one begins to see how James, the consummate cosmopolitan, explores modernity's mechanisms of destabilizing self-identity, folding without assimilating alien otherness into modern self-constitution.

References and Further Reading

Anderson, Amanda 1998: Cosmopolitanism, Universalism, and the Divided Legacies of Modernity. In, Pheng Cheah and Bruce Robbins (eds.), *Cosmopolitics*. Minneapolis: University of Minnesota Press, 265–89.
Barrish, Phillip 2001: *American Literary Realism, Critical Theory, and Intellectual Prestige, 1880–1995*. New York and Cambridge: Cambridge University Press.

Berman, Jessica 2001: *Modernist Fiction, Cosmopolitanism, and the Politics of Community*. Cambridge and New York: Cambridge University Press.

Cahan, Abraham [1917] 1960: *The Rise of David Levinsky*. Intro. John Higham. New York: Harper and Row.

DeLillo, Don 2003: *Cosmopolis*. New York and London: Scribner.

Dos Passos, John 1925: *Manhattan Transfer*. Boston: Houghton Mifflin.

Dos Passos, John 1988: *John Dos Passos: The Major Nonfictional Prose*. Ed. Donald Pizer. Detroit: Wayne State University Press.

Dreiser, Theodore [1900] 1990: *Sister Carrie*. New York and London: Viking Penguin.

Dreiser, Theodore [1923] 1996: *The Color of a Great City*. Syracuse: Syracuse University Press.

Flanner, Janet [1926] 1974: *The Cubical City*. Carbondale and Edwardsville: Southern Illinois University Press.

Glickman, Lawrence B. 1997: *A Living Wage: American Workers and the Making of Consumer Society*, Ithaca and London: Cornell University Press.

Hales, Peter B. 1984: *Silver Cities: The Photography of American Urbanization, 1839–1915*. Philadelphia: Temple University Press.

Higham, John 1984: *Send These to Me: Immigrants in Urban America*. Rev. edn. Baltimore and London: Johns Hopkins University Press.

Hollinger, David A. 1995: *Postethnic America: Beyond Multiculturalism*. New York: Basic Books.

Jacobson, Matthew Frye 1998: *Whiteness of a Different Color: European Immigrants and the Alchemy of Race*. Cambridge, MA and London: Harvard University Press.

Johnson, James Weldon 1968: *Black Manhattan*. New York: Atheneum.

Michaels, Walter Benn 1995: *Our America: Nativism, Modernism, and Pluralism*. Durham and London: Duke University Press.

Miles, George (ed.) 1892: *The World's Fair from London 1851 to Chicago 1893*. Chicago: Midway Publishing Co.

Park, Robert and Ernest Burgess 1967: *The City: Suggestions for Investigation of Human Behavior in the Urban Environment*. Chicago and London: University of Chicago Press.

Posnock, Ross 1998: *Color and Culture: Black Writers and the Making of the Modern Intellectual*. Cambridge, MA and London: Harvard University Press.

Roosevelt, Theodore 1898: True Americanism. In *American Ideals and Other Essays Social and Political*, 2nd edn. New York and London: Putnam's Sons, 15–34.

Ross, Dorothy 1991: *The Origins of American Social Science*. Cambridge and New York: Cambridge University Press.

Roth, Henry [1934] 1991: *Call It Sleep*. Intro. Alfred Kazin. New York: Noonday.

Steffens, Lincoln [1903] 1957: *The Shame of the Cities*. Intro. Louis Joughin. New York: Hill and Wang.

Wharton, Edith [1905] 1990: *The House of Mirth*. Ed. Elizabeth Ammons, New York and London: W. W. Norton.

Wilson, Christopher P. 1985: *The Labor of Words: Literary Professionalism in the Progressive Era*. Athens: University of Georgia Press.

Wirth, Louis [1938] 1964: *On Cities and Social Life*. Intro. Albert J. Reiss, Jr. Chicago and London: University of Chicago Press.

Yezierska, Anzia [1920] 1997: *Hungry Hearts*. Intro. Blanche H. Gelfant, New York and London: Penguin.

Chapter 13

Other Modernisms

John Carlos Rowe

The remarkably diverse essays in this collection help us understand how literary culture changed in the United States in the first 50 years of the twentieth century. The editors and other contributors refer often to the notoriously difficult task of defining modernism, given its many different versions. Although I agree that there are many different understandings of modernism and modernity, I want to begin with a basic definition: between 1900 and 1950 (more or less), various modernisms vigorously criticized the modernization process we identify with economic, technological, and political changes in this period. These changes are usually identified with "second-stage industrialization," in order to distinguish them from those associated either with the earlier "industrial revolution" or the later "post-industrial" transformation of first-world economies. Second-stage industrialization includes production we identify with Henry Ford's assembly-line processes (Fordism), Frederick Winslow Taylor's development of managerial practices for improving the efficiency of production (Taylorization), the integration of marketing and advertising into the manufacturing processes, and responses to these economic changes, such as the international organization of labor in union movements, as well as communism and socialism. These economic, technological, and political changes had far-reaching consequences for the inhabitants of industrialized nations, like the USA. The regimentation and automatization of industrial manufacturing and their social effects are represented critically in many different media and their sub-genres. When viewed in such broad terms, modernization has consequences for everyone, so considering many different responses makes good sense if we hope to understand modernism in the context of such widespread socio-economic changes.

"Art is a way out!" Miss Lonelyhearts' merciless editor, the aptly named Shrike, shouts at him as if his satire were a bannered headline, in Nathanael West's *Miss Lonelyhearts* ([1933] 1962). The essays in this collection amply attest to the diverse alternatives offered by modernist artists to the problems of urban work and life, which included: dehumanization, alienation, ennui, mystification, and exploitation. It is thus little wonder that modernism represents a "history of the dead," to borrow from the titular subject of Michael Szalay's essay, because modernization involved death on a grand scale from the mechanization of military conflict in two world wars to systematized and bureaucratized genocides, such as the Holocaust and Stalin's "purges." Although his first works are published a few years after the end of the period covered by this volume, Thomas Pynchon represents effectively the death-drive of the modernization process in his pseudo-scientific accounts of humanity's entropy, with its psychic complements alienation and paranoia.[1] Despite his reputation as a postmodern skeptic and anti-aesthete, Pynchon affirms the traditional claims of modernist artists to offer vital alternatives to the death-drive of modernization. Szalay notes how both Eliot and Hemingway invoked art's timeless qualities (and the bonus of authorial immortality) as motives for their metaphors, but most of the modern art produced under the shadow of modern capital offers few genuine social and political options. Shrike is in many respects right: art became a mere slogan or headline, an advertiser's ploy to sell us another dubious cathartic mass-produced by the culture industry. Scholars of modernism often complain that art protests vigorously the modern situation, either closely charting our commodification or offering wild escape routes, but too rarely provides alternatives beyond its own imaginative spaces. In the 1970s, Helen Reddy yearned to escape another terrible historical period by trying to "find a good book to live in," but most of us know that the imagination can be inhabited on a permanent basis only by the clinically insane. The conventional difficulty of defining modernism has much to do with the imbrication of modernist art with the modernization process, the object of its critique. Roiling about like Jacob and the Angel, they depend upon each other for life and death.

Since the late 1980s, scholars have confronted this problem by elaborating "other" modernisms which do not so much challenge modernization from within as offer social alternatives that, if adopted, would dramatically change both our understanding and the practices of modernization. Among the many different "modernisms," I want to consider the following versions in this essay: African American, Native American, Asian American, Chicano/a, New Media, Pan-American, and Postcolonial modernisms. This combination of ethnic studies, critical theories, and media and communications studies by no means covers the many different modernisms we might use to map the terrain of the new scholarly approaches to the historical period treated in this volume. Because feminist, gay, and lesbian approaches are treated at length by Jennifer L. Fleissner and Kathryn R. Kent in their contributions to the volume, I do not include them in my discussion, even though they are appropriately central to more diverse approaches to US modernism. In this brief essay, I can only offer the most abbreviated remarks, and also plead my limited expertise in some areas, so my purpose will be to follow the editors' suggestion that the "multiple interpretive approaches" in this volume will be "provocative" and "useful" for readers' "own critical practices" (p. 000).

African American responses to modernization and its systemic racism are often treated in terms of how the Harlem Renaissance responded to the "high" modernism represented by James, Pound, Eliot, Stein, Fitzgerald, Hemingway, and Faulkner. The problem with such approaches is that they tend inevitably to subordinate African American cultural production to the aesthetic concerns of white avant-garde artists, ignoring the very particular responses of African American intellectuals and artists to the political economy of modernization. Is Countee Cullen's neoclassicism in his poetry traceable to that of the London Imagists, like Pound and Eliot, or is Cullen developing a different modern poetic tradition within the Harlem Renaissance? Does Langston Hughes's combination of short lyrics into the long poem *Montage of a Dream Deferred* ([1951] 1990) build upon the poetic montages and rhetorical collages of Pound's *Hugh Selwyn Mauberley* ([1920] 1957) and Eliot's *The Waste Land* ([1922] 1962), or is Hughes relying on the rhythms and motifs he adapted from African American jazz, be-bop, and dance? By putting such interesting questions in exclusively aesthetic terms we forget how directly African Americans had to struggle against economic and political racism in Jim Crow America.

In *Black Reconstruction in America* ([1935] 1992), W. E. B. Du Bois argues that the Reconstruction of the South following the Civil War was accomplished by an African American leadership fundamental to subsequent struggles for civil, economic, and human rights in the United States. He also claims that Black Reconstruction worked not only for the full emancipation of African Americans but for a thorough transformation of the United States, especially in its relationship to the rest of the world. Du Bois understands Reconstruction as an opportunity for the USA to reject the European imperialism that was deeply involved in global slavery and continued to exploit peoples of color in the "equatorial black belt."

This utopian reconstruction of the US nation was formally and abruptly ended by the US government in 1876, and instead of the US leading the "modern world" toward a genuinely democratic future

> Americans saw throughout the world the shadow of the coming change of the philanthropic attitude which had dominated the early nineteenth century, with regard to the backward races. International and commercial imperialism began to get a vision. Within the very echo of that philanthropy which had abolished the slave trade, was beginning a new industrial slavery of black and brown and yellow workers in Africa and Asia. (Du Bois [1935] 1992: 632)

When federally supported Reconstruction was dismantled in 1876 the promise of a new US democracy, which might have been a model for the rest of the world, waned: "If that part of the white South which had a vision of democracy and was willing to grant equality to Negroes of equal standing had been sustained long enough by a standing Federal police, democracy could have been established in the South" (ibid.). At once a global and a local issue, the full emancipation of African Americans in the postbellum South is for Du Bois a fundamentally modern question. In *The Souls of Black Folk* ([1903] 1989), Du Bois had famously claimed: "The problem of the twentieth century is the problem of the color-line – the relation of the darker to the lighter races of men in Asia and Africa, in America and the islands of the sea" ([1903] 1989: 13). In *Black Reconstruction in America*, Du Bois rephrases the "Negro Problem": "How far [the South] dare let the Negro be a modern man" ([1935] 1992: 633).

Other African Americans pursued the transnational issues of African American modernity in the global directions Du Bois suggested. Celebrated for her Southern African American regionalism in *Mules and Men* ([1935] 1990) and *Their Eyes Were Watching God* ([1937] 1990), since 2000, Zora Neale Hurston has been recognized as an advocate of postnational thinking about African Americans (Rowe 2000: 253–4). In *Moses, Man of the Mountain* ([1939] 1991), she reconstructs the diasporic roots of African Americans in Egypt and that sacred figure of the Judeo-Christian tradition, Moses, even as she pushes him toward his West African and Caribbean avatar, Damballah, a divine figure who shares Moses' rhetorical powers (Rowe 2000: 266–8). Read in conjunction with her account of Haitian Voodoo in *Tell My Horse* ([1938] 1990), the regionalism and even the controversial African American dialect in *Mules and Men* and *Their Eyes Were Watching God* can be reinterpreted not as the products of provincial, rural folklore but as the results of the complex migrations of Egyptian, West African, and African American cultures, hybridized with local Native American spiritual practices, and thus integral forces in modern globalization. Not only were slave labor and the exploitation of the labor of peoples of color in the aftermath of slavery crucial in the formation of first-world nations, but the cultural hybridization and cosmopolitanism of diasporic and immigrant people are integral to most nations' modernity. Exoticized as "natural primitivism" by many white intellectuals or as simply reactive expressions of psychic alienation and despair, Spirituals, Rag-Time, Jazz, the Blues, and be-bop are defining modernist musical forms, the rhythms of which are as much critiques as they are reflections of modernization. T. S. Eliot could sneeringly refer to the "Shakespeherian rag" in *The Waste Land* ([1922] 1962) in the same context in which he mocks working-class figures like Lil and Albert, but Eliot's defensiveness has much to do with his awareness that modernist culture was deeply influenced by the musical innovations we identify with African American culture in its global circulation ([1922] 1962: 34).

Understanding the history of America in terms of these diasporic and immigrant cultural routes recasts America as African American as much as it is Euroamerican, and Hurston argues in her explicitly transnational works that modernist cultural hybridization can be traced successfully back to the seventeenth-century harbors of Port-au-Prince and Habana and the eighteenth-century maroon communities on Jamaica and Haiti, where African slaves combined West African spiritual beliefs with Carib, Arawak, and other indigenous practices to create Voodoo. Still identified in the popular Western imagination with pre-modern, primitive forms of worship, Voodoo and its US variant Hoodoo exemplify for Hurston a protest against modernization that offers a social alternative in the communities formed around their practices (Rowe 2000: 274–80).

Like her high-modernist contemporaries, Hurston works deliberately to shock her readers, but her claim in "How It Feels to Be Colored Me" ([1928] 1979) that African American cultural "primitivism" may in fact be a modernist strategy goes far beyond the trumpeted iconoclasm of Eliot and Pound. The latter borrowed broadly from different cultural traditions; Eliot's *Waste Land* concludes with a dizzying array of references to Hindu scriptures, Dante's populist Catholicism, Elizabethan and Jacobean drama and their Anglicanism, and French Symbolist gnosticism. Yet Hurston suggests that the celebrated cultural collages of the high moderns were finally aesthetic indulgences when measured against the living and working African American and Afro-Caribbean communities whose culturally hybrid practices include ancient Egyptian, West African, Native American, and Euroamerican elements. Du Bois famously invokes African American "double consciousness" at the beginning of *The Souls of Black Folk* as both a curse and a blessing, thinking in the latter regard of how the historical experiences of African Americans have enabled them to think and live with different cultural epistemologies ([1903] 1989: 5–6). Could it be that the African American's capacity for double consciousness is, in effect, a truly modern talent?

That iconoclastic idea has considerable relevance for Native Americans, who since Europeans first arrived in the Americas have suffered imperial violence, systematic genocide, and the usually unintentional but certainly convenient devastation of the diseases carried by Europeans and other non-indigenous peoples. Following the Mexican historians Enrique Dussel and Edmundo O'Gorman and the Argentine historian Rodolfo Kusch, Walter Mignolo argues that global "modernization" begins in the fifteenth- and sixteenth-century European voyages of exploration and conquest of the Western Hemisphere. Linking modernization less with technological innovation or complementary industrial processes – Columbus and Cortés sailed from Spain using traditional navigational techniques and naval vessels – than with the emergence of imperial expansion, Mignolo and other scholars advocating the "early modern thesis" insist that modernization cannot be understood without studying the methods of imperial domination: religious legitimation of invasion and theft, consequent missionary zeal, strategic xenophobia to construct the colonized subaltern as "primitive," the privileging of print literacy and the destruction of other literacies, and the "civilizing" vocation of the colonizing pirates.

Thanks to the work of archaeological biologists and anthropologists armed both with awareness of ethnography's role in colonialism and new scientific tools, scholars are recovering the extraordinary demographic, social, economic, and technological diversity of the Americas prior to the arrival of Columbus. Charles Mann's *1491: New Revelations of the Americas before Columbus* (2005) represents effectively the "modernization" projects successfully undertaken by the Clovis people in middle of North America, the environmentally sophisticated society of the Marajóara in Amazonia between AD 800 and 1400, and countless other complex civilizations flourishing throughout the populous continents prior to the military and microbial destruction brought by the Europeans (Mann 2005: 167–78; 323–9). By 1893, Frederick Jackson Turner could announce at the Columbian Exposition that the North American "frontier" was "closed," on the grounds that however tragically or inevitably indigenous cultures had been defeated and were doomed to extinction. Native American Studies in the first half of the twentieth century is the conflicted story of native peoples struggling to survive and Euroamerican society insisting upon their disappearance.

Theodora Kroeber's *Ishi in Two Worlds* was not published until 1961, but it tells the story of Ishi (ca. 1860–March 25, 1926), the last Yahi – and arguably the last "Indian" – living in the California "wild," who was studied by the anthropologists Alfred Kroeber (Theodora's husband) and Thomas Talbot Waterman and given a job at the University of California, San Francisco's Museum of Anthropology between 1911 and 1916, the year of his death from tuberculosis. Still one of the University of California Press's all-time bestsellers, *Ishi in Two Worlds* depends upon the Myth of the Vanishing American. In his great trilogy about the myth of the West, Richard Slotkin shows us how this particularly destructive myth developed from the "fatal environment" of nineteenth-century Manifest Destiny to the global frontier of American imperialism in the twentieth century. For the first half of the twentieth century, then, modernization and Native American cultures were locked in a death struggle whose end would be the post-World War II "termination" policies of the Bureau of Indian Affairs and its advocacy of the complete assimilation of indigenous peoples into the US nation.

The term "termination" is used in federal Indian law to denote "a massive drive to assimilate Indians once and for all and thus to end the responsibility of the federal government for Indian affairs" (Prucha 1984: 1013). Although the US effort to end Indian sovereignty and nationalize as well as assimilate native peoples has a very long history, the specific policies of termination begin in 1945–46, after John Collier, advocate of the Indian Reorganization Act (Wheeler-Howard Act) of 1934 and Director of the Bureau of Indian Affairs, left office in 1945 followed by his "strong supporter Harold Ickes" who "resigned as secretary of the interior in 1946" (ibid.). Federal programs to bus Native Americans to large urban areas, like Los Angeles, encouraging them to find employment and housing among the general population, were motivated by the desire to assimilate native peoples completely.

Although such programs cannot be compared with the genocide of the Holocaust or Stalin's purges or with the imprisonment of Japanese Americans during World War II, these "termination" policies do suggest a general tendency in the modern period to eliminate human and cultural differences. It is not too extreme to suggest that industrial standardization influenced social and political attitudes in many areas, urging conformity and resemblance to such a degree that personal and cultural "differences" were increasingly viewed as "problems," often solved in violent ways.

A bumper sticker for the Tongva people of California (misnamed "Gabrielinos" by the Franciscans) declares proudly: "The Tongva Nation. We still exist!" The cultural stories of Native American survival, and in some cases success, warrant reconsideration of how Native American cultures ought to be configured in relation to modernization and modernism in the first half of the twentieth century. Caught between the allotment and assimilation policies of the Dawes Act (1887–1934) and compromise policies advocating Indian sovereignty in the Indian Reorganization Act (1934–1945), native peoples living in the USA in the first half of the twentieth century had to be extraordinarily adaptive and skillful to negotiate contradictory and often downright murderous federal Indian policies. When asked why he had converted first to Protestantism during his employment in Buffalo Bill Cody's Wild West Show, then to Catholicism on the Catholic dominated Pine Ridge Reservation in South Dakota, the Lakota holy man, Nick Black Elk, answered simply "My children had to live in this world" (Rowe 2000: 229). Scholars are beginning to understand that native peoples had their own "double consciousness," which in some cases drove them effectively mad and in others enabled them to represent themselves publicly against overwhelming odds. Whatever criticisms we may direct today at John Neihardt and Nicholas Black Elk's *Black Elk Speaks* ([1932] 1979), the text remains a powerful criticism of second-stage industrialization and the modernization process, as well as offering a viable social alternative in Lakota communalism. Guiding Black Elk to the top of Mt Harney, a peak in the heart of *paha sapa* (the Black Hills) sacred to the Lakota people, Neihardt urges his native witness to enact a virtual "rain dance" to conclude *Black Elk Speaks* in accord with the Myth of the Vanishing American:

> A scant chill rain began to fall and there was low, muttering thunder without lightning. With tears running down his cheeks, the old man raised his voice to a thin high wail, and chanted: "In sorrow I am

sending a feeble voice, O Six Powers of the World. Hear me in my
sorrow, for I may never call again. O make my people live!" (274)

The sentimental and staged conclusion of *Black Elk Speaks* belies the
powerful influence of Black Elk and his Lakota colleagues' defiance of
Euroamerican imperialism. Long before Dee Brown's *Bury My Heart at
Wounded Knee: An Indian History of the West* (1981), the rural poor Lakota
men interviewed by Neihardt in 1931 offer their own Lakota history
of the West, invoking the pan-Indian power that "wiped out" Custer
and the Seventh Cavalry at the Battle of Little Big Horn and inspired
the spread of the Paiute Wovoka's Ghost Dance Religion from Nevada
across the Midwest and beyond in the 1880s and 1890s. With its
magical buckskin shirts, reputed to protect the wearers from bullets,
and its hybridization of Christian, Paiute, and other indigenous spiritual rites and symbols, the Ghost Dance is itself an act of resistance to
second-stage modernization as radical as the most avant-garde poem or
painting. In *The Culture Concept: Writing and Difference in the Age of Realism*,
Michael Elliott points out that no one in the 1890s "engaged the
Ghost Dance as a legitimate form of religious and political activity,"
although he concedes that "those who came closest may have been
those representatives of the U.S. government, including members of
the Army and the Office of Indian Affairs, who attempted to repress it"
(2002: 118). Yet, when members of the American Indian Movement
reoccupied "Wounded Knee" in May 1973, they explicitly invoked the
resistance of native peoples to the US government in the performance
of the Ghost Dance and the subsequent Wounded Knee Massacre of
1890 (Matthiessen 1992: 19–21). Fond as we are of citing the successful legal test of James Joyce's *Ulysses* against charges of pornography
as one memorable case in which modernism's daring message was nearly
censored, we should remember that both the Sun Dance and Ghost
Dance *were banned* because they threatened the hegemony of the US
nation. Dangerous dances! They look quite modern to me, just as the
"frenzied" dances of Haiti appealed to that pioneer of modern dance,
Katherine Dunham, who first visited Haiti in 1936 to "study primitive dance and ritual in the West Indies and Brazil" while she was a
"graduate student in anthropology" (Dunham 1969: vii).

Considering *Black Elk Speaks* as part of modernism requires us to see
it as part of a much larger effort on the part of anthropologists and
native peoples to be heard in a time when cultural self-representation
for many minorities was extremely difficult. Reading today Frank B.
Linderman's many popular books about the Crow – *Plenty-coups: Chief*

of the Crows ([1930] 1957) and *Pretty Shield: Medicine Woman of the Crows* ([1932] 1972) are the most famous – and Mourning Dove's (Hum-Ishu-Ma's) *Cogewea, the Half-Blood* ([1927] 1981), which she completed with the help of her "literary mentor and coauthor, as well as personal friend and confidant for twenty years" Lucullus V. McWhorter, we are tempted to judge such texts to be primarily the ideological products of cultural commodification and remembrance, effects of the Myth of the Vanishing American (Fisher 1981: v–xxix at v). Yet if they are viewed as part of a larger pan-Indian movement that increasingly included concerned and informed non-Indian editors, authors, anthropologists, and social activists, then this "modern" record of Native American writing leads directly to the extraordinary vitality of today's native American writing by authors as diverse as Scott Momaday, Gerald Vizenor, James Welch, Louise Erdrich, Leslie Marmon Silko, and countless other native artists, intellectuals, and writers who have done far more than "survive" but have transformed our understanding of what it means to be a modern American.[2]

Maxine Hong Kingston's *China Men* was published in 1980 and thus falls outside the historical scope of this volume, but the Chinese American culture she recreates from 1848 to 1975 overlaps the period treated by the essays in this collection. Like other subalterns, whether in their home countries or immigrants to the imperial center, "Chinamen" were stereotyped as premodern primitives, suited only for the most dangerous or undesirable labor, and paid the lowest possible wages. For these racialized, effeminized, and demonized "Chinamen" to become the "China Men" of Kingston's title, they must be granted the productive agency they earned by helping to build the Transcontinental Railroad, as well as many of the other post-bellum rail networks in the USA and the urban infrastructures required for rapid modernization. Chinese Americans indeed contributed to what Kingston terms "The Making of More Americans" ([1980] 1989: 163), playing off Gertrude Stein's modernist account of her own German–Jewish–American heritage in *The Making of Americans* (Stein [1925] 1962).

In her survey of "Asian American Literature" between 1910 and 1945, Elaine Kim notes that the "first published works by American-born Asians are two Chinese American autobiographies, Pardee Lowe's *Father and Glorious Descendant* (1942) and Jade Snow Wong's *Fifth Chinese Daughter* ([1945] 1950), which "appeared in print at a time when Chinese, like Filipinos, were viewed as American allies and enjoyed unprecedented popularity" (Kim 1988: 813). Of course, one reason for the historically late appearance of literary texts by American-born

Chinese is the consistent policy of excluding Asians from legal immigration between 1882, when the US Congress passed the first Chinese Exclusion Act, and 1943, when the wartime alliance of China and the USA against Japan caused the US Congress to repeal the Chinese Exclusion Acts (Kingston 1989: 152–9). In the 61 years of formal Exclusion, China men and women lived and worked in the United States, but in conditions we might describe as "culturally invisible."

Recovering that cultural history is the work of late-modern writers like Kingston and historians, like Iris Chang, whose *The Chinese in America: A Narrative History* (2003) complements Kingston's *China Men* by demonstrating the wide range of literary means ordinary Chinese immigrants employed to represent themselves, often resisting the US modernization process to which they also, contradictorily, contributed. Kingston refers often to the letters illiterate immigrants dictated to professional scribes to communicate with families in China; Kingston and Chang note the sophistication of the "paper villages" and imaginary "families" Chinese immigrants "memorized" in order to trick US Immigration officials into believing they qualified for legal admission during Chinese Exclusion (Kingston 1989: 46–7; Chang 2003: 150, 155). When the 1906 San Francisco Earthquake destroyed legal records, many Chinese immigrants claimed to be American born (Kingston 1989: 150). Marlon K. Hom has collected the popular rhymes (poetry and songs) of oral culture in San Francisco's Chinatown, and he opens his collection with a " 'Wooden Barracks' poem," which is one of the few verses to survive from the numerous poems written by Chinese immigrants on the walls of the Angel Island Immigration Station (Hom 1987: vii). How do we assess these everyday literary acts in the terms of the high modernists' valorization of the fictive and imaginary? Wallace Stevens may calmly place his "jar in Tennessee," where its poetic form makes the "slovenly wilderness" cohere, but what of the desperate Chinese immigrant at Angel Island reciting the details of a village he has never visited and family members he has never met (Stevens 1972: 76)? What *Notes toward a Supreme Fiction* did the Chinese immigrant write (1947 in Stevens 1972: 380–408)?

Elaine Kim treats "published creative writing in English by Americans of Chinese, Filipino, Japanese, Korean, and Southeast Asian (for now, Burmese and Vietnamese) descent" in her scholarly survey of "Asian American Literature" (Kim 1988: 811). I would add "South Asian" to include Indian, Pakistani, and Sri Lankan (Ceylonese in the period of this volume) immigrants to the USA. Chinese American cultural responses to US modernization should not be allowed to represent the many different peoples and cultures reductively treated as "Asian" in the popular imagination. Chinese Exclusion ended in 1943 in the same wartime period the US government forcibly relocated American citizens of Japanese descent to the euphemistically named "internment camps" scattered throughout the western states from California's Manzanar to Wyoming's Hart Mountain.

Franklin D. Roosevelt's Executive Order 9066, issued on February 19, 1942, attempted not only to clear all people of Japanese ancestry from the western states and intern them in military-style concentration camps, but also to exclude them from the vicinity of US military bases. For Japanese Americans, criminalization and incarceration for mere "ancestry" was experienced not only as racism but as a peculiarly modern version. Miné Okubo's extraordinary account of internment, *Citizen 13660*, which combines her line drawings and memoir, locates the fantastic not so much in her own artistic talents as in the perverse imagination of the modern US state, which renders its own citizens foreign. Okubo's remarkable text, rediscovered by a new generation of scholars, is just one example of the many Asian American texts written between 1900 and 1950 deserving greater attention for their sophisticated responses to US modernization.[3]

New scholarly studies of Hispanophone US culture, especially Mexican American literature, have pushed its cultural history back to the early modern era and up through the "invention" of Mexican American identity with the US invasion of Mexico (1846–8) to the problematic terms of the Mexican American War's Treaty of Guadalupe Hidalgo. In Mexican American culture, the primal scene of imperial conquest is Hernán Cortés' employment (as translator and cultural go-between) and seduction of the Mexica woman, Doña Marina, mythologized in much Mexican and Mexican American literature as "la Malinche." A combination of "her Nahuatl birth name, Malinal, and the Spaniards' name for her, Marina, given at her Christian baptism," her very name represents an enduring problem central to Mexican American literature (Brickhouse 2004: 68). Mexican American identity is historically the product of at least three different and competitive imperialisms: Spanish, Mexican, and US. Like the fractured, multiple selves that populate much modernist literature, "La Malinche" is both "la madre" and "la chingada," the mythic origin of *mesitzo/a* identity and the perpetual sign of her betrayal of indigenous peoples (Brickhouse 2004: 68). Indeed, the mythologized "Malinche" appears to confirm the arguments of Dussel, O'Gorman, Kusch, and Mignolo that our modern contradictions are inextricably tied to our imperialist origins.

This connection between "traditional" Hispanic culture and the Chicano culture that just begins to emerge at the end of the 1940s is by no means obvious in Mexican American literature published between 1900 and 1950. In his survey of Mexican American literature and culture from 1900–45, Raymund Paredes stresses how many Mexican American writers in this period responded to US modernization by cultivating a Southwest, Hispanic regionalism directly at odds with wartime modernization (Paredes 1958: 803). Works like Josephina Niggli's related stories in *Mexican Village* (1945) play upon certain US expectations of charmingly provincial villagers living timeless premodern existences "in the mountains of Northern Mexico" (804). But the premodern agriculture of Mexican and Southwest villagers hardly represented the changing social realities of Mexican Americans living in urban *barrios* in Los Angeles, Tucson, Albuquerque, Santa Fe, and the growing cities of the San Joaquín Valley. Paredes traces the use of the term "chicano" – "a short way of saying *mexicanos*" – to the barrio fiction of Mario Suárez, whose "sharp portrayals of barrio life" in the 1940s "are enhanced by his effective rendering of *caló* – a combination of English and Spanish particularly popular among teenagers" (Paredes 1958: 805). Like later African American hip-hop and other hybridized ethnic argots, *caló* suggests in advance of scholarly "border studies" how important language politics were in everyday responses to the alienating processes of modernization.

Such avant-garde defiance is particularly visible in the Zoot suiters of the 1940s and the infamous Zoot Suit Riots of 1942–3, in which sailors and soldiers stationed in Los Angeles during World War II clashed with Mexican American youths. Luis Valdez's play, *Zoot Suit* (1978), as well as the 1981 film inspired by his play, and Thomas Sanchez's *The Zoot Suit Murders* (1991) are beyond the historical period of this volume, but the avant-garde fashion, anti-establishment style, and gangster *macho* of the Zoot suiters belongs decidedly to modernism. Late in Ralph Ellison's *Invisible Man* ([1952] 1995) the narrator encounters three young black men on a New York subway platform, "walking stiffly with swinging shoulders in their well-pressed, too-hot-for-summer suits, their collars high and tight about their necks; . . . their coats long and hip-tight with shoulders far too broad to be those of natural western men," listens to them "speak a jived-up transitional language full of country glamour," and imagines they "think transitional thoughts" (440–1). These young black men are not wearing Zoot suits, but their fashion and speech declare they choose not to *be* "natural western men" (440). They are literally young and fashionable, and they are allegories:

they are African American modernists, even though they read comic books on the subway train and have not heard of Zora Neale Hurston or W. E. B. Du Bois. In the Zoot Suit Riots, the Los Angeles Police left rioting soldiers and sailors alone, but they arrested scores of Mexican Americans, African Americans, and Filipino-Americans (many of whom had nothing to do with the conflict) for "disturbing the peace." Indeed, the Zoot suiters in LA, like Ellison's subway youths in New York, disturbed the "peace" of wartime America.

The Chicano Zoot suiters and Ellison's three young black men pose another problem for our efforts to understand American literature between 1900 and 1950. Ellison's young men are "outside historical time" (440), in part because they belong with those "who write no novels, histories or other books" (439). This period not only depends upon the growing competition print media faced from new media, such as radio, film, and television, but also on the different media, traditional and new, employed by the increasingly diverse peoples of the mulitcultural USA. Oral story-telling and song, ritual and dance, dress and other forms of body art, drawing, photography, street art and graffiti, public murals, car culture, and gang signing are only a few of the numerous media employed by ordinary people in response to their modern urban situations.

Visiting Mexican artists, like José Clemente Orozco, Diego Rivera, and Miguel Covarrubias produced public murals at Dartmouth and in Detroit critical of the US capitalist system that supported them, and they illustrated books by other people of color, as Covarrubias did brilliantly with his wood-block prints for Hurston's *Mules and Men*. Is Orozco's great fresco in the Reserve Room of Dartmouth's Baker Library, *The Epic of American Civilization* (1932–4), a Mexican, Mexican American, or US cultural work?[4] One of Ellison's young black men takes three rolled-up comic books from his jacket pocket and passes them to his friends (Ellison [1952] 1995: 442). Was Orozco, a Mexican Marxist, thinking of such youths potentially reading his hieratic "cartoons" of indigenous conflict and the imperial *Conquista* in his *Epic*? Traditional Mexican American *corridos* (ballads) of the Southwest border regions were adapted in the modern period to protest US racism, colonization, and economic exploitation. From the classic *corrido*, "Gregorio Cortez," in which a *tejano vaquero* avenges his brother's murder by shooting the sheriff in 1901, to the *corridos* composed and sung by United Farm Workers in support of César Chávez in the mid-1960s, oral and theatrical works for those "who write no novels, histories or other books" have enabled many people to enter history (Paredes 1988: 801, 806).[5]

In another context, how can we read the scene in *The Great Gatsby* where Daisy and Gatsby make passionate love by way of his "beautiful shirts" without recalling the 1920s' Arrow Shirt Man with his stylishly slicked-back hair? As Dr T. J. Eckleburg's demi-divine billboard for eye-glasses looms over the Valley of Ashes, Fitzgerald reminds his readers that *reading* is no longer a private activity and by no means restricted to words on the page. We should not read Faulkner's fiction without thinking of his contributions to such *noir* films as *The Big Sleep*, however jarring the conjunction of the Luddite Boon Hoggenbeck and Chandler's savvy urbanite Philip Marlowe may be. In short, how do we account for the complex cultural, economic, and political entanglements of the different, competitive media in the modern era? Writers for the Communist Party of the United States of America's popular front also wrote scripts for Hollywood films and in many cases were subsequently black-listed by Hollywood studios as a consequence of Senator Joseph McCarthy's House Un-American Activities Committee's hearings.

Of course, the period covered by the essays in this volume is also an extraordinarily multimedia era. Okubo's *Citizen 13660* is not unusual for its combination of picture and text. Muriel Rukeyser's leftist poem, *The Book of the Dead* ([1938] 1992), about Union Carbide's cover-up of the industrial scandal at Gauley Bridge, West Virginia, was almost certainly intended to be accompanied by Nancy Naumberg's lost photographs of the people and conditions in which they lived, worked, and died (Rowe 2002: 138).[6] Rukeyser's avant-garde documentary poetry anticipates by three years James Agee's and Walker Evans's more celebrated *Let Us Now Praise Famous Men* ([1941] 1988), a combination of modernist text and photographs about the Ricketts, Woods, and Gudgers: desperately poor white sharecropper families in Alabama. Agee's and Evans's multimedia text is itself profoundly influenced by Erskine Caldwell's and Margaret Bourke-White's *You Have Seen Their Faces* (1937), which also combines print and photographs to publicize the plight of Depression-era Southern sharecroppers. These documentary works are unimaginable without the great innovations in politically left-wing documentary films produced in the 1930s, which are generically beyond the subject of this volume and yet crucially bear upon its literary subjects.[7]

In the same vein, it is impossible to understand many literary works written in this period without also "hearing" their musical counterparts. West African music and African American jazz thrum through Hurston's *Their Eyes Were Watching God* ([1937] 1990); Langston Hughes's *Montage of a Dream Deferred* ([1951] 1990) is metrically and thematically organized around be-bop and the Blues. In his Imagist phase, Ezra Pound insisted upon "melopoeia" as a crucial poetic value, but he himself only vaguely gestures toward this union of sound and figuration in the "Envoi" to *Hugh Selwyn Mauberley* ([1920] 1957), where he recalls pedantically how Edmund Waller's Renaissance poem, "Go, Lovely Rose" was set to music by Henry Lawes (Pound [1920] 1957: 70). Yet, if it was musical poetry Pound wanted, then he should have spent less time in the library and more at the jook-joints, where John Coltrane, Muddy Waters, or Led Belly might have taken him away. Eliot never matches musically the "O O O O Shakespeherian Rag" he mocks as modern decadence in *The Waste Land*; Scott Joplin's fast-paced compositions are not only more memorable, but they may express better than Eliot a popular protest against modernization (Eliot [1922] 1962: 34).

I have touched briefly on how African American, Native American, Asian American, and Chicano/a modernisms challenge and broaden our traditional understanding of modern American literature. We should not understand these ethnic or minority cultures as additions to the American literary canon occasioned by the changing demographics of the United States in the first half of the twentieth century. Not only does each culture transform our understanding of "America" as a unified field but it ought also to be understood in contestation and interaction with others. If we fail to miss these multiple intersectional relations, then we reproduce misleading dualities, like the famous "black–white binary" often criticized by scholars as yet another means of occluding the multicultural and polylingual complexities of the United States. Each of these "other" modernisms also draws on cultural heritages that go far beyond the geopolitical and social boundaries of the United States. As US foreign policies became increasingly global and imperialist in the course of the Spanish–American (1898–9) and Philippine–American Wars (1899–1902), so many of the leaders within those communities internally colonized in the nation built political and cultural coalitions with peoples around the world. In the years leading up to the US involvement in World War II, the Japanese made special appeals to US minorities, especially African Americans, on the grounds that Japan advocated equality without regard to race or ethnicity. Cedric Robinson has shown how powerful this appeal was for African American intellectuals like Du Bois, who speaks often of the shared destinies of Japanese and African Americans (Robinson 2000: 137). In a similar fashion, Soviet communism made special appeals to ethnic minorities colonized by the US within and outside its borders. Of course, the Japanese leadership was lying, as its viciously racist policies during World

War II toward many other Asians, notably Koreans, Chinese, Burmese, Vietnamese, and Filipinos, attest; Soviet communism's oppression of gays, Jews and members of organized religions of all sorts, and countless minorities within its vast empire also reveals its claims for a trans-racial utopian state to be sheer propaganda.

Nevertheless, the rapid globalization of US power, thanks in large part to its economic and technological leadership in second-stage industrialization, hardly paved the way for what Francis Fukuyama optimistically terms "the end of history" as a consequence of triumphant global capitalism. Quite the contrary, US globalization has prompted a growing number of diverse groups to work independently and across traditional boundaries to resist one-way modernization with "modernist" alternatives increasingly anti-national or post-national in character. Will it be possible twenty years from now to speak of "American Literature, 1900–1950" as a cohesive, albeit complex, suite of cultural productions tied closely to the US nation? I hope *not* and that instead we will have to imagine the "Americas" and "Canada" in their his-torically conflicted, polyglot, transcultural intersections within the Western Hemisphere and then in the dizzying flows and currents – that wide Sargasso Sea – wherein these worlds inevitably acknow-ledge others.

Notes

1 Pynchon's "Entropy" was published in 1960 and anticipates his efforts to use thermodynamic and informational "entropies" as both scientific theories and metaphors for modern societies.

2 The idea of "native modernism" is well established in the visual arts, as evidenced by such works as Bill Anthes's *Native Moderns: American Indian Painting, 1940–1960* (2006) and the exhibition "Native Modernism: The Art of George Morrison and Allan Houser" at the Smithsonian National Museum of the American Indian (September 12–21, 2004).

3 See, for example, Robinson and Tajima (2005).

4 See Jacquelynn Baas (2002: 142–85).

5 The *corrido* of Gregorio Cortez is famously analyzed by Américo Paredes in *"With a Pistol in His Hand": A Border Ballad and Its Hero* (1958).

6 Jessica Bremmer, a PhD candidate in English at the University of Southern California, has uncovered archival photographs of the dam project, the workers and their families, and living conditions in the Gauley, West Virginia region that suggest how scrupulously Rukeyser was trying to represent verbally the visual details of the region. Although Bremmer's archival work

has not yet been published, it gives even more credibility to the idea that Rukeyser imagined her poem would be published with Nancy Naumberg's photographs.

7 See Barnouw (1974: 120–45) for a good overview of 1930s' documentary films.

References

Agee, James and Evans, Walker [1941] 1988: *Let Us Now Praise Famous Men*. Boston: Houghton Mifflin.

Anthes, Bill 2006: *Native Moderns: American Indian Painting, 1940–1960*. Durham: Duke University Press.

Baas, Jacquelynn 2002: "*The Epic of American Civilization*: The Mural at Dartmouth College (1932–1934)." In Renato González Mello and Diane Meliotes (eds.), *José Clemente Orozco in the United States, 1927–1934*. New York: Hood Museum of Art in Association with W. W. Norton and Co.,

Barnouw, Erik 1974: *Documentary: A History of the Non-Fiction Film*. New York: Oxford University Press.

Brickhouse, Anna 2004: *Transamerican Literary Relations and the Nineteenth-Century Public Sphere*. New York: Cambridge University Press.

Brown, Dee 1981: *Bury My Heart at Wounded Knee: An Indian History of the American West*. New York: Washington Square Press.

Caldwell, Erskine and Bourke-White, Margaret 1937: *You Have Seen Their Faces*. New York: Modern Age Books.

Chang, Iris 2003: *The Chinese in America: A Narrative History*. New York: Penguin Books.

Du Bois, W. E. B. [1903] 1989: *The Souls of Black Folk*. New York: Penguin Books.

Du Bois, W. E. B. [1935] 1992: *Black Reconstruction in America: 1860–1880*. New York: Atheneum.

Dunham, Katherine 1969: *Island Possessed*. Garden City, New York: Doubleday.

Dussel, Enrique 1995: *The Invention of the Americas: The Eclipse of "the Other" and the Myth of Modernity*. Trans. Michael D. Barber. New York: Continuum.

Eliot, T. S. [1922] 1962: *The Waste Land and Other Poems*. New York: Harcourt, Brace and World.

Elliott, Michael A. 2002: *The Culture Concept: Writing and Difference in the Age of Realism*. Minneapolis: University of Minnesota Press.

Ellison, Ralph [1952] 1995: *Invisible Man*. New York: Vintage Books.

Fisher, Dexter 1981: "Introduction." *Cogewea, the Half-Blood*. Lincoln: University of Nebraska Press.

Fitzgerald, F. Scott 1925: *The Great Gatsby*. New York: Charles Scribner's and Sons.

Fukuyama, Francis 1992: *The End of History and the Last Man*. New York: Avon Books.

Hom, Marlon K. (ed.) 1987: *Songs of Gold Mountain: Cantonese Rhymes from San Francisco Chinatown*. Trans. Marlon K. Hom. Berkeley: University of California Press.

Hughes, Langston [1951] 1990: *Montage of a Dream Deferred. Selected Poems*. New York: Vintage Books.

Hurston, Zora Neale [1928] 1979: "How It Feels to Be Colored Me." *I Love Myself When I Am Laughing . . . And Then Again When I am Looking Mean and Impressive: A Zora Neale Hurston Reader*. Ed. Alice Walker. Old Westbury, NY: Feminist Press.

Hurston, Zora Neale [1935] 1990: *Mules and Men*. New York: Harper and Row.

Hurston, Zora Neale [1937] 1990: *Their Eyes Were Watching God*. New York: Harper and Row.

Hurston, Zora Neale [1938] 1990: *Tell My Horse: Voodoo and Life in Haiti and Jamaica*. New York: Harper and Row.

Hurston, Zora Neale [1939] 1991: *Moses, Man of the Mountain*. New York: Harper and Row.

Kim, Elaine 1988: "Asian American Literature" (1910–1945). *Columbia Literary History of the United States*. Eds. Emory Elliott et al. New York: Columbia University Press, 811–21.

Kingston, Maxine Hong 1989: *China Men*. New York: Vintage Books, 811–21.

Kroeber, Theodora 1961: *Ishi in Two Worlds*. Berkeley: University of California Press.

Kusch, Rodolfo 1962: *América profunda*. Buenos Aires: Hachette.

Linderman, Frank B. [1930] 1957: *Plenty-coups: Chief of the Crows*. Lincoln: University of Nebraska Press.

Linderman, Frank B. [1932] 1972: *Pretty-shield: Medicine Woman of the Crows*. Lincoln: University of Nebraska Press.

Lowe, Pardee [1942] 1943: *Father and Glorious Descendant*. Boston: Little, Brown and Co.

Lowe, Truman T. (ed.) 2004: *Native Modernism: The Art of George Morrison and Allan Houser*. Seattle: University of Washington Press.

Mann, Charles 2005: *1491: New Revelations of the Americas before Columbus*. New York: Vintage Books.

Matthiessen, Peter 1992: *In the Spirit of Crazy Horse*. New York: Penguin Books.

Mignolo, Walter 1995: *The Darker Side of the Renaissance: Literacy, Territoriality, and Colonization*. Ann Arbor: University of Michigan Press.

Mourning Dove (Hum-Ishu-Ma) [1927] 1981: *Cogewea, the Half-Blood*. Lincoln: University of Nebraska Press.

Neihardt, John G. and Nicholas Black Elk [1932] 1979: *Black Elk Speaks: Being the Life Story of a Holy Man of the Oglala Sioux*. Lincoln: University of Nebraska Press.

Niggli, Josephina 1945: *Mexican Village*. Chapel Hill: University of North Carolina Press.

O'Gorman, Edmundo 1961: *The Invention of America: An Inquiry into the Historical Nature of the New World and the Meaning of Its History*. Bloomington: Indiana University Press.

Okubo, Miné 1946: *Citizen 13660: Drawings and Text by Miné Okubo*. New York: Columbia University Press.

Paredes, Américo 1958: *"With a Pistol in His Hand": A Border Ballad and Its Hero*. Austin: University of Texas Press.

Paredes, Raymund 1988: "Mexican American Literature" (1910–1945). *Columbia Literary History of the United States*. Eds. Emory Elliott et al. New York: Columbia University Press, 800–10.

Pound, Ezra [1920] 1957: *Hugh Selwyn Mauberley. Selected Poems*. New York: New Directions.

Prucha, Francis Paul 1984: *The Great Father: The United States Government and the American Indians*. 2 vols. Lincoln: University of Nebraska Press.

Pynchon, Thomas 1984: *Slow Learner: Early Stories*. Boston: Little Brown.

Robinson, Cedric J. 2000: *Black Marxism: The Making of the Black Radical Tradition*. Chapel Hill: University of North Carolina Press.

Robinson, Greg and Tajima, Elena (eds.) 2005: *A Tribute to Miné Okubo*. Seattle: University of Washington Press.

Rowe, John Carlos 2000: *Literary Culture and U.S. Imperialism: From the Revolution to World War II*. New York: Oxford University Press.

Rowe, John Carlos 2002: *The New American Studies*. Minneapolis: University of Minnesota Press.

Rukeyser, Muriel [1938] 1992: *The Book of the Dead. Out of Silence: Selected Poems*. Ed. Kate Daniels. Evanston: TriQuarterly Books.

Sanchez, Thomas 1991: *The Zoot-suit Murders*. New York: Vintage Books.

Slotkin, Richard 1985: *The Fatal Environment: The Myth of the Frontier in the Age of Industrialization, 1800–1890*. New York: Atheneum.

Slotkin, Richard 1992: *Gunfighter Nation: The Myth of the Frontier in Twentieth-Century America*. New York: Atheneum.

Stein, Gertrude [1925] 1962: *The Making of Americans: The Hersland Family*. New York: Harcourt Brace and World.

Stevens, Wallace 1972: *The Collected Poems of Wallace Stevens*. New York: Alfred A. Knopf.

Valdez, Luis 1978: *Zoot Suit*. Los Angeles: Center Theater Group, Mark Taper Forum.

West, Nathanael [1933] 1962: *Miss Lonelyhearts and The Day of the Locust*. New York: New Directions.

Wong, Jade Snow [1945] 1950: *Fifth Chinese Daughter*. New York: Harper.

Index

DH

813.
520
9
CON